Showdown

ALSO BY LARRY ELDER

The Ten Things You Can't Say in America

Confronting Bias, Lies, and the

SHOWDOWN

Special Interests That Divide America

Larry Elder

ST. MARTIN'S PRESS

NEW YORK

www.stmartins.com

BOOK DESIGN BY JENNIFER ANN DADDIO

Reprinted by permission of the Middle East Media
Research Institute (p. 76).
Permission granted by Ann Landers and Creators Syndicate (p. 249).
Reprinted with permission—The Toronto Star Syndicate (p. 249).
Reprinted with permission of *Insight*. Copyright 2002 News
World Communications, Inc.
All rights reserved (p. 294).

LIBRARY OF CONGRESS CATALOGING-IN-PUBLICATION DATA
Elder, Larry.
    Showdown : confronting bias, lies, and the special interests that
divide America / Larry Elder.—1st ed.
        p. cm.
    Includes bibliographical references.
    ISBN 0-312-30179-0
    1. United States—Social policy—1993–   2. United States—Politics
and government—2001–   3. Discrimination—United States.   4.
Social problems—United States.   I. Title

HN65 .E437 2002
361.6'1'0973—dc21

                                                2002068391

First Edition: September 2002

10   9   8   7   6   5   4   3   2   1

To Viola and Randolph, my mom and dad

ACKNOWLEDGMENTS

I want to thank my first and best role models—my mom and dad, Viola and Randolph—for their hard work and sacrifice.

I want to again thank my excellent, diligent, and loyal staff, led by Dana S. Riley, and her assistants Pinky Winters-Hardaway and Jennifer Hardaway.

I also want to thank Jasmine Takeshita for encouraging me to do *Moral Court*, and her steadfast belief in my vision, and in me.

Thanks once again to attorney James Wilcox for reviewing the manuscript and making suggestions, and also to Justin Gelfand for pitching in at the last minute.

And finally, I wish to again thank my wise and patient editor, Elizabeth Beier, for agreeing to tee it up one more time.

CONTENTS

PREFACE

On September 11, 2001, our government failed to live up to its most important responsibility—to protect its citizens. It failed because the federal government uses its $2 trillion budget to meddle in our personal and financial affairs and to provide goods and services that Americans can and should provide for themselves.

A federal government that promises education, health care, and retirement neglects its most sacred obligation—to protect its citizens from foreign and domestic enemies.

America has become a nation of excuse-making, blame-pointing, government-dependent people—victicrats. Our victicrat nation hurts our war against terrorism. We fight this war on several fronts—military, political, diplomatic, and financial. But we also must engage in a domestic war against the welfare state—the victicrat mindset that says government knows best, and that has created a citizenry increasingly less inclined to accept personal responsibility.

After September 11 Americans asked, "Why do so many hate us?" *Showdown* traces the roots of Arab-Muslim resentment toward Israel, the United States, and the West. Ignorance, envy, jealousy, and scapegoating—and an Arab victicrat mind-set—caused the September 11 terrorist attacks.

A nation divided by special interests screams, "Life is unfair"; "The rich get richer while the poor get poorer"; "Big business and multinational corporations exploit the poor, powerless workers." Nonsense. But the us-against-them nature of the mostly liberal mainstream media helps to support and advance this mind-set. *Showdown* reveals how the media misleads and confuses us on issues ranging from global warming to the "fact" of racial profiling. Similarly, a left-leaning academia converts our children into uncritical supporters of the welfare state. This book asks Americans to roll back the modern welfare state. The Founding Fathers envisioned a country whose citizens provide for themselves—and for each other—to the fullest extent possible. A self-sufficient society that assumes personal responsibility is not only more prosperous but more humane.

Showdown explains how people can and would cope better in a world without a government-provided so-called "social safety net." The Founding Fathers clearly established a limited federal government. They assumed a society smart enough, mature enough, and moral enough to run its own affairs. This book shows that they were right.

Federal government involvement in spending our nation's health-care dollars virtually guarantees that the number of uninsured Americans goes up. The Food and Drug Administration (FDA) "ensures" safe medicines. But the FDA stops or delays promising drugs from going to market, causing more deaths and greater suffering. The Federal Aviation Administration "guarantees" safe air transportation. But inefficient government management of airports and air traffic control systems creates delays and compromises safety. The Equal Employment Opportunity Commission (EEOC) claims it "levels" the playing field in hiring and promotion. But threats of lawsuits from women and minorities make private employers skittish about hiring the very people the government designed the EEOC to help.

Showdown exposes the feminist, black, and civil rights leadership that cripples blacks and other "underrepresented" minorities by supporting unfair programs like affirmative action and insultingly pushes for reparations for slavery. This book exposes how black racism makes society worse off and paves the way for black leadership to replace affirmative action with affirmative attitude. It also shows whites and other nonblacks how to fight unfair charges of racism.

Showdown also explores the who, what, when, where, and why of a free society. Without a federal Environmental Protection Agency, how can we ensure a clean and safe environment? Assume the elimination of the Internal Revenue Service. How would the government fulfill its limited constitutional duties and obligations? If all states allowed citizens to carry concealed weapons, how could we prevent guns from getting into the hands of bad guys? If government did not force savings through Social Security, wouldn't we have irresponsible seniors sleeping on storefronts and diving in dumpsters? If taxpayers didn't provide public education, how would poor people afford their kids' schooling? Without a federal Occupational Safety and Hazard Agency, how would it be possible to police unscrupulous, exploitative employers who force employees to work under dangerous, unsanitary conditions?

A world of limited government and maximum personal responsibility scares people. *Showdown* says: Do not fear a country that trusts its people, that refuses to rob its citizens of their income and their freedoms. History shows Americans are good enough, smart enough, competent enough, and forward-thinking enough to control their own lives with little government interference. Government now takes about *forty percent* of our national income. This is an assault on the very principles of the Constitution that set forth a small, limited federal government that trusts its citizens with their money, their freedom, and their spirit.

Showdown says that while the country's two major political parties differ in rhetoric, their behavior endorses the growth and expansion of the welfare state. *Showdown* urges all Americans to renounce the welfare state, the status quo, and the collectivism of today's mainstream" political parties. *Showdown* is a challenge to you to vote your conscience, stand up for your principles, and fight for a limited, responsible government that trusts its people.

Showdown

1.

LIBERAL FASCISM

Stealing Freedom With Compassion

Against individualism, the Fascist conception is for the State; and it is for
the individual in so far as he coincides with the State. . . . Liberalism
denied the State in the interests of the particular individual; Fascism
reaffirms the State as the true reality of the individual.[1]
—BENITO MUSSOLINI, *FASCISM: FUNDAMENTAL IDEAS*

Of all tyrannies, a tyranny exercised for the good of its victims may be the
most oppressive. It may be better to live under robber barons than under
omnipotent moral busybodies. The robber baron's cruelty may sometimes
sleep, his cupidity may at some point be satiated; but those who torment
us for our own good will torment us without end, for they do so with
the approval of their own conscience.[2]
—C. S. LEWIS

Every day, well-meaning liberals sacrifice America's freedom under the guise of benevolent protection. The United States faces real danger in following this perilous path—where liberalism quietly, softly, and sneakily becomes fascism.

The Founding Fathers envisioned a country where the individual restrained the government. But today, feel-good policies, well-intentioned politicians, and "caring" special interest groups conspire to rob us of our personal and financial freedoms.

West Hollywood, California, requires bar and tavern owners to display fishbowls full of condoms and provide safe-sex literature to patrons! Combating AIDS and other communicable diseases somehow falls outside of the responsibility of individuals. Instead, tavern and bar owners must ensure that their beer- and booze-guzzling patrons engage in responsible "safe sex."

Meanwhile, the Screen Actors Guild (SAG) has inked a new deal with Hollywood studios. Citing legal concerns, SAG no longer uses the term "affirmative action" in its contracts with studios. Instead of requiring studios to use "best efforts" at diversification, the new contract language says studios "shall" engage in diversity. "Shall?" How ironic that Hollywood, a community full of allegedly freedom-loving liberals, sees no contradiction in mandating presumably "racially insensitive" employers to hire based on race or ethnicity.

In Santa Monica, California—sometimes called the People's Republic of Santa Monica—the city recently passed a "living wage ordinance," mandating a minimum wage of $10.50 an hour! When businesses protested and predicted layoffs, the Santa Monica City Council simply shrugged and said, "Too bad."

Now, get ready for "visitability." Visitability? The term means the ability of "disabled" friends, neighbors, and solicitors to visit your house. The Santa Monica City Council authorized a study to determine whether to *mandate* handicapped accessibility in *private homes*. If this law goes through, homeowners face a requirement to install at least one handicap-accessible ground-level entrance, thirty-six-inch-wide hallways, and at least one bathroom with a thirty-two-inch-wide doorway. This would apply to all new Santa Monica homes as well as those undergoing extensive renovation.

"This is a movement toward something that is inclusive," said Santa Monica resident Alan Toy, also a member of the Santa Monica Rent Control Board. Mary Anne Jones, the executive director of the Westside Center for Independent Living, said the ordinance is necessary "because we can't go see our friends." And Santa Monica Mayor Michael Feinstein said, "There's no question that there's value in universal access."[3]

And then there's the new Santa Monica "rehiring law." After September 11, many businesses faced layoffs and the belt-tightening induced by any economic downturn. In hyper-liberal Santa Monica, restaurateurs laid off over three hundred workers. What does any self-respecting collectivist city council do? It passes legislation requiring—repeat, *requiring*—employers to first rehire those laid off. Not only that, employers must rehire them in the same order in which they laid workers off. In other words, a restaurateur, who first laid off Harry, the most expendable employee, must first rehire Harry, the most expendable employee! In a classic example of liberal fascism, Santa Monica Mayor Michael Feinstein said, "Businesses always operate within a social context defined by any municipal and state law. In this case, we have to look at September 11. It created an extraordinary situation in this country."[4] Within a "social context"? Feinstein also suggested rent control for *commercial* properties, making Santa Monica the only city in the country to cap prices on commercial real estate.

Tearful articles about people struggling to survive on minimum wages spark demands to force employers to artificially boost wages. In a recent *Wall Street Journal* cover story, for example, the newspaper followed Pat Williams, a nurse's aide attempting to piece together a life based on $5.55 an hour. Not until deep in the article do we learn about Ms. Williams's three grown children (there is nothing in the *Wall Street Journal* article that suggests her grown children financially assisted her), that she never married the father(s) of her children, that she dropped out of high school in the tenth grade, that she cares for her seven-year-old grandson, that she once left for a higher-paying job but returned to the nursing home that paid her the minimum wage because she preferred that atmosphere.[5] So Ms. Williams—a card-carrying victicrat—becomes the poster child for laws forcing employers to pay artificially higher prices for wages.

HOW DID WE GET HERE?

For the first 150 years of our nation's history, the Supreme Court interpreted the Constitution the way the Founding Fathers wrote, explained, and intended it—as a restraint on government. What happened?

Franklin Delano Roosevelt.

While FDR rallied American spirits and brilliantly prosecuted World War II, he also deserves the damning title of principal architect of the modern welfare state. Angered by Supreme Court decisions striking down major parts of his New Deal legislation, FDR fought back, proposing a law to add more justices to the Supreme Court. He threatened to pack the court with justices who deemed the Constitution a "living, breathing document," versus the "strict constructionist" outlook held by the anti–New Deal justices, who had determined that an activist, benevolent government was unconstitutional.[6]

Even FDR's legal advisor, Felix Frankfurter (whom FDR later appointed to the Supreme Court), advised FDR against his court-packing scheme. In the well-received biography *Franklin D. Roosevelt: A Rendezvous With Destiny*, author Frank Freidel discusses the profound shift in constitutional interpretation that occurred during the dramatic years of the Roosevelt administration. "Frankfurter," wrote Freidel, "had hastened to Washington and had advised . . . [FDR] to bide his time before clashing with the Supreme Court: let more adverse decisions accumulate and then propose a constitutional amendment. Roosevelt ignored the advice and set forth upon his own course of action."[7]

The Constitution, despite the '30s circumstances of a depression and 25 percent unemployment, did not permit the kind of income redistribution New Deal legislation required, no matter how popular or desirable. If you want to pull this off, advised Frankfurter, change the Constitution. "From Roosevelt's standpoint," wrote Freidel, "the emotion was not pique but outrage. His target was not the Constitution but rather the outmoded Supreme Court interpretation of it."[8]

Following his second inauguration, Roosevelt remarked to one of his speechwriters, "When the Chief Justice read me the oath and came to the words 'support the Constitution of the United States' I felt like saying: 'Yes, but it's the Constitution as *I* understand it, flexible enough to meet any new problem of democracy—not the kind of Constitution your court has raised up as a barrier to progress and democracy.' "[9]

FDR's court-packing scheme angered liberals, moderates, and conservatives alike. Many members of Roosevelt's own party, while supporting the New Deal, hated his naked attempt to alter the court's historic structure. "One of the unhappier aspects of the proposal was its deviousness," said Freidel. "No sophisticated person took Roosevelt seriously when he insisted afterward that what he wanted was to speed the business of the court through providing additional aid to superannuated justices. That smacked of the trickery of demagogues."[10]

But the court-packing scheme worked. Shortly after Congressional hearings on the court-packing bill began, the court blinked. Justice Owen J. Roberts, who previously ruled against New Deal legislation, switched sides. Chief Justice Charles Evan Hughes reportedly congratulated him on "saving the court." Eventually, through replacement appointments, Roosevelt built a New Deal–friendly "Roosevelt Court." And thus began a staggering invasion of federal authority that would have stunned the Founding Fathers. "From this standpoint," wrote Freidel, "the court fight had brought the great end Roosevelt sought. The end was far more acceptable because he had not attained even a compromise; the legitimation of the New Deal reforms came from a court with the traditional nine justices, and it came fundamentally before even the first Roosevelt appointee took his seat. *A momentous turning point had come in constitutional law* [emphasis added]."[11]

Never mind that state-sponsored welfare violates Economics 101 while diminishing the initiative of both the giver and the givee. No, the crime of the modern welfare state is more basic. The Founding Fathers drafted the Constitution to limit government, expecting citizens to assume responsibility for the rest of their lives. As James Madison put it, "I cannot undertake to lay my finger on that article of the Constitution which granted a right to Congress of expending, on objects of benevolence, the money of their constituents."[12]

Today's liberals, as with the well-intentioned Roosevelt, bulldoze over the constraints placed by the limited-government-supporting Founding Fathers. The it-takes-a-village crowd simply pours it down our throats like castor oil while telling us that it's good for us. Article

I, Section 8 of the Constitution outlines the duties and responsibilities of the federal government, leaving all other powers to the states and to the people. It's a good read.

CONSERVATIVE-BASHING FOR
FUN AND PROFIT

"Wake Up Democrats! Take Back the Country," became the rallying cry for the June 24, 2001, conference sponsored by the liberal Americans for Democratic Action. Its attendees included a who's-who list of extremist, emotional, angry, "compassionate" liberals. The theme? Post–George W. Bush, Americans need to regain their moral center and kick out those evil Republicans, who seek to reenact slavery and chain women to hot stoves.

At the conference, actor Warren Beatty trumpeted the need for campaign finance reform, calling it "the transcendent issue of American democracy in our time." He also urged those on the left to put aside factionalism in order to write a simple "one-page Democratic Contract With America" that would be "short enough to accommodate the attention span of the channel surfer."[13]

Former prosecutor Vincent Bugliosi, author of the over-the-top *The Betrayal of America: How the Supreme Court Undermined the Constitution and Chose Our President*, bashed the U.S. Supreme Court conservative majority's legal reasoning in *Bush v. Gore*, charging that they "belong behind bars" since they committed "one of the biggest and most serious crimes in American history when they stopped the recount in Florida."[14]

House Minority Leader Dick Gephardt (D-Missouri) attacked the Bush tax cut as "a horrible mistake for the future of the country" and accused Republicans of "blowing the fiscal responsibility which . . . [the Democrats and President Clinton] stood for."[15]

Reverend Jesse Jackson condemned the very concept of federalism, calling the nation's greatest problem "a separate and unequal system" of "50 separate and unequal states and 3,067 separate and unequal counties [that] must be rooted out root and branch. . . . The enemy here is the Tenth Amendment, the unenumerated rights" which permits inequalities to exist.[16]

Robert Borosage, co-director of the Campaign for America's Future, called Bush a latter-day William McKinley and accused the president of creating an alliance of robber barons against the people, given Bush's policies of "tax cuts for the wealthy," "arsenic in the water," and "salmonella in the food."[17]

Representative Maxine Waters (D-Los Angeles), typically blunt, said, "If George W. Bush does not wake us up, we are literally dead!"[18]

Former Green Party California senatorial candidate Medea Benjamin, in a panel on the California power crisis, described President George W. Bush as "marinated in oil." S. David Freeman, adviser to California Governor Gray Davis (Democrat), said "Deregulation is a bad idea [and] the common good requires governmental action." Representative Dennis Kucinich (Democrat) of Ohio proposed a constitutional amendment to bar anyone from operating an electric power system for profit.[19]

Representative Henry Waxman (Democrat) of West Los Angeles flatly announced, "We belong to a community where we want to take care of everyone. . . . We must guarantee everyone access to health care, universal coverage."[20] Former Labor Secretary Robert Reich urged the Democrats to retake power by promising health care, child care, education, and "no more tax cuts."[21]

A "mole," attorney and journalist Edgar B. Anderson, attended the affair. In ten hours of speeches, Anderson said he never once heard the word "taxpayer."[22] He saw a room of "toe-tag" liberals. These are people who live cradle-to-grave, apparently believing in the existence of something called "the government" as a source of funds separate and apart from the taxpayers, who, in fact, provide the money for these feel-good programs. Taxpayer? Who's that? Personal responsibility? What's that?

NONLIBERALS = BAD PEOPLE

Twenty years ago, former pro-life California state legislator John Schmitz blasted feminist attorney and radio talk show host Gloria Allred. The senator held hearings on a proposed anti-abortion measure. Several pro-choice people appeared to testify, some apparently at Allred's behest. The state senator issued an angry press release, headlined "Senator Schmitz and His Committee Survive 'Attack of the Bulldykes.' " The release described Allred's witnesses as "imported lesbians from anti-male and pro-abortion queer groups in San Francisco and other centers of decadence" and called those in attendance "a sea of hard, Jewish and (arguably) female faces." As for Allred, he called her "a slick butch lawyeress."[23]

Allred sued for defamation and won $20,000 and a public apology. "I specifically apologize to Gloria Allred for any embarrassment or harm the release may have caused her. . . . Based upon my past relationships with Gloria Allred, her husband and her family, I have never considered her to be and recognize that she is not a 'slick butch lawyeress.' " He also apologized to women, gays, and Jews.[24]

But Allred's sensitivity for slights doesn't always apply when *she* refers to others. After George W. Bush's election, he named Colin Powell the first black to hold the powerful cabinet position of secretary of state; Norman Mineta, the first Asian to hold a cabinet position to be secretary of transportation; and Condoleeza Rice, the first black woman to serve as head of the National Security Agency. He also appointed Roderick Paige as education secretary and six more blacks to important posts just below Cabinet rank. On Allred's radio show, a caller complained about Bush's minority appointees, "This is an alleged diversified cabinet by Bush. What is extraordinary about Republicans is they always manage to find those minorities who are not in the least representative of minority viewpoints. What the Republicans keep doing is they find the one black, the one Latino, the one whatever, who is not in step at all with the vast majority of the minorities they represent."

Allred agreed with the caller, "That's a great point . . . in other words, Uncle Tom types." Uncle Tom types?! So, it's not OK for Schmitz to call Allred "a slick butch lawyeress," but it's perfectly OK for Allred to refer to Colin Powell, perhaps the most respected public figure in America, as an "Uncle Tom type."[25]

A decade ago, Representative Pete Stark (D–California) verbally attacked Louis Sullivan, a black man then serving as Health and Human Services secretary. Stark accused Sullivan of "being used by the administration and [that he] does not have the strength of his convictions." Stark further called Sullivan "a disgrace to his race" and said that "he's being programmed [what] to say by the overseers on the [White House Chief of Staff John] Sununu plantation."[26] One would expect a huge outcry to follow, marches on Washington, demands for Pete Stark's head, right? Wrong. You see, Sullivan served in a Republican—not a Democrat—administration. Thus making Sullivan, as Gloria Allred might have put it, an "Uncle Tom type."

The "kid glove" treatment of Democrat Pete Stark caused then-ABC White House correspondent Brit Hume to comment, "Could you imagine the outpouring in this town had [Republican] John Sununu, for example, said that some black member of Congress was a disgrace to his race? I mean, people would be lying down in front of automobiles on Pennsylvania Avenue. It would be an unbelievable outrage and the media would be exploding."[27] Hume was right. Liberals can get away with outrageous, contemptible remarks that, if they came from a conservative's mouth, would get that conservative metaphorically hanged from the highest tree.

Representative Eliot Engel (D–New York) introduced legislation directing the Federal Communications Commission (FCC) to establish a "clearinghouse" where folks offended by the television or movie portrayal of blacks, Hispanics, Jews, Arabs, Italians—or any ethnic or minority group—can lodge an official complaint with the government.

The Ethnic, Minority, and Gender Bias Clearinghouse would track and report incidences of bias in the news and the entertainment media. "This bill in no way seeks to censor any form of American media," said an Engel spokesman. "It simply creates a clearinghouse for the American public's concern about being stereotyped."[28] Hmmm. Does that include terms like "Uncle Tom types," too?

See, Democrats, good; Republicans, bad. Even an ostensibly non-partisan professional group like the American Bar Association (ABA) revealed their liberal, partisan hand after Northwestern University law professor James Lindgren analyzed the way the ABA rates judges. Lindgren looked at judges appointed by Bill Clinton and George Bush senior—the forty-first president—controlling for objective qualifications, such as prior experience, to determine if subjective factors explained the ratings.

Lindgren found that Clinton appointees were *seven to ten* times more likely to be given the highest "well-qualified" rating than their comparably qualified Bush appointees. "Just being nominated by Clinton instead of Bush," said Lindgren, "is better than any other credential or than all other credentials combined." In fact, the ABA gives higher ratings to Clinton appointees with *fewer* credentials than Bush appointees. And Bush appointees without prior judicial experience effectively had no chance of being rated "well-qualified," while Clinton's nonexperienced appointees had at least an 80 percent chance of getting the highest rating.[29]

"When one controls for being minority or female and all measured criteria," said Lindgren, "the Clinton appointees have 10.7 times higher odds of receiving the highest rating from the ABA. . . . Amazingly, a Bush appointee with the top credentials has a slightly lower probability of getting the highest ABA rating than a Clinton appointee who has none of these credentials."[30]

Wow—just being nominated by a Republican taints judges in this country. Suppose you accidentally find yourself sitting next to a Republican at a baseball game? Is Republicanism communicable?

HOLLYWOOD VERSUS REPUBLICANS

Pre–September 11, Hollywood celebrities jumped on Republicans like a linebacker on a fumble.

Rosie O'Donnell, while hosting a fundraiser for Hillary Clinton, called New York Mayor Rudolph Guiliani a "village idiot."[31] Martin Sheen pronounced the president a "moron."[32] Actor Robert Redford, referring to the president's views on the environment, called George W. Bush "ignorant" and said that he "does not have a clue."[33] Singer-actress Cher said, "If you're black in this country, if you're a woman in this country, if you are any minority in this country at all, what could possibly possess you to vote Republican? . . . You won't have one f—king right left."[34]

Some stars promised to leave the country rather than suffer a Republican president. In September 2000, actor Alec Baldwin announced his intention to leave the country should voters elect Bush. Baldwin's wife, actress Kim Basinger, confirmed her husband's refusal to stay in the country under a Bush presidency. "Alec is the biggest moralist I know," said Ms. Basinger. "He stands completely behind what he says." She added, "I'd probably have to go, too." And director Robert Altman intended to bug out, also. "If George Bush is elected president, I'm leaving for France," said Altman. "He is not smart, not educated, just the son of a powerful politician and does what dad tells him. . . . No matter what, it would be a catastrophe for the whole world if George Bush is elected."[35]

What happened to the exodus of the stars? Both Altman and Baldwin quickly denied ever making such statements! For Altman, this proved to be somewhat troublesome, since someone taped his remarks. Altman backpedalled, now claiming he really meant Paris . . . the city in Texas, "because the state would be better off if [Bush] is out of it."[36] Oh.

Actress Julia Roberts, at a Radio City Music Hall political fundraiser, said she looked up the word "Republican" in the dictionary and found that it fell somewhere between "reptilian" and "repugnant."[37] Later, when the president's daughters faced charges of underage drinking, Roberts compassionately "defended" them: "We all need to take a deep breath and think about being a Bush daughter and having that cross to bear. I'd go out and have a couple of drinks, too."[38]

Do these people think things through?

Guns and the Second Amendment so disturb actor Tim Roth that he felt uncomfortable costarring in the remake of *Planet of the Apes* with National Rifle Association (NRA) president Charlton Heston. "I have disagreements with everything he stands for," said Roth.[39]

But Mr. Roth suffered no difficulty working with another costar in *Planet of the Apes,* Mark Wahlberg. Wahlberg, too opposes guns, "Being from the 'hood, I've got my own views on guns."[40] The 'hood? *People* magazine says Wahlberg grew up in "Boston's working-class Dorchester section."[41]

People magazine also reports that Wahlberg spent forty-five days in prison for assaulting a Vietnamese man, calling him a "slant-eyed gook." Actually, *People* appears to have pulled its punches, for, according to other sources, Wahlberg not only assaulted the man but also struck him with a stick, blinding the man in one eye.[42] In 1986, at age 15, police arrested Wahlberg when he and two others threw rocks and screamed at blacks "intruding" into his neighborhood. Wahlberg and his companions allegedly yelled, "Kill the niggers! Kill the niggers!" The state issued a judgment, signed by Wahlberg and his mother, prohibiting Mark from committing further hate crimes and from "assaulting, threatening, intimidating, or harassing . . . persons or property . . . because of that person's race, color or national origin."[43]

In 1992, a man accused Wahlberg of "without provocation or cause, viciously and repeatedly [kicking the plaintiff] . . . in the face and jaw."[44] And more recently, Wahlberg's bodyguard filed a $2 million lawsuit, claiming that Wahlberg "maliciously and intentionally, and without just cause or provocation, assaulted, beat and bit him" in November 2001 outside a New York City restaurant.[45]

Similarly, Roth found no difficulty filming a movie with Tupac Shakur. Remember Tupac? He was sentenced to four-and-a-half years after a sex attack on a female fan and spent fifteen days behind bars for assaulting the director on a music video set.[46] Shakur also allegedly assaulted a Los Angeles limo driver. A court convicted him of assault for a baseball bat attack on another rapper. Other run-ins included a gun battle with two off-duty Atlanta policemen, but the charges were later dropped.[47]

Roth says his status as a father makes him sensitive to the issue of guns. What would Roth's kids think of Daddy's role in *Pulp Fiction,* where Roth played a thuggish lowlife who pulled armed robberies? Wahlberg and Tupac are one thing, but Roth draws the line at working with a member of the NRA. Hey, an actor's gotta have standards, right?

Actor Sean Penn apparently prefers Al Qaeda's Osama bin Laden to Fox's Bill O'Reilly. "I think that people like the Howard Sterns, the Bill O'Reillys, and to a lesser degree the bin Ladens of the world are making a horrible contribution," the forty-one-year-old star told *Talk* magazine. "I'd like to trade O'Reilly for bin Laden. . . .[O'Reilly] is not a man sitting on the toilet with a smile on his face. He's a grumpy, self-loathing joke. There's a long history of people who capitalize on the lowest common denominator of people's impulses, Adolf Hitler being one of them. Not everybody wants to hit the wall in a violent rage and break their knuckles, so [O'Reilly] does it for them. He'll get very rich and get his rocks off that he's powerful. . . . These guys—Joe McCarthy, Bill O'Reilly—die like everyone else. And when they do, their legacy is one of damaging the spirit of good things, and they become rather broken, pathetic figures. And that is what is going to happen to him."[48]

Former *NYPD Blue* actress Sharon Lawrence appeared in a photo spread on the Bush inaugural. Now, Lawrence, mind you, did not attend the Bush inaugural. Instead, she attended a soiree for the Creative Coalition, an advocacy organization of the arts and entertainment community. *People* magazine simply put her photo next to a series of

Bush inaugural photos, thus giving a not-so-careful reader the impression that Lawrence received an invitation to and attended the Bush inaugural. Although Lawrence calls herself a lifelong Democrat, some in Hollywood falsely assumed her a Republican based on her inclusion in the *People* spread. Lawrence received hate mail, and people confronted her on the streets. Lawrence also said she "was chilled" when one producer queried her during a business meeting, "I have to ask, are you really a Republican?" Lawrence said, "If one is ever perceived to be a Republican in Hollywood, there can be an excluding reaction and people genuinely resent you!"[49]

And it's not just the actors. According to Liz Smith, the late makeup-artist-to-the-stars Kevyn Aucoin insisted he would never touch the face of a Republican celebrity: "It would be like a Jew doing makeup for Eva Braun!"[50]

Republicans appear to be an endangered species in Hollywood. I received this letter from a lonely Republican off-camera worker:

> I work as a dolly grip in the movie business. I've heard some of your comments regarding the lack of tolerance for opposing views among the liberals of Hollywood. I was working on The Princess Diaries during our last presidential election. I'm a Republican and intended to vote for George Bush, and I don't like to make politics a big deal at work. But one day about a week before the election, Gore/Lieberman stickers and buttons started appearing everywhere. Someone even came to the set from the campaign. I didn't want this to go unanswered, so I put a Bush/Cheney sticker that I got from the NRA on the dolly. It didn't last twenty minutes. While not a single Gore sticker was touched in any way, the Bush sticker was written on, torn and ultimately covered with several Gore stickers, all on my piece of equipment. I was also called a "racist, white supremacist redneck" by the cameraman (who's a 6'3" blond German, oddly enough), because he says that's the only way he can explain wanting to vote for Bush or own a gun.

Actor Richard Gere objected to Bush's declaration of war against terrorism. He offered this solution: "It's all of our jobs to keep our minds as expansive as possible. If you can see [the terrorists] as a relative who's dangerously sick and we have to give them medicine, and the medicine is love . . . there's nothing better."[51] How about a bumper sticker—"Have You Hugged a Terrorist Today?" Why bother dropping daisy-cutters when we can just drop love bombs?

Even after September 11, director Robert Altman continued his attack on the administration. In an interview with a London newspaper, Altman said, "This present government in America I just find so disgusting, the idea that George Bush could run a baseball team successfully—he can't even speak! I just find him an embarrassment. I was over here when the election came on and I couldn't believe it—and I'm seventy-six years old. Then when the Supreme Court came in and turned out to be a totally political animal, the last shred of any naïveté that was left in me has gone. When I see an American flag flying, it's a joke."[52]

Love the terrorist, hate the conservative.

SHALLOW HOLLYWOOD
DOUBLE STANDARD

Look out, here comes the National Association for the Advancement of Fat Acceptance. Calling obesity a "civil rights issue," the organization protested the movie *Shallow Hal*. Hal, an ordinary-looking guy, prefers dating only unbelievably attractive women. He meets the morbidly obese Gwyneth Paltrow. The sight of her, of course, simply repels him. But wait, Hal undergoes hypnosis to overlook her obesity, and voilà, now sees the obese Gwyneth Paltrow as slender and sleek.

When the spell wears off, Hal realizes, much to his dismay, that his new love makes Jabba the Hutt look dainty. And shallow Hal being shallow Hal, he recoils from the woman to whom he once proclaimed love. But, after soul searching, Hal rejects his own superficiality and embraces Gwyneth Paltrow, all 300 pounds of her.

The movie passes no judgment on a habit—overeating—that affects almost 57 percent of the American population. Almost 20 percent are obese.[53] For the most part, obesity results from too much food and too little exercise. The *Journal of the American Medical Association (JAMA)* says that obesity accounts for something like 300,000 deaths per year. According to *JAMA,* "Our current findings indicate that most U.S. adults (more than 56 percent) are overweight, about one in five is obese, and 7.3 percent have diabetes. . . . The weight-related behaviors of U.S. adults are clearly linked to these continuing epidemics. We found that 27 percent of U.S. adults in 2000 did not engage in any leisure-time physical activity, and another 28.2 percent were not regularly active."[54]

But when it comes to cigarette smoking, Hollywood slams the hammer down. Jack Valenti, president of the Motion Picture Association of America, and Sherry Lansing, chairwoman of Paramount Pictures, in conjunction with a cancer-fighting campaign, headed a task force devoted to finding "new ways . . . to reduce tobacco use" in films.[55] Producer-director Rob Reiner led a California fight to put a fifty-cent tax on cigarettes to provide monies for childhood development. (Only the impolite, of course, point out that characters smoked in the Reiner films *This is Spinal Tap* and *Stand by Me.*)

Imagine the following plot line. An average-looking guy, Superficial Sam, seeks a lifelong female companion. But Sam adamantly adheres to one rule—no cigarette smoking. He meets an attractive, smart, witty, vibrant person of good character. But, gasp, he discovers that despite the health risks, despite the noxious odor, why, she . . . smokes! What to do, what to do?

So a friend hypnotizes him into ignoring her loathsome habit. Now, undaunted by her post-dinner filters, he falls hopelessly, madly in love and connects with her on a deeper, spiritual level. But the spell wears off, and, much to his horror, he discovers he now loves a smoker with a three-pack-a-day jones! Oh, sure, he huffs off for a time and pouts a bit, but then loneliness and realization set in. He learns to look past her loathsome habit and to consider the total package. He commits. Love triumphs.

What's the diff? We condemn one habit—smoking—while urging "understanding, acceptance, and tolerance" of another at least equally "deadly" habit—overeating.

In proposing a law outlawing smoking in public parks, Los Angeles Councilwoman Jan Perry didn't bother with health arguments, "When kids see adults smoking in a family-friendly place like a park, it normalizes smoking and causes it to be approved behavior."[56]

But why doesn't this apply to obesity? After all, when the kids see Uncle Ned scarfing down a Hostess Ding Dong, doesn't this "normalize" overeating and "cause it to be approved behavior"?

America faces far more daunting problems than obesity. Cigarette smoking, while certainly unhealthful, ranks low on the list of things that damage America. But when the antismoking zealots energize legislatures to pass laws that restrict the freedom of others, this becomes our business. In San Francisco, for example, "fat acceptance" activists succeeded in getting a law passed to prevent employers from engaging in "size-ism." If an employer seeks to hire, and an obese person applies for the job, that employer cannot "discriminate" by refusing to hire an obese applicant. Now, an employer, citing health concerns and rising medical insurance premiums, may refuse to hire a chain smoker. But the very same employer, citing health concerns and increased insurance premiums, cannot refuse to hire someone who is obese.

In Montgomery County, Maryland, right outside Washington, D.C., the city council passed the nation's most sweeping, invasive antismoking law. A private homeowner could face a fine of 750 bucks if a neighbor complains about the homeowner's cigarette smoke. If you're kickin' back on your lounge chair in the den, and you decide to fire up a Winston, beware if the smoke wafts out of your window and winds its way into the nostrils of your neighbor. He'd be entitled to call the authorities and get you slapped with a $750 fine! The city council bases this legislation on "science."

Science? Montgomery County's Michael Subin, who voted against the bill,[57] said proponents failed to come up with scientific data to support their contention. "I think that, yes, at some point there is an impact," said Subin, "there is an effect, but this one is so tenuous that I don't believe that there was any health data. . . . You are telling somebody that, on their own property, that they can't do something if it bothers somebody. . . . [Something] that is not illegal, not immoral, that is not unethical and as a non-smoker or as a former smoker, it's silly."[58] The Montgomery County Council ultimately backed down, but they had made their point.

Both cigarette smoking and obesity, for the most part, come from voluntary behavior. We demonize one habit, while erecting a no-fly zone over the other.

THE AMERICANS WITH DISABILITIES ACT: "PROTECTING" THE HANDICAPPED BY CRIPPLING THEM

"During the last eleven years," President George W. Bush recently said, "we have opened the doors of opportunity to millions of people with disabilities. And, together, we can ensure that everyone with a disability enjoys the respect that all citizens deserve."[59] He praised the 11-year-old Americans with Disabilities Act, saying it made the United States "a stronger, more productive nation"[60] by providing disabled workers a chance.

But "protecting" the underdog exacts a high price. Altruistic "protection" often cripples those it intends to protect while eroding our freedoms.

Aside from the takeover of authority by the Feds, the Americans with Disabilities Act (ADA) backfires on practical grounds. Since passage of the ADA in 1990, unemployment for the so-called disabled has actually increased!

"Since the highly touted Americans with Disabilities Act passed . . . a decade ago," said Los Angeles Times' Bill Bolt, "supposedly offering new protections for the disabled, things have worsened significantly. . . . During the Clinton Administration, unemployment of working-age people with disabilities has soared from a horrendous 66 percent to a disastrous 75 percent. For those with severe disabilities, for example those who cannot walk, the unemployment, once 87 percent, is rising."[61]

What explains the uptick in unemployment? After all, the ADA supporters assured us that the Act provides incentives for both the employer and the prospective handicapped employee. But, once again, the law of unintended consequences kicked in. Employers worry, "Will I face a lawsuit should I need to fire a disabled person? How much must I spend in order to 'accommodate' a disabled employee?"

"It's likely that the ADA led to people with disabilities being perceived as more expensive for employers," said a University of Chicago public policy professor, "both because of the potential litigation and the costs of accommodations."[62] Economists from the Massachusetts Institute of Technology (MIT) reached a similar conclusion. "The existing evidence suggests that although some accommodations are reasonably cheap," said the MIT professors, "there are some quite expensive accommodations as well. One possibility is that since employers aren't sure what the costs will be, they shy away from hiring disabled workers."[63]

So what to do? Why, expand the Americans With Disabilities Act, of course! Given the ADA's "success," Bush wishes to expand it even further. He now proposes something called a "New Freedom" initiative. This would, among other things, encourage private companies to develop "technologies" to improve the prospect of handicapped employment.

Astoundingly, the Supreme Court recently sided with disabled golfer Casey Martin, in a 7–2 ruling, saying that the federal disability-bias laws require the PGA Tour to waive its requirement that golfers walk the course during tournaments. Martin suffers from a circulatory disorder which obstructs blood flow to his right leg and heart, making it painful to walk long distances, and he sought the right to compete while using a golf cart.[64]

But pro golfers call walking and the fatigue it induces part of the game. "We have believed from the beginning of this situation," a PGA Tour statement said, "that the issues involved go well beyond considerations involving an individual player."[65] The Supreme Court begged to differ. In a dissent, however, Justice Antonin Scalia wrote, "In my view today's opinion exercises a benevolent compassion that the law does not place it within our power to impose."[66]

What greater way to ensure dependency than to pass a law that says you can't cope? Consider a letter I received from a "handicapped" woman:

I am an American with a disability. I have a very rare genetic deletion that has rendered me legally blind. (20/200 best corrected.) I have been told all my life that I should rely on the Welfare State for my subsistence. After all, a "handicapped" person should not be expected to support themselves, now should they?

Well guess what? This "blind" person is a successful SOFTWARE ENGINEER! Gee, imagine that. I have had people tell me all my adult life that my commitment to my career and to supporting myself is threatening other people's "benefits" from The Welfare State. You see, since I have shown, for the past thirteen years, that a "handicapped" person CAN have a successful career AND support themselves AND their family, then other "handicapped" people may be forced to WORK for their living, (OH GASP!!! HORROR OF HORRORS!!!)

I COULD be the Poster Child for The Welfare State. INSTEAD, I am the poster child for what the "disabled" can do if they WANT to. The more I hear about victimhood, about the Social Safety Net, about how the Government OWES people a life and a living, about how the Government should provide a retirement plan for us, the more I talk about my "disability." I do this in the VAIN hope that ONE other person with a "disability" will rise to the challenge and take responsibility for their OWN life and living. If I can get one "disabled" person, one "victim," one person trapped in the Social Safety Net to open their eyes and realize THEY are the key to THEIR success, I have succeeded.

—Mary B.

MASSACHUSETTS GOVERNOR JANE SWIFT SAYS WOMEN CAN HAVE IT ALL—WITH A LITTLE HELP FROM THE STATE

Will someone please tell the victicrats that life consists of trade-offs?

Acting Massachusetts Governor Jane Swift (Republican) gave birth to twins in 2001. Confined by doctor's orders to bed rest, the governor made arrangements to continue legislative business while in the hospital. During her political career she saw her family, two-and-a-half hours away, on weekends and perhaps once or twice during the week. Would anyone dare suggest pregnancy and motherhood incompatible with the demands of running a state? Apparently not. Governor Swift says, "It does make an important statement to young girls, particularly in Massachusetts, that you can achieve a position of authority without sacrificing your personal life."[67] Without sacrificing your personal life?

The Family and Medical Leave Act requires employers to continue paying medical benefits for an employee absent to care for a "family matter." But suppose an employee cannot afford to take time off from work? Not a problem, says Governor Swift, who supports *paid* parental leave. Under a current proposal, Massachusetts employers would make "contributions" to a fund, with the state providing millions of dollars in tax credits. The proposal allows an employee, following the birth of a newborn, to take up to twelve weeks off while "earning" as much as $477 per week.[68]

Here's a thought. Why not relieve the typical American family's tax burden instead? People would have more choices, employment prospects for women wishing to work outside the home would increase, and it would become easier for stay-at-home moms to do so without economic sacrifice. If the governor wants women to know they can "achieve a position of authority without sacrificing your personal life," how about giving taxpayers back their money and increasing their options? But to tell women they can run a state, have family and children, and be equally attentive to all—is a lie.

CRYING OVER THE SHATTERED
GLASS CEILING

I once spoke at a high school in liberal Santa Monica. During the question-and-answer session, a female student broke down while arguing with me about the "obstacle" of the glass ceiling. She later told her school newspaper, "I got emotional not because of how he responded to what I said but because I couldn't believe that someone could ignore the fact that sexism and racism still exist."[69] You see, by pointing out the relative lack of sexism or racism or any other "ism" to hold her back, I undermined her comfortable view that blamed problems she encountered in the world on sexism. It's always safe and reliable to assess blame elsewhere. I took this away from her.

The tearful young lady argued that sexism prevented more females from becoming legislators. Well, why not elect them? After all, women voters outnumber male ones. If, in fact, women perceive electing women to be a compelling need, then why don't more females vote for females?

What about the glass ceiling faced by poor Matt Lauer, cohost of the *Today Show*? Certainly he demonstrates NBC's obvious glass ceiling. Katie Couric just signed a multiyear deal with NBC with a price tag estimated at $60 million.[70] Let's see. The *Today Show* stays on two hours, with Katie Couric and Matt Lauer splitting hosting duties. Thus, per minute, Katie works no harder than her cohost. Where's Lauer's multiyear $60 million deal? Quick, somebody call the EEOC!

Similarly, female heavy hitters Barbara Walters and Diane Sawyer clock in at the $13 mil range,[71] dwarfing the money paid most of their male colleagues. Where, when you need them, is NOM, the National Organization for Men?

And what about poor Lindsay Davenport, 2001's No. 1–rated female tennis player? Who gets the endorsement money? Why, none other than Russia's beautiful and sexy Anna Kournikova, who in her years on the tour has produced exactly zero professional singles wins.

Call her the Susan Lucci of tennis—except that Lucci ultimately did win an Emmy. To date, Kournikova has never won a singles tournament, yet earns more money than any of the women tennis stars and most of the men. Quick, somebody call the Civil Rights Commission!

Shedding tears over the "lack of female progress" results from activist-driven ignorance about the success of today's women. For example, Democrats elected the first-ever female House minority whip, self-described progressive Nancy Pelosi of California. How did the National Organization for Women (NOW) greet this liberal's ascension to power? "Whoo-hoo!" gushed Kim Gandy, president of NOW. "It's a breakthrough for women. Her election to this post gives real hope to women who aspire to positions of public leadership."[72] Did Gandy scream "Whoo-hoo!" when nonliberal female Condoleeza Rice became the head of the National Security Agency? Of course not, for right after Gandy's election to the NOW presidency, she said, "One of the things at the top of my agenda is sending George Bush to Texas," vowing to oppose "right-wing political extremists" from infiltrating the federal bench.[73]

Yet good news for women in the workplace and public life abounds. Betty Heidesch cofounded the Women in Sports Careers Foundation and notes the wealth of opportunities for women in sports, and not just as athletes. "Now we see women from areas like marketing and technology bringing their business skills to their jobs and having an impact. There are tremendous opportunities for women to get involved in sports and do significant things through a variety of channels, channels *they may not have even been aware of.*"[74] [Emphasis added.]

The Santa Monica high school student's attitude rests on a false premise. She believes that, but for sexism, women would likely comprise close to 50 percent of most professions, including politics. Really?

How many *men*, let alone women, possess the stomach and, like the characters in the brilliant David Mamet play, *Glengarry Glen Ross*, the amorality to cold call and sell like mercenaries? How many *men*, let alone women, could survive in a full-throated, take-no-prisoners sales atmosphere like that portrayed in the not widely-released, but fascinating movie *Boiler Room*, which depicted aggressive, hard-core, ice-water-in-the-veins sellers of junk equities? In that movie, experienced salesmen counseled younger ones not to "pitch to the bitch," meaning avoid selling to women, arguing they were too cautious to buy into a telephone, cold-call pitch. Now, how many women do you know who want to sell in an environment like that? Is it the "glass ceiling" that made the movies' casts of salespeople 100 percent male?

Vanderbilt University recently concluded a long-term study of "gifted children," boys and girls equally exposed to intellectually challenging pursuits and studies. They tracked children identified as gifted from the ages of twelve and fourteen and followed up with them for twenty years. What kind of occupations did these high-achieving students choose? Although both groups were identified as "mathematically gifted," boys and girls still chose different fields, with more females than males receiving degrees in life sciences, health, or medicine. Boys were more likely to go into physical sciences and engineering. And 15 percent of the females were homemakers at age 33.[75]

The study also found that men attached greater importance to money and work, while women gave higher ratings to spiritual life, friendships, and living near their parents and relatives. The study concluded that men and women simply make different choices: "Finally, if the United States is to remain true to the ideals that all students be given access to opportunities for developing their potential and that people be allowed to choose their life paths freely, this might require questioning whether males and females should be equally represented across the full educational-vocational spectrum."[76]

In other words, don't assume a 50 percent female role in everything, even given "a level playing field." Men and women are different, and make different life choices.

SEXISM IN FUNDING?

Women now succeed in business at a phenomenal rate. According to a recent *USA Today* article, between 1992 and 1997, 70 percent of all new jobs came from female-headed start-up companies. Yet while women owned 26 percent of all companies, they received "only" 4.4 percent of investment money.[77] Sounds like the landscape looks pretty grim. Is sex discrimination at work here?

Well, not exactly. A female venture capitalist said, "I don't care if the entrepreneur's name is Sam or Susan. I care about: Have they done it before? Are they credible? Can they come in and defend their business case?" It turns out that women receive only 12 percent of doctorate degrees in engineering and 39 percent of business degrees, credentials looked upon favorably by venture capitalists. Also, female businesses tend to concentrate in the service and retail areas, smallish businesses not likely to appeal to home-run-seeking venture capitalists.[78]

But the *USA Today* article implies unfairness, if not discrimination. How? Well, some venture capitalists—get this—dare ask these female entrepreneurs whether they intend to have children. One female entrepreneur sought advice from a male mentor: "When [Christine] Warren, 32, was planning her start-up near Philadelphia, a man she approached for advice asked if she had any children. She said she had a 4-year-old and a 1-year-old. 'So you're done?' he asked. Warren recalls thinking: 'Are you really asking me that?' "[79] Yeah, he was really asking you that. And why not?

When a venture capitalist ponies up tens of millions of dollars to invest in a start-up or expansion, he wants to safeguard his investment. Suppose Danny Daredevil approaches you for millions for his high-tech start-up. He presents a detailed, if optimistic, business plan that shows gradual increase in revenues with a huge payoff in five to ten years. But Danny, on the weekends, enjoys competitive stunt skiing. He also likes to drag race, again, just on the weekends, mind you.

Question: Do you insert a clause forbidding Danny Daredevil from engaging in his enjoyable, but high risk, weekend hobbies? Of course you do. In fact, many professional sports contracts forbid baseball, football, and basketball players to engage in hazardous conduct not related to their sport. Call it protecting an investment.

Are there legitimate business reasons for a venture capitalist to ask a female entrepreneur whether and when she intends to have children? Hell, yes. In fact, *USA Today* quotes a professor who says, "Some women may be slowed by child-rearing. But others start companies so they can better control their schedules to spend more time with their kids." In the article, one female entrepreneur admits that if she had never had kids, she "absolutely" would have begun a company sooner.[80] Doesn't the fact that "some women may be slowed by child-rearing" warrant an obvious, sensible question? Are you committed?

Forget about venture capitalists. How about regular ol' employers? Why can't they ask the same questions? Many businessmen and businesswomen deal with this reality every day: Will the woman who applies as a sales manager give me enough steady, committed time on the job to warrant my investment? Employers also face the mandatory Family and Medical Leave Act, allowing an employee, after the birth of a child or for a family emergency, to keep his or her job and take time off with employer-paid medical benefits. These laws, quite simply, increase the cost of hiring women, and the expense is passed on to consumers. But ask a woman if she intends to have children and expect a hot call from the Equal Employment Opportunity Commission.

A heavy thing, asking somebody for dough. Along with a solid business plan, venture capitalists seek an all-hands-on-deck commitment. Are you dedicated? Will you give me 24/7?

Sissies need not apply. Or can I not say that?

PROTECTING US TO DEATH

A bicycle helmet helps to protect the rider from the possibility of injury. Sounds logical enough. So logical, in fact, that in the last nine years, nineteen states passed mandatory helmet laws. These statutes cover almost half of the children under fifteen in the country. About half of all riders use bike helmets today, compared with less than 18 percent ten years ago. Researchers say helmets reduce brain injury by as much as 88 percent.[81] Therefore, given the number of states passing helmet laws, one would reasonably expect that head trauma injuries should be less than they were a decade ago, right? Wrong.

The number of head injuries sustained while bicycle riding has *increased* 10 percent since 1991. Worse, the number of injuries has spiked even as the number of bicycle riders has declined. Thanks to the increase in activities like in-line skating, skateboarding, and the like, overall bike usage has declined about 21 percent during the same time period. So the rate of head injuries for cyclists has actually increased 51 percent![82]

What's going on here? Fewer people riding, more of them wearing helmets, yet one-and-a-half times more injuries sustained than before mandatory laws. Specialists in risk analysis say that wearing a helmet gives the rider an elevated feeling of security, and therefore the rider is inclined to take more risks. Call it "the daredevil effect": the cyclists feel safer so they ride faster and take more chances on riskier maneuvers.[83]

Scientists call it "risk homeostasis." Insurance companies deal with it all the time. They call it "moral hazard." Once a person feels "safely" covered by an insurance policy, or in this case, by a helmet, he takes more risks. People believe the safety net will be there to catch them if they fall. "People tend to engage in risky behavior when they are protected," says Robert Hartwig, chief economist for the Insurance Information Institute. "It's an ubiquitous human trait."[84]

Doesn't this apply to proliferation of single moms and dads? Doesn't the expectation of welfare benefits affect sexual behavior? When states imposed "family caps" after the Welfare Reform Act of 1996, young people and teens changed their behavior, and the welfare rolls declined.

Yet the well-meaning liberal fascists continue to legislate for our protection, even though the human tendency toward risk causes some "protected" people to engage in still-riskier behavior. They don't seem to realize the unintended consequences caused by their "You can't make the proper decision to protect yourself, so I'm gonna impose a law to force you to be safe" edicts.

THE GLOBAL HIJACKING OF COMMON SENSE

Environmental activist and actor-director Robert Redford recently attacked George W. Bush's environmental policies, saying the president is "ignorant" and "does not have a clue."[85]

In an appearance on *Larry King Live*, *Politically Incorrect* host Bill Maher, too, expressed his supreme disappointment at Bush's environmental policies:

KING: "How's George W. doing . . . as a uniter?"

MAHER: "He is a uniter. Did you see that 178 countries lined up against the one, us, 178 to one on the Kyoto protocol. Even Hitler didn't unite people like that. When Hitler used to do what he was doing there were still some countries, Bulgaria, South America, Spain, that were like 'Well, you know, I don't know.' A hundred seventy-eight to one. That is a uniter. You would think—see that is the arrogance of that administration."[86]

Wow, all this only a mere six months into his presidency.

Unlike other members of the human species, Republicans apparently neither breathe air, nor drink water, nor enjoy nature. On the environment, Republican critics believe the party operates under this motto: capitalism to Earth—drop dead.

In criticizing President Bush's environmental policy, Congress-woman Nancy Pelosi (D-California) pronounced, "Here, the environment is not an issue—it's an ethic. It's protecting creation."[87] Echoing a similar theme, a former official with the Wilderness Society of California said, "Many, many people feel almost religious about the environment. It really does touch their inner souls."[88]

Actor Martin Sheen, who called Bush a "moron," recently received the Sierra Club's Distinguished Environmentalist Award. Sheen sees Armageddon coming: "I don't know if we can repair what's been done already. I really don't know, and I don't know if anyone does. With global warming and the gases that are already trapped, and with no real awareness in sight, with the nuclear proliferation and with the cutting down of the forest in the Third World just to burn fuel, to cook food, to keep warm, I mean it's just horrible."[89] My, my.

Let's examine the indictments.

"Can I please have some more arsenic in my water, Mommy? More salmonella in my cheeseburger, please."[90] So begins a Democratic National Committee commercial attacking George W. Bush's policy on arsenic levels in the water. In the commercial, a cute little girl fills a glass of water from the sink and asks for not only more arsenic but also salmonella. To paraphrase former President Ronald Reagan, "There they go again."

For seven years, eleven months, and twenty-eight days in office, Clinton kept the arsenic levels exactly where they had been since 1942—at fifty parts per billion. In the waning hours of his administration, Clinton reduced the allowable parts from fifty to ten. Bush put it back to fifty. The water industry argued that the new Clinton standard required an investment of $600 million per year, plus billions in capital expenses.[91] Whether the water industry exaggerated the cost misses the point. For Clinton's eight years, Americans somehow, some way, struggled with the same arsenic levels Bush wishes to retain.

But does the environmental policy of the Bush administration truly depart from that of the Clinton administration? Not according to Gregg Easterbrook, writing for the left-leaning magazine, *The New Republic.* "On almost every environmental issue," wrote Easterbrook, "Bush has upheld the Clinton-Gore position. . . . All [Bush has] done," says Easterbrook, "is delay the date on which trace levels of arsenic are cut. This is *precisely* what Bill Clinton and Al Gore did for almost eight years—postponing any tightening of the standard until just before leaving the White House."[92] But, but, this is, after all, arsenic. However, Easterbrook says, "Arsenic is not one of America's leading environmental problems. It occurs in drinking water at worrisome levels in only a few areas of the country, and public health estimates show at worst a 1 percent increase in the odds of late-life cancer for someone who consumes such water for decades."[93]

What about carbon dioxide emissions? Didn't candidate George Bush promise to retain the Clinton-imposed standards? Yes, during the campaign, Bush promised to retain the recently reduced Clinton standard for carbon dioxide emissions. He broke the promise and now is charged with attacking the planet. Yet again, for most of the Clinton years, the country survived under the new Bush standard. Somehow the planet survived while supporters hailed the Clinton administration's environmental activism.

A 1999 *Boston Globe* investigation concluded that the worst polluter in the country is . . . the United States government. Most of the worst pollution on land, lakes, and rivers occurs on government property.[94]

Recently, President Bush sought modest changes to the Endangered Species Act (ESA) to slow down civil lawsuits aimed at getting animals and plants listed as threatened or endangered. He also sought to reign in the process by which federal regulators, citing environmental concerns, restrict the use of private property. "Foul," cried environmentalists.

But even former Secretary of the Interior Bruce Babbitt found such changes worth discussing, and he chastised the environmentalists for their absolutism: "Environmentalists resist any change, fearful of giving opponents of the Endangered Species Act any openings. But on this matter, they are overreacting."[95]

While the ESA sounds noble and just, proponents ignore the law's unintended side effects. Since the government can halt land development and does not compensate a landowner for "preserving" his land, the act creates an unintended problem—landowners destroying habitats before the government can restrict the land's use. The National Center for Policy Analysis, a nonprofit organization seeking private-sector solutions for problems, says, "Even environmentalists are beginning to acknowledge that the ESA may endanger some species by giving people an incentive to engage in what people in the Pacific Northwest call the 'shoot, shovel and shut-up' phenomenon."[96]

But hasn't the Endangered Species Act "worked"? Not according to the National Center for Policy Analysis, which, in 1997, said, "For all of its power, the ESA has not worked well. Of the 1,524 species listed as either endangered or threatened during the ESA's more than twenty years of existence, only twenty-seven had been delisted by the end of 1995. Seven of the twenty-seven had become extinct, eight others had been wrongly listed and the remaining twelve recovered with no help from the ESA. In fact, no species recovery can be definitively traced to the ESA."[97]

And what about private property rights? How much should regulations cost per life saved? Does sound science back regulations supported by the "green" people? Legitimate questions deserve careful thought—something difficult to achieve when legislators like Congresswoman Pelosi feel "almost religious about the environment." Fine. Praise the Lord and pass the sanity. Environmentalists look at "saving the environment" as a religion. Never mind the tradeoffs.

How, I recently asked Vice President Dick Cheney, do we break this environment-as-religion mind-set? Cheney said, "We're trying to get people to come down off the ceiling, if you will, and listen carefully to the discussions and enter into the debate, recognize that we do have to do both, that we've got a solemn obligation to protect and preserve the environment and pass it on to our kids and grandkids in better shape than we've had it. But also, that if we're gonna have any kind of economic growth in this country and maintain the standard of living for our people, we have to have adequate supplies of energy. Now, you have to do both, and we can do both. We can do both in a safe and sane fashion at a price we can afford. But you need to get people to sort of calm down and engage on the substance, not start throwing grenades at one another, because that doesn't get us any place."[98] Now pass the water.

Americans give Bush overall favorable poll numbers, except in one area—the environment. As the media continues to misinform on issues like arsenic in drinking water, global warming, and drilling in the Arctic National Wildlife Refuge, expect this to continue.

The National Academy of Sciences (NAS) released its long-awaited report on "global warming" in June 2001. In the body of the report, the scientists disagreed about the extent of global warming and how best to address it. Yet a CNN reporter waved the report around like a smoking gun, saying that it confirmed "a unanimous decision that global warming is real, is getting worse, and is due to man. There is no wiggle room."[99]

This CNN broadcast, among others, so angered Dr. Richard Lindzen, one of the eleven scientists who compiled the report, that he wrote an article in the *Wall Street Journal* saying, "I can state that this is simply untrue. . . . The NAS never asks that all participants agree to all elements of a report, but rather that the report represent the span of views. This the full report did, making clear that there is no consensus, unanimous or otherwise, about long-term climate trends and what causes them."[100]

The Media Research Center (MRC) examined how the major news networks have covered the global warming debate. They examined the fifty-one news stories appearing on the major networks from January 20, 2001, through April 22, 2001. When presenting global warming theories, NBC, ABC, CBS, and CNN failed to question the theories 97 percent of the time. Only the FOX channel showed some balance, but even there, 63 percent of the global warming stories went unchallenged. The MRC study also found that when covering the Senate-defeated Kyoto Protocol, ABC, CBS, and NBC favored the protocol 78 percent of the time, compared to 56 percent of the time by CNN and 67 percent of the time by FOX.[101]

When it comes to global warming, unpleasant evidence simply gets ignored.

A rare, evenhanded article on global warming in the *Los Angeles Times* says, "Global warming is far from an established phenomenon. Ground-based and atmospheric measurements have yielded conflicting results: While Earth's northern hemisphere has warmed about two degrees Fahrenheit since the Industrial Revolution began, there is equally compelling satellite data suggesting that the rest of the world is actually cooling."[102] Professor Richard Alley serves as chairman of a panel on climate change at the National Academy of Sciences. Alley says, "We are reasonably confident now that a whole lot of the things we have been getting excited about are not [caused by] global warming; we aren't sure what they are."[103]

Few know about the Oregon Petition. "You may have heard that 1600 scientists signed a letter warning of devastating consequences [of global warming]," says ABC's John Stossel. "But I bet you hadn't heard that 17,000 scientists signed a petition saying there's no convincing evidence that greenhouse gases will disrupt the earth's climate."[104]

Signed by 20,000 people, 18,000 of whom have degrees in science—most of them advanced degrees—the Oregon Petition urged the United States to reject the so-called Kyoto treaty, signed by Al Gore, aimed at reducing levels of carbon dioxide. The petition said, "We urge the United States government to reject the global warming agreement that was written in Kyoto, Japan in December 1997, and any other similar proposals. The proposed limits on greenhouse gases would harm the environment, hinder the advance of science and technology, and damage the health and welfare of mankind.

"There is no convincing scientific evidence that the human release of carbon dioxide, methane, or other greenhouse gases is causing or will, in the foreseeable future, cause catastrophic heating of the Earth's atmosphere and disruption of the Earth's climate. Moreover, there is substantial scientific evidence that increases in atmospheric carbon dioxide produce many beneficial effects upon the natural plant and animal environments of the Earth."[105]

In the ABC TV special, *Tampering With Nature*, correspondent John Stossel punctured many of the myths advanced by "environmental activists."

Stossel talked to a group of schoolchildren, all of whom believed the planet faced environmental holocaust. Stossel told the kids that, according to the government, the quality of the air and water had actually *improved* over the last thirty years. To which the kids shouted in unison, "They're lying!"[106]

"Why don't they know the facts?" asked Stossel. "The EPA says, over the last thirty years, the air has been getting cleaner. Smog days, even in Los Angeles, are now rare. How many of you even know that? Nitrogen dioxide, sulfur dioxide, carbon monoxide, lead. Every major pollutant the government measures is decreasing. And the EPA says our lakes and rivers are cleaner now, too. But the kids don't believe it."[107]

And the money for the "environmental movement" continues to pour in. There's money in them thar environmentally sensitive hills. "Money is flowing to conservation in unprecedented amounts," says *Sacramento Bee* writer Tom Knudson, "reaching $3.5 billion in 1999, up 94 percent from 1992. But much of it is not actually used to protect the environment. Instead, it is siphoned off to pay for bureaucratic overhead and fund-raising, including expensive direct-mail and telemarketing consultants."[108]

Environmentalists know how to get folks to open their wallets. "What works with direct mail? The answer is crisis. Threats and crisis," according to Daniel Beard, chief operating officer of the National Audubon Society. "So what you get in your mailbox is a never-ending stream of crisis-related shrill material designed to evoke emotions so you will sit down and write a check. I think it's a slow walk down a dead-end road. You reach the point where people get turned off. But I don't want to say direct mail is bad because, frankly, it works."[109]

Ronald Bailey, environmental journalist and author of the book *Earth Report 2000: Revisiting the True State of the Planet*, says, "Environmental groups make a living by scaring people. They say they're merely exposing the terrible truth about the trends; in my opinion, they're misinforming people in order to scare them."[110] Hysterics, pure and simple.

Professor Jerry Franklin, an ecologist at the University of Washington, says, "A lot of environmental messages are simply not accurate. But that's the way we sell messages in this society. We use hype. And we use those pieces of information that sustain our position. I guess all large organizations do that."[111]

Former Greenpeace environmental activist Bjorn Lomborg threatens to do to the green movement what Professor John Lott, author of *More Guns, Less Crime*, did to the gun control movement. Lomborg tells the truth.

In his book, *The Skeptical Environmentalist: Measuring the Real State of the World*, Lomborg took up a challenge. He read an interview in which the late economist Julian Simon said that environmentalists exaggerate conditions. Lomborg said, "I thought no, it can't be true. But he said, 'Go check it yourself,' . . . so I'll have to get his book, to see that it was probably wrong. And it was sufficiently good, his book, and it looked sufficiently substantiated that it would probably be fun to debunk. So I got some of my best students together and we did a study course in the fall of 1997. . . . We wanted to show, you know, this is entirely wrong, this is right-wing American propaganda. As it turned out over the next couple months, we were getting debunked for the most part."[112]

Lomborg now says, "The world in decline is a litany we have heard so often that another repetition is, well, almost reassuring. There is just one problem: It does not seem to be backed up by the available evidence."[113]

The "available evidence" debunks a number of myths. The *London Times* summarized Lomborg's findings:

> We are not running out of energy or natural resources.
> Ever fewer people in the world are starving.
> Food is increasing per head of the world's population.
> The world's species are not disappearing at an alarming rate.
> Acid rain does not kill forests.
> Air and water supplies are becoming less and less polluted.
> Forest cover across the world has increased.
> Oil spills and toxic chemicals in the sea have declined.
> Nearly every indicator shows man's lot vastly improved.
> Global warming will cost 5 trillion pounds over the century.
> The Kyoto protocol adds a further $4 trillion to this bill.
> The protocol only postpones a 2C temperature rise by six years.
> The money should be spent on new technology and the Third World.
> Human health could benefit from higher temperatures.
> Antarctica will decrease the sea level by about 3 in.[114]

Lomborg, a self-admitted liberal, chastises fellow scientists who put agenda ahead of fact: "If we start thinking, we can't say this because I'm gonna help somebody, for instance Bush, somebody I might not like, so I should keep it back, then I become a small politician instead of being a scientist. So in that respect, I say it's an occupational hazard of being a scientist that you sometimes end up supporting what you in your own personal, political views, you would think of as the wrong people."[115]

Lomborg better brace himself. In a recent issue of *Scientific American* four scientists blasted Lomborg's book. The scientists included Stephen N. Schneider, John P. Holdren, John Bongaarts, and Thomas Lovejoy. But, according to the Center For the Defense of Free Enterprise, *Scientific American* failed to disclose the scientists' leftist ties.

The Center calls Stephen Schneider "a long-time radical anti-capitalist dubbed 'the greenhouse salesman' by *Discover* magazine and the 'guru of gloom' by many others. He worked for two decades at the activist National Center for Atmospheric Research. His science is so good that in the early 1970s he rejected a global warming theory and even predicted a 'Little Ice Age.' It didn't happen. Many have questioned Schneider's devotion to factual accuracy, and have quoted his remarks advocating 'a balance between effectiveness and honesty.' We thought honesty didn't need a counterbalance in science."[116]

Scientist John P. Holdren, of the Center For the Defense of Free Enterprise, serves as "director of the John T. and Catherine C. Mac-Arthur Foundation with the power to submit grants for those he agrees with and deny money to all others. He's also tight with Teresa ('the Ketchup Mafia') Heinz's foundations, holding a chair at Harvard endowed by Heinz money. He also received a tidy $250,000 Heinz Award for environmental wonderfulness in 2001. Oh, yes, and a medallion. And he's a political flak, too, having served as a Clinton administration advisor on the President's Committee of Advisors on Science and Technology."[117]

Scientist John Bongaarts, notes that the Center For the Defense of Free Enterprise is a member of an "activist group founded in 1952 by John D. Rockefeller III, and since then funded massively by the Rockefeller Foundation, Ford Foundation, Turner Foundation, and other rich folks who think there are too many poor folks in the world and have an agenda to control their populations."[118]

Thomas Lovejoy, *Scientific American* writes, is a "senior adviser to the president of the United Nations Foundation." But, according to the Center, what *Scientific American* doesn't mention is that "Ted Turner (who funds radical environmental groups such as the Ruckus Society) is the foundation's chairman and money bags. *Scientific American* tells us that Lovejoy served as assistant secretary of the Smithsonian Institution. They don't tell us that he was a part of the Clinton administration as Science Advisor to Secretary of the Interior Bruce Babbitt and was project leader of the Interior Department's National Biological Survey. . . . He is a partisan Democrat with a partisan Democrat agenda, and a partisan Democrat donation record."[119]

Do facts matter? "Know-nothing science sees unpleasant facts as mere details, and the overall philosophy as everything," says physicist Michio Kaku. "If the facts do not seem to fit the philosophy, then obviously something is wrong with the facts. Know-nothing science comes in with a preformed agenda, based on personal fulfillment rather then objective observation, and tries to fit in the science as an afterthought."[120]

Apparently, environmental activists assume Americans too stupid, too lazy, and too emotional to care about evidence. In his book *Capitalism*, economist George Reisman says some activists practically brag about their ability to use scare tactics to grab the attention of the public. Reisman quotes activist Stephen Schneider himself, who in 1989 told the science magazine *Discover*, "To [grab the public attention] we need to get some broad-based support, to capture the public's imagination. That, of course, entails getting loads of media coverage. So we have to offer up scary scenarios, make simplified, dramatic statements, and make little mention of any doubts we may have. This 'double ethical bind' we frequently find ourselves in cannot be solved by any formula. Each of us has to decide what the right balance is between being effective and being honest."[121]

The "right balance between being effective and being honest"?

THE CREEPING SEIZURE OF THE HEALTH CARE INDUSTRY

Mandates, however well-intentioned, often trigger unintended consequences. After thirty-one deaths, the Bayer Corporation unilaterally pulled a cholesterol-lowering drug, Baycol, off the market in 2001. Yet the FDA—the agency designed to prevent bad products from reaching the market—had approved the drug. According to the *Los Angeles*

Times, "Baycol . . . is the twelfth prescription drug to be withdrawn for safety reasons within the last four years. Nine of the drugs were approved since 1993, when the FDA has been under strong bipartisan pressure in Washington to accept more products developed by the $100 billion pharmaceutical industry."[122]

What does this tell you? It shows that the FDA, like all government agencies, yields to political pressure. And, after FDA approval, the manufacturer, not the agency, demonstrated more concern about potential risks to consumers. Manufacturers do not need government prodding to remove a dangerous product from the market, given liability exposure should consumers continue to suffer harm. Not to mention that dead customers make poor repeat buyers.

Surely a just government can, at the very least, establish minimum standards? But who sets the guidelines? Who sets the standard and conducts the cost/benefit analysis? Who stands to lose more if things go south—a job-protected government bureaucrat or a hapless product manager who, amidst consumer complaints about product quality and effectiveness, gets canned?

In a *Los Angeles Times* editorial, the paper praised an "audacious new bill" to provide health-care for the 7 million Californians without it. "At first glance," said the editorial, "[the bill's] price tag—up to $1.8 billion a year—will cause heart palpitations among the budget-conscious. But a raft of public health research makes it clear that the bill would pay for itself by reducing the $6 billion to $7 billion that the state and counties now spend treating sick people in hospitals and clinics."[123] They call this preventive medicine? Get it? More taxpayer money spent now means less taxpayer money spent later. Rather than call this taxation, tax-grabbers prefer the term "investment."

But even if money spent now saves money later, so what? Why do taxpayers foot the bill for health care for other people at all? By assigning the job of health care to government, we say to people, "Health care is a right, an obligation to be borne by fellow taxpayers. Government exists to provide you, your family and your children health care."

Constitutional arguments aside, what part of "Price controls don't work" do people fail to understand? Care to trade our health-care system for that of Great Britain's? According to an article in the *New York Times*, on August 26, 2001, "At present, about a million Britons are waiting for treatment from the state-financed Health Service, and more than 40 thousand wait more than a year for operations."[124] The solution? The government just agreed to pay for the medical care for Britons who leave the country and go elsewhere for treatment. Oh.

How about the Canadian universal health-care system so vaunted by Bill and Hillary Clinton during the first few years of their White House tenure? Kerri Houston, writing in *Investor's Business Daily*, says:

> *Canada's health care is so bad that even the most liberal of politicians there are now calling the system a failure, screaming for complete overhaul, and even proposing—gasp!—private-sector solutions. . . .*
>
> *The assault on Canada's sick people comes from several fronts. Lack of access to drugs, shortages of doctors and other health care professionals and closing of beds are all real problems. . . .*
>
> *Ontario has a critical shortage of radiation therapy machines and technicians. This year, not a single new graduate qualified to become a radiation technologist. The one lone radiation clinic in all of Manitoba reported a waiting list of 371 last summer. . . .*
>
> *From April 1999 to July 2000, more than 1,400 patients in Ontario alone were sent to the U.S. for treatment at a cost to Ontario taxpayers of $15,000 Canadian each. . . .*
>
> *In the meantime, patients in some provinces are waiting one month to see a general practitioner, and up to seven for CT scans, MRIs and other diagnostic tests that take only a few days to receive here in the U.S.*[125]

Third-party paying systems condition people into *not* thinking about the cost of health care. After all, a faceless third party assumes the cost. Columnist Mona Charen writes, "Before the government began permitting companies to deduct the cost of providing medical insurance (and before the government began paying the bills of the elderly outright), individuals either purchased their own insurance or paid for medical expenses out of pocket. In either case, they had an incentive to use medical services prudently.

"But after medical insurance became a fringe benefit—after a third-party payer forked over 80 percent or 100 percent of the price of a visit to the dermatologist or psychiatrist or podiatrist—the individual had little or no incentive to curb his appetite for medicine. If the same system applied to food expenses, who wouldn't choose filet mignon and caviar every night?"[126]

Meanwhile, the cost of health care spirals upward. During World War II the government imposed wage controls. With their ability to lure and reward good employees hampered by wage limitations, employers convinced the government to allow employer-provided health-care benefits.

But the medical–spending floodgates really opened after the creation of Medicare. Medical spending in 1960 was 5 percent of our gross domestic product, and by 1997 it was 14 percent.[127] According to government projections done in 1992, which assumed a modest growth rate of 1.1 percent a year (a much lower rate than we actually managed in the 1990s), health-care spending could reach 27 percent of Gross Domestic Product (GDP) by 2020 and 32 percent by 2030.[128]

Dr. Vern Cherewatenko and Dr. Dave MacDonald took steps to stop this government-driven runaway train of higher health-care costs. Under the guidelines of managed care, their Renton, Washington, practice was losing $80,000 a month. How? They charged $79 for a ten-minute visit. But the insurance companies would only pay an average reimbursement of $43, and it cost them up to $20 to chase down that $43 payment. That left them with just $23 to pay their $30 over-head—a loss of $7 per visit.[129]

Fed up, the doctors started SimpleCare. They offer their patients a "best price" fee of $35 for a ten-minute visit if the patient pays in full at the time of the visit. You know, the same way you pay for groceries, or to get your car repaired, or virtually any other product or service. The doctors, now making a reasonable profit for their services, report that their patients, especially the uninsured, seem delighted.[130]

Imagine that. Pay-as-you-go. Fee-for-services between customer and provider. No third party or government needed. What a novel idea.

I recently received this to-the-point letter from a Maryland doctor:

There's all this talk of protecting patients' rights. I'm not against patients' rights. But doesn't the fact that patients' rights seem to be getting violated raise serious questions about our whole health-care system in the first place?

If the government didn't interfere so much in medicine, patients' rights would be protected by the value doctors and patients would otherwise have for each other. Doctors would be invested in pleasing their patients and doing good work. These are rational incentives required both to make money and achieve excellence in the field of medicine.

Because of government involvement in medicine, third parties have intervened so much in the doctor-patient relationship that rights have gone by the wayside. Doctors must increasingly answer either to Medicare, a government agency, or heavily regulated quasi-private companies such as HMOs. Doctors have increasingly been put in a position of conflict of interest: If the patient's needs conflict with the wants of the third party, then the third party must win—or else the doctor goes out of business. It's also hard for doctors to fully consider the dignity and rights of the patient when working through the maze of regulations generated by government bureaucracy.

This is the real problem in health care today. No patients' bill of rights is going to fix it. At best, such a bill will do nothing and at worst it will harm things even more, driving up the costs of health care due to legal damages. Until patients are given more freedom and responsibility, in the form of now-forgotten proposals such as Medical Savings Accounts and tax incentives, they are not going to experience the rights they want. Rights are not things which can be wished or legislated into existence by feel-good proposals. Rights can only be actualized by leaving people alone, by not interfering in doctor-patient relationships except in the cases of objective malpractice or fraud. If our government would just stop trying to impose a one-size-fits-all solution on medical care in this country, the medical marketplace would be as affordable and rational as the marketplace for computers, cellular phones, cars, and houses.

—*Michael J. Hurd, Ph.D. (www.DrHurd.com)*

But the nanny-staters—those who believe the government should care for us as if we were children—remain undaunted.

Congress recently passed, and the president signed, a Patients' Bill of Rights. A Patients' Bill of Rights? In any other normal setting, the business provider seeks to please the consumer, and therefore has no need for a "Bill of Rights." I recently visited an "In-N-Out Burger" and did not notice the posting of a "Fast Food Customers' Bill of Rights." I then got my car washed, but I didn't see anything called a "Car Wash Customers' Bill of Rights." Is there a "Department Store Service Bill of Rights"? A "Personal Computer Users' Bill of Rights"? "Grocery Store Shoppers' Bill of Rights"? "Gas Station Customers' Bill of Rights"? "Barber and Beauty Shop Bill of Rights"?

If we patients want better service, let's tell the government to stop practicing medicine.

2.

SELF-DEFENSE IS JOB
NUMBER ONE

*We now have a government that tries to do everything for everyone. In the
weeks preceding the [September 11] attack, Congress was debating inane
subjects such as whether the government should pay for expensive prescription
drug benefits for senior citizens, the richest age group in America; whether Uncle
Sam should be providing day-care subsidies for working moms; whether the
Justice Department should break up Microsoft.*[1]
—STEPHEN MOORE, PRESIDENT, CLUB FOR GROWTH

*[Congress's] motto is, "Don't just stand there, spend something."
This is the only way they feel relevant.*[2]
—MITCH DANIELS, DIRECTOR, OFFICE OF
MANAGEMENT AND BUDGET

On September 11, 2001, government failed.

As nineteen terrorists hijacked four commercial planes, President George W. Bush sat reading to schoolchildren at Booker Elementary
School in Florida. Nice photo op. But the scene serves as a microcosm
for "what went wrong."

On that day, government failed to do its job—national defense—while
the president performed a task outside of his job description—education.
A government exists, first and foremost, to ensure the safety of its citizens.

Why, on September 11, did government fail? Our welfare-state-driven
Congress spends its time and money on federal education programs, federal
involvement in health care, federal involvement in retirement benefits—
all functions citizens can and should handle themselves. The tragedy of

September 11 demands that Americans rethink their relationship with government. Why does government spend so much of its $2 trillion budget on matters outside the federal government's job description?

The FBI, the CIA, the National Security Agency, the Federal Aviation Administration (FAA), and the House and Senate military oversight committees all failed to prevent nineteen terrorists from hijacking not one, but four, commercial airplanes. And, more galling, all the hijackers apparently entered the country legally, but they overstayed their visas, and no one bothered to look into their activities. Indeed, two of the hijackers were mailed approvals for student visas six months after September 11.

Yet, during the 2000 presidential race, both candidates fell all over themselves promising to spend more and more of taxpayers' money to create the all-time largest nondefense government. Pre–September 11, our "limited-government" president signed a budget increasing government spending by 5 percent, well above the rate of inflation.

Whether the spending "works" seems irrelevant. As a presidential candidate, George W. Bush promised to fundamentally alter education and to allow parents to opt out of the monopolistic public school system. But the final budget excluded vouchers and increased spending. In 1965, Congress passed the Title I program, designed to close the performance gap between urban public school districts and suburban districts. Candidly, George W. Bush's secretary of education, Rod Paige, admitted the program was a failure. "After spending $125 billion of Title I money over twenty-five years, we have virtually nothing to show for it. Fewer than a third of fourth-graders can read at grade level."[3]

But, voilà, the final budget *increased* Title I by 20 percent.[4]

Now some forty states face spending deficits, even though nearly all have laws or constitutions requiring a balanced budget. During the economic boom of the nineties, states spent and spent some more, burning through their surpluses as if they possessed licenses to print money.

Secretary of the Treasury Paul O'Neill, only months into the new administration, made a bold and politically incorrect statement. This plain-talking businessman, the former CEO of Alcoa, sounded almost like one of the Founding Fathers when he said, "Able-bodied adults should save enough on a regular basis so that they can provide for their own retirement and, for that matter, for their health and medical needs."[5]

O'Neill argues that a moral, principled, constitutional society celebrates personal responsibility and free enterprise. But under the Bush administration, government *continues* to grow.

For a time, Republicans controlled the White House and both chambers of Congress. With what result? Stephen Moore, author and president of the Club for Growth and current senior fellow and former director of Fiscal Policy Studies for the Cato Institute, says, "Over the past three years—a period of Republican control of both House and Senate—the rate of growth of federal domestic spending has accelerated from 6 percent to 8.5 percent, during a time of nearly zero inflation."[6]

"So far this year [through early September, 2001]," says Moore, "legislators have requested an all-time-record number of pork-barrel special interest projects—bicycle paths, county courthouses, railroad museums, shark-research funds, money for onion growers, and the like. At least half of these slabs of taxpayer-funded bacon would be delivered to Republican districts. The Office of Management and Budget calculates that if every one of these requests were approved, the price tag would reach $280 billion. That's a figure equal to the entire defense budget."[7]

Even worse, some Republicans privately call much of the spending wasteful, unnecessary, and even harmful. Take the Department of Education and the growth of its budget. Moore said, "Between 1996 and 1999, the department's budget shot up 38 percent, to $33 billion. In 2000, its funding grew by another $6 billion; and this year Bush's education reforms call for a doubling of the federal education budget over five years. *White House officials admit—anonymously and off-the-record* [emphasis added]—that these funds will do almost nothing to help schoolchildren, but will do a lot to help Republicans save their jobs."[8]

A month and a half before September 11, Congress busied itself with at least ten bills related to airline customer service matters. Why? Congresspersons fly often, becoming the most frequent of the frequent flyers. Many dash off back home after the day's last vote has been taken—right around the busiest time of the day as planes begin to back up on the tarmac. Of course, congresspersons have the right—just like the rest of us—to patronize carriers with strong ontime records and better customer service. But, no. Personally inconvenienced, many undoubtedly say to themselves, "There oughta be a law."

Inconveniencing a congressperson, it appears, is a sure path to additional government regulation. Unlike your ordinary unhappy traveler who found his bag didn't make it to his destination, *these* disgruntled fliers believe they have the right and the power to do something about the inconvenience. Members of Congress "can't let their personal single bad experience dominate the development of policy for the industry," says Representative John Mica (R-Florida). Yet they do. "If you're in a position to do something about it," says Carol Hallett, president of the Air Transport Association, "you're going to do it whether or not it's the fair thing to do." Hallett says she urges the irritated lawmakers to call the airlines' special service desks for VIPs. "The airlines want to work with them, but sometimes they don't get the opportunity."[9]

Representative James Oberstar (D-Minnesota) suggested a law to require people to put their bag in the bin above their own seat. Representative Peter DeFazio (D-Oregon) doesn't believe the stats indicating that customer service complaints are lower. He fumes that both a United Airlines 800-number operator and a Red Carpet Club employee refused to take one of his complaints. Representative Robert Menendez (D-New Jersey) groused that an airline lost one of his bags on a February trip to Mexico. Senator Dianne Feinstein (D-California) called for a two-drink limit on domestic flights, threatening legislation if the airlines don't "volunteer" the alcohol limit. Representative John Dingell (D-Michigan) thinks airlines should pay travelers 200 percent of the ticket price for a flight delayed over two hours. For a delay over three hours, his legislation proposes a 100 percent penalty for every hour of the additional delay. And this would apply to delays beyond the control of the airlines, including bad weather.[10]

Doesn't Congress have better things to do—like protecting this country?

GOVERNMENTAL POWER GRAB IN
WARTIME WASHINGTON

Bush declared a War Against Terrorism. Now both Democrats and Republicans use the war to justify expanding the scope, power, and intrusiveness of government.

Congress quickly approved $40 billion in emergency spending following September 11, but financial losses for affected businesses continued to mount. Citizens face unparalleled domestic security threats from terrorist cells, or enemies from within. Our CIA spends too little on intelligence. Our defense establishment has few fluent Arabic speakers on the payroll.

Now is the time to re-embrace the Founding Fathers' vision of limited government. Now is the time to focus our time, energy, and resources on government's number 1 job, self-defense.

Instead, Congress uses national security to rationalize the bailout of some industries while browbeating and coercing others into doing the government's bidding.

Consider what the *Wall Street Journal* called "The Cipro Circus."[11] Following the anthrax scares, Congress urged stockpiling of the anti-anthrax drug Cipro. But Cipro's manufacturer, Bayer AG, holds the patent. Politicians from both sides of the aisle demanded that Bayer make Cipro available at "affordable" prices, threatening to strike down Bayer's patent if the manufacturer failed to go along! New York Senator Charles Schumer (Democrat) urged Congress to ignore Bayer's patent. Republican Health & Human Services head Tommy Thompson also threatened to override Bayer's patent if the manufacturer refused to lower its prices.[12]

Clearly intimidated, Bayer took out a full-page ad in the *Washington Post,* promising, "We will meet this threat head on."[13] Bayer agreed to sell the government 100 million pills at 95 cents each, a savings of nearly $100 million of Bayer's customary price. Bayer also substantially increased production. "Bayer is fully committed to supplying America in its war on bioterrorism," said Bayer President Helge H. Wehmeier.[14]

The *Wall Street Journal* said, "What makes the Cipro circus doubly disturbing is that it seems to have been motivated by concerns over price and not supply. Bayer seemed able to produce enough Cipro, and even if it were not it makes more sense to allow Bayer to license production to other companies rather than bust a patent."[15]

AMERICA GOT MUGGED

After September 11, the airline industry asked Congress for "emergency aid." Since the feds grounded them for several days, said the airlines' CEOs, the government needs to step up and help the industry. But the airlines had experienced a downturn before the terrorist attacks. And regarding the federally ordered grounding, the airlines themselves projected losing only $5 billion from September 11 through September 30 due to the closing of the airports and the gradual resumption of scheduled service.[16]

The former chairman of American Airlines pleaded, "My guess is that the airlines will have to raise something between $10 [billion] to $11 billion on the low side and perhaps $25 billion on the high side, of new cash. Now that's simply more than the airline industry on its own can manage."[17]

"No," should have been the answer from Congress.

Incredibly, the airline industry received $15 billion in "emergency aid" from Congress despite the fact that airlines began suffering before September 11 because of the softness of the economy. Airlines, even in the best of times, remain a notoriously cyclical business with thin profit margins. Did the CEOs base their request on the disaster of September 11 or was it an effort to mask earlier structural problems their management failed to heed? Yet by a vote of ninety-six to one, the Senate passed this "emergency" aid package. They don't use the term "bailout." Nor do they use the term "corporate welfare."

Supporters of the airline bailout point to the "successful" Chrysler bailout. *Successful?* From the time Chairman Lee Iacocca pulled the company back from the brink, it consistently got into further financial difficulties. In 1998, Daimler-Benz bought Chrysler. But suppose more than two decades ago Congress had allowed Chrysler to fail? Wouldn't Ford or Chevrolet have scooped up their assets, possibly producing a more efficient and productive domestic automotive industry?

Suppose the terrorist attacks substantially, and maybe even permanently, altered people's willingness to fly? Should we bail the airlines out because their customers now make different choices? Many Israelis, for example, simply go out a lot less because they feel safer at home. If people decide to fly less often, why should taxpayers step in and make up for the shortfall? Chapter 11 allows a company with financial difficulties to continue operating while shielded from creditors. The airline CEOs could take to the media airwaves and explain their financial difficulties and make a direct appeal to consumers: Buy an airline ticket now, even if you intend to fly much later. If Americans deem the airlines' plight legitimate, expect them to open their hearts and wallets as they have done for the American Red Cross and countless other charities and fundraisers set up for post–September 11 disaster relief.

Certainly, the airline bailout spells good politics. But it is in the heat of emotion that good people must remember to stand on principle.

According to industry analysts, before September 11, U.S. airlines faced losses of $1.5 billion in 2001 from the continuing slump in business travel.[18] Government spending on airlines simply subsidizes sloppy management with money-losing operations. A government bailout merely postpones the hour when airlines will have to come to grips with the obvious: fewer people want to fly following September 11. When business revenues decline, business people running *real* businesses cut costs, downsize, sell, merge, or liquidate. It ain't pretty, but we call it capitalism.

The bottom line? A business, simply because of its large size, deserves no special protection from failure. Protecting businesses from failure, especially with taxpayer money, means money spent on propping up failure while costing lost opportunities. Whatever you call it, don't call it patriotism.

PRIVATIZATION

Why not privatize, with the federal government retaining oversight for national security purposes?

New Zealand privatized their air navigation system in 1987, creating Airways Corporation of New Zealand Ltd., an autonomous, state-owned enterprise operating that country's network of control towers, radar stations, and air traffic control. While the new corporation reports to the ministers of finance and state-owned enterprises, Airways Corporation can't borrow from the Crown or use the Crown to guarantee any debt.[19]

The result? In the five years before the creation of Airways Corporation, the state-run system had run up $120 million in losses. Within less than eight years, the independent company cut its operating costs by 25 percent—even while going into debt to pay for a massive overhaul of key radar and computer systems—and also paid $80 million in taxes and dividends back to the government. "The basic element to achieving the proper commercial approach," said Airways Corporation CEO Pierre Proulx, "is to recognize that governments are not necessarily the best people to run an organization that provides a service to paying customers."[20]

Robert Poole of the Reason Foundation says, "Private ownership has given us the world's finest high-tech phone system. A user-owned, user-funded air traffic control corporation would have the resources and motivation to modernize our deficient system—fast. No longer held hostage to the federal budget process, procurement rules or civil service restrictions, it could give us the kind of high-tech air traffic control U.S. aviation desperately needs."[21]

But what about the FAA? Surely it provides security and protection for travelers? John Strauchs, CEO of Systech Group Inc., an engineering and consulting firm specializing in security, *blames* the FAA for the September 11 terrorist attacks. "These events could have been prevented. I don't think there is anybody who has worked in airport security who does not believe that the FAA should have been dismantled and rebuilt years ago. No doubt there are a few dedicated people who lack resources, funding and support. But most of the people there are fundamentally incompetent. The FAA provides no useful leadership, and the Department of Transportation shares that fault. About sixteen years ago, DOT shut down its office of security. It shocked everybody. The FAA and DOT have never taken security very seriously. They conduct inspections, find inefficiencies, and nothing gets corrected."[22]

To improve airport safety, Congress passed a bill federalizing 28,000 airport security workers, supposedly to ensure a better-educated and higher-quality workforce. But, according to the *New York Times,* "After stoking high expectations that the federal takeover of airport security would lead to a new breed of airport security screener, one who was better educated and more qualified to assume a position of increased responsibility, the Department of Transportation has decided not to impose rules that would displace thousands of current screeners.

"Most significantly, the department will not insist that screeners be high school graduates, a requirement that would have disqualified a quarter of the present work force of 28,000."[23]

What about our FAA-controlled air traffic control system? Subject to military-type federal procurement regulations, it takes years to upgrade computers or purchase badly needed new high-tech radar systems. With technology moving forward at lightning speed, by the time an upgrade is finally approved and purchased, the system is practically obsolete. Several European countries restructured their air traffic control systems years ago into corporations, wholly or partly government-owned, paid for by users—airlines, airports, and private pilots' groups—with great success.

Under the FAA, pre–September 11, 95 percent of airline baggage never got scanned by a bomb detector. Again, this calls into question the meaning, adequacy, and enforceability of FAA rules.

Rather than wait for FAA directives, San Francisco International Airport (SFO) took action. SFO plans to spend $50 million for "explosives detection screening," or EDS, for all bags, whether domestic or international.

According to Ray Bernard, an airline and airport security consultant:

> The SFO International Terminal features the highest level of security for international travelers found anywhere in the world. . . . This level of baggage scrutiny is far in excess of what is required by the FAA.
>
> . . . What makes the SFO International Terminal baggage-screening initiative remarkable is the fact that under FAA regulations it is the airline companies, not the airports, which have responsibility for baggage screening.
>
> So why did the airport undertake this initiative? First of all, by providing common use baggage screening, equipment costs can be shared by the airlines, making a higher level of technology and security available to all airlines at a lower cost than if each airline were to independently try to establish a similar system. Second, it allows the airport itself to establish the security standard.
>
> SFO has a distinct advantage over many other airports . . . The SFO business model minimizes red tape and encourages airport initiative for the airport's sake and for the sake of its airline tenants and passengers. They are able to define objectives and mobilize personnel without the hindrances that are typical of most governmental bureaucracies.
>
> The City and County of San Francisco's appointed Airport Commission operates the airport as a separate enterprise department of the city. The airport is an independent economic entity and receives no direct taxpayer revenue.
>
> The airport sets the standards for all airport facilities and operations. The airport realizes the full economic value of its assets. Airport assets are defined to not only include land and facilities, but also the right to access airport passengers. . . . By owning facilities and controlling airport standards, the airport can maximize facilities usage and profits while limiting inefficient capital investments.[24]

The solution lies in the opposite direction from the one in which we're heading. Privatize airports, cut taxes on airlines, and allow the privatization of the air traffic control system. Let airlines compete not only on on-time performance but on safety as well. The car manufacturer Volvo markets itself first and foremost as a safe vehicle. Why can't airlines do the same?

SFO built the safest, most technologically advanced airport in the country, without the direction of the Feds, because they cut their cumbersome governmental ties and are free to operate like a private enterprise. All other American cities take note: Set your airports free!

DON'T JUST STAND THERE, SPEND SOMETHING

The war against terrorism, says President Bush, promises to be long, arduous, and expensive. To ensure America's security, the public and the private sectors need to spend more money on security, preparation, and self-defense. Where will the money come from? The government already takes about 40 percent of the nation's income at the local, state, and federal level. Add in the cost of regulation—estimated to be $500 to $800 billion—and the government now takes nearly half of America's money.

What's next? Well, hold on to your wallets.

After the airlines succeeded in shaking down Congress, other industries and individuals stepped up with pockets turned inside out.

Politicians from steel-producing states demanded import restrictions against "cheap" foreign steel. "Without steel, we cannot guarantee our national security," says Senator Jay Rockefeller (D-West Virginia). "Without steel, we cannot build from our tragedy."[25] Too bad he never explained how artificial shortages and higher prices caused by import restrictions would help us "guarantee our national security."

Then came the leaseholder of the World Trade Center, who, despite holding insurance, asked Congress to help cap his payout to claimants and subsidize his plan to rebuild the World Trade Center—initial construction of which depended upon taxpayer subsidies in the first place.

The farmers came next. The farm industry, too, declared its survival a matter of national security. Farming lobbyists told their congressmen that "terrorist attacks have bolstered the argument that food production is vital to the national interest."[26] So Congress passed an emergency farm bill, a multibillion-dollar package of subsidies, price supports, and controls. But didn't Congress pass a $5.5 billion "emergency" farm aid package only a couple months earlier? And now an additional "emergency fund"? Yep. The House voted 291–120 to award farmers $170 billion over ten years! That's right, $170 billion over ten years, including $73 billion in new spending.[27] Actually, Congress revamped an earlier bill, titled the Agriculture Act of 2001, tacked on an extra $69 billion in handouts, and renamed it the Farm Security Act of 2001.[28] Southern catfish growers even managed to get a restriction on the importation of competitive Vietnamese fish into an agriculture appropriations bill.[29]

Representative Jim Nussle (R-Iowa) justified the bill by noting the post–September 11th economic stress on farmers, "It's time to react to a very serious situation in farm country. . . . How do you expect farmers to survive under this kind of situation?"[30] Well, how do we expect anyone to make it "under this kind of situation"? What about plumbers, dishwashers, carpet layers, trash haulers, receiving clerks, sales consultants? Do we all get taxpayer money, given our struggle "under this kind of situation"?

The Department of Agriculture expects 2001 farm revenue to reach a record $61 billion.[31] Of that amount, what percentage comes from government payouts? The answer is a whopping 50 percent.[32]

Senator Richard Lugar (R-Indiana) calls farm aid a taxpayer rip-off, noting that the lion's share of "emergency aid" goes to wealthy, quite solvent agribusiness people. "We see that 80 percent of the payments go to farms that have sales of $100,000 or more each year," said

Senator Lugar, "meaning they are farms of sufficient acreage to be worth $1 million or more. The money is going to millionaires."[33] But a fellow Republican defended the funding for large operations. "The reason that some people get more money is they produce more," said Representative Larry Combest (R-Texas). "They are not hobby farmers; they are heavily at risk."[34]

Heavily at risk? The five-year take of some of the current beneficiaries of taxpayer largess to "farmers" include Ted Turner, at $176,000; basketball great Scottie Pippen, $131,000; David Rockefeller, $352,000; Representative Doug Ose (R-California), $149,000; Representative Marion Berry (D-Arkansas), $750,000; and Hancock Mutual Life Insurance, $211,000.[35]

Michael Lynch, a *Reason* magazine national correspondent, says, "Taxpayers might well wonder what happened to the free-market farm policy that was enshrined in the 1996 Freedom to Farm Bill. That law freed farmers of row crops such as corn, wheat, cotton, rice, and soybeans from much federal regulation in exchange for giving up guaranteed payments from D.C. It turns out that farmers did like being free from the dictates of bureaucratic planners. *However, they didn't like having to rely on their farms for income.*"[36] [Emphasis added.]

Our farm subsidies hurt Third World countries. Poor countries start growing an economy with agriculture. Basic farming requires little in the way of education and training and provides the foundation upon which a poor economy evolves. But we protect our farmers against competition by instituting price controls and guaranteeing farmers' profits. This shuts out foreign competition, often from Third World countries. Taxpayers go along with this nonsense because in our minds we conjure up a farm image as depicted in Grant Wood's *American Gothic* painting. But what's American about a farmer picking up a government check that rewards him for *not* farming?

The insurance industry promised not to use the war as an excuse to avoid payouts. Yet they, too, soon knocked on Congress's door for help. The House voted for a package for the insurance industry, similar to the one the airlines received. They voted a $7.5 billion reparations package of grants and loans for "general aviation entities," including flight schools, skydiving companies, and small aircraft manufacturers.[37]

Shipbuilders—not satisfied with the federal subsidy increase already granted—requested a deferral of income taxes owed on payments for building of Navy ships.[38]

What about the bus industry? The industry benefited as the tragedy of September 11 boosted bus service, when wary passengers shifted from planes to ground transportation. Still, the American Bus Association said, "The American motorcoach industry is in the midst of an economic crisis." The industry came to the Hill asking for a grant program, low-interest loans, tax credits, repeal of the federal fuel tax, and a new government program to promote tourism.[39] How can you blame them for groveling at the trough since legislators opened up the purse strings nice and wide?

Amtrak, already heavily subsidized, called on Congress for a $3 billion emergency infusion of cash—50 percent more than its annual $2 billion in revenues. The National Association of Railroad Passengers (NARP), an Amtrak support group, pressed Congress to pass the High Speed Rail Act of 2001, at a taxpayer cost of $19.1 billion. All in the best interests of the nation, of course. "Our transportation system and economy would be far stronger and more resilient," according to NARP, "if we had a world class passenger rail system.[40] But Amtrak already has a new "high-speed" train service, which—due to congestion and poor track quality—averages only 66 miles per hour between Boston and New York, about the same speed cars travel on the Interstate.[41]

Next up, the travel industry. On *This Week With Sam & Cokie*, billionaire Marriott hotel CEO J. W. Marriott, Jr., said, "Everybody who travels in America is sort of a frontline soldier in the war" and expressed his enthusiastic support for the $500-per-person tax credit for travel. "This has caused us," said Marriott, "for the three-month period [following September 11] to be down around 25 to 30 percent. . . . In fact, people at Eastman Kodak say they're selling less film because people are not taking vacations, and when they take vacations, they buy a lot of film. So the ripple effect of this is tremendous. There are 18 million people employed in travel and tourism in the United States. This is the number one industry in twenty states—number one, two or three in twenty-eight states and the District of Columbia. So it's a huge industry impacting a lot of people and a lot of jobs."[42]

The American Society of Travel Agents petitioned Congress for $4 billion in grants and no-interest loans, because—despite the existence of the Internet travel services—they believe that without actual travel *agencies* "the nation's travel industry cannot function."[43]

Before September 11, the U.S. Postal Service expected a $1.35 billion loss for 2001 and planned a rate increase for the fall of 2002. The postal service now says it needs $5 billion to cover the costs of recovering from the anthrax attacks and making the mail safe, but it sought $7 billion dollars from Congress. The post office says it needs $2 billion to offset decreased mail usage post September 11. Postmaster General John E. Potter told a Senate Appropriations Committee, "They should be considered costs of homeland security. Users of the mail should not be burdened with these extra costs through the price of postage."[44] Incredibly, despite their fiscal problems—undoubtedly exacerbated by the terrorist attacks—Potter said the postal service has no plans to lay off workers.[45]

In his book *Human Action,* economist Ludwig von Mises describes the problem: "If the government itself owns and operates plants, farms, forests, and mines, it might consider covering a part of the whole of its financial needs from interest and profit earned. But government operation of business enterprises as a rule is so inefficient that it results in losses rather than in profits. Governments must resort to taxation, i.e., they must raise revenues by forcing the subjects to surrender a part of their wealth or income."[46]

Supporters of the airline bailout called the industry "vital" to America, especially during the war against terrorism. But certainly eating falls into the "vital" category as well. What about housing? Expect laid-off workers to experience stress and pressure in meeting their rent and mortgage.

Mitchell Daniels, the beleaguered director of the Office of Management and Budget, said of Congress post September 11, "Their motto is, 'Don't just stand there, spend something.' "[47]

But the spending continues. Undoubtedly pressured, Daniels retracted much of his statement, and apologized: "That was one of those moments when my brain went on vacation and left my mouth in charge."[48]

The cash register is running.

WARTIME: GOOD NEWS FOR THE WELFARE STATE

Doesn't government spending stimulate the economy? No. Government spending takes money out of the pockets of taxpayers while spending the money less efficiently, less effectively, and often less humanely than private citizens do.

"More fundamentally, does fiscal stimulus stimulate?" asked Nobel laureate economist Milton Friedman. "Japan's experience in the '90s is dramatic evidence to the contrary. Japan resorted repeatedly to large doses of fiscal stimulus in the form of extra government spending, while maintaining a restrictive monetary policy. The result: stagnation at best, depression at worst, for most of the past decade. That has also been the experience in the U.S. and other countries that have tried to use government spending to jump-start the economy."[49]

Wartime provides excuses for Congress to ignore this basic lesson, again savaging the Founding Fathers' principle of limited government. Even before the war against terrorism, the often-Republican-dominated Congress taxed, spent, and regulated almost as much as their "Big Government" brethren across the aisle.

Administration budget director Mitchell E. Daniels said that lobbyists, legislators, and even members of his own administration proposed "national security" spending proposals totaling $120 billion. "It might be autumn everywhere else," said Daniels, "but in Washington it's springtime for big spenders. . . . With a little imagination, any straight-faced advocate can recast his pet program somewhere under the inviting headings of war, recession or disaster recovery."[50]

To fight this war against terrorism, we need to rearrange our priorities and spend the necessary money and resources to protect us against our foreign and domestic enemies.

Shortly after the tragedies, I interviewed liberal California Senator Barbara Boxer (Democrat). "Senator," I said, "I heard one of the news anchors ask a politician the following question, 'Do we have enough money for the billions of dollars we need to spend in order to improve our security *and* for all the domestic programs?' Doesn't this suggest that our priorities are wrong and that we ought to put at the top of the list the protection of American people and property, and perhaps we're spending far more money on social programs that should be done and could be done by people themselves?"

"Well, I just think that you're painting a horrible picture of what we're about," Senator Boxer replied. "We're the greatest country in the world, and, in fact, we have always, always, made sure that defense was number one. What we have not done was to focus on terrorism, and we have failed in that regard, and yes, we need to do that. But do we have to educate our children and make sure that we find a cure for cancer, and Alzheimer's? You bet. So the answer to that is: We are the greatest nation on earth and if we turn away from that, then the terrorists will have won."[51]

What a government. Not only does it "educate our children," but it also discovers cures for cancer and Alzheimer's. We don't need no stinking pharmaceutical companies.

Americans do not need government to teach compassion. Americans watched when, on September 11, about 3,000 people died in the World Trade Center tragedies, 189 died when a jet crashed into the Pentagon, and 44 died in western Pennsylvania. The Red Cross alone, in the first month following the tragedy, raised enough for a $30,000 cash grant for every victim's family.[52]

Less than one month after the terrorist attacks, the *Los Angeles Times* wrote about the astonishing amount of money that had been donated to terror-relief funds in those first few weeks: "Almost as soon as terrorists struck the World Trade Center and the Pentagon, Americans began donating money—and then asking each other to keep giving. More than $840 million has been donated so far, the Chronicle of Philanthropy estimates. Fundraising experts say there's no end in sight, as long as Americans feel threatened and anxious about terrorism and the war to end it."[53] Surprise, surprise. Americans care about, well, other Americans.

After September 11, people asked, "Why do so many hate us?" It's not because of Americans' lack of generosity. Before September 11, American taxpayers already planned to provide $174 million in aid to Afghanistan, more than any other country promised to give.[54]

Americans committed the lives of our sons and daughters to defend Muslims in Somalia, Bosnia, Kosovo, and the Persian Gulf War. Yet many, like former President Bill Clinton, argue that September 11 demands still more foreign aid for Third World countries. The principles of individual rights, free markets, free trade, and rule of law apparently take a back seat to simply providing more money. "We ought to pay for these children to go to school," said the former president. "A lot cheaper than going to war."[55] Or, as actor Richard Gere might have put it, why not just drop love bombs?

AMERICA THE NAÏVE

Arrogance in America, suggested former President Bill Clinton, contributed to the terrorist attacks on September the eleventh:

Here in the United States, we were founded as a nation that practiced slavery, and slaves quite frequently were killed even though they were innocent. This country once looked the other way when a significant number of native Amer-

icans were dispossessed and killed to get their land or their mineral rights or because they were thought of as less than fully human. And we are still paying a price today. . . .

In the first Crusade, when the Christian soldiers took Jerusalem, they first burned a synagogue with 300 Jews in it and proceeded to kill every woman and child who was a Muslim on the Temple Mount. I can tell you that story is still being told today in the Middle East and we are still paying for it. . . .

We've got to defeat people who think they can find their redemption in our destruction. And then we have to be smart enough to get rid of our arrogant self-righteousness so that we don't claim for ourselves things we deny for others.[56]

Arrogant? Name a superpower, through all of human history, that exercised more restraint, more humility, and more concern for the downtrodden than the United States. From the end of World War II until several years later, the United States alone possessed the mightiest, most destructive weapon known to humankind—the atomic bomb. Did the United States pillage, plunder, colonialize? Did America use it to conquer and dominate its neighbors? Despite anticipated hostilities with the Soviet Union, did Harry Truman decide to "get it over with" by attacking that country? The gap between America and the world's second mightiest country is the widest in history. Yet America gives more aid, provides more humanitarian relief, gives more "debt relief," and continuously demonstrates a restraint of power that is historically unique.

Did America's foreign aid to Afghanistan win friends? Did the risking of American lives on behalf of Muslims in Kosovo, Bosnia, Somalia, and Kuwait earn us brownie points in the Arab world?

The generosity and good faith of America causes us to naïvely assume good faith and fairness in others. Twenty-five years ago, former Soviet dissident Aleksandr Solzhenitsyn, in his treatise, *A Warning to the West,* warned America against naïvely trusting in the good faith of others. The world, he notes, remains dangerous, and we cannot allow our goodness to blind us from recognizing evil in others:

It is precisely because I am a friend of the United States, precisely because my speech is prompted by friendship, that I have come to tell you: "My friends, I'm not going to tell you sweet words. The situation in the world is not just dangerous, it isn't just threatening, it is catastrophic."

. . . Now, in the West, we hear many voices saying, "It's your fault, America." And, here, I must decisively defend the United States against these accusations. I have to say that the United States, of all the countries of the West, is the least guilty in all this and has done the most in order to prevent it. The United States has helped Europe to win the First and Second World Wars. It twice raised Europe from post-war destruction—twice for ten, twenty, thirty years it has stood as a shield protecting Europe while European countries were counting their nickels, to avoid paying for their armies (better yet to have none at all), to avoid paying for armaments, thinking about how to leave NATO, knowing that in any case America will protect them anyway. These countries started it all, despite their thousands of years of civilization and culture, even though they are closer and should have known better. I came to your continent and for two months I have been travelling in its wide open spaces and I agree: here you do not feel the nearness of it all, the immediacy of it all. And here it is possible to miscalculate. Here you must make a spiritual effort to understand the acuteness of the world situation. The United States of America has long shown itself to be the most magnanimous, the most generous country in the world. Wherever there is a flood, an earthquake, a fire, a natural disaster, disease, who is the first to help? The United States. Who helps the most and unselfishly? The United States. And what do we hear in reply? Reproaches, curses, "Yankee Go Home." American cultural centers are burned, and the representatives of the Third World jump on tables to vote against the United States. . . .

I have traveled a lot around the United States and this has been added to my earlier understanding of it; what I have heard from listening to the radio, from talking to experienced persons. America—in me and among my

friends and among people who think the way I do over there, among all
ordinary Soviet citizens—evokes a sort of mixture of feelings of admiration
and of compassion. Admiration at the fact of your own tremendous forces
which you perhaps don't even recognize yourselves. You're a country of the
future; a young country; a country of still untapped possibilities; a country of
tremendous geographical distances; a country of tremendous breadth of spirit;
a country of generosity; a country of magnanimity. But these qualities—
strength, generosity and magnanimity—usually make a man and even
a whole country trusting, and this already several times has done you a
disservice.

I would like to call upon America to be more careful with its trust and
prevent those wise persons who are attempting to establish even finer degrees
of justice and even finer legal shades of equality—some because of their
distorted outlook, others because of short-sightedness and still others out of
self-interest—from falsely using the struggle for peace and for social justice to
lead you down a false road. Because they are trying to weaken you; they are
trying to disarm your strong and magnificent country in the face of this fearful
threat—one which has never been seen before in the history of the world.
Not only in the history of your country, but in the history of the world.[57]

TO THE VICTICRAT, FREEDOM IS A "DANGEROUS THING"

Why do some countries prosper while others suffer?

UCLA Business School Professor Richard Roll recently examined
wealth disparities between rich countries and poor ones. After all, some
countries existed long before others, yet a country's age does not seem
to correlate with its wealth. Some countries enjoy abundant natural
resources, while others occupy rather barren territory. Yet Hong Kong,
which rests on a rock, enjoys greater prosperity than many African
countries sitting atop high-demand natural resources.

Professor Roll looked at several variables that factor into a country's success: democracy, trade barriers, property rights, corruption, monetary policy, political instability, civil liberties, and cultural values.

His conclusions? First, dictators hurt. "War is a more immediate and disastrous economic result of maintaining too much power in too few hands. A dictator can send his country to war over the slightest infraction or insult to his ego. The average citizen, the one at risk, has no voice. By contrast, in a democracy, the immediate families at risk decide whether to fight."[58]

But what about a benevolent dictator—one who tempers an iron fist with keeping his citizens' interests at heart? Roll says this presents four problems: "First, there is no assurance that a benevolent dictator today will be benevolent tomorrow, and once political rights are surrendered, they can be very difficult to reacquire; Second, many non-benevolent dictators, who are doing great harm to their economies and their citizenry, hide behind the false label of benevolence; Third, even if a dictator has the best intentions, without the feedback mechanisms of open democracy, he will not have easy access to the information essential for success; Finally, a benevolent dictator may simply be inept, regardless of intentions. Democracy provides a mechanism for the periodic, and peaceful, replacement of ineffective leaders."[59]

Prosperity, Roll finds, remains linked with political and economic freedom. "In a seminal work on the subject, [economist] Milton Friedman argues that political freedoms go hand in hand with economic development. Our empirical results confirm Friedman's views, though again, we cannot be sure from the regression analysis which is the cause and which is the effect. Many . . . believe higher income makes it possible for people to become better educated and more involved in their government. In other words, higher incomes can cause democracy."[60]

But what about the role of government expenditures? Can't a wise government spend money to jump-start prosperity? Again, take the recent experience of Japan. An *Investors Business Daily* editorial says, "Since 1991, Japan has enacted ten separate government spending stimulus plans. They've pumped more than $254 billion into the economy, mostly in the form of infrastructure projects so favored by the U.S. Senate's Democrats. What do the Japanese have to show for it? An average annual growth rate of 1 percent versus a 3.8 percent average in the United States."[61]

Professor Roll agrees: "A developing government should probably not conclude from this result that it could spend its way to prosperity."[62] On the importance of property rights, Roll said, "Because property rights are weak in many developing countries, foreigners, fearful of expropriation, eschew direct capital investment. Smugglers resort to the black market for imported goods. Multinationals are slow to build factories and plants for fear that they will be nationalized."[63]

About Third World property rights, Hernando de Soto, the Peruvian economist, said, "The poor inhabitants of these [developing] nations—five-sixths of humanity—do have things, but they lack the process to represent their property and create capital. They have houses but not titles; crops but not deeds; businesses but not statutes of incorporation. It is the unavailability of these essential representations that explains why people who have adopted every other western invention, from the paper clip to the nuclear reactor, have not been able to produce sufficient capital to make domestic capitalism work."[64]

Moral to the story? Roll concludes, "Data for 1995 through 1999 indicate that more than eighty percent of the cross-country variation in wealth [Gross National Income per capita] can be explained by nine separate influences. The most significant and consistent positive influences are strong property rights, political rights, civil liberties, press freedom, and government expenditures. The negative significant influences include excessive regulation, poor monetary policy, black market activity, and trade barriers.

"When countries undertake a democratic change such as deposing a dictator, they enjoy a dramatic spurt in economic growth, which persists for at least two decades. In contrast, an anti-democratic event is followed by a reduction in growth. This verifies that democratic conditions really are *causes* of cross-country differences in wealth and not the endogenous effects of wealth."[65]

The solution is to confidently, persistently, and loudly proclaim the values that made Western civilization great. Italian Prime Minister Silvio Berlusconi said, "We should be conscious of the superiority of our civilization, which consists of a value system that has given people widespread prosperity in those countries that embrace it, and guarantees respect for human rights and religion. This respect certainly does not exist in the Islamic countries."[66]

The Islamic-Christian Summit delegates condemned Berlusconi for his "racist" remarks. The Arab League demanded a retraction and an apology. A Turkish paper called Berlusconi "a new Mussolini."[67] Cardinal Carlo Maria Martini, the archbishop of Milan, said, "The terrorists must be identified and disarmed, but that cannot be done if an entire culture, religion or nation is held responsible."[68] How dare Berlusconi suggest a superiority of the West, where the people elect their representatives, and where citizens enjoy individual rights such as the freedom to worship any God, or no God? How dare he argue the inherent superiority of freedom? Who does he think he is? Berlusconi apologized.

The statement made by Abdulrahman Awadi, formerly a high-ranking official in Kuwait, reflects the mind-set of many in the Middle East who call freedom perilous. When Kuwait learned that Sulaiman abu Ghaith, a Kuwaiti citizen, had become a top lieutenant with Osama bin Laden, Kuwait revoked abu Ghaith's citizenship. Awadi said, "This is a wake-up call that we have to be very careful with freedom. Democracy and freedom of choice may be good for Western cultures, but for the Gulf countries, those are dangerous things. These people are using freedom to achieve their ends."[69]

ARAB ISLAMIC TERRORIST-VICTICRATS

We "need to understand the mind of an terrorist," goes the refrain. No, we do not need to understand the mind of a terrorist so much as we need to understand the mind of an Arab Islamic "terrorist-victicrat."

Ramzi Ahmed Yousef now serves a life sentence for the 1993 attack on the World Trade Center. Before his sentencing, Yousef told the court, "Yes, I am a terrorist and I am proud of it. And I support terrorism so long as it was against the United States and Israel, because you are more than terrorists. You are the ones who invented it. You are butchers, liars and hypocrites."[70]

Investigative reporter Steve Emerson produced a video documentary, *Jihad in America,* which PBS aired in November 1994. He talked about how Islamic extremists came to America to recruit money and urge *jihad,* or "struggle," against America. Before Osama bin Laden, writes Emerson in *American Jihad: The Terrorists Living Among Us,* came Sheikh Abdullah Azzam, a Palestinian refugee, who, according to Emerson, "laid the groundwork for bin Laden's rise to power."[71]

At the First Conference of Jihad, held in Brooklyn in 1998, Azzam declared, "Every Moslem on Earth should unsheathe his sword and fight to liberate Palestine. The jihad is not limited to Palestine. . . . Jihad means fighting. . . . You must fight in any place you can get. . . . Whenever jihad is mentioned in the Holy Book, it means the obligation to fight. It does not mean to fight with the pen or to write books or articles in the press or to fight by holding lectures."[72] That same year, at a conference of the Muslim Arab Youth Association in Oklahoma City, Azzam said, "O brothers, after our experience in Afghanistan, nothing in the world is impossible for us anymore! Small power or big power, what is decisive is the willpower that springs from the religious belief. It has been revealed that you should perform Jihad with your lives and your wealth. . . . The Palestinian youth came here to Afghanistan, and also non-Palestinians, and they were trained, and their souls became prepared, and the paranoia of fear disappeared, and they became experts. Now, every one of them returns . . . ready to die."[73]

The terrorist Osama bin Laden, considered the mastermind behind the September 11 attacks, blames the United States for, well, practically everything. Bin Laden rails against the West for its evil acts—imperialism, militarism, exploitation, and manipulation. Bin

Laden issued a declaration of jihad to all Muslims in 1996 based in part on America's support of Israel and the presence of the American military in the holy land of Saudi Arabia. He later said that "terrorizing the American occupiers [of Islamic holy places] is a religious and logical obligation."[74]

This angry, historically warped worldview screams one thing: victim.

Following the 1998 bombings of two American embassies in Africa, *Time* magazine interviewed Osama bin Laden. *Time* asked, "What can the U.S. expect from you now?" Bin Laden said, "Any thief or criminal or robber who enters another country in order to steal should expect to be exposed to murder at any time. For the American forces to expect anything from me, personally, reflects a very narrow perception. Muslims are angry. The Americans should expect reactions from the Muslim world that are proportionate to the injustice they inflict."[75]

In 1998, Osama bin Laden issued a fatwa—a religious edict—which decreed to all Muslims, "The killing of Americans and their civilian and military allies is a religious duty for each and every Muslim to be carried out in whichever country they are until Al Aqsa mosque has been liberated from their grasp and until their armies have left Muslim lands." He called on Muslim scholars, leaders, and youths to "launch an attack on the American soldiers of Satan. . . . We—with God's help—call on every Muslim who believes in God and wishes to be rewarded to comply with God's order to kill Americans."[76]

Shortly after his fatwa was issued, bin Laden was interviewed by ABC News correspondent John Miller. Bin Laden explained the fatwa to Miller:

> *Allah ordered us in this religion to purify Muslim land of all non-believers, and especially the Arabian Peninsula where Ke'ba is. . . .*
>
> *We must use such punishment to keep your evil away from Muslims, Muslim children and women. American history does not distinguish between civilians and military, and not even women and children. They are the ones who used bombs against Nagasaki. Can these bombs distinguish between*

infants and military? America does not have a religion that will prevent it from destroying all people.

Your situation with Muslims in Palestine is shameful, if there is any shame left in America. In the Sabra and Shatilla massacre, a cooperation between Zionist and Christian forces, houses were demolished over the heads of children. Also, by testimony of relief workers in Iraq, the American-led sanctions resulted in the death of over one million Iraqi children.

. . . We believe that the biggest thieves in the world and the terrorists are the Americans. The only way for us to fend off these assaults is to use similar means.

We do not differentiate between those dressed in military uniforms and civilians; they are all targets in this fatwa.[77]

The West, according to bin Laden, assumed its military, financial, and cultural dominance through cheating, lying, "exploitation" of the less privileged, corruption, stealth, and brutality. Does the United States come to the table with completely clean hands? Of course not. Name a country that does.

The Arab Islamic-victicrat premise says, "Western world bad, Muslim world good." But 4,000 years of recorded human history show conquest, invasion, commerce, religious conversion, and war. The Middle East is no exception. In his book *Conquests and Cultures*, part of a trilogy on the history and culture of the world, author, economist, and social commentator Thomas Sowell says, "The Ottoman Turks became Moslems after conquering Islamic nations, as the Slavs became Christians after invading Christian Europe, as the Manchus adopted Chinese culture wholesale even before conquering China, and as the ancient Romans absorbed the culture of the Greeks whom they conquered."[78]

Osama bin Laden and his followers call America "the great Satan." But, according to Sowell, "By the time the Europeans discovered the Western Hemisphere at the end of the fifteenth century, Moslem merchants already dominated the slave trade in West Africa, as they did in East Africa and North Africa. The Islamic *jihads* of the eighteenth and nineteenth centuries created new Moslem states in West Africa, which in turn promoted enslavement on a larger scale. Altogether, between 1650 and 1850, at least 5 million slaves were shipped from West Africa alone."[79] And while slavery ended in the West, says Sowell, "In some Islamic countries in Africa and the Middle East, slavery lasted even longer. Saudi Arabia, Mauritania, and the Sudan continued to hold slaves on past the middle of the twentieth century."[80]

Slavery *still* thrives. "Slaves are cheaper today than they've ever been in human history," says Professor Kevin Bales, an expert on contemporary slavery, who estimates that 27 million people in the world live as slaves. "When they're that cheap, they're like plastic pens. You use them, you throw them away when they run out."[81]

The United Kingdom's *Sunday Telegraph* claims that Osama bin Laden buys Ugandan children for use as slave laborers. Radio intercepts, according to the *Telegraph,* show that bin Laden pays one Kalashnikov rifle for every child. The paper says that overseers force the children to work on his marijuana farms in the Sudan, the country where bin Laden lived from 1994 to 1996. According to Ugandan intelligence, bin Laden "has a wide range of business interests [in Sudan], covering farms, banks, factories and infrastructure. These are used to fund terrorism in Africa and elsewhere."[82]

Bin Laden's followers speak of American "imperialism," the bombs we dropped on Hiroshima and Nagasaki, the enslavement of blacks, American support of Israel, and our support, for national security reasons, of unpopular regimes in the Middle East.

Osama bin Laden paints a Muslim world victimized by an unclean, unjust superpower. But Sowell points out, "Morally reprehensible behavior has been all too widespread among all branches of the human race, rather than being localized in those who happened to achieve greater success in conquest or in economic activities. . . . Once again, the mundane reality is that productivity creates wealth, so that trade with and investment in more productive countries is a far more important source of wealth than 'exploitation' of the Third World, however that elusive term might be defined."[83]

So as we learn more about the mind of terrorist-victicrats, let us demand that they, in turn, learn that Italian Prime Minister Berlusconi was right. The West's dominance results from respect for private property, the rule of law, individual rights, no state-sponsored religion, a Constitution that limits the power of the government, and free markets and international trade.

Yet, anger, bitterness, ignorance, and a warped and unbalanced view of history, combined with manipulative, scapegoating Arab leaders, create the mind-set of a terrorist-victicrat. Can one reason with that kind of worldview? Only a fool sits around waiting for the answer.

THE ISRAELI-PALESTINIAN DISPUTE

To understand the Palestinian–Israeli dispute, one must distinguish between the arsonists and the firefighters.

What part of "attacked" don't people understand? Some say September 11 is a wake-up call for more "balance" in the Israeli–Palestinian dispute. But, at the last "peace talks" Prime Minister Ehud Barak offered terms unthinkable only years earlier. Palestine Liberation Organization head Yassir Arafat turned down an offer that would have given Palestinians 95 percent of the West Bank, control over East Jerusalem and most of the Old City, along with the eventual recognition of an independent Palestinian State.

In *O Jerusalem,* authors Larry Collins and Dominique Lapierre describe the Arab world's reaction to the United Nation's 1947 vote that partitioned the area into a Jewish State and a Palestinian State:

> *Half a century behind their Zionists neighbors in the development of their own nationalist aspirations, industrially and socially underdeveloped, having just emerged from centuries of repressive colonial rule, the Arabs responded to the situation simply and unsophisticatedly. They consistently refused every compromise offered them, insisting that since the Jewish claim to Palestine*

was invalid in the first place, any discussion of the subject would merely give it a validity it did not have. Repeatedly, their attitude, made unbending by the fanaticism of their leaders, lost them opportunities to set a limit on Jewish growth in Palestine and to define with precision their own rights there.[84]

But, at the very least, can the Palestinians justifiably claim moral superiority? Palestinian Liberation Chairman Yassir Arafat insisted on "repatriation" of Palestinians who left during the 1948 war. But who told them to leave?

In the book, *From Time Immemorial: The Origins of the Arab–Jewish Conflict Over Palestine,* author Joan Peters initially set out to write about the tragic situation of "Arab refugees." When she started out, Peters said, "The deprivation of Arab refugees' human rights and the political manipulation of their unfortunate situation were unconscionable to me, particularly because it seemed their plight had been prolonged by a mechanism funded predominantly by contributions from the United States."[85]

But after exhaustive research examining the history and politics of the Israeli–Palestinian dispute, she reversed course:

The Arabs had initiated hostilities in Palestine upon the November 1947 United Nations' partition of Palestine into a Jewish and Arab state, employing outside forces and arms from Arab states as distant as Iraq to prevent the creation of the Jewish state, "a series of killings and counterkillings that would continue for decades." Thousands of Arabs, including the more affluent, left for nearby Arab states before Jewish statehood. When Israel's independence was declared in 1948, the Arab forces combined to crush it. . . ."[86]

After the Arabs' defeat in the 1948 war, their positions became confused: some Arab leaders demanded the "return" of the "expelled" refugees to their former homes despite the evidence that Arab leaders had called upon Arabs to flee. At the same time, Emile Ghoury, Secretary of the Arab Higher Command, called for the prevention of the refugees from "return." He stated in the Beirut Telegraph on August 6, 1948: "It is inconceivable that the refugees should be sent back to their homes while they are occupied by the Jews. . . . It would serve as a first step toward Arab recognition of the state of Israel and Partition."[87]

. . . Ever since the 1967 Israeli victory, however, when Arabs determined that they couldn't obliterate Israel militarily, they have skillfully waged economic, diplomatic, and propaganda war against Israel.[88]

Indeed, Peters said that the prime minister of Syria wrote in his memoirs: "Since 1948 it is we who demanded the return of the refugees . . . while it is we who made them leave. . . . We brought disaster upon . . . Arab refugees, by inviting them and bringing pressure to bear upon them to leave. . . . We have rendered them dispossessed. . . . We have accustomed them to begging. . . . We have participated in lowering their moral and social level. . . . Then we exploited them in executing crimes of murder, arson, and throwing bombs upon men, women and children—all this in the service of political purposes."[89]

The surrounding Arab states refused to absorb the Arab "refugees." She quotes King Hussein of Jordan, who, in 1960, said, "Since 1948 Arab leaders have approached the Palestine problem in an irresponsible manner. . . . They have used the Palestine people for selfish political purposes. This is ridiculous and, I could say, even criminal."[90]

What about the property seized by the Israelis when Arabs departed? Peters writes:

One crucial truth, among many that have been obscured and depreciated, is that there have been as many Jewish refugees who fled or were expelled from the Arab countries as there are Arab refugees from Israel, and that the Jews left of necessity and in flight from danger.

. . . By coincidence, even the total number of Arabs who reportedly left Israel is almost exactly equaled by the number of Jews exchanged. There has been a completed exchange of minorities between the Arabs and the Jews, and a more-than-even tradeoff of property for the Arabs. The Jews who fled Arab countries left assets behind in the Arab world greater than those Arabs left in Israel. Jewish property that the Arabs confiscated in Iraq, Syria, Libya,

and Egypt apparently has more than offset Arab claims of compensation from Israel.[91]

Peters concludes:

If the Arab World's political and unjustified discrimination against its refugee-émigré brothers were to cease, and if the camp indoctrination could no longer act as a catalyst to the rejection of peace with Israel, if the Jordanian-Palestinian state, the Arabs' "displacement" of Jews, and the exchange of populations that took place between the Jews and Arabs are all finally understood and recognized by the free world, then the Arab "rejectionist" front dedicated to the jihad (holy war) against Israel may finally realize that the program of propaganda deception cannot succeed. They may then accede to a policy of genuine moderation, of a kind which in the Western sense means toleration and peace.[92]

Arab anti–Semitism remains a staple fare of Arab–world newspaper articles and columns as well as television shows. Abu Dhabi television recently aired a series of programs attacking Prime Minister Ariel Sharon. In one episode, a Sharon-like character drinks the blood of Arab children. Later, Dracula takes a bite out of Sharon's neck, but Dracula himself dies.[93] Bad blood, you know.

SEPTEMBER THE ELEVENTH AND THE ARAB MEDIA

After September 11, newspaper stories in the United States soon appeared bemoaning the "rash" of hate crimes against Arab-Americans, Middle Easterners, and those who "look" Middle Eastern. Robin Toma, executive director of the Los Angeles County Human Relations Commission, said, "As you can see, a wave of hate followed September 11. This is a huge jump from previous years." The entire year of 2000 saw approximately twelve hate crimes toward Middle Easterners, but ninety-two hate crimes were reported in the two months following September the eleventh.[94] Certainly we object to any kind of hate crime. But how about a little perspective?

Dr. Muqtedar Khan, an Indian Muslim and director of International Studies at Adrian College in Adrian, Michigan, shudders at the possible fate of minority Muslim groups elsewhere in the world whose Muslim members committed the terrorist act of September 11. "If what happened on September 11 had happened in India, the biggest democracy, thousands of Muslims would have been slaughtered in riots on mere suspicion and there would be another slaughter after confirmation. But in the U.S., bigotry and xenophobia has been kept in check by media and leaders."[95]

Indeed, President Bush calls Islam a religion of peace and calls for a War Against Terrorism, not against the Muslim religion. Bush points out that most Muslims worldwide want neither America nor Israel destroyed. Fourteen percent of India's 1 billion people live in relative peace as minority Muslims. And in Christian countries, Muslim minorities enjoy greater civil liberties than enjoyed by their Muslim-majority coreligionists in countries like Saudi Arabia, Syria, Lebanon, Iran, and Iraq. But Bush's message gets filtered through the Arab—mostly state-run—media. And, all too often, the Arab media lie.

The Middle East Media and Research Institute (MEMRI), an independent, nonprofit organization, provides translations of stories in the Arab media and original analysis on developments in the Middle East. On their web site, www.memri.org, it describes this chilling "account" of America, post September 11, that appeared in the Arab press:

The Egyptian Sheikh Muhammad Al-Gamei'a, the Al-Azhar University representative in the U.S. and Imam of the Islamic Cultural Center and Mosque of New York City, was interviewed [following his return] to Egypt after September 11 because he was being "harassed."

GAMEI'A: Following the incident, Muslims and Arabs stopped feeling that it was safe to leave [their homes] . . . They stopped feeling that it was safe to send their wives to the market or their children to the schools. Muslims do not feel safe even going to the hospitals, because some Jewish doctors in one of the hospitals poisoned sick Muslim children, who then died.

Q: The media has reported firing on mosques and harassment of Muslim women, and the situation has gotten so bad that Arabs are murdered in the streets. What about harassment you and your family have suffered?

GAMEI'A: It's true. The Muslims are being persecuted by the people and the federal government. This is the result of the bad image of Muslims created by the Zionist media, and of their presenting Islam as a religion of terrorism. That is why the Americans have linked the recent incidents to Islam. I personally have suffered; my home was attacked and my daughters were harassed.

Q: What did you do about this harassment?

GAMEI'A: When a group of people attacked my home, I went out to them and asked why they were doing this. They said that because we were Muslims we were linked to terrorism. I explained to them that what they were doing was uncivilized and was, in effect, a twofold crime, you let the criminals go free and attack innocents. This does not suit a modern state and a modern people, and is opposed to human values. During my conversations with this group, it became clear to me that they knew very well that the Jews were behind these ugly acts, while we, the Arabs, were innocent, and that someone from among their people was disseminating corruption in the land. Although the Americans suspect that the Zionists are behind the act, none has the courage to talk about it in public.

Q: Why can't they talk about it? It's their country, and the Jews are a minority.

GAMEI'A: When I asked them whether they had the courage to talk about it openly, they said: "We can't." I asked why, and they said: "You know very well that the Zionists control everything and that they also control political decision-making, the big media organizations, and the financial and economic institutions. Anyone daring to say a word is considered an anti–Semite" . . . All the signs indicate that the Jews have the most to gain from an explosion like that. They are the only ones capable of planning such acts. First of all, it was found that the automatic pilot was neutralized a few minutes before the flight, and the automatic pilot cannot be neutralized if you don't have command of the control tower. Second, the black boxes were found to contain no information; you cannot erase the information from these boxes if you do not plan it ahead of time on the plane. Third, America has the most powerful intelligence apparatuses, the FBI and the CIA. . . . How did [the perpetrators] manage to infiltrate America without their knowledge? Fourth, Jews control decision-making in the airports and in the sensitive centers in the White House and the Pentagon. Fifth, to date America has presented no proof incriminating Osama bin Laden and Al-Qa'ida.[96]

MEMRI also posts the following translations from Arab journalists blaming September 11 on everything from Japan to the Israelis:

Many columnists in the Arab media have discussed the identities of the perpetrators of the New York and Washington, D.C., attacks. Some chose to disregard the findings of the FBI investigation (that the perpetrators were Arabs and/or Muslims), presenting instead a series of American and international elements that they believe carried out the attacks.

BUSH AND POWELL DID IT

The possibility that the U.S. attacks were a conspiracy hatched by President Bush and Secretary of State Powell was presented by Samir Atallah, a columnist for the London daily Al-Sharq Al-Awsat. He wrote: "I have a sneaking suspicion that George W. Bush was involved in the operation of September 11, as was Colin Powell."

ISRAEL, INTERNATIONAL ZIONISM, OR THE JEWS DID IT

This theory has been very popular among various columnists in the Arab media. Columnist Ahmad Al-Muslih, for example, stated: "What happened is, in my opinion, the product of Jewish, Israeli, and American Zionism, and the act of the great Jewish Zionist mastermind that controls the world's economy, media, and politics."

Jordanian columnist Rakan Al-Majali wrote that "it is clear that Israel is the one to benefit greatly from the bloody, loathsome terror operation that occurred yesterday, and that it seeks to benefit still more by accusing the Arabs and Muslims of perpetrating this loathsome attack. . . . Only Israel does not fear the discovery that the Jews are behind this operation, if indeed it was so; who in the U.S. or outside it would dare to accuse them, as every blow to them means talk of a new 'Holocaust'? They, more than anyone, are capable of hiding a criminal act they perpetrate, and they can be certain that no one will ask them about what they do."

AMERICAN EXTREMISTS, JAPAN, CHINA, RUSSIA, OR OPPONENTS OF GLOBALIZATION DID IT

The Arab media presented a lineup of other suspects who are neither Arab nor Muslim. Syrian columnist Hassan M. Yussef wrote: "There is a possibility that this was an [act of] ancient retribution. . . . The U.S. declared war on Japan, and used the atomic bomb for the first time, against Hiroshima and Nagasaki. [The bomb] killed more than 221,983 Japanese, and was

the cause of the Japanese defeat and the end of the war in 1945. Has the
tragedy of Hiroshima and Nagasaki been resurrected sixty years later?"[97]

A widely believed Arab urban legend claims that four thousand Jews
failed to show up for work at the World Trade Center on September 11.
They received a warning alerting them to the tragedy, according to the
rumor. An opinion poll commissioned by a Pakistani web site reported
that only 13 percent questioned it as a "rumor," 71 percent thought it
a "possible fact," while only 16 percent found the rumor "baseless."[98]

Never mind that Osama bin Laden all but publicly performed a victory dance. In one of his post–September 11 video appearances, he said:

Here is the United States. It was filled with terror from its north to its south
and from its east to it west. Praise be to God. . . .

When Almighty God rendered successful a convoy of Muslims, the van-
guards of Islam, He allowed them to destroy the United States. . . .

But if the sword falls on the United States after 80 years, hypocrisy
raises its head lamenting the deaths of these killers who tampered with the
blood, honor, and holy places of the Muslims.

The least that one can describe these people is that they are morally
depraved. They champion falsehood, support the butcher against the victim,
the oppressor against the innocent child.

May God mete them the punishment they deserve.

I say the matter is clear and explicit. In the aftermath of this event and
now that senior U.S. officials have spoken, beginning with Bush, the head
of the world's infidels, and whoever supports him, every Muslim should rush
to defend his religion. . . .

As for the United States, I tell it and its people these few words: I swear
by Almighty God who raised the heavens without pillars that neither the
United States nor he who lives in the United States will enjoy security before
we can see it as a reality in Palestine and before all the infidel armies leave
the land of Mohammed, may God's peace and blessing be upon him.[99]

We have a word for this—terrorism.

THE BATTLE OVER ISLAM

Americans expected to hear this kind of reaction from Arab leaders, Middle Eastern clerics, scholars, and others: "The terrorist acts of September 11, committed in the name of my religion, constitute a sin, a sin that absolutely, unquestionably, denies the sinner's entrance into Paradise."

Certainly some in the Middle East publicly condemned not only the tragedy of September 11 but also denounced the terrorists in religious terms. Sheik Yusef al Qaradawi of Qatar condemned the attacks as a "grave sin," saying that even if the terrorists were fueled by anger over the Palestinian–Israeli conflict, Islam does not permit the shifting of the confrontation outside the region.[100] But elsewhere the silence was deafening.

It took a month after the attacks before one of the first prominent Arab-world Muslim scholars stepped up to publicly denounce bin Laden and the Taliban. "Bin Laden is not a prophet that we should put thousands of lives at risk for," said Tahirul Qadri, head of the Pakistani Awami Tehrik Party. "Bombing embassies or destroying non-military installations like the World Trade Center is no jihad, and those who launched the September 11 terrorist attacks not only killed thousands of innocent people in the United States but also put the lives of millions of Muslims across the world at risk." Qadri also said he holds the Taliban responsible "for the deaths of hundreds of innocent Afghans," and he urged them to hand bin Laden over to the United Nations.[101]

But for the most part, few Arab leaders and Muslim clerics pronounced the September 11 terrorist attacks a sin that would deny the perpetrators admission to paradise. A senior Saudi Foreign Ministry official, speaking anonymously, while admitting that "we should punish the guilty and bring them to justice," also said, "Israel is a terrorist state, based on occupation and is ruled by a world famous terrorist." The official expressed concern that the United States would adopt "the

Israeli version of terrorism, which defines resisting occupation as a form of terrorism."[102]

Remember the fatwa issued against Salman Rushdie, the heretic who dared write *The Satanic Verses*, a book that "blasphemed" Islam? The former commissioning editor of Channel 4 UK, Farrukh Dhondy, an Indian-born writer now living in London, wrote:

> *In 1989 came the most significant divide in the multicultural history of Britain: the Rushdie affair, which uncovered a multicultural fifth column, whose literary criticism entailed book-burning and death threats. The British Muslim community echoed the call of the Ayatollah Khomeini to hunt down and kill the writer. There were denunciations of Rushdie in every mosque by mullahs and crowds who had only handled a copy of the book to burn it. Not one mullah raised a voice in support of the principle of freedom of creativity; no mullah ventured the opinion that the fatwa was wrong or against Islamic teaching. Though the supposedly liberal Muslim commentators whom the British press retains were not in favor of the death sentence, none would extend himself to a defense of the book. . . .*
>
> *But in the 1980s, a new Muslim leadership of mullahs inspired and paid for by various Islamic powers around the world was entering the country and setting up bases in Britain, thanks to an immigration-law loophole that allows religious personnel open-ended permission to stay. Iranian money, Saudi money from worldwide foundations for the promotion of Islam, was establishing mosques and setting up madrasas, schools that purvey primitive religious instruction and teach the Quran by rote. Adolescents attracted to this new radical preaching, young people whose childhood religious observances had already set them apart from their British contemporaries, came under the domination of a stricter observance with the allure of an ideology. The new mullahs were . . . promising membership in an organization that would dominate the world. . . .*
>
> *If you prostrate yourself to an all-powerful and unfathomable being five times a day, if you are constantly told that you live in the world of Satan, if those around you are ignorant of and impervious to literature, art, historical*

debate, and all that nurtures the values of Western civilization, your mind
becomes susceptible to fanaticism. Your mind rots.[103]

Salman Rushdie says that extremist "Islamists" hijacked the Muslim
religion:

> *These Islamists—we must get used to this word, "Islamists," meaning those*
> *who are engaged upon such political projects, and learn to distinguish it from*
> *the more general and politically neutral "Muslim"—include the Muslim*
> *Brotherhood in Egypt, the blood-soaked combatants of the Islamic Salvation*
> *Front and Armed Islamic Group in Algeria, the Shiite revolutionaries of*
> *Iran, and the Taliban. Poverty is their great helper, and the fruit of their*
> *efforts is paranoia. This paranoid Islam, which blames outsiders, "infidels,"*
> *for all the ills of Muslim societies, and whose proposed remedy is the closing*
> *of those societies to the rival project of modernity, is presently the fastest*
> *growing version of Islam in the world. . . .*
>
> *An Iraqi writer quotes an earlier Iraqi satirist: "The disease that is in*
> *us, is from us." A British Muslim writes, "Islam has become its own en-*
> *emy." A Lebanese friend, returning from Beirut, tells me that in the after-*
> *math of the attacks on September 11, public criticism of Islamism has become*
> *much more outspoken. Many commentators have spoken of the need for a*
> *Reformation in the Muslim world.*[104]

BLAMING AMERICA

In Afghanistan, a teacher holds up a pie chart showing the wealth of
the world. He depicts the United States with a huge slice of the pie,
leaving only a tiny sliver for Afghanistan. The not-so-subtle point? We
Afghans suffer poverty because America enjoys so much wealth. It's
the Arab-victicrat mentality. The wealth of the United States comes at
the expense of the rest of the world, especially the Arab world.

Countries like Saudi Arabia and Egypt suffer double-digit unemployment rates estimated to run as high as 25 percent. Grinding poverty and religious zealotry, wrapped around a blanket of government-led scapegoating of Israel, the United States and the West—combine to form a dangerous and deadly Third World victicrat mind-set. Blame defeats enlightenment, and anger defeats reason.

So, who to blame?

"I don't have the knowledge to blame a government," said Bakhtiar Khan, an Afghan man in his midtwenties. "I don't know about politics, but for our problems I blame the world community. All humans should be equal, but we are not. You ask me who is to blame. You find out who is to blame."[105]

Khan, according to a recent *New York Times* piece on the origins of Islamic extremism, earns a subsistence-level income making bricks in a pit outside the city of Peshawar, an Afghan city of two million, nearly 50 percent of them refugees. Khan works twelve hours a day, six days a week, producing 1,000 bricks a day. He has been working in the brick pits since he was 10 years old. When asked about his life, he says, "Life is cruel. You can see for yourself. You wear nice clothes and are healthy. But look at us. We have no clothes to wear and we are not healthy. Your question is amazing."[106]

But Khan lacks the "knowledge to blame a government." For, through knowledge, Khan would discover that his poverty stems from corrupt, dictatorial governments, the absence of capitalism and free trade, and the lack of individual rights and the rule of law. But who, in the Arab world, spreads this message?

Dr. Muqtedar Khan, of Adrian College, challenges American Muslims to set the masses straight:

> *While we loudly and consistently condemn Israel for its ill treatment of Pa-
> lestinians, we are silent when Muslim regimes abuse the rights of Muslims
> and slaughter thousands of them. Remember Saddam and his use of chemical
> weapons against Muslims (Kurds)? Remember the Pakistani army's excesses
> against Muslims (Bengalis)? Remember the Mujahideen of Afghanistan and
> their mutual slaughter? Have we ever condemned them for their excesses?*

Have we demanded international intervention or retribution against them? Do you know how the Saudis treat their minority Shiis? Have we protested the violation of their rights? But we all are eager to condemn Israel; not because we care for rights and lives of the Palestinians, we don't. We condemn Israel because we hate "them."

Muslims love to live in the U.S. but also love to hate it. Many openly claim that the U.S. is a terrorist state but they continue to live in it. Their decision to live here is testimony that they would rather live here than anywhere else. As an Indian Muslim, I know for sure that nowhere on earth, including India, will I get the same sense of dignity and respect that I have received in the U.S. No Muslim country will treat me as well as the U.S. has. . . .

It is time that we acknowledge that the freedoms we enjoy in the U.S. are more desirable to us than superficial solidarity with the Muslim World. If you disagree, then prove it by packing your bags and going to whichever Muslim country you identify with. If you do not leave and do not acknowledge that you would rather live here than anywhere else, know that you are being hypocritical.

It is time that we faced these hypocritical practices and struggled to transcend them. It is time that American Muslim leaders fought to purify their own lot.[107]

CONGRESSWOMAN CYNTHIA MCKINNEY'S
LETTER TO A DESPOT

Prince Alwaleed bin Talal bin Abdul Aziz al Saud of Saudi Arabia offered a donation of $10 million for the survivors of the victims of the World Trade Center attacks. New York Mayor Rudolph Giuliani told the Saudi Arabian prince to take his $10 million and shove it.

Why? The money came with this foreign policy "lecture" delivered by the prince: "I believe the government of the United States of America should re-examine its policies in the Middle East and adopt a more balanced stance toward the Palestinian cause. . . . Arabs believe that if the U.S. government wanted, it could play a pivotal role in pushing Israel to sign and fully implement a comprehensive peace treaty."[108] The prince also said, "Our Palestinian brethren continue to be slaughtered at the hands of the Israelis while the world turns the other cheek. At times like this one, we must address some of the issues that led to the criminal attack."[109]

In other words, the Israelis also engage in "terrorism" against the Palestinians, and the United States turns a blind eye. Never mind the absence of Israeli suicide bombers, or that Israel defends itself by attacking military targets. Israel, victorious in war, dramatically expanded her boundaries, only to give back much of the conquered area for peace. No, this "moderate" Arab ally, Saudi Arabia, outrageously and offensively considers the Israelis' defense of her very existence against hostile neighbors the moral equivalent of what happened on September 11.

But, wait, Congresswoman Cynthia McKinney (D–Georgia) to the rescue! McKinney wrote the prince a letter essentially apologizing for the mayor's rude behavior, "I was disappointed that Mayor Giuliani chose to decline your generous offer and instead criticize you for your observations of events in the Middle East. . . . Let me say that there are a growing number of people in the United States who recognize, like you, that U.S. policy in the Middle East needs serious examination."[110]

The McKinney letter gets worse. "Your Royal Highness," she said, "the state of black America is not good." She then uncorks a litany of black America's grievances including but not limited to poverty; homelessness; hunger; an unfair criminal justice system that disproportionately imprisons blacks; "health disparities"—with blacks less likely to receive surgery than whites; and the demise of affirmative action. "As you can see," she tells the prince, "the statistics are very grim for black America." She then magnanimously offers to provide names of charities that might benefit from the $10 mil that Rudy turned down.[111]

Complaining to a Saudi Arabian royal about a lack of civil rights is like taking an anger management course from Charlie Manson. In a recent *Newsweek* article called, "Why Do They Hate Us?" the magazine assesses the level of civil liberties in countries in the Arab world. On a scale from 1 (most free) to 7 (most repressive), Saudi Arabia ranks 7. There is no free press in Algeria, Tunisia, Libya, Egypt, Yemen, Oman, United Arab Emirates, Iran, Iraq, Syria, Lebanon, or Saudi Arabia.[112]

"This [Saudi Arabia] is a regime where, if you steal, you'll have your hand cut off publicly. They have public beheadings," said the former Justice Department lawyer who supervised the prosecution of espionage and terrorism cases.[113] Congresswoman McKinney complains about black homelessness, about black poverty and other social problems. Yet America's 32 million black Americans are simply the best-educated, best-fed, most healthy, and most prosperous blacks in the world. If black America were a separate country, its half-a-trillion dollar economy[114] would make it one of the world's top fifteen wealthiest nations.[115]

Comically, after the prince's offensive statement, he went on *Larry King Live* for damage control. Surely you knew, asked King, that your statement would "inflame" people? Incredibly, the prince replied, "Not necessarily, because I understand that in America the free speech is something paramount over there, and especially in New York."[116] Yes, a free press here, in America, not there, in Saudi Arabia. Suppose a Saudi Arabian citizen stood on a soapbox, at high noon in downtown Riyadh, and criticized the concentration of wealth in the hands of, say, Prince Alwaleed bin Talal? What result? Never mind. We already know.

SENATOR SCHUMER AND THE
BURKA SALESMAN

Where does it end? On September 11, government failed to exercise its most important task—that of protecting America, Americans, and American interests. Now that the War Against Terrorism requires Americans to spend far more on safety, will we rethink our ever-growing welfare state? Not if Senator Charles E. Schumer (D-New York) has anything to say about it.

Schumer argues that in fact September 11 demonstrates the need for yet *more federal government.* "For the foreseeable future," said Schumer, "the federal government will have to grow. . . . Our society will have to examine the vulnerable pressure points in our country—air travel, nuclear power plants, public health systems, power and computer grids, border crossings—and work to protect each from terrorist attack. . . . Only one entity has the breadth, strength and resources to lead this recalibration and pay for its costs—the federal government.

"To ask each town and village to guard all the power lines, gas lines and aqueducts is too much; to ask large private-sector companies such as airlines and food processors to be wholly responsible for the security of their products is also too much. It is not just that Washington is the only entity with the ability to raise the resources our new situation requires; the notion of letting a thousand different ideas compete and flourish—which works so well to create goods and services— does not work at all in the face of a national security emergency. Unity of action and purpose is required, and only the federal government can provide it. The era of a shrinking federal government has come to a close."[117] Wow.

After September 11, thousands of businesses suffered. Many expected the government to make them whole. Well, Senator Schumer, meet Mohammed Isaq, the burka salesman in Afghanistan.

Isaq's import business collapsed in 1990 after the Soviets invaded Afghanistan. Isaq, with a family, asked himself, "What to do?" Since the Islamic extremists mandated the wearing of burkas, Isaq reasoned, why not sell them? So, over the next several years, Isaq began to make burkas, garments that require seven yards of fabric to make and cover a woman from head to toe, leaving only a screen for the eyes. The burka business did well, and Isaq employed forty to fifty people, including two neighboring extended families and his own three teenage daughters.[118]

Then came September 11 and America's declaration of war against terrorism, including Al Qaeda terrorist leader Osama bin Laden and the Taliban, Afghanistan's ruling body. The Taliban fell, and, along with it, the requirement that women wear burkas. Once again, Isaq's business collapsed. Indeed, even his daughters shed their burkas, and they plan to attend school in the fall.[119]

So what will become of the hapless burka salesman in war-torn Afghanistan? Will Isaq get a bailout consisting of cash, loan guarantees, and tax credits? Isaq accepts the new reality with the grit of an entrepreneur. "My business will die," he said, "because women will start walking around open-faced. *I will just have to find something else to do.*"[120] [Emphasis added.]

In a post–September 11 climate, who better embodies the true-blue American spirit of hard work and self-reliance—Senator Schumer, or Isaq the burka salesman?

3.

EDUCATION BIAS

No Wonder Johnny Can't Read

*Ideas are far more powerful than guns. We don't let our people
have guns. Why should we let them have ideas?*[1]
—JOSEPH STALIN

At one high school, the teacher required an essay on the root causes of poverty. One student attributed poverty to three things—violent crime, government programs, and irresponsible breeding. He backed up his position with statistics and analyses. The student, in part, wrote, "In the United States, over the last thirty years, five trillion dollars (equated) have been spent battling poverty with no noticeable improvement. . . . Furthermore, according to the same study, when benefits for poor families are increased by one percent of the average personal income, the number of poor people living in a state increases by .8 percent."

A defensible point of view, right? No, his teacher, a Bush-bashing, self-described liberal, gave this A student a low score of fifty-eight out of seventy. How does the student know the teacher shafted him? Well, the student approached another student in the class, one who usually made poor grades. "May I see your exam?" The "bad" student happily complied: "Economics is another reason that there is [sic] a lot of homeless people in the world, no job offers or anything. Some people are getting paid really low wages and they need the money sometimes so they can feed their kids or even thereselves [sic]. welfare [sic] is really hard to get. . . ." Guess what that student received? The very same grade—fifty-eight. What's worse, this student admitted that he began and finished his essay, barely over a page double-spaced, at around 4 o'clock that very morning!

Some months earlier, at the same A student's request, I spoke at his high school. Before my speech an adminstrator informed me that they intended to invite a liberal speaker to "provide balance" to my non-liberal views. I later learned that, since my appearance, the school invited several liberal speakers, with no non-liberal speaker apparently necessary to provide "balance."

This politically incorrect student appeared on my radio show, sparking a meeting with one of school's administrators. Why, asked the student, does an Elder speech require "balance," but non-liberals need not follow campus appearances by liberals? "The administrator," reported the student, "said that you [Elder] were more aggressive, that you were paid to incite emotion, and that liberal speakers . . . [one of whom] led a march that required police intervention, weren't trying to change minds, but were recounting life experiences."

According to the student, the administrator spent nearly half the session accusing the young man of untrustworthiness for airing dirty linen. "How do I know I can trust you?" said the administrator. The official further warned the teen not to be so "narrow-minded." And, incredibly, the administrator then suggested that the student not "latch on to causes."

Do "conservative" speakers face discrimination at colleges and universities? In 2001, sixteen politicians were invited to address graduates at the nation's top twenty-five colleges. Three were Republican. Two of the three received offers only because of recent political events. Yale invited alumnus George W. Bush, who just happened to have been elected president a few months earlier. But the university invited Senator Hillary Clinton (D–New York) to precede Bush and to address the senior class the day before the president. Bush's former presidential rival, "maverick" Senator John McCain (R–Arizona), spoke to University of Pennsylvania grads but shared the stage with Democratic former Congressman Floyd Flake. Besides, John McCain hardly shares the alleged core values of the Republican Party. David Horowitz, of the Center for the Study of Popular

Culture, says, "It's a given that 95 percent of college speakers will be liberals, but it's unacceptable."[2]

Horowitz commissioned a survey of Ivy League college professors and found that 84 percent of those in the humanities voted for Al Gore. Only 3 percent called themselves Republicans. Seventy-four percent opposed development of a missile defense system, versus 70 percent of Americans who support a missile defense system.[3]

MICROSOFT MONOPOLY BAD, PUBLIC EDUCATION MONOPOLY GOOD

The National PTA, according to their own mission statement, serves to "support and speak on behalf of children and youth in schools," to "assist parents in developing the skills they need to raise and protect their children," and to "encourage parent and public involvement in the public schools of this nation." Good, worthwhile stuff. "We are a nonpartisan group," according to their spokeswoman. "We don't take political sides on issues."[4]

Then how does the PTA explain its membership in the Fair Taxes for All coalition, an ensemble of hundreds of liberal interest groups opposed to George W. Bush's proposed tax cuts? The liberal People for the American Way leads the Fair Taxes for All group. The People for the American Way spearheaded the attack on John Ashcroft's nomination for attorney general.[5] Not exactly "nonpartisan."

But of course the PTA, which, after all, wants only the best for our children, must surely support school choice and vouchers, right? They wouldn't want parents to be forced to send their kid to an underperforming school simply because their residence puts them in an undesirable school district, would they?

No, the PTA *opposes* vouchers. The National PTA claims vouchers and tuition tax credits "would promote division and separation within the community and negate the long struggle to desegregate our schools and our society." The National Federation of Teachers agrees, claiming

that "educational choice leads to greater socioeconomic and racial segregation of students." And the Center on Education Policy, a Washington, D.C., "independent advocate for public education," warns that,
"Without public schools, children would most likely today attend
schools that reflected their own racial, ethnic, religious, or economic
background, much as in churches, social organizations, and other
groups that people join voluntarily."[6] So?

What about parents who don't like the public school to which the
government assigned their child? Shouldn't a parent be able to send a
child to whatever school he or she wants and can afford, up to and
including private schools?

Some offer the "melting pot" rationale for public schools, arguing
that public schools teach tolerance, acceptance, and association with
other ethnicities and cultures. But the data fail to support the widely
held view of private schools as islands of segregation.

Researchers Jay P. Greene and Nicole Mellow of the University of
Texas at Austin devised a simple way to look at the extent of integrated
social interaction at nineteen public and nineteen private schools. They
observed the interactions of students in school lunchrooms, recording
where and with whom students sat by race. At private schools, almost
two-thirds of kids integrated themselves in the lunchroom, while at
public schools less than one-half of the children did so. "If we are
serious about the benefits of racially heterogeneous school experiences," say Green and Mellow, then policies that "detach schooling
from housing," such as school choice programs, should be seriously
considered. Unfortunately, the PTA and many others continue to use
private-school segregation as a key argument against voucher programs.[7]

What is it the antivoucher people don't understand? Affluent minorities apparently reject the "melting pot" theory of public education.

Director Spike Lee, for example, sends his kid to private school.
Reverend Jesse Jackson sent his to chichi St. Albans, the same tony
prep school to which Al Gore sent his kid. A Heritage Foundation poll
found that 14 percent of the Hispanic Congressional Caucus place their

kids in private school versus 8 percent of the Hispanic population in general. Similarly, of the Black Congressional Caucus, 28 percent of their kids attend private schools, versus 8 percent of the black population in general.[8]

Yet, the National Association for the Advancement of Colored People (NAACP), the Democratic Party, the Reverend Jesse Jackson, and teachers' unions all adamantly, consistently, almost pathologically oppose vouchers. Of course, vouchers are not a panacea. With vouchers the government will place strings, in effect semiregulating the private education industry. And a rush of money will likely spur fly-by-night operations, leading many to scream, "Free enterprise in education does not work!"

But a state of emergency exists in inner-city public education in America. Two-thirds of inner-city kids cannot read, write, and compute at grade level. Recently the NAACP launched a campaign to "end racial disparities in the nation's public schools, colleges and universities" and placed the blame for a wide "achievement gap" on the usual suspects—lack of money, racial insensitivity, blah, blah, blah. "Racial inequality persists in too many of our nation's educational systems," according to NAACP President Kweisi Mfume. He also said that many inner-city and predominantly minority schools lack qualified teachers and adequate educational resources and have higher rates of suspensions and expulsions.[9]

But the primary culprit, the principal reason for the low academic standards in urban education, the reason for the acceptance of a disproportionately high number of unqualified or marginal inner-city schoolteachers, the reason the board of education consistently misspends money? The parents! When the parents don't care, their kids won't care, and all bets are off.

It's like this. A friend and I once ate dinner in a nice restaurant. Across the room, a couple sat, toying with a cell phone. The man pushed a button, the phone rang, and they laughed. He pushed it again, a different ring, again, a different ring. Each ring became increasingly annoying.

The noise bothered others, but whether because of excessive politeness or timidity, no one said anything. Eventually, my friend said, "Could you get the waiter so that I can ask him to do something about that?" I called the waiter over, but he seemed timid and afraid to go to the table and address the rude diners.

If the waiter wouldn't, I would. So I bellowed from halfway across the room, "Sir, do you mind?!" He promptly folded the phone, and he never bothered anybody again.

Even though the other diners had said nothing, all had seemed indignant, angrily fidgeting and darting poisoned looks at the telephone couple. Why? We paid for what was proving to be an inconvenient part of our collective experience. All of us chose this restaurant, willing to spend our hard-earned money for a dinner out. No one paid for a rude telephone ringer serenade. How dare he waste *our* money.

Whether it's a bicycle, a home, or an education, we value what we purchase. We furthermore demand that others respect our investment. Would parents, if they paid directly from their hard-earned salaries, tolerate the waste, inefficiency, poor discipline, and low academic standards that we see in inner-city public education? Wouldn't paying customers demand quality, value and service?

My parents paid for piano lessons for my two brothers and me. My little brother, Dennis, soon lost interest in playing piano, and when it came to practice time, he and my mother battled constantly. Dennis dragged his feet at school homework, too. But, when it came to piano lessons, my mother said, "Boy, don't you make me waste my money!" To get him motivated for homework, however, she talked about his future and how the quality of his adult life depended on how he spent time now. But she never told him that his failure to study *cost her money*. And, yes, while she was paying for the piano lessons, Dennis did, indeed, practice.

The same formula applies to education. One seldom achieves excellence without competition or without pressure to produce results. Would paying customers tolerate outbursts and lack of discipline in the classroom?

Incredibly, researchers seldom study the effect of bad discipline on the learning curve in education. Edward Lazear, an economist at the Hoover Institute and Stanford Graduate School of Business, produced a study showing how a student who is disruptive or who takes up teacher time in ways that are not useful to other students affects not only his own learning but also that of others in the class. "For example, if the class has one student or thirty students, the time available for learning is 100 percent if there are no disruptions. But if, on average, each student disrupts the class 1 percent of the time, the time available for learning drops to 99 percent for a one-student class . . . and to just 74 percent for a class size of thirty."[10]

THE MIND-SET OF A TOE-TAG LIBERAL EDUCRAT

The UCLA Graduate School of Education publishes something called the *Center X Forum*. The Spring/Summer 2001 issue featured a cover story co-authored by Peter McLaren, one of the school's professors. The article, called "Critical Literacy for Global Citizenship,"[11] displays blatant, open hostility to capitalism. "Following in the wake of push-cart, no-frills, bootstrap capitalism," said McLaren, "is the cultural flotsam and jetsam produced by the Starbucking and Wal-Marting of the global landscape, as the tyranny of the market ruthlessly subjects labor to its regulatory forces of social and cultural reproduction in the unsustainable precincts of the capitalist market."[12] Down with cultural flotsam and jetsam!

McLaren dismisses free-market economists like economic Nobel laureates Milton Friedman, author of *Free to Choose*, and Friedrich von Hayek, author of the brilliant *Road to Serfdom*. According to McLaren, "Under the tutelage of neoliberalism's economic engineers, Milton Friedman and Friedrich Von Hayek, the 1980s and 1990s became a showcase for an orchestrated conservative and right-wing backlash against the civil rights of working-class minority groups, immigrants, women, and children. Recently in the United States we have witnessed a series of democratic 'victories' for proponents of Propositions 21, 209, and 227 in California, propositions aimed at welfare 'reform' and managed 'care' as well as increasing the executions of criminals and massively expanding the prison industry."[13]

McLaren, not too surprisingly, belongs to the healthcare-as-a-right crowd.[14] He also takes a whack at those who oppose race-based preferences and denounces opponents of "bilingual education." In fact, as Professor McLaren sees it, the pursuit of the buck threatens life as we know it, "The world runs amok as global carpetbaggers looking to become the world's latest centillionaires take advantage of the results of increasing rights for business owners worldwide—privatization, budget cuts and labor 'flexibility' due to the engineered absence of government constraint on the production, distribution, and consumption of goods and services brought about by global neoliberal economy policies."[15] Greed kills, right, prof?

This wouldn't be so bad, except that teachers train in these leftist departments of education. Given this kind of socialistic, collectivist indoctrination, newly minted teachers enter their field with a victicrat, it-takes-a-village mind-set, devoid of any understanding of basic principles of economics.

A letter from 16-year-old Alec nicely summarizes the problem:

> I am merely sixteen years old, and attend a public high school. Already, I have experienced excessive stomach-churning liberal bias in school. So I accept and even appreciate this, since I have no problem with openly arguing their misinformed beliefs. (Albeit 85 percent of my fellow peers in that school have socialist and left-wing extreme ideas already instilled in their head by . . . years of public schooling.)
>
> My problem and endless rage enters when comments are made by my extreme-liberal teachers, and my response is literally cut off. These teachers constantly avoid allowing me to contradict their senseless preaching. I know I have to learn to accept this, because liberal bias in high school is only a fraction of the liberal bias in college. However, it is becoming extremely tougher

*to deal with, when more and more of my peers are thinking that socialism
and communism are the "fairest" answer. This ignorance is mind-boggling,
because these kids, teachers, etc. have never lived under socialism and communism. I have constantly offered to buy them a one-way ticket to Cuba,
but shockingly they refuse. . . . These people are hypocrites, and their answers
to my arguments are never backed-up and are completely childish. The shadow
of logic, reason and common sense is frightening to these teachers. Look no
further, this is the problem with the public school system.*

—*Alec Mouhibian*

TEXTBOOKS: LIBERALISM
BY-THE-BOOK

Save our youth!

They start early, with textbooks that reek of socialism. *Civics: Participating in Government*, by James E. Davis and Phyllis Maxey Fernlund,
is a popular history textbook used in many of the nation's middle
schools.

In a section called "The Limits of Free Enterprise," the authors
offer the classic, statist view of big government: "As the economy has
developed, however, Americans have become increasingly aware that
the free enterprise system may not always serve the common good.
While it has made the United States one of the wealthiest countries in
the world, it has also led to problems that cannot be solved by letting
the market system work entirely on its own."[16]

No mention in the textbook of the fact that many prominent economists would argue the exact opposite: from the havoc wreaked on the
health-care industry by the imposition of Medicare, to the regulation,
then deregulation, and sometimes re-regulation of industries such as
electric power, cable service, and airlines, government intervention in
most areas has actually *created* problems that simply could not exist in
a free-market system.

The text continues, "These problems have caused Americans to look to government for solutions. Six problems are listed below to help you understand why government has become involved in our economy."[17] It is certainly true that many Americans—most of whom have good hearts but do not actually comprehend how the free market works—turn to their elected officials at every slight or perceived unfairness, and cry, "Fix this!"

Let's examine the six instances that Davis and Fernlund say warrant government intervention:

1. Businesses have sometimes earned profits unfairly. *They have driven competitors out of business or made secret agreements with competitors to fix prices at high levels. Businesses have also fooled customers through false or misleading advertising.*[18]

"Businesses have sometimes earned profits unfairly"? Sure, and some people commit murder. Bad people exist, bad business people exist. And, yes, government serves to protect us against force, fraud, and deceit.

The Justice Department's lawsuit against Microsoft is a case in point. Through tenacious marketing of products that consumers want, Microsoft attained a dominant position. When competitors like Oracle, Sun Microsystems, and IBM screamed unfairness, the government stepped in. Yet Helen Chaney, a policy fellow at the Pacific Research Institute, compared the government break-up of AT&T to the Microsoft case: "To be sure, the AT&T break-up settlement benefited consumers. Between 1984 and 1994, prices for long-distance service fell by a real 66 percent. . . . But the increased competition following the settlement was not a result of new regulations imposed upon the company. Instead, competition flourished because the settlement forced the government-regulated telephone monopoly into the throes of private-sector competition. A break-up of Microsoft would achieve the opposite effect. It would turn a private company, conceived in a garage by college dropouts, into a government-regulated company."[19]

Juan C. Ros, the executive director of the California Libertarian Party, says the audacity of the government in trying to "take over and micromanage a privately owned company" is "thuggery of the worst sort." "If the government wants to look for monopolies," says Ros, "it only needs to look in the mirror. The U.S. Postal Service has a monopoly on the delivery of first-class mail. State lotteries enjoy a monopoly in most states over other forms of gambling. Many government services are provided without the benefit of private competition."[20]

Perhaps the Justice Department doesn't understand the free-market system. "There is no such thing as a private monopoly," says Edwin A. Locke, a senior writer for the Ayn Rand Institute. "Only the government can forcibly prevent competitors from entering a market. Microsoft has attained dominance in the software industry, but dominance is not a monopoly. Market dominance has to be earned by a long struggle, by providing better products and better prices than anyone else.

"Once-dominant companies that falter (like Xerox, IBM, General Motors, and Eastman Kodak) find their market share can erode very quickly. There is no monopoly threat from these dominant players so long as their competitors are legally permitted to enter the field, invent products and combine with each other to gain market power. . . . A private company has no power to force consumers to do anything. Did . . . Microsoft threaten to beat people up or throw their bodies into the East River if they bought another Web browser? Of course not. The only leverage Microsoft has is the leverage it has earned by producing a product that people want to buy."[21]

The next economic problem that requires government intervention, according to the Davis–Fernlund textbook:

2. Conditions for workers have sometimes been unsafe and inhumane. . . . *Workers have sometimes been badly treated. Some have been required to work long hours with low pay, while others have had to use dangerous machinery or chemicals without protection.*[22]

Hold the phone. "Some have been required to work long hours with low pay"? *Required*? A willing supplier of labor voluntarily contracts with a willing payer for that labor. The term "required" is flat-out wrong unless it pertains to slavery. This kind of mischaracterization makes young people buy into the notion of the big, benevolent government.

"Others have had to use dangerous machinery or chemicals without protection"? This perpetuates the notion that an employer, having invested money in training personnel, wishes to mistreat his most valuable asset—his employees. In his book *The Jungle*,[23] Upton Sinclair exposed unsanitary work conditions at meatpacking factories. Under common law, employers already owe employees a duty of reasonable care. True, "pro-labor laws" mandated better factory conditions. But politicians drafted laws in response to the growing power and clout of employees. The laws themselves did not suddenly create an improvement in factory conditions. Government-imposed "improvements"—whether reduced maximum hours or regulated physical working conditions—become costs borne by the employer. This reduces money otherwise available for hiring, increased wages, research and development, or lower prices. Better working conditions, on the whole, came with better technology and improved productivity.

3. Unsafe products have harmed consumers. *Foods have sometimes spread diseases and caused other health problems. Household products have injured people, and toys have hurt children.*[24]

Food processors and restaurateurs see little incentive in killing their customers. Bad publicity and lawsuits quickly whip negligent manufacturers into shape; or one can simply stand by and watch them go bankrupt. Why do manufacturers seek the Good Housekeeping Seal of Approval? Manufacturers know—*without* a government dictate—that the seal conveys safety and reliability to the consumer, qualities that translate into sales and profits.

Government exists to outlaw force and fraud and police against them. But a line exists between defense and babysitting. Take, for example, the government's pizza rules. That's right—for decades, the government has promulgated rules that determined the ingredients of frozen pizza. The rules, called "standards of identity," exist to promote the eating of meat and cheese. Department of Agriculture regulations dictate that a meat pizza must possess crust, a tomato-based sauce, and between 10 and 12 percent meat by weight. Even consumer advocate Carol Tucker Foreman, who served as an administrator in the department under President Carter, says the standards of identity don't "make sense in today's society."[25]

The regulatory burden shouldered by Americans is staggering. According to the Competitive Enterprise Institute, regulations cost Americans $700 billion each year—equal to a "hidden tax" of $7,500 per year for the typical two-income family.[26] And politics rather than science often drives the decisions to regulate.

4. Not all Americans have had economic security. People who lose their jobs or cannot work due to sickness, injury, or old age have faced hunger and homelessness. Discrimination has made it hard for others to get jobs to support themselves.[27]

Addendum to the textbook: Life isn't fair. Not all of us chose wealthy parents to give birth to us. Of course "not all Americans have had economic security." Therefore, what? Taxpayer A does not owe taxpayer B a nice lifestyle. But what if taxpayer B, through no fault of his own, suffers a setback or injury? That's why we have charity, neighbors, friends, and family.

"Discrimination has made it hard for others to get jobs themselves." Yes, bigots exist. But in the year 2002, can discrimination halt the person willing to work hard from finding a job? Hard work and perseverance reap rewards, but the relentlessly victicrat media remind us how bad things truly are.

A recent *Los Angeles Times* article, for example, screamed "Jobless Blacks Face Steepest Challenge." The article said the rate of black unemployment is 9.7 percent nationally in October, 2001, up from a low of 7.5 percent in February, 2001. And the rate for whites rose from its low of 3.6 percent in January to 4.8 percent in October.[28] If you read the graph at the bottom of the page, however, you will note the white unemployment rate is increased 33 percent from its low, compared to the lower 29 percent increase for blacks. But the focus of the article remains on blacks.[29]

And if it's discrimination, how, then, to explain the following sentence: "Young black men are less likely to be working today than they were twenty years ago."[30] So blacks today face *more* racism than twenty years ago? Please.

In fact, the very same *Los Angeles Times*, only months earlier, touted the progress of Los Angeles area Hispanics who started out at the entry level in fast-food restaurants. "In an unlikely industry now often shunned by middle-class teens," said the article, "many have found stability and careers, and fast-food jobs have helped push unemployment among Latinos to record lows in California and elsewhere. . . . And over time, they have learned, fast-food jobs can carry them further, make them more financially secure and employ their family and friends. New immigrants see the work as a way to hone their English skills, and some crave the stability often found in the industry's structured workplace."[31]

José Hernandez began mopping floors at McDonald's in 1990 for $3.35 an hour. He now earns $50,000 a year—up to as much as $60,000 with incentives—supervises fifty-five employees, and "boasts that he is the luckiest man in the world." Hernandez owns his own home and drives his family around in a minivan. "I have a career, a real career, and I am supporting my family," says Hernandez. "My children can be proud of me."[32]

Hernandez worked hard to get there. When he started mopping floors ten years earlier, Hernandez spoke very little English. "The restaurant's owner, Isabelle Villasenor," said the *L.A. Times*, "encouraged Hernandez to improve his English beyond 'the McDonald's lingo.' He read training manuals and insisted that other co-workers speak to him only in English. Villasenor quizzed him on his vocabulary and kept the radio on in the back of the restaurant so Hernandez could listen to the words." Villasenor says, "He wanted so desperately to succeed."[33]

"I can't believe how far I've come," says Hernandez. "Next stop, supervisor. After that, who knows? I feel like nothing's out of reach anymore."[34] José Hernandez understands that success is about attitude and work ethic. If you have that, then indeed, "nothing's out of reach." Of course, a student wouldn't learn that essential truth by reading the Davis–Fernlund textbook.

5. The economy has been unstable. *Periods of economic slowdown have put many people out of work and caused great hardship. Periods of inflation have reduced the buying power of the dollar.*[35]

The economy experienced booms and busts before and after the founding of the Federal Reserve Board. Economies go through recessions. Economies go through recoveries.

Inflation, however, results from bad government policy. During the Depression, President Roosevelt removed this country from the gold standard. What is the gold standard? It means that someone holding a piece of paper can redeem it for gold. Until the Depression, this country operated on a gold standard. Economist George Reisman, in his comprehensive book, *Capitalism,* says, "The ideal monetary system would be a *100-percent-metallic-reserve system.* Under this system, all paper currency and checking deposits would be 100 percent backed by gold or silver. The advantage of such a system would be that not only would it be immune from inflation, but unlike the first decades of . . . [the twentieth century], it would also be immune from *deflation.* Because once gold or silver money comes into existence, it *stays* in existence. It is not wiped out by the failure of any debtor."[36]

Reisman further explains that, "It was government interference over a period of more than two centuries that brought about the abandonment of the use of gold and silver as money and thus the powerful restraint on the increase in the quantity of money that a gold or silver money entails. In the last sixty years or more, the government of the United States . . . has had unlimited power to expand the quantity of fiat paper money and has made ample use of the power. Thus, the whole problem of an inflationary rise in prices reduces to an increase in the quantity of money at a rate more rapid than the increase in the supply of gold and silver or, to what is equivalent in view of its role in their abandonment as money, an increase in the quantity of money *caused by the government.*"[37]

> 6. The environment has been damaged. *Businesses and consumers have polluted the air, water, and land upon which we depend for our basic life needs. Many animals and plants are also in danger.*[38]

Typical "green people" rhetoric, the type schools expose kids to every day in these environmental boot camps. Yes, the government plays a legitimate role in protecting the environment, especially in cases of air and water pollution, where one cannot easily determine property lines.

But even the Environmental Protection Agency (EPA) admits that air, lakes, and rivers have grown cleaner over the last thirty years. Every major pollutant the government measures—nitrogen dioxide, sulfur dioxide, carbon monoxide, lead—is decreasing. And while the government wants to pat itself on the back for this improvement, which has cost taxpayers billions, for the most part *voluntary* actions of businesses and consumers made the difference. Businesspeople understand the public relations nightmare (whether based on sound or junk science)— and the possible loss of sales—if customers perceive them as insensitive to the environment. As for the plants and animals, maybe the environmentalists need to reread Darwin's theory. It's called survival of the fittest. Circle of life. Species of plants and animals go extinct eventually. It happened before humankind came along, and it will happen long after. Just ask the dinosaurs.

On the whole, *Civics: Participating in Government* is not the worst textbook ever written. But the errors, omissions, and not-subtle skewing of facts should not be presented as an accurate picture of reality to impressionable middle-school kids. After all, inaccuracy, bias, and distortion abound out in the real world in many venues. If parents and teachers perform their jobs well, and produce young men and women capable of critical thought, people can detect bias and deal with it. But they shouldn't have to find it in their civics textbook.

GET GOVERNMENT OUT OF EDUCATION

Government must, goes the argument, serve at the very least as a last resort to provide education for the poor. But Llewellyn Rockwell, Jr., president of the libertarian Ludwig von Mises Institute, says, "The per-pupil cost of public schools averages $6,000, compared with $3,100 for private schools. In other words, all else being equal, we could abolish all public schools and the taxes that support them tomorrow, let the market replace them with private schools and cut the total cost of education by nearly half."[39] That's nationwide. The Los Angeles Unified School District spends $8.9 billion and schools over 720,000 students. This works out to $12,300 annually per student![40] The Catholic schools in the Archdiocese of Los Angeles educate 100,000 students, the third-largest system in California. Its cost per pupil? $2,800. And they produce student test scores that average at or above grade level.[41]

The home-school movement, growing at 11 percent a year, makes a powerful statement about the quality of public education. In a cover story on home schooling, *Time* magazine said, "According to a new federal report, at least 850,000 students were learning at home in 1999, the most recent year studied; some experts believe the figure is actually twice that. . . . While politicians from Washington on down to your school board have been warring over charter schools and vouchers in recent years, home schooling has quietly outpaced both of those more attention-getting reforms (only half-a-million kids are in charter schools, and just 65,000 receive vouchers). In many ways, in fact, home schooling has become a threat to the very notion of public education."[42]

But until the last couple of decades, laws in many states flat-out banned home schooling. Some feared home schooling created kids devoid of social skills. But according to *Time*, "In 1992 psychotherapist Larry Shyers did a study while at the University of Florida in which he closely examined the behavior of 35 home schoolers and 35 public schoolers. He found that home schoolers were generally more patient and less competitive. They tended to introduce themselves to one another more; they didn't fight as much. And the home schoolers were much more prone to exchange addresses and phone numbers. In short, they behaved like miniature adults."[43]

But parents of home schoolers must make more money, thus providing time and the resources necessary to educate their own children, right? Wrong. According to a study by the Department of Education, while parents of home schoolers tend to have more education than other parents, household income averages less than $50,000 a year, with many earning under $25,000. Laura Derrick, president of the Home Education Network, says, "These are families that have one income and have sacrificed to live on one income."[44]

And the primary reason parents give for home schooling? Not religion, as many assume. In fact, parents cite religion as the second reason for home schooling. Parents gave quality of education as the number one reason. Perhaps parents want to avoid misleading, deceptive, error-ridden textbooks such as *Civics: Participating in Government*. The publisher of *Home Education Magazine* says, "The primary reason is that it's a great way to raise kids. Any way you slice the American pie, you're going to find home-schoolers sticking out of it."[45]

KIDS SPEAK OUT

Still don't believe kids get a liberal indoctrination in our high schools and colleges? Consider this letter from a Santa Monica High School student:

Dear Mr. Elder:

I live in Santa Monica, California, and attend Santa Monica Public High School. My school indirectly, but thoroughly, supports terrorism. To describe my school as being liberal would be an understatement. I could write hundreds of pages detailing the left-wing activities and positions of my school, but I am writing now to discuss the behavior of my school regarding the Taliban and terrorism, and just how appalling and detrimental that behavior has been. I apologize in advance for the length this letter must be.

First of all, I would like to mention that the last time one of the public schools I have attended said the Pledge of Allegiance every day . . . was in kindergarten. In high school, we never say the Pledge of Allegiance. After we began bombing Afghanistan instead of leading us in the Pledge of Allegiance, our principal got on the PA system, and announced to the school his doubts about the morality of our air campaign in Afghanistan.

On our day of national prayer and remembrance following the terrorist attacks, I wore an American flag shirt to school. The student sitting in front of me in English wore a shirt with an American flag crossed out and burning American icons. He was not the only student in our school wearing such attire. I was, however, the only one in the school who seemed to care about it, among teachers and students alike. Not a single American flag was put up in the school, but when Mexican Day of the Dead rolled around our entire school was ornately decorated with symbols of Mexican culture and pride. There was a celebration at lunch. While we did have a school-wide assembly about the horrible catastrophe of September 11th, the continual message given by the faculty and students hosting the assembly was, "To forgive and to understand; to seek out non-violent solutions." The way they would have it, we would just censure bin Laden and make him promise not to do it again.

Another response our school had to deal with the attacks was to invite a Muslim leader to the school to explain how the Islamic religion is a noble and righteous one. Unfortunately, they never brought anyone to the school to tell us how the United States is a noble and righteous country.

What finally prompted me to write this letter, though, was the barrage of downright insulting, practically treasonous comments made in our school newspaper. The newspaper is not student run, but is an actual class, which is funded by the government, and supervised by a teacher. The following statements from the newspaper have been quoted exactly as they appear, and the opinions they so clearly express went unopposed.

"I think that Bush should change his mind on going to war . . . and just accept the fact of what's happened and just leave it like that to avoid war and other tragedies."

"If America wants terrorism to cease, then it must respond with non-violence."

"Reverend Jesse Jackson was invited by the Taliban's religious leader to negotiate a deal to hand over bin Laden. Powell replied that doing so would serve no purpose. Jackson may have proved successful. Negotiation would be one non-violent step towards a solution in the present situation."

"America is Afghanistan's greatest threat. The principles of the United States government dictate that a helpless country cannot be attacked."

"After the Columbine school shootings . . . Bill Clinton spoke to a school in Virginia about a non-violent approach to life. On the same day Clinton hypocritically ordered a large bombing in Belgrade . . . Americans should be non-violent, but the government has a right to?"

"The only way to solve the ongoing spiral of terrorism is to stop it with its antithesis: peace. If America bombs terrorists, their cells, or their camps, the violence will continue moving in a circle with no solution."

"Dear SUV drivers, your cars are big, ugly, and useless. For the most part you cannot drive. In addition, as if that weren't enough, you manage to simultaneously ruin the environment, and help drive the United States to war."

"I am especially angered nowadays when I see those of you who drive through streets with an American Flag attached to the window of your SUV. You act as if you are patriots, but in reality, you are quite the opposite. If it weren't for you petroleum sucking-monsters, the U.S. might not be in this mess. Although our dependence on foreign oil is not the sole determiner of American Middle East policy, it is certainly a major factor."

The first school newspaper issued after the attacks did contain a picture of the American flag, except covering our beautiful stars and stripes was the Afghanistan flag, and to the right a message urging tolerance. It should also be noted that in mine, and presumably many other student's history classes, we are told that our country is not actually the land of the free, that the Revolutionary War was motivated purely by economics, the Mexican-American war is described as the "North-American Invasion," our Founding Fathers are called "bigots," and the United States is depicted as the evil invader of this continent. Again, as I have said before, I could write hundreds of pages detailing the incredibly liberal and politically correct opinions spewed out by my school. Opinions that, I might add, are not correct, but merely political. However, I shall digress no further.

The problem is that many of the faculty and students of my school fail to make a distinction between what the Taliban and Al Qaeda have done, and the military response that is currently underway. We are good, the terrorists are evil. For good to triumph, it must fight evil, not negotiate with it. People are entitled to their opinions, but as logic would dictate, students are very limited in their freedom of speech. It would seem though, that they can say whatever they wish when it comes to America bashing, but beliefs like mine—that the United States has an obligation to persecute and even kill terrorists at home and abroad—are most unwelcome.

What's the bigger picture? That the new generation of adults being bred in public schools lack not only any patriotism, but are instilled with a dislike, and in many cases hatred, of the United States. Many students in my school are very privileged, and have no understanding or appreciation for the sacrifices that have been made by our American ancestors in wars. What I see happening is thousands of students from my school graduating with the belief that as a country, the United States has no right to wage war, no right to *discriminate against the immigration of Arab-Muslims into our country, no right to self-preservation. In this way my high school is indirectly supporting terrorism, and I don't know what to do.*

Needless to say, I am angered by the comments in my school newspaper, the opinions of my teachers and administrators, the stunning lack of American pride, but the overwhelming embrace of all foreign cultures. This is an issue of national importance, and I thought an inside perspective would be useful in combating the problem.

I feel something must be done, which is why I wrote this letter, and I hope that I have helped to create awareness of this dilemma. I thank you, truly, from the bottom of my heart.

—*Stephen M.*

At nearby UCLA, things appear no better. During the anti-affirmative-action battle for California's Proposition 209, to eliminate race and gender as factors in public hiring and university admissions, most of the UC regents publicly professed support for affirmative action.

Dear Larry,

I am a graduate student at UCLA. I spend my days in classrooms learning about public policy, community development, and social responsibility. Yet I find myself continually frustrated with the consistent portrayals of landlords as greedy, ethnic minorities as disadvantaged, and government as the solution. Class issues are routinely discussed in terms of race. The victim mentality is pervasive, as ethnic-minority status is equated with disenfranchisement.

Inside the classroom, rent control is offered as the obvious answer to the housing crisis. My law professor never discussed legal arguments against rent control, such as the infringement on private property rights. My economics professor never mentioned that few economists agree with rent control, which often hurts the very people it purports to help. "Affordable housing" is proposed in every mock development project, while there has been no discussion about how affordable housing is funded, the notion of government subsidies, or the increased burden on taxpayers. I suggested to one professor: "Perhaps *instead of demonizing landlords as greedy, we ought to look at the broader issue. The landlord can charge $1,500 for a one-bedroom apartment because there are dozens of people willing to pay it. The real problem is our severe housing shortage." I naïvely expected to be complimented for my insight into the overall cause of this urban dilemma. Instead, students were silent, and my professor dismissed my comment as "interesting." The minimum wage issue is treated in a similarly one-sided manner.*

During one class discussion, I remarked that a proper evaluation of any public policy requires an analysis of the costs and benefits. A classmate balked at my suggestion: "We should just do what is right."

In a School of Public Policy, professors and students alike refuse to discuss the consequences of their proposed planning solutions, the effects of government intervention, and results of regulation. So much for diversity.

Second-year political science student Ben Shapiro writes of his experiences battling the toe-tag liberals at UCLA:

Universities have a serious problem. The type of liberalism so heavily favored by the intellectual elite has crossed the line. Professors throughout the educational world are supporting murderers and terrorists; they are justifying despicable actions because of the political philosophies of the actors. Murder, slaughter, and terrorism are OK, they say, as long as they are directed at law-enforcement officials or civilian Westerners. It's fine as long as the murderer is anti-capitalist, anti-establishment, or anti-conservative.

This frightening ideology has not only blurred the line between liberalism and radicalism—it has destroyed it. This ideology cannot truly be called liberalism—it can only be called evil. And this evil must be eradicated before it spreads and engulfs the aspiring youth of our nation in its dark and shadowy tentacles.

The case of Sara Jane Olson has revealed the ugly and dangerous thought processes of the professorial ilk [sic]. . . . Prosecutors say that the former member of the radical Symbionese Liberation Army planted bombs under the cars of two police officers in a "wide-ranging conspiracy to overthrow the government" in 1974 ("Judge May Reject Olson Guilty Plea," LA Times, Nov. 2). Olson pleaded guilty to this charge on November 1, signing an agreement stating that she "is pleading guilty because she is in truth and fact guilty." However, she stated immediately afterward, "I pleaded to something of which I am not guilty." Why this sudden reversal?

Ostensibly, she fears that the terrorist attacks of September 11 would hinder her ability to get a fair trial. With broad public support for government institutions, she fears that her attempted murder of police officers would seem like . . . (gasp) attempted murder. . . .

Despite Olson's guilty plea, support from her comrades in the educational community comes streaming in. "I support Sara Olson," says Mary Brent Wehrli, a professor of social work at UCLA. A self-described radical, Wehrli has taught at UCLA for eight years. "Olson has been denied the right to a fair trial," says Wehrli. Erwin Chermerinsky, a professor of law at USC, concurs—his name, as well as Wehrli's, is on the Sara Olson Defense Fund Committee's official web site.

Would these passionate defenders of public justice support an anti-abortion radical suspected of murdering an abortion doctor? Highly doubtful. Support for Olson is not based on an underlying fear of the criminal justice system. It is based on nothing less than support for Olson's anti-government, anti-establishment, radical ideals. These ideals can, according to the educational establishment, justify even murder.

Support for Mumia Abu-Jamal is another example of dangerously twisted thinking among the intellectuals at universities. Abu-Jamal is a former member of the Black Panthers and an influential writer and radio host, as well as a backer of the radical black group MOVE. He is also a murderer. He murdered Philadelphia police officer Daniel Faulkner, shooting him in the chest and in the neck. A jury of 12 citizens, two of them black, all 12 accepted by Abu-Jamal himself, sentenced him to death, and he currently awaits execution on death row. The Pennsylvania Supreme Court and U.S. Supreme Court have both heard Abu-Jamal's evidence and upheld the judgment of the jury.

On campus, Mumia Abu-Jamal is a hero. Wehrli says, "His case is a blight on the democratic process we all believe in." If so, how was he convicted? "Information which would have changed the outcome of the trial was not admitted," she states, "and the judge appeared to be racist and not open-minded—not unbiased." This despite a strong case against Mumia, including eyewitnesses, people who heard Abu-Jamal scream, "I shot the motherf___er and I hope he dies," and powerful scientific and ballistic evidence.

Still, Albert Boime, a professor of art history who has taught at UCLA since 1978, maintains, "Mumia is definitely innocent—he deserves another trial. He was unjustly persecuted, no doubt about it. He was probably persecuted for reasons ranging from personal reasons, such as his frequent verbal attacks on the police department, to political reasons, such as his defense of MOVE, which infuriated the police. They had a vendetta against him." This faith in the innocence of a convicted murderer is touching to be sure— it is highly unlikely that these same professors would support the killers of James Byrd. Only professors would be able to excuse the murder of a policeman by a Black Panther on ideological grounds.

This perverse and twisted thought process has been stuffed down the throats of the students with respect to the Sept. 11 attacks—and it has to stop. University professors blame the attacks on American foreign policy, American prosperity, the capitalist system, or any other Western ideology. The killing of more than 6,000 [sic] Americans is dismissed by saying that America has been asking for it. Says Marc Trachtenberg, a professor of political science at UCLA, "Despite the death of millions in the Middle East, we opted instinctively from the very start to turn a blind eye." Aamir Mufti, a Muslim professor of comparative literature at UCLA, states, "I am skeptical that we have even learned anything from this attack . . ."

These are the people who will shape the youth of this country. These are the men and women who will forge college students into adults. They excuse murder. They promote terrorism. They stretch their arms toward their vulnerable students, leading them into moral oblivion. This is not a free speech issue; free speech cannot justify the willful endorsement of murder. This is an issue of good versus evil.

Their thoughts and actions cannot justify hatred and violence. Promoting these can only indoctrinate the students with hatred toward America, morality *and Western values. Now is the time to demand that those shaping the future elite consider the ramifications of their actions.*

—Ben Shapiro[46]

Do you know an organizaiton called MEChA—Moviemiento Estudiantil Chicano de Aztlan? One concerned high-schooler sent me the following article, outlining her views about MEChA and its activities, submitted and rejected for publication by her school newspaper:

THE CASE AGAINST MECHA

. . . Currently, junior high schools, high schools, and universities are harboring anti-American organizations, namely MEChA. . . . The sole purpose of the organization is to "liberate" the Chicano population from oppression. While putting on the façade of attempting liberation from socioeconomic, educational, and occupational oppression alone, MEChA's true purpose is to achieve complete political liberation.

At the foundation of MEChA is the concept of Aztlan. Aztlan is roughly defined as the Southwestern states of California, Arizona, New Mexico, Texas, Colorado, and Utah. . . . MEChA, at the national level, works to infiltrate the educational system to promote their ideals of liberation and revolution.

Taken from MEChA's own literature, they state, "We are free and sovereign to determine those tasks which are justly called for by our house, our land, the sweat of our brows, and by our hearts. Aztlan belongs to those who plant the seeds, water the fields, and gather the crops, and not to the foreign Europeans. We do not recognize capricious frontiers on the bronze continent."

MEChA strongly believes and advocates reclaiming Aztlan for the Chicano population, being that population of indigenous people of the Southwestern United States. They claim that this area defined as Aztlan was "stolen" by the United States, a statement that gives no recognition to the Treaty of Guadalupe Hidalgo wherein the United States paid Mexico 15 million dollars for the land. Through various techniques of lies and propa-

ganda, MEChA has been successful in creating chapters across the country, brainwashing students into believing the United States is a country of racist "gringos" who exploit the Chicano population for greedy capitalist purposes.

Having MEChA on any public school campus directly violates education codes. Section 31835 of the California Educational Code states, "Any use, by any individual, society, group, or organization for the commission of any act intended to further any program or movement the purpose of which is to accomplish the overthrow of the government of the U.S. or of the state by force, violence, or other unlawful means while using school property pursuant to the provisions of this chapter is guilty of a misdemeanor." Furthermore Section 31835 states, "No governing board of a school district shall grant the use of any school property to any person or organization for any use in violation of Section 31835." If Aztlan is to be reclaimed, the U.S. government must be overthrown. Therefore, MEChA directly violates Section 31835. . . .

The facts prove MEChA to be an anti-American organization and as citizens of the United States it is our duty to protect our land and our freedom. The decision is ours whether to take action . . . or to stand idly by in complicity. I call on the administration and faculty to take action to correct the error of allowing MEChA on our campus, and we as a student body must educate ourselves so this mistake will not repeat itself. May God bless America.

—Marci Deever, age 18

At first the editor of the school newspaper assured her that he intended to publish the letter. Then they decided that, no, the article lacked balance, and that the paper intended to make it part of a pro and con feature. But then, even as a pro and con feature, the article remained too controversial. The school paper then decided to publish the article as a letter to the editor. But, oops, the term ended, and the last newspaper published omitted the submission, either as an article, as part of a pro and con piece, or even as a letter to the editor. As a senior, this high-schooler graduates before the publication of the next newspaper. In short, they ran out the clock.

THE ONLY FREE SPEECH IS
LIBERAL SPEECH

And what about higher education? Do college campuses even teach the First Amendment anymore? Writer Nat Hentoff says the precious Amendment is being trampled at our institutions of higher learning:

Twice, at prestigious Cornell University, many copies of the conservative Cornell Review *were stolen—first because of a parody of Ebonics (black English) and later in indignant response to a syndicated pro-life editorial cartoon.*

Cornell's dean of students initially told me that the first theft never happened, but I told him I had a photograph of a group of vigilantes standing beside a bonfire fueled by the Cornell Review. *Standing among them was this very dean of students. He didn't appear to be restraining them. And a spokeswoman for the university insisted that the pillaging was simply "a form of free expression."*

When I was invited by Cornell's American Studies department to speak there on—of all subjects—the First Amendment, I asked, at a faculty luncheon, why the professors, including First Amendment scholars at Cornell's law school, had been silent. There was more silence, except from a blustering public-relations administrator. As I was leaving, a dean took me aside and softly said, "I'm glad you said that—because I can't."[47]

When David Horowitz, president of the Center for the Study of Popular Culture, surveyed Ivy League professors, he found that 40 percent of professors support reparations, versus 11 percent of the general public.[48]

Horowitz calls the reparations for slavery movement the Super Bowl of all shakedowns. Because of the growing support for reparations on college campuses, Horowitz sent an ad, "Ten Reasons Why Reparations for Slavery Is a Bad Idea—and Racist Too," to thirty-five college newspapers around the country. Most refused to print the ad, even though Horowitz accompanied a check with each submission. But a handful of student publications did run it.[49]

The fit hit the shan. Brown University students stole a 4,000-copy press run of their school's *Daily Herald*.[50] At UC-Berkeley's *Daily Californian*, students stormed the paper's offices, some crying, some tearing up copies of the paper.[51] The next day the newspaper, in full retreat, ran an editorial, apologizing for the "offensive" ad: "The full-page ad . . . was not condoned by the Senior Editorial Board, but we realize that the ad allowed the *Daily Cal* to become an inadvertent vehicle for bigotry. The board regrets that the ad was published, and that the standard approval or rejection process was not carried through."[52]

But black senior Jacquelyn Lindsey insisted that the apology did not go far enough. "I was extremely upset and disappointed that the so-called apology seemed more like a list of excuses and procedures that should have been followed instead of an apology."[53]

At the University of California-Davis, the campus newspaper the *Aggie* also carried the ad. A shocked black sophomore, Charmayne Young, said, "The advertisement was intended to inflame a certain group of people. This just re-emphasizes an opinion that I and the other students don't belong here."[54] In a next-day editorial, the paper apologized, blaming a procedural breakdown. "It came as a total surprise to me when I opened up the paper," said Editor-in-Chief Eleeza V. Agopian. "That ad completely violated our ad policy. Had we seen this ad beforehand, we never would have published it. . . . It's really unfortunate that it happened on the last day of Black History Month. This hinders any sort of effort to create an open environment, and we're working very hard to build back the trust that we lost today."[55]

Is the Horowitz ad racist? He sets forth ten reasons for opposing reparations:

- There is no single group clearly responsible for the crime of slavery.
- There is no one group that benefited exclusively from its fruits.

- Only a tiny minority of white Americans ever owned slaves, and others gave their lives to free them.
- America today is a multi-ethnic nation and most Americans have no connection (direct or indirect) to slavery.
- The historical precedents used to justify the reparations claim do not apply, and the claim itself is based on race not injury.
- The reparations argument is based on the unfounded claim that all African-American descendants of slaves suffer from the economic consequences of slavery and discrimination.
- The reparations claim is one more attempt to turn African-Americans into victims. It sends a damaging message to the African-American community.
- Reparations to African-Americans have already been paid.
- What about the debt blacks owe to America?
- The reparations claim is a separatist idea that sets African-Americans against the nation that gave them freedom.[56]

In its apology, UC Davis *Aggie* editor Agopian said the ad "in no way reflects the feelings or climate of our staff."[57]

I interviewed Ms. Agopian, questioning the necessity of her paper's apology.

ELDER: "How do you know how the rest of your staff feels? Have you polled them on how they feel?"

EDITOR: "I couldn't exactly give you a straight answer on the way that the staff feels because from what I've heard from numerous discussions with our entire staff is there's about 100 different opinions."

ELDER: "Then how do you say 'It in no way reflects the feelings or climate of my staff'?"

EDITOR: "Because that one statement does not reflect the exact sentiment of over 100 people who work for a newspaper. How could it? I ask you, how could it? How could those statements reflect one staff?"

ELDER: "I thought you just told me your staff had divergent
    points of view?"

EDITOR: "Yes, there are divergent points of view, so how can
    one point of view reflect 100 people?"

ELDER: "In other words, the students reading your paper are so
    stupid as to think that if there's an advertisement, it reflects the
    views of you and your staff and, therefore, you have to let
    them know it doesn't?"

EDITOR: "No, I didn't say that. I think that we wanted to rein-
    force to our campus community that advertisements don't rep-
    resent the views of the *Aggie*, just as any other newspaper
    would enforce that in their own newspaper's advertising pol-
    icy."[58]

Whew. Glad we got *that* straightened out.

Mr. Horowitz called the *Daily Cal* apology "a really black day for
the First Amendment. . . . It's important to have a dialogue of many
voices. The reality at UC is that there is only one voice on these issues
because people are afraid of being called racist."[59]

Well, I hope Horowitz at least got a refund.

4

MORE DADS, LESS CRIME

The Welfare State's Devastating
Impact on Families

The attachment between father and son may be the key [to responsible boys].
Fathers teach their sons lessons, directly and indirectly, about what it
means to be a man. When boys identify with fathers who are loving and
available, the likelihood lessens that they will define their masculinity in
terms of rebellion and antisocial aggression.[1]
—SOCIOLOGIST MAGGIE GALLAGHER

Fathers are models for manhood. If not dad, who or what will form a boy's
understanding of who he is and how he should act? As for girls, they need their
father's guidance and knowledge about boys and men. A girl spends much of her
adolescence trying to figure out how to relate to boys. Teen childbearing occurs
more often with girls from single-parent, female-headed households.[2]
—ELOISE ANDERSON, DIRECTOR, CLAREMONT INSTITUTE'S
PROGRAM FOR THE AMERICAN FAMILY

Irresponsible breeding—not crime, racism or bad schools—remains America's number-one problem. An uninvolved or absentee father creates undeniable damage to a child's psyche. An absent or uninvolved father hurts children, making them less trusting and less capable of committing to others. Dads matter.

Consider this letter I received from a grateful son:

The most important thing that my father has given me has nothing to do
with money. It is his passion for life and the belief that I can accomplish
what I set out to do.

If only people followed their own inner curiosity like my father does . . .
if only people wondered more whether they might accomplish something and
dared to give it a try . . . if only more people knew the secret: You can rise
to the occasion. From wherever you are, you can rise and achieve something
wonderful.

A listener to my radio program sent me a copy of an opinion piece she'd written, titled, "To All the Dads I've Loved Before," that had been published in her local paper, the *Palisadian Post,* a few days before Father's Day. It said, in part:

"To All the Dads I've Loved Before" [is] a love song to all the fathers
who've coached my children in basketball, soccer, baseball, and swimming.
It's a love song to all the men who've taught my children in school and
Sunday school. They bring something to the table that women can't. Men
understand boys better. They love their daughters because they're everything
they aren't. It's a politically incorrect view, but if you doubt what men bring
to a family and to relationships, and the stability they give, then look to the
inner cities where dads aren't present and tell me it's a functional environment.

I know it's a vogue thing among some stars to have a baby without the
dad in the household, making it seem that men are superfluous. Before I had
children and a husband, I too thought briefly about sperm donation. Then,
in my usual opinionated manner, I decided if I wasn't smart enough to have
a relationship with a man, I wasn't smart enough to raise a child.

Yesterday, my opinion was confirmed. My two boys were making a racket
in the living room. I went in to tell them to stop, instead I quietly backed
out. You see, it was a three-way wrestling match between my husband, my
seven- and four-year-old. Everyone was laughing as they rolled around. Dads
give children something different than women do, and our children desperately
need it.

The writer received mail calling her "insecure" and "insulting to single parents"! One writer said, "We're proud of being single parents, it's a sign of our independence."

Independence? Certainly a woman has the *right* to have a child without the benefit of marriage. But what about the rights of the child, thrust into the world and denied the right to a dad? As the saying goes, "You've come a long way, Baby." But in their triumph women shouldn't assume that having the freedom and the right and the ability to "do it all" means that doing it all on your own is necessarily a good thing—*especially* for your kids.

Will ending welfare ensure responsible, hands-on dads? Of course not. But welfare does promote premature motherhood and fatherhood. Remove the government-provided "social safety net," and teens and young men and women would make different decisions about when (and with whom) to become parents.

A recent article in the *Raleigh News & Observer* notes a 1990 North Carolina out-of-wedlock birthrate for black children of almost 65 percent that rose to 66 percent by the year 2000. During that same period, Hispanic out-of-wedlock births grew from about 23 percent in 1990 to almost 43 percent; with whites, it was 14 percent to 19 percent; and for Asians, 6 percent to 13 percent.[3]

Speaking of personal responsibility, the article contained these gems: " 'I have to be the mother and father,' said [LaQuinta] McKoy, 25, who says things just didn't work out with the men who fathered her children. . . . Looking professional in a gray vest and white blouse, McKoy said she dearly wants to get off welfare and back on her feet. But 4½ months pregnant, she knows many challenges lie ahead."[4]

Or how about this one? "At least once a week, Karl R. Whitley of Knightdale visits his 8-year-old daughter, Carolyn, who lives with her mother in Raleigh. . . . Whitley said he can't provide financial support right now. But, he said, he makes sure his daughter knows she's loved."[5] Hey, let's run him for "Father of the Year."

And here's the poverty-excuses-deviant-behavior line: "Black women are more likely to have children outside marriage mainly because many live in poverty, experts say."[6]

And this from an "expert": "When you don't have available, employed men, you have women who have families anyway," said Barbara Risman, sociology professor at NC State University, who is co-chairwoman of the Council for Contemporary Families, a national think tank. "If your choice as a woman is to have a stable, loving, two-parent family with a husband who participates as a breadwinner and a co-parent, but if one of those isn't available and you still want to have a family, you still have a family."[7]

After reading yet another victicrat article urging social programs to address the "plight" of troubled inner-city youths, an eighth-grade inner-city math teacher wrote:

> As an African-American public school educator in a school that serves an urban demographic, I'm intimately familiar . . . [with] the genesis of these irresponsible fathers. There is little the government can do to help these men. They must first help themselves, and their communities must help them help themselves.
>
> This year, 95 percent of the black boys I educate are failing my 8th grade algebra class, despite all of them being at least as capable (if not more) than those that are passing. These 95 percent waste most of their class time, do little or no homework, are preoccupied with sports and girls, deride the 5 percent passing my class as "weak" or "soft," are consumed with wearing the latest "gear," only read when their teacher pleads, and laugh when they get Fs. While I love them as intensely as I love my own son, I loathe their academic skills, attitude, and commitment. I have no doubt the public school system has ruined them with years of inexperienced/uncommitted teach-ers who haven't demanded or expected the level of performance I have of them. Not surprisingly, none of these boys have fathers in their home (con-versely, the 5 percent that are passing do). Very few of them are promising athletes . . . combined with their poor academic performance and social skills (many of the girls find them quite undesirable), you have the recipe for gang-bait. The help these young men need starts at home.
>
> I deplore single mothers with multiple children who rely on the older siblings to "help with" the younger kids. I share this anger with my students,

*and it always strikes a nerve. Just because you're 13–14 doesn't mean you
don't have needs, too. An adolescent needs love and attention as much as a
five-year-old, yet so many of my young men don't get it, and thus turn to
other things. We are foolish if we expect these young men to grow up as
responsible men without any models of responsible men in their lives. I take
little pride in being the first black man they've known who a) went to college;
b) doesn't smoke, do drugs, or abuse alcohol; c) doesn't try to be a "playa";
d) consistently speaks standard English; e) doesn't have a criminal record.
Black people must simply stop having children that cannot be responsibly
reared, period. It's obvious to me why this issue is never emphasized by the
social service advocates: you can't get government money for something most
people should learn at home. The black community must create an environment that promotes responsible rearing of children. We always speak of the
power of the black church. The black church should be even more vocal ex-
tolling the virtues of sacrifice, discipline, and responsibility regarding sex and
creating life.*

In algebra, students learn that factoring really involves taking out *and*
separating, *not* putting *in, and* gathering. *We could not spend enough
money on these dads until we separate and identify the spiritual and personal
commitment required by those intimate with these young men. Change starts
with the individual, not from some outside entity. When these young men
decide to educate themselves, ignore the pop-culture free-market barrage of
half-truths, and accept their obligation to their future children and community,
they will not need to be part of the welfare equation, for they will be the
solution.*

—Pete F.

What about personal responsibility? Child rearing remains the most
serious task undertaken by an adult short of combat. Don't blame poverty. Don't blame the schools. Don't blame "the system." Blame the
parent.

I receive letter after letter from frustrated public school teachers
who say that they confront the identical, disturbing, it's-not-my-

responsibility pattern time and again. When a student is failing, cannot concentrate, and lacks motivation, that is often a student whose parents—either due to work or a lack of concern—fail to take an active role in their child's education. When a student's classroom behavior is unacceptable, that's a student whose mother never bothers to come to a parent-teacher conference or whose father is not living in the home. All too often, when the father is not in the picture, male students show no discipline and have little direction. They seem to abound in rudeness and disrespect.

The location of the school does not matter. The problems remain the same. When parents take no responsibility, even though their children are acting out in the classroom and failing as students, teachers become frustrated. Their anger is understandable.

Pace University philosophy professor Andrew Bernstein notes that in New York in 1905, more than 80 percent of black families included a black father in the home. "By 1980," he writes, "48 percent of black babies were born to single mothers, compared to 17 percent in 1950. In that same year, 82 percent of all children born to black girls aged 15–19 were illegitimate. By 1998, the illegitimacy rate for black children stood at a staggering 70 percent."[8]

What happened? Bernstein blames the I-feel-your-pain-we-think-of-you-as-a-victim contemporary liberal attitude, "The government's post-1960s policies must be examined in their cumulative effect. The state made welfare a more lucrative short-term option than full-time minimum-wage employment. It made chronic illegitimacy a superior financial alternative to marriage and a self-supporting family. It increasingly refused to discourage unruly behavior in school. By promoting even those who failed to learn, it undercut the motivation to study and get an education. By permitting disruptions, it made learning as difficult as possible in the urban public schools. By decreasingly punishing youthful offenders, it encouraged crime. Government policies encouraged indolence, illegitimacy, lack of family supervision, disruptive school behavior, diminished education and crime."[9]

We often talk about divorce's impact on children. Seldom, however, do we consider the impact of the welfare state on families. Social Security, Medicare, and Medicaid all sound beautiful in theory, but in reality they discourage family solidarity, unity, and interdependence. With a government-provided "social safety net," families rely and depend less on each other. This means they need to work less hard on their relationships and need to stay in touch less often. For a supposedly "it-takes-a-village" country, isn't this the opposite of what we expect families to do?

By giving money to people who make irresponsible decisions—such as bearing a child before being morally, spiritually, and financially ready to assume the responsibility—we reward their irresponsibility while shielding them from its bad, behavior-changing effect.

MY DAD

Critics call this "hard work" formula simplistic.

My own father, Randolph, was born in 1915, in Athens, Georgia. He does not know his biological father, and various men passed in and out of his and his mother's life. At age 13, my father came home one day and, according to his mother's boyfriend, "made too much noise." My father and the boyfriend verbally squabbled, with the mom siding with the boyfriend.

His own mother threw him out of the house. As he walked down the street, she yelled, "You'll be back—either that or in jail." Not much of a start. A black Southerner without a father, disowned by his mother, during the Depression.

He began a series of Dickensian jobs—hotel boy, shoeshine boy, valet, and cook for a white family. He became a Pullman porter for the railroad and a member of the Brotherhood of Sleeping Car Porters. He traveled all across the country and visited California, a sunny place that seemed more liberal. When World War II broke out, he joined the Marine Corps, became a cook in the military, and fed thousands of GIs. He rose to the rank of sergeant and spent some time on the island of Guam awaiting a possible military invasion of the island of Japan. But, at the end of the war, he returned to the South, seeking work as a short-order cook.

"Sorry," restaurant after restaurant told him, "You have no references." References? How about that wartime stint on the island of Guam, cooking for and serving soldiers while awaiting the invasion of the island of Japan? No one hired him. They all said he "lacked references." Disgusted, my father, who had just married my mother, packed up and left for California, vowing to find a job and send for her. My father again sought work as a short-order cook. Sorry, owners repeatedly told him, we need references.

So my dad went to the local unemployment office, and informed the clerk that he intended to take the first job that walked in the door. He literally sat for hours in the office until something came through.

The Nabisco Company, the clerk eventually advised him, needs a janitor. The work included cleaning toilets. "Would that be acceptable?" the lady asked my dad. Within a few months, Nabisco promoted him from janitor to supervising others. He also began a second job as a janitor, and, on weekends, cooked for a wealthy white family in the suburbs. He also attended night school three nights a week to get his high school equivalency.

By the age of forty-seven, my father had scraped together enough money to start a café, a lifelong dream. At first, he kept his regular job, covering his bets in case the restaurant failed. It didn't. For over thirty years, my father awakened shortly after 4 A.M. to open the restaurant at 6:30. He never missed a day, never arrived late, and never served a bad meal.

The restaurant sat in the Pico-Union area, an increasingly gang-infested part of town. One of the city's most notorious gangs, the Eighteenth Street Gang, calls Pico-Union their turf. But my father studied Spanish, employed Spanish-speaking locals, served good food, and watched a generation of youth grow up, get married, and have children. Graffiti vandals sometimes wrote on the restaurant's walls, but my dad never got robbed, mugged, or otherwise physically harassed. People respected him.

No, my dad and I did not always get along. Gruff and blunt, my dad often intimidated my two brothers and me. But we never doubted his love or his commitment to his family. Yes, he knows racism, and experienced it during a demeaning, in-your-face era of white bigotry. Still, my father never railed against "racist" America. He now says, "Son, sky's the limit."

My mom and my father recently celebrated their fifty-third wedding anniversary. Through example, my father taught me the value of hard work, of perseverance, and of not making excuses.

Dad closed the doors on Elder's Snack Bar, 1230 South Valencia Street, Los Angeles, California, about five years ago. He seldom took a vacation, and he built a successful business with a loyal, grateful clientele. He now busies himself, at age eighty-five, with Spanish lessons and takes a one-mile walk every day. But then, no one who knew him expected any less.

DAD: A FATHER, NOT A FRIEND

Benjamin Cooper, a black man from Texas, recently died. Mr. Cooper never made the cover of *Time* magazine, nor did the local newspapers print a large obituary about him. Mr. Cooper was my Little League coach for two years.

Tough, gruff Mr. Cooper reminded me of my dad. A product of that Depression/WWII generation, Mr. Cooper drove a city bus until he retired. Two times during the week we'd practice at Van Ness Park in South Central, Los Angeles, and we played a game every Saturday. Mr. Cooper served not merely as a coach, but also as a mentor, leader, and taskmaster. Once Mr. Cooper saw me giddily running on the field, and he complimented me: "Larry, you certainly are exuberant today."

To which I replied, "What does exuberant mean?" Mr. Cooper barked, "Look it up."

One Saturday, after I'd had a particularly good game, I decided that, no, I really didn't need to show up to practice during the week. I did, however, promptly show up for the game that next Saturday. For some reason Mr. Cooper didn't start me, and I began the game on the bench. By the third inning, I remained on the bench. Fifth inning, still ridin' the pine. Game over, Mr. Cooper came up to me, looked me in the eye and said, "Larry, I don't know how good you think you are, but no one is good enough to miss practice and then have the nerve to show up for a game. If you're too good to practice, you're too good to play. Pull that again, and don't bother ever showing up." I never missed practice again.

Mr. Cooper raised two fine sons. No one was surprised when one of the bus driver's sons became a doctor, the other a lawyer. And Mr. Cooper helped to shape young ballplayers like myself who stood on the verge of manhood. I've never forgotten his lessons.

Ask Jesse Jackson or Al Sharpton this question. Which causes more difficulty and creates more pain—the presence of white racism, or the absence of black fathers? But the welfare state provides financial incentives for women to marry the government, all too often reducing would-be Mr. Coopers to economic fifth wheels.

Former UCLA basketball standout and pro star turned sports analyst Marques Johnson explained the adjustment problems of some black NBA players: "People talk about the external or internal factors. Some of these guys—a lot of African-American players today come from single-parent homes where there's no strong father figure in the home. You might have a situation where there's some animosity between the father and the mother in that situation . . . and so I think a lot of it is just acting out frustration, full of anger on life conditions that we know nothing about. A guy like [this young star] who I know has a strong mother—don't know a whole lot about the father situation—but I think a lot of this you're seeing is acting out."[10]

When have you heard Jesse Jackson, NAACP president Kweisi Mfume, or the chairman of the Black Congressional Caucus say anything remotely that obvious, commonsensical, and important?

Michael Jordan, following yet another frustrating loss with his young Washington Wizards, blasted his team about their lack of work ethic, "When they take that paycheck twice a month, along with that comes responsibility, accountability and the expectation of them working hard. If they're not ready for that, they should give back the money, go to school or do something else."[11]

And what about Los Angeles Clippers' black coach Alvin Gentry? His 2001–2002 team, the youngest in the NBA, nearly blew a twenty-one-point lead against the Houston Rockets. Angered by the near miss and by his perception that his team lacks commitment, Gentry laid down the law that we seem to apply to sports but not to academics or to life. Very little of it was fit to be printed in a newspaper. But the bottom line was that it's time for the Clippers to grow up and act like adults.

"The thing I'm most disappointed in is that I think our focus and our attention spans are not very good," Gentry told reporters. "The difference between a good team and a bad one is the good ones come to practice after a win and work even harder. For some strange reason, we seem to think we've got this entitlement thing going. We think we're entitled to be a good team. The only thing we're entitled to is working our tails off.

"We're not going to be a good team until we put all the horseplay behind us. We'll have our moments and we'll win some games when we look great, and then we'll take a big step backwards. It's all focus. Or lack thereof."[12]

When a reporter noted that the Clippers' average age of 24.8 years was the youngest of any NBA team on opening night, Gentry said, "It's no excuse. I refuse to use it as an excuse. That was cute last year.

"We all know the difference between right and wrong," Gentry said. "We all have children who know the difference between right and wrong. All that being young stuff won't play anymore. I think we're immature. We've got to work on it. Nothing comes easy. Except failure."[13]

A single-parent household does not equal a death sentence. My father does not know his biological father, yet he married and raised three law-abiding boys in a marriage that is fifty-three years plus and counting. But while moms provide the heart, dads provide the muscle.

Face it—mothers and fathers play different roles.

Remember the movie *Boiler Room,* in which a young man tries to please his successful father? At first the boy tries, much to his father's disapproval, an illegal gambling operation. So he ultimately abandons the gambling business and becomes a stockbroker. But the boy's company does not resemble anything like Merrill Lynch. In fact, he now works for a "chop shop" that sells junk to "lay-downs" or stupid investors. When his father learns of son's shady business, the son arranges for a sit-down in a coffee shop with dad.

> SON: I don't know why we can't just discuss this. I mean, I mean, maybe you just don't see my side.
>
> FATHER: Look, you know, I'm not your best pal, that's your mother's side. I'm your father. I tell you when you screw up. I mean, my God, if I woulda called my father to meet me for a cup of coffee to talk about my screwups, he probably would have laughed. We didn't have nice little chats about why I was a bad boy—I got smacked. And I didn't do it again. Much simpler.
>
> SON: Look, you know, I'm just trying to restore what's left of our relationship. I mean—
>
> FATHER: —Relationship? Are we dating? I'm not your girlfriend, I'm your father.

The father in the movie got it right. A parent and a buddy are two different things. This dad gets it:

Dear Larry,

As I was growing up I thought my dad was the toughest dad around, and certainly not "my buddy." In those days, every kid thought dads were supposed to be Ward Cleaver or Robert Young, so I was often disappointed that my dad could not be like that. Even in my twenties, I thought I could be more mellow and understanding with my kid, but I found myself more concerned with how she would manage and survive in the world as an adult, than with being her friend and making things easier for her.

My daughter and I were often at odds during her adolescence, but as I grew older I realized I was "becoming" my father in some ways. And, I began to more fully appreciate the job he had done in raising me. He taught me to work hard, be responsible, ambitious and to stand up for myself (among other things!). I don't know if we ever had a "Ward Cleaver" moment, but I do know that he helped immeasurably in preparing me for what was to come in the real world. We are probably closer now than we have ever been. Was he perfect? No, far from it. But he was tough when he had to be and generous when he could be and now I feel lucky to have had him as my father.

My daughter is now twenty-five and still trying to find her niche in life. But she has a science degree from a major, private university and has never been in any problems that affect the kids today, such as substance abuse. As her dad, I wish I could wake up 5–10 years from now and know that everything turned out OK! But, I'm confident that it will, and that she's better prepared than she even realizes for what the world will throw at her. Our relationship has seesawed over the years, but we are getting closer as the years go by. I now realize that, as her father, my ultimate reward is to know that she can take care of herself and compete in whatever field she enters. I also now realize/believe, that she will appreciate her dad more as she gets older.

—Peter K.

What do basketball star Shaquille O'Neal and Los Angeles murder suspect Samuel Sharad Shabazz have in common? Fathers.

Last year, the Los Angeles Lakers basketball team won their second championship in two years. The principal credit goes to their seven-foot, three-hundred-pound-plus center, Shaquille O'Neal.

The previous year the Los Angeles police arrested eighteen-year-old Samuel Sharad Shabazz on suspicion of murdering Police Chief Bernard Parks's granddaughter, Lori Gonzalez. Accompanied by a friend with gang affiliations, Ms. Gonzalez had pulled into the driveway of a fast-food restaurant. The suspect walked up to Gonzalez's car and began pumping bullets into the vehicle. Her companion, the apparent target, ducked, and the assailant's bullets struck and killed Ms. Gonzalez.

O'Neal's biological father abandoned his family. Shaquille's mother married a former military man, affectionately known as "Sarge," who helped raise young Shaq from the age of three. O'Neal cites Sarge as his toughest but most important teacher, inspiring *Los Angeles Times* sportswriter Bill Plaschke to write about Sarge's "tough love."

Once, writes Plaschke, the police called Sarge when his ten-year-old elementary-school stepson got into trouble as a result of hanging around with the wrong type of kids. The police told Sarge that O'Neal and friends set off a fire alarm. Sarge ran down to the school, paddle in hand. The cops saw him when he came through the door, and they said, "If you hit him, we're going to lock you up!" Said Sarge, "I told them, 'then lock me up right now!' " A whipping followed, and Sarge says he barked to his young charge, "I told him, 'Better I do it now than have the police do it later.' . . . I told him, 'You've got to be a leader, not a follower.' "[14]

Three years later, Sarge attended a parent–teacher conference where teachers complained that Shaq wasn't "taking care of business" in school. One teacher told Sarge that Shaq spent his time goofing off and break-dancing in shop class. Sarge promptly took Shaq to a nearby bathroom, where Sarge "beat his ass." But Sarge adds, "That was the last time I ever had to do that to my son. The last time. After that, he grew up."[15]

Boys who spend their developmental years without fathers pose a special challenge. As boys grow, they become difficult for their mothers to control physically. Their increasing strength renders the threat of a spanking almost laughable.

For all of Shaquille O'Neal's power and physical intimidation, most in the game find him mature, level-headed, and even-tempered. Assist to Sarge, a man who, by the way, never uses the term "stepfather" or "stepson." "What do you mean, stepson?" bellowed Sarge. "Bull! No such thing! You love the mother, you love the child, you raise the child. I would die for my family."[16]

A salute to the Sarges of the world. They can—and do—make a difference, sometimes *the* difference.

And what of Mr. Shabazz? After the murder of the chief's granddaughter, the investigation led to Mr. Shabazz's home. A SWAT team surrounded the teenager's home and arrested him, charging him with one count of murder and one count of attempted murder. After police searched the suspect's home, they reportedly also arrested *his father* on an "outstanding unrelated warrant for parole violation."[17]

Shaquille O'Neal turned out just like his father. As for murder suspect Samuel Sharad Shabazz, you make the call.

Dads matter.

DADS AND CRIME

Years ago, the Reverend Louis Farrakhan led the Million Man March, where he properly urged black men to assume their parental responsibilities to their children and their moral responsibilities to their wives and girlfriends. According to the Washington, D.C., police, crime in Washington, D.C., that day fell dramatically. One experienced officer called the march the most peaceful demonstration he had ever seen. Why? Moral pressure.

AT&T tells us that, on Mother's Day, Americans generate about 150 million phone calls, compared to approximately 120 million for Father's Day. Interestingly, Father's Day generates more collect calls than any other day of the year. The greeting card industry observes a similar disparity, reporting sales of nearly 150 million Mother's Day cards, compared to 95 million for Father's Day. What does this tell us about our relationships with moms versus dads?

A recent study blames absentee, noninvolved fathers for increasing the odds of a life of crime. Each year a boy spends without dad at home raises his odds of future incarceration by 5 percent. Boys without dads more frequently father children out of wedlock and drop out of school. Yet the same study shows that a boy living with his single father—as opposed to his single mother—has *no* higher risk of incarceration than does a boy from a two-parent family.[18]

Eloise Anderson, former director of California's Department of Social Services, says, "Fully 70 percent of all prison and reform school inmates come from fatherless homes."[19] Of young suicides, 63 percent come from homes without fathers. And of homeless children, including runaways, nearly 90 percent come from homes with absent fathers.[20] This is not good news.

Anderson says, "Boys fare the worst. They are the majority of youthful drug abusers, homeless children and kids in foster care. A boy in a single-parent home is twice as likely to be incarcerated as his peer living with both parents, regardless of race, income or education level."[21] Dads matter.

Dominic Fowler, a thirty-year-old black man and a self-described member of the "hip-hop generation," recently sent me an essay. He entitled his wake-up call, "All of My Friends Are Dying":

My name is Dominic. I am thirty years old. . . . My parents divorced when I was in the sixth grade. . . .

Every family memory I have begins at the end of fifth grade, when my parents were on the road to divorce. . . . After my parents got divorced, I do remember moving to southeast San Diego with my mother, older brother, younger brother, and baby sister. I remember being injected into the heart of a low-income neighborhood with heavy gang activity. This is where I grew up. On Thirty-third St., "Tha' Coast."

. . . It was here that I learned that welfare is as common as working. It was here that I learned all plans, goals, victories, defeats—any emotion you possess—could and should be celebrated or deadened with alcohol. It was here that I learned that absolutely nothing was expected of me, that mediocrity in the tired form of just trying to make it in the white man's world was all that was required. These are not the teachings of my mother or father. But it was a weird, unstable period. Sometimes, when your home base is turbulent, you tend to start picking up the teachings of your friends and neighbors. There were some kids whose parents *had been simmering in this poisonous atmosphere since their own birth. Am I telling you that no hard-working people existed in my neighborhood? Absolutely not! But we were where we were and "positivity" was not plentiful. . . .*

You see, our friends are dying. Some are dead now—literally. Most are on the death path. Out of the ten I can think of right now, one is dead (rest in peace), nine are alcoholic, five are regular drug users, five are unemployed, none have college degrees and everyone has fly-ass clothes.

. . . I was sixteen years old the first time I drank a "forty" on my homies' porch. My brother tells me that the homies are still drinkin' "forties." Everyone is at least thirty years old. *What kind of future do my friends have? If this is the total sum of young, black thought, how successful as a people are we going to be? . . .*

My friends and I were once sixteen-year-old boys drinking "forties." Can we teach the next batch of children a little bit of balance? Can we, who are now grown, say something to the kids who are on the same path? Can we maybe do things differently inside of the home where our kids are watching our coping skills? . . . I don't know. I do not have all of the answers to all of the problems. But I do know all of my friends are dying. And all of my friends are someone's children.

Peace,

—Dominic Fowler, a.k.a. "THA' Veteran"

CHINO BLAMES THE MAN

"Society pushes you back in to the same pile of sh—t you came out of. Back into the 'hood, drinking, kicking and selling drugs to a bunch of young kids, preparing them to take your place."[22] Chino, a Los Angeles gang member, provided this answer for why he and others join gangs. You know, the Man.

Time magazine, in its September 3, 2001, issue, featured a story on Los Angeles gangs. It stated that while the city saw an overall drop in some crime figures, gang-related murders increased 143 percent in 2000. Three hundred thirty-one people died because of gang violence, in contrast to 136 in 1999. And, according to *Time,* even though gang-related property crimes decreased, "Felony assault by gangsters is up 9.7 percent, attacks on police officers are up 35.5 percent, witness intimidation is up 50 percent. In other words, there is less drug dealing and theft, more violence for the sake of violence."[23]

Why the rise in crime? *Time* says that criminologists point to two reasons. "First, veteran gang members jailed a decade ago during the crack epidemic are getting out of prison—and returning to reinfect their neighborhood with violent habits hardened and reinforced in prison," says the magazine. And, says Jack Riley, director of the criminal-justice program at the RAND Corporation, "The next generation of gang homicides is going to have a different construct [from the crack epidemic]. . . . Locals in South Central and East L.A. think it is people returning from prison and trying to re-establish their authority."[24]

"There are 100,000 gang members in jail in California, and they are getting out at a rate of about 3,000 a month," says *Time.* "Social workers call them 'spoons'—people who get out of jail and stir things up."[25]

Time claims that the second reason for the rise in gang violence is that the police are backing out of these gang-infested neighborhoods. "Immediately after the dissolution of CRASH (Community Resources

Against Street Hoodlums) there was a lull," says LAPD Detective Chuck Zeglin, a gang specialist. "Morale plummeted and many cops moved to other police departments in other cities. Then a lot of the more hard-core gangsters came to believe we were not going to be as proactive as before, and they went a little crazy."[26] As for the second reason, thank the Los Angeles Police Department scandal, but, more broadly, the constant attack on the police. Racial profiling. DWB—Driving While Black.

But Chino blames society. The racist power structure, the "oppressor," conspires to hold him down.

Blaming others—the victicrat mentality—means Chino accepts the idea of powerlessness over his circumstances. But the powerlessness is an illusion. In the movie *Slam*, a black female motivational speaker goes to prison and delivers a powerful, tearful soliloquy to hardened convicts: "You know, it's really f——ked up that you were born in South-East, in the ghetto, it's really f——ked up that you were born black, it's really f——ked up that you had the hard time you had in your life. Whatever your story is—whatever it is that brought you here in your life, if you keep shoving the anger and the pain and the frustration down, and you keep saying, 'That's all right, f——k it, I'm gonna do what I gotta do,' and you don't let it come out, that keeps pushing you down. *That* is your prison. You gotta let that shit out. 'Cause once you let that frustration out, it doesn't hold you back anymore. It doesn't lock you down. And then you can stand up with some courage and say, 'OK, but *I* am not gonna live like this. *I* am gonna take my destiny into my own hands. That's the only way to go now.' "

Who's the enemy? The white man? The FBI? J. Edgar Hoover? Republicans? I asked gang members to call my radio show and answer that question.

An ex-gang member, who admitted starting a gang, said he grew up "confined" to public housing. He felt "the white man put us there." Now, he calls his analysis "dumb," "stupid," and he urges his "running buddies" to denounce that worldview.

Another ex-gang member, who said he started listening to my show while in prison, said, "I knew that this was not the place I wanted to be. I knew that this was no place for no man, no matter what race, or what socioeconomic background he comes from. The primary thing that I would say that drives a lot of us to the streets is—number one— no father in the home. No positive male influence, whether it be father, brother, uncle, grandfather—it's not there. And when you have the majority of us being raised by females—and that's no disrespect to females of any race or caliber—when I go to my homie's house, it's a female, when I go to my cousin's house, it's a female. Females all around. The male is affected by that. He grows up trying to handle male encounters in life, but his only example of how to deal with this is by a female. And that doesn't work. And vice versa, it won't work if you have a group of girls being primarily raised by men."

There is hope. The cycle can be broken. Craig, a twenty-five-year-old ex-gang member, repaired his relationship with his father, who broke up with his mother when Craig was eleven. "I thought I was cool," Craig now says. "I thought I was crazy, I thought I was wild, but on the real side, you know, and we—who been there—we all know that, the life is rough, man. It's not fun. On the real, it's stupid. There is no explanation for it. And for me, I got out. I moved away. Now I do inside sales. I moved out of the warehouse, you know, they gave me chance."

What turned Craig around? "I had kids," said Craig. "And I don't want my kids to go through things I went through. I thought I had to prove something to people, and I don't have to prove nothing to no one but me and my family. So I turned it around. You know what? It's not society. We just have to blame something on another person. If you work hard, and you do everything that you're supposed to do, you're gonna go past that person. You know, Larry, I attended one semester of college, and everyone around me has a college degree. You know how I got where I'm at? I took it. If I want something hard enough—just like I wanted to join a gang, I wanted to gang-bang— if I want something so bad, I'm gonna take it. I took it, and I got it, and now you can't take it from me, 'cause I'm a hard worker, and I'm teaching my children that. You don't need to run no streetcorner. You know what? One day, I'm gonna *own* that streetcorner. And that's the way we have to look at it. Us as black people, we gotta step up, and think past all that. The white man ain't doing nothing, and we need to stop pointing the finger. It's all about us. You want someone to respect us, but we don't even respect ourselves. So how can we expect someone else to respect us?

"We are our own worst enemy, and if we hold down ourselves, we'll never be nothin'. But don't compare me to the other person out there. Compare me as an individual. I'm scarred, I have tattoos, so when I wear a tank-top, people look at me in another light. But as soon as I open my mouth to them, it's like, 'Wow, you're a nice guy.' Yeah, because I'm a person, I'm a human. I just made wrong choices. And you know what? We *can* change. As long as we want to change, we will change. And who cares what the next man thinks about you. As long as you have high self-esteem, you can go a long way, as long as you always have your goals."

Following that show, I received this letter from an ex-gang member:

I'm listening to a replay of your show on gangs, and you say, or ask, "Why? Why join a gang?" I was in a gang between the ages of 15 and 27, and yeah, I can understand how you would pity a gang member's lifestyle. It's a loser's lifestyle. Like you said, you either end up dead or in prison—the sad part is gang members who have kids who grow up in the same lifestyle. It's pathetic. I got out, after I got sick of the near misses on my life, the near misses at getting busted. I was at a point where I was always carrying heat, and that's no way to live. I got out of the lifestyle around the same time I got out of drugs, I wanted a life. I still have weapons, and I think that's why my ex-homies didn't bother me when I dropped out, I did get death threats, but I put out the word I was packing a 12-gauge sawed off, and they left me alone.

Yes, my dad was absentee. My mom was always working, never home.

So I got into trouble, but I wised up. I got a job I been at for sixteen years. I own my own home. But I still got the tattoos and I still get mad-dogged by gang members, mostly young punks out to impress, and I'm forty-four now. I still get harassed by cops. I get looks by people that seem to be afraid or intimidated by me. I heard hearsay at work just tonight that I look like a hoodlum and like I just got out of prison, so you see, you never lose that look.

But I'm clean, and proud of it. As you can see, some of us are smart enough to get out and be productive members of society. But, to be honest, Larry, I think because of the tattoos, and my history, it will eventually catch up with me. You know the ol' saying: Live by the sword, die by the sword. I will either get shot or I shoot a rival in self-defense, and then my life will be over. Everything I worked hard for will be lost. I can feel it coming. Kinda sucks.

—George

The truth will not set you free, if delivered without hope. Craig overcame the handicap of a difficult relationship with his father. He now has hope. But this begins with the assumption of personal responsibility and the willingness to assume the consequences of our own actions. No matter the circumstances, everyone has a moral obligation to try.

5.

BLACK VICTICRATS

Whining and Exaggerating Racism
for Fun and Profit

*The tragic truth is that the language of "victimization" is the true victimizer—
a great crippler of young minds and spirits. To teach young people that their
lives are governed—not by their own actions, but by socio-economic forces or
government budgets or other mysterious and fiendish sources beyond their control—
is to teach our children negativism, resignation, passivity and despair.*[1]
—LOUIS W. SULLIVAN, FORMER SECRETARY OF
HEALTH AND HUMAN SERVICES AND PRESIDENT OF THE
MOREHOUSE SCHOOL OF MEDICINE

I shall allow no man to belittle my soul by making me hate him.[2]
—BOOKER T. WASHINGTON

Black leaders" use hysterical, inflammatory, and absurd language to trumpet the "poor-me" line. The victicrat mentality says you-owe-me. It says that forces conspire to pull me down and to hold me back. Thus the black victicrat mentality demands not just equal rights, but equal results, a goal that damages the psyche of both blacks and nonblacks. Black leaders teach blacks to think of themselves as victims and of whites as victimizers.

Most blacks, despite tremendous social, economic, and political progress, expect race relations to remain a problem in this country. Frank Newport, the Gallup Poll's editor in chief, blames the negative perception on economic pressure, the Republican administration, and media-highlighted racial profiling incidents.[3]

This black victicrat mentality hurts. The "black leadership," however, continues to fight racism, while placing less emphasis on improving schools, the rewards of hard work, and avoiding irresponsible breeding.

Black leaders demand "fairness" in hiring. So they push for antidiscrimination laws intended to ensure "fair treatment" in the job market. But, while well-intentioned, these laws make the private sector wary of hiring blacks. Employers fear lawsuits, and worry that hiring a minority may later lead to facing charges of discrimination.

Black leaders also defend the government monopoly on education even as a majority of inner-city elementary school kids cannot read, write, or compute at grade level. Ending the government monopoly means better-educated students, which means more livable neighborhoods, which means less crime and greater economic development.

Ignoring far more pressing issues, black leaders continue fighting against white racism as if conditions remain unchanged from those in the days of the Jim Crow South. NAACP Chairman Julian Bond, at a pre–September 11 gathering, likened the Republican Party to the totalitarian Taliban regime in Afghanistan: "[Bush] has selected nominees from the Taliban wing of American politics, appeased the wretched appetites of the extreme right wing, and chosen Cabinet officials whose devotion to the Confederacy is nearly canine in its uncritical affection."[4] And, in December 2001, *after* the terrorist attacks, Bond repeated the charge, again likening the Republicans to the Taliban![5]

In May 2001, two white police officers in Seattle, Washington, shot a black man. A local black activist group called for a citizen board of inquiry, an end to racial profiling, and—get this—a boycott of Starbucks. A boycott of Starbucks? Locals blame dot-com professionals for driving up housing prices and edging poor families out of revitalized downtown areas. The corner Starbucks led the way for the likes of Walgreens and Hollywood Video to move in. And when companies move in, they want an aggressive police to protect their assets. Thus, Starbucks, at least indirectly, causes police brutality. "African-Americans need to wake up and recognize who the villains are in this," said Reverend Robert Jeffrey. "The police are hired guns."[6] Poor Starbucks.

In April 2001, a Cincinnati police officer shot and killed a nineteen-year-old unarmed black suspect. Several days of riots followed, with graphic images in the media of black thugs beating whites. Black Cincinnati defense attorney Ken Lawson, who specializes in police brutality cases, said the rioting "gave whites a better understanding of what it feels like to be a random target of violence just because of the color of your skin."[7] Oh, if only whites saw blacks' pain!

Predictably, NAACP President Kweisi Mfume jetted to Cincinnati. "I'm here because there's Cincinnatis in every state of this union. Every state of this union!"[8] Bullhorn in hand, Mfume called for the grand jury investigating the matter to act swiftly, "Because without any justice there's not going to be any peace."[9]

That April 2001 shooting brought the total number of blacks killed by Cincinnati cops since 1995 to fifteen. But in six of the cases guns were drawn on officers; in four officers were threatened with other instruments; and one case resulted in a Cincinnati officer being killed with two others being injured. The police actions seem, if not entirely defensible, certainly far short of clear-cut police brutality, racial profiling, or "random targeting."[10]

The result? Cincinnati now sees a staggering rise in crime. After a spate of shootings and other violence, one community leader said, "It's like the OK Corral around here anymore."[11] Hamilton County Prosecutor Mike Allen said, "It's like the killing fields, it's like the Wild West down here. There is still the same lawlessness that went on during the riots. And the criminals know that police are now reluctant to take action."[12]

In the three months following the riots and during the intense scrutiny and federal investigation focused on the police department, there were seventy-five gunshot victims—most of them black—compared to eleven in the same three months the previous year. One analyst said, "The city's cops, fearful of being accused of racism, have simply pulled back from aggressive policing. Arrests are down 50 percent since mid-April."[13]

Still, Cincinnati activists chant the victicrat party line. The Reverend Clarence Wallace said, "They have created the criminal culture. We have asked for help in these pockets of the city and so far we have heard nothing. We know it will not be a quick solution, but until some of these communities are strengthened, you are going to have this crime."[14] The reverend also noted that lawlessness would subside when the city's black community is given financial help.

Money? Lack of opportunity? The previous summer, an amusement park just outside the city imported one thousand young Eastern Europeans for summer jobs because too few locals applied. Still, following the violence, leaders demanded the creation of thousands of summer jobs to forestall another rampage.[15]

Memo to Reverend Wallace: Which causes the bigger problem for the black community—The "absence of financial help" or the absence of black fathers? Get back to us on that.

CAN WE TALK?

I have extended countless invitations to many of America's liberal "black leaders" to discuss the issues facing the black community. With few exceptions, they have declined.

One recipient of multiple invitations has been Congresswoman Maxine Waters (D-California). No response. Finally, in 2001, I wrote her a letter outlining my concerns. I promised to keep the communiqué private, pending her reply. I know she's a busy lady, but I think after nine months, I'm probably not going to get one. So here is the letter that merited no response:

Dear Congresswoman Waters:
I write this letter directly to you. No one else received copies.

Your power in America, and especially in the black community, is substantial. I honestly, and sincerely, urge you to rethink your positions on several issues. I have, so far, kept this letter private. I hope that after you read this letter, you will agree to have a one-on-one, sit-down, private conversation with me about the future and direction of black America.

But given the stakes, our personal feelings towards each other are incon-

sequential. I reach out in good faith, based on my sincere concern for the black community. I see an erosion of community standards, values, hopes and aspirations.

By the way, despite my acknowledged harsh criticisms of you, I never once attacked you personally. I said, on many occasions: I don't question her heart, but I question her head. I called you a hardworking, tireless warrior for your views.

I'm not grandstanding, not doing this for ratings. Again, at least, until I hear from you, I am reaching out. I hope to hear from you soon.

I recently received an invitation to an event at a private residence to celebrate the election of Los Angeles Mayor James Hahn.

Frankly, the invitation surprised me, given my harsh criticism of the then-candidate Hahn's position on several issues. Nevertheless, I accepted, only to receive a phone call, dis-inviting me. I understand that the host received pressure from you, among others, that I be barred from the event.

Again, as I said, the invitation surprised me, and I don't blame you or others for not wanting me there. After all, this presumably celebrated your hard work in getting Hahn elected.

I hoped, by accepting, to finally talk with you and other black "leaders" about problems in the black community. My producer called your office on several occasions to get you on my show, but each time you refused. Recently, a caller to my show said that she called your office in hopes that she might convince you to appear on the show. She said your office told her that "you had never heard of Larry Elder." Again, I think I understand the tactic— the tactic of ignoring me, in hopes to minimize what I suspect you perceive as a growing influence. Again, I understand.

I write this letter, however, to issue a call. Your position on major issues affecting the black community is simply, and flat out, wrong. Not only do your positions fail to advance the interests of blacks, but also, in many cases, they actually hurt them. Let's go over them.

Gun Control

You, the NAACP, and the majority of the "black leadership" routinely call for more gun control legislation. Powerful evidence, however, indicates that restrictive gun laws do nothing to deter bad guys, while making it more and more difficult for good people to defend themselves. Violent crime rates have fallen faster and further, for the most part, in the thirty-three states allowing citizens to carry concealed weapons, vs. non-carry states. Japan and England now see crime rates increasing, despite bans on private ownership of guns. Washington, D.C., a city with perhaps the nation's most restrictive gun laws, ranks No. 1 in per capita murders. As former D.C. mayor Marion Barry once incredibly put it, "Outside of the killings, Washington has one of the lowest [crime] rates in the country."[16]

Crime in America remains disproportionately an urban affair. Therefore, those who most need protection from bad guys remain—due in large measure to your policies—most vulnerable to crime.

Affirmative Action

In America in Black and White, *Stephen and Abigail Thernstrom clearly show that the black middle class preceded affirmative action. Moreover, it insults the hardworking black men and women of this country who, since slavery, built the black middle class, day by day, brick by brick, backache by backache. The first black member of the Federal Reserve Board, Arthur Brimmer, studied affirmative action's impact. By affirmative action, I mean preferences, the lowering of standards to achieve "diversity" or "multiculturalism" or "inclusion." I do not include outreach, or using efforts to inform others, irrespective of race, gender, etc., of available opportunities. Brimmer concluded, "I would say that most blacks I know did not get [their jobs] because of affirmative action, but it's impossible [to determine the exact number]."*[17]

In 1963, Ebony magazine ran a series of motivational articles called, "If I Were Young Today." Each month, they asked a black achiever— Federal District Judge Herman Moore, union leader A. Philip Randolph, famed Los Angeles architect Paul Williams—to provide advice to today's youth. Each spoke of drive, vision, hard work, and preparation. Not one even implied the need or desire for preferential treatment.

In 1963, Whitney Young, then head of the Urban League, proposed a kind of a "Marshall Plan" for blacks. A member of the league, however, objected to what he called "the heart of it—the business of employing Negroes [because they are Negroes]." Moreover, Whitney Young suggested his "Marshall Plan" for a period of ten years. This means, if Young prevailed, affirmative action would have ended in 1973![18]

The Detroit News recently wrote that, at seven Michigan colleges and universities, blacks within six years graduate at a rate of 40 percent compared to 61 percent for whites and 74 percent for Asians.[19] Blame lowered standards to achieve campus "diversity." This mismatching of students—placing someone in a major league school when he or she would have been better in a Triple A league—causes, according to one study—a loss of $5.3 billion a year to the black community.[20] Moreover, affirmative action, in the educational field, masked the real problems, substandard education K–12. Yet you, the Democratic Party, and the unions all resist many changes urban parents want, including vouchers.

Besides, hard work wins. Back in 1901, thirty-six years after slavery, Booker T. Washington said, "When a Negro girl learns to cook, to wash dishes, to sew, to write a book, or a Negro boy learns to groom horses, or to grow sweet potatoes, or to produce butter, or to build a house, or to be able to practise [sic] medicine, as well or better than some one else, they will be rewarded regardless of race or colour. [sic] In the long run, the world is going to have the best, and any difference in race, religion, or previous history will not long keep the world from what it wants.

"I think that the whole future of my race hinges on the question as to whether or not it can make itself of such indispensable value that the people in the town and the state where we reside will feel that our presence is necessary to the happiness and well-being of the community. No man who continues to add something to the material, intellectual, and moral well being of the place in which he lives is long left without proper reward. This is a great human law which cannot be permanently nullified."[21]

Welfare

You fight any attempt to roll back the welfare state, and voted against the Welfare Reform Act of 1996. This act caused a 50 percent reduction in the welfare rolls,[22] without a corresponding increase in abortion. It reduced teen *pregnancy, without a corresponding increase in abortion. Census records from 100 years ago found blacks, in some cases, more likely than whites to marry and have children within a traditional family structure. As recently as 1960, 22 percent of black children were born to unwed parents.*[23] *Today, the figure stands at 70 percent, with 80 percent spending at least some time living without a father in the house, at least for part of their lives.*[24] *Racism? Blame Lyndon Johnson's War on Poverty, coupled with a "you-owe-me" victicrat mindset that creates dependency and fosters irresponsibility.*

In 1985, the Los Angeles Times *conducted a poll, asking poor people whether poor young women "often," or "seldom," have children in order to get on welfare. More poor people (64 percent) than non-poor (44 percent) agreed that welfare recipients "often" have children to get additional benefits.*[25] *More poor people than non-poor people agreed that welfare fosters dependency.*

War on Drugs

You recently condemned the CIA for its alleged role in the creation of urban America's drug problem, bellowing at a Town Hall meeting: "If I never do anything else in this career as a member of Congress—I'm gonna make somebody pay for what they've done to my community."[26] *Never mind that the* New York Times, *the* Washington Post, *and the* Los Angeles Times *all wrote stories debunking the notion that the CIA had played anything other than an incidental role in the creation of a drug war. Furthermore, what about personal responsibility? Did some strange mystical racist force cause black people to ingest or inject drugs?*

Many young blacks, convicted of drug-related offenses, waste away in jail. Many never committed violent crimes. Yet, you do not call for the end of the War on Drugs.

You claim you condemn drugs, but you wrote a letter to Janet Reno to back off of a joint federal Justice Department local DEA probe. The probe centered on James A. Prince, a childhood neighbor of your husband's. The authorities suspected him of drug trafficking, and some DEA agents working on the probe suddenly got yanked off. Some, on the record, accused you of interfering with a legitimate probe.[27] *For these reasons, I suspect that you* question the legitimacy of the government's War on Drugs. Why not, then, publicly call for an end to this expensive, unfair, corrupting War on Drugs?

In 1973, former Black Panther Joanne Chesimard gunned down a New Jersey State Highway Patrol Officer. A jury convicted her of murder, and sentenced her to life in prison. In a daring breakout, Chesimard escaped from prison and fled to Cuba. Congress passed a unanimous resolution urging Castro to send Chesimard back to America and face charges.[28] You, however, wrote Castro a letter, urging him to let her stay, stating she was persecuted for her political beliefs and affiliations.[29] You further likened her to Martin Luther King![30]

The War on Drugs requires a growing use of informants, thus compromising the integrity of our criminal justice system. Under the guise of fighting the War on Drugs, President Clinton authorized more wiretaps and asset forfeitures than under the Bush and Reagan administrations combined. Economist Milton Friedman said, "Today in this country, we incarcerate 3,109 black men for every 100,000 of them in the population. Just to give you an idea of the drama in this number, our closest competitor for incarcerating black men is South Africa. South Africa—and this is pre–Nelson Mandela and under an overt public policy of apartheid—incarcerated 729 black men for every 100,000."[31]

Many experts estimate that nearly half of all street crime is directly related to criminals seeking money to support drug habits. I urge you to take a courageous stand and publicly pressure the government to end this war.

Racism

Black leaders refuse to acknowledge the good news: Racism no longer remains a potent threat in American life. Most blacks remain solidly middle class, with blacks forming businesses at a faster rate than whites.

Harvard's Orlando Patterson, a liberal Democrat, said, "The sociological truths are that America, while still flawed in its race relations . . . is now the least racist white-majority society in the world; has a better record of legal protection of minorities than any other society, white or black; offers more opportunities to a greater number of black persons than any other society, including all those of Africa."[32]

Studies show three out of four blacks, with SAT scores between 1250 and 1300, receive admissions into the nation's most elite colleges. Only one in four whites with comparable SAT scores receive admission.[33]

The Screen Actors Guild reports prime-time TV roles going to blacks exceed the percentage of our population in the nation.[34] *Unemployment rates for married black men just about equal those for married white men.*

Yes, black net worth remains but a fraction of white net worth, but government programs cannot close that gap without forcibly taking money away from somebody and giving it to someone else. Instead, hard work, personal responsibility, avoiding slovenly behavior, getting an education, and focus create growth and opportunity. You display precisely these qualities in your life and career, and they form the basis for your success.

As mentioned before, 70 percent of today's black children are born outside of wedlock. Nearly one-third of young black men are in the criminal justice system.[35] *In many urban schools, the dropout rate exceeds 50 percent. Because of these problems, there are only 100 eligible, marriageable black men for every 111 eligible, marriageable black women.*[36] *Nearly three-quarters of inner-city kids at the elementary school level fail to read, write, and compute at grade level.*[37]

In America, we see two black Americas. The majority black world reflects increased prosperity, growing homeownership, and steady asset accumulation. The other, the so-called black underclass, remains disturbing. Quite simply, we see too many children having children. It stands, far and away, as America's No. 1 problem. Whatever role racism played, the complete abolition of white racism would leave these problems unresolved.

I await your response.

Sincerely yours,
Larry Elder

THE REPARATIONS HUE AND CRY

Incredibly, many of today's "black leadership," including Jesse Jackson, now demand reparations for slavery.

But how do the reparations proponents handle the sort of nagging problem of African and Arab involvement in the slave trade? Yes, dirty hands belong to African and Arab slavers. African chieftains sold blacks into slavery, and Arab slavers sold more slaves to South America and to the Middle East than to the United States.

Follow the reasoning here. Even though Europeans enslaved Europeans and Asians enslaved Asians, and black Africans enslaved black Africans, the West owes reparations to the countries from which slavers took and transported slaves.

Muslim merchants dominated the slave trade for centuries. It was the West that first began to reject slavery as inhumane. Indeed, in parts of Africa and the Middle East—Chad, Mauritania, and United Arab Emirates—slavery continues to this day!

Nation of Islam Minister Louis Farrakhan and others claim pride in the architectural, cultural, and scientific achievements of Egyptians. But doesn't the Bible tell us that Egyptians enslaved Jews? Does this mean that Egyptians and, therefore, blacks owe the Jews reparations?

The United Nations held a conference on racism in August 2001. Among other things, the conference provided a forum for Israel haters to condemn Zionism as equivalent to racism. Quite properly and understandably, the United States refused to send more than a token delegation to the South African U.N. conference. In South Africa, Reverend Jackson said, "In our own Constitution, we pointed out African descendants as three-fifths of a human being. No immigrant, no other body of Americans were named in our Constitution as three-fifths of a human being." Jackson also said, "Indeed it was [Colin Powell's] duty to be there as the secretary of state and as an African American. The United States sent in a low-level delegation late, never took a seat and left early."[38]

Although CNN did cover the conference, Jackson blasted the major American TV networks for their "boycott" of the event, saying the media moguls still considered blacks "three-fifths sub-human," and therefore unworthy of news coverage. "If this conference was being held in Germany and dealing with anti-Semitism, no one would beg the major media to be there. But their politics took over and . . . [the media moguls] acted as an extension of the U.S. government."[39]

Jesse Jackson called reparations for slavery his number-one priority.[40] Saying that "we must make crooked ways straight," Jackson explained the need for reparations: "We have fewer services and less education. We are disproportionately jailed and killed by the state. We have shorter life spans. We have less access to capital."[41]

Jackson said, "An apology is in order. But you must not only apologize with your lips. Repent, repair, and remedy go together. . . . If you don't feel apologetic for slavery, if you don't feel apologetic for colonialism, if you feel proud of it, then say that."[42] Color some of us confused. Does this mean we grant a waiver to a white guy who is maybe apologetic, but not here's-some-money type apologetic? Even the "first black president of the United States," Bill Clinton, while open to the idea of an apology for slavery, rejected a claim for reparations.

Jackson's position lacks perspective. Slavery, at least in the West, has been reduced to a historical monstrosity. Today is today, and slavery played at best a tenuous role in the creation of the black American "underclass." Rather than tell kids, "Seize the day," Jackson says, "The world remains hostile. The forces conspire against you. Remain in a perpetual state of anger."

But at the United Nations conference on racism, Abdoulaye Wade, the president of Senegal, demanded sanity. "It's not the Europeans of today or the Americans of today who brought slavery. It's the ancestors. Me, personally, how can I be responsible for what my ancestors did in the thirteenth, fourteenth, fifteenth, sixteenth, seventeenth centuries?"[43]

President Wade admitted, "If one can claim reparations for slavery, the slaves of my ancestors, or their descendants, can also claim money from me. Because slavery has been practiced by all the people in the world."[44]

And what about the problem of Liberia? American ex-slaves helped found Liberia in 1822. Freed American slaves settled there, and they and their descendants held power for a century and a half. But the freed ex-American slaves battled indigenous tribes, forcing them, often with the complicity of the tribal chiefs, into slavery under threat of flogging or incarceration.[45] Exactly who owes reparations to whom in Liberia?

Instead of a U.N. conference on racism, how about something likely to produce real results? How about a conference where delegates can discuss and understand free-world markets versus repressed markets.

Hong Kong, devoid of natural resources, has dramatically outperformed mainland China economically. Led for years by British free-market stewardship, Hong Kong trusted free markets and sensationally outperformed its larger, resource-rich neighbor.

Many African countries found themselves *worse* off postcolonialism. And what does the reparations-for-slavery crowd say about the current Zimbabwe government seizure of white-owned farms in order to "relocate them" to their "rightful owners"? Never mind that this very same government, only years earlier, urged whites to stay and spoke about a multicultural Zimbabwe. Once the Zimbabwe economy hit the skids, it threatened President Robert Mugabe's political survival and Mugabe turned into a black David Duke. Ah-h, power.

Black leaders call for reparations to improve the conditions of the so-called underclass. But they make the following assumption: It's about the money. Without focus, drive, and a willingness to assume responsibility, what exactly will the money accomplish?

Similarly, Third World leaders ask for money. Never mind that repressive, dictatorial regimes rule much of, say, sub-Saharan Africa, creating conditions that suppress the work ethic, drive, and creativity of their citizens. But does international aid help or hurt? Incredibly, according to Doug Bandow, many of the countries are worse off. He says, "Since World War II, the United States alone has provided one trillion (in current dollars) in foreign aid to countries around the world. The result? According to the United Nations, 70 countries, aid recipients all, are poorer today than in 1980. An incredible 43 are worse off than in 1970."[46] No, it ain't about the money.

How about a U.N. conference on "The Connection between Free Markets, Rule of Law, Respect for Private Property and Prosperity"?

Perhaps delegates could learn how West Germany outperformed East Germany, despite the fact that both countries possessed the same people, the same culture, and the same history. How, the delegates might ask, does Taiwan outperform mainland China, despite having the same people, the same culture, and the same history? What about South Korea versus North Korea—same people, same culture, same history.

But playing victicrat always trumps hard work and the acceptance of responsibility.

HAIL MARY OF THE U.S. CIVIL RIGHTS COMMISSION

Mary Francis Berry, a black attorney, serves as chairwoman of the U.S. Civil Rights Commission. She received her commission appointment in 1980, and President Clinton elevated her to chairwoman. She presides over this board, originally established to make recommendations on civil rights matters.

During the Bush/Gore Florida election contest, she called Florida Secretary of State Katherine Harris and Governor Jeb Bush "grossly derelict" and accused them of conducting an election pervaded with "a pattern and practice of injustice and ineptitude." She further charged "widespread voter disenfranchisement" and implied that racism had been employed against minority voters in Florida. Yet after a lengthy investigation, she failed to support the claims. Her commission's report failed to find any evidence of deliberate discrimination to deny an eligible minority Floridian the right to vote.[47]

Berry's actions fail to surprise any observer of her career. Berry calls herself an independent, but over the years she contributed $25,000 dollars to Democrats, including Al Gore.[48] During an NAACP speech, after she learned of then-Republican James Jeffords's intention to switch parties, she said, "Before that I was wondering when Strom Thurmond was gonna die."[49] (Jeffords's switch created a Democrat majority, something obviously cheered by the "independent" Berry.)

Berry faced accusations of generating and leaking politically moti-
vated reports such as ones leaked in 2000 attacking the affirmative
action records of Governors George W. Bush of Texas and his brother
Jeb of Florida. And someone on the commission leaked a draft report
harshly criticizing the New York Police Department just as Mayor
Rudolph
Giuliani was preparing a U.S. Senate bid against Hillary Clinton. Ms.
Berry, by the way, contributed $1,250 to the Clinton campaign.[50]

In 1982, Berry cowrote *Long Memory: The Black Experience in America*. In the book she says about KGB chief Yuri Andropov: "Blacks
shared so many of the economic goals of the communists that many
of them might be described as fellow travelers. . . . Subjected to a massive barrage of propaganda from the American news media, few know
about Russia's constitutional safeguards for minorities, the extent of the
equality of opportunity or the equal provision of social services to its
citizens."[51] About the condition of black America in the mid '60s, she
said, "The threat of genocide was real. It was roughly comparable to
the threat faced by the Jews in the 1930s."[52]

Michael Horowitz, who served as general counsel of the Office of
Management and Budget under Reagan, describes Ms. Berry as "one
of the shrewdest operatives in Washington," and an ideologue who is
"ten degrees left of the extreme left." Horowitz says, "I've never seen
a person with a more unacceptably radical set of views manage to gain
credibility in public life."[53]

President George W. Bush nominated and had sworn in black conservative Cleveland labor lawyer Peter Kirsanow to an expiring seat on
the civil rights board. The addition of Kirsanow stood to change the
liberal-to-conservative ratio on the commission, which now stands at
5–3. "Foul," cried Berry, who argued that no available seat existed.
Before President Clinton left office, he appointed someone to finish
out an unexpired six-year term scheduled to end November 29, 2001,
but Berry maintained that Clinton's appointee had received a *fresh* six-
year term, not just an unexpired term—therefore no such vacancy existed.

But records show that the Clinton White House expected the appointee's term to end in 2001, as confirmed in a legal opinion by the Justice Department Office of Legal Counsel.[54] That, of course, did not deter Ms. Berry. She promised to stonewall Kirsanow's appointment, saying his selection was "about muzzling us, and it's scary to have them take all this time and energy. It makes me even more afraid for the preservation of the commission."[55]

The White House accused Ms. Berry of violating the law by keeping the Clinton appointee on the commission. Still, Berry remained defiant. "She said that she would refuse to seat any new people appointed by President Bush," said White House Press Secretary Ari Fleischer. "She further said that the only way that she will let . . . [Peter Kirsanow] be seated is if the United States marshals show up and force her to do so."[56] Ms. Berry filed a lawsuit, which a Clinton-appointed federal judge upheld, blocking the Kirsanow appointment. The Justice Department immediately appealed, and won. Finally, Mr. Kirsanow was seated. Stay tuned.

Berry's term ends December 5, 2004. We're all just going to have to hold on.

JESSE JACKSON: RACE CARD SHAKEDOWN ARTIST

Harvard's new president, Lawrence Summers, recently criticized Harvard's so-called Afro-American Studies "dream team." Professor Henry Louis Gates Jr. chairs the department, which includes his star recruits, including Cornel West, formerly of Princeton, and Anthony Appiah, a nationally respected philosopher.

But trouble in Cambridge. According to the *Boston Globe,* newly empowered President Summers failed to "make a strong statement in support of affirmative action" during a meeting with members of the department. "In the meeting, according to senior faculty members who spoke with the *Globe,* Summers rebuked West for recording a rap CD, for leading a political committee for the Reverend Al Sharpton's possible presidential campaign, and for writing books more likely to be reviewed in the *New York Times* than in academic journals. He also reportedly criticized West for allowing grade inflation in his introductory course on black studies. Grade inflation has been a contentious issue this year at Harvard, which recently reported that nearly half of all grades given are As."[57]

The article speculated that Cornel West, one of fourteen out of Harvard's 2,200 faculty members named a university professor—the university's highest faculty post—may leave given the "climate" at Harvard (which later he did). Black Harvard University law professor Charles Ogletree, who also represented Anita Hill, seemed ready to do battle: "It would be a shame and a miscarriage of justice if for any reason Cornel were no longer at Harvard," he said, calling West "my client in these matters." According to the *Globe*, another Harvard faculty member said, "People are willing to give a new president a grace period, but if in that time he acts like a bull in a china shop, it makes people very worried. It appears as if he has deliberately set himself on a collision course with faculty members."[58] Jesse Jackson interjected himself into the dispute, and Al Sharpton threatened to sue Summers for interfering with West's involvement in Sharpton's presidential campaign.[59] President Summers retreated and professed his support of "diversity."[60]

Reverend Jesse Jackson also attacked Toyota for its alleged racial insensitivity. In a marketing campaign, Toyota distributed postcards to black establishments like restaurants and bars. The ad featured a close-up of a black person's large smile. On one of the teeth appeared a gold Toyota Rav4. Racism, yelled Jackson, "The only thing missing is the watermelon."[61] He threatened a boycott. Never mind that Toyota, on its own, pulled the ads before Jackson's charge of racial insensitivity.

Soon, nervous Toyota executives met with Jesse Jackson. Toyota agreed to do a better job at minority outreach, promising to spend hundreds of millions yearly to hire and train more minorities, buy from minority companies, expand the use of minority banking firms, and spend with minority advertisers. The deal calls for Toyota to spend more than $7.8 billion over ten years, including a goal to recruit more minority auto dealers.[62] All this over a gold tooth.

Don't tell Jackson, but a Reebok ad in *Sports Illustrated* recently featured a photograph of Edgerrin James, the great running back for the Indianapolis Colts. In one of the pictures, however, Edgerrin James sports a broad smile—with gold in his teeth. Don't tell Jackson, but this presents at least two juicy targets. First, Reebok deserves a dressing-down for designing the ad, and certainly *Sports Illustrated* should get the Toyota treatment for running the ad in the first place.

Why do these companies cave in to Jackson? "Nowadays, a corporation would rather be accused of child molestation than racism," says Eric Dezenhall, a D.C.-based corporate consultant. "I think Jackson's efforts have blown out of something very legitimate. When he started, there were these disparities. But now, there are black CEOs, and that's one reason Jackson hasn't been doing so well. They got to the top through hard work and taking risks."[63]

Reverend Jackson started the "Wall Street Project" in an effort to promote greater minority participation in corporate America. But he made his Wall Street supporters nervous when, after George Bush's contested election, Jackson vowed to "take to the streets" with a "civil rights explosion." After the Supreme Court's December 12, 5–4 ruling placing Bush in the White House, Jackson said he rejected Bush's succession "with every bone in my body and every ounce of moral strength in my soul."[64]

But Jackson's new Wall Street buddies feared unstable markets given the attacks by Jackson and others challenging Bush's legitimacy. According to Peter Noel of the *Village Voice,* Jackson's money buddies told Jackson to halt the "blistering attacks" and put in a telephone call of reconciliation to the new president-elect! One financial insider said the contributors told Jackson, "You better hold this down because we won't back you anymore if you are adverse to the new administration in Washington. . . .We certainly can't give you the floor of the New

York Stock Exchange and all these other perks if you are out there taking shots at a president we now have to lobby to get what we want."[65] So who's singing, who's dancing?

Similarly, a few years ago, the NAACP attracted ugly headlines when its embattled executive director, Ben Chavis, faced allegations of sexual discrimination and harassment. The Ford Foundation held up its contribution of $500,000 until the NAACP cleaned up its act and installed suitable leadership.[66] Again, who's singin', who's dancin'?

Businessman Harold Doley Jr., head of Doley Securities and one of America's wealthiest blacks, says Jackson's tactics amount to "racketeering." As one of the first blacks to purchase a seat on the New York Stock Exchange, Doley at first reacted enthusiastically to Jackson's Wall Street Project. But he watched how Jackson went after the pension industry, persuading them to place funds they brokered or managed with minority firms. "What worried me was the way he operated, dealing with these veiled threats," said Doley, who realized that Jackson was directing an enormous income from pension funds that was being channeled to about ten qualifying firms. Doley expressed his doubt that most Americans realized "that they were paying and putting money in Jesse Jackson's coffers to the tune of $170 million in commissions a year, 10 percent of which is going to Jackson."[67]

Doley also says he saw first-hand how "Jesse in effect stiffed the poor people of America" by giving political cover to a bank merger that cut $330 billion over a ten-year period to poor communities. According to Doley, the merger failed to meet the minimum standards of the Community Reinvestment Act, but Jackson's representatives from PUSH and the Wall Street Project, testifying before the Federal Reserve Board, pronounced the deal in America's best interests. Doley says that Jackson supported a merger which "fell short by $330 billion going into communities in terms of mortgages and services provided by financial institutions. . . . [Jackson] knew the mega mergers were not meeting the guidelines . . . but Jesse was getting contributions because of his support" for the deals.[68]

"What he was doing was a kind of RICO operation, both criminal and civil," argued Doley. "It was racketeering." Doley, who severed relations with Jackson, now calls him a "Civil Rights Entrepreneur." Doley notes that in 1996, PUSH had a corporate income of $695,000. By 2000, PUSH's revenues had grown to $17 million. "He's done better than any goddamn dot-com stock that I am aware of," Doley says.[69]

Kenneth Timmerman wrote a book called *Shakedown: Exposing the Real Jesse Jackson,* in which he exposes the Jackson "empire." Jackson, according to Timmerman, shocked the Wall Streeters supporting his Wall Street Project with post–September 11 remarks widely perceived to be anti-American. "When the entire country is in a state of grief and patriotic resurgence," said Timmerman, "he wasn't flying [the flag] at his home. It wasn't on his car, it wasn't on his lapel, it wasn't on stage behind him. In front of the cameras, there wasn't visible a flag in the whole place. There was no sense or expression of either mourning or grief or even sympathy for the victims of September eleventh."[70]

Jackson, according to the Cybercast News Service (CNS), said, "Too many have been intimidated by flag wearing and flag waving."[71] Jackson also called Attorney General John Ashcroft a terrorist "suspect [because] he threatens democracy."[72] These remarks do not please Wall Streeters.

Another Jackson business associate defected and said, "Jackson is going to go in and talk about not waving the flag? In all of America you can't exceed the patriotism that exists on the trading floors and in the New York Stock Exchange. The terrorist attacks happened in their neighborhood. Having him host an event on Wall Street amounts to money from the stock exchange being used to subsidize sedition."[73]

Jackson's perceived anti-American statements cost him dearly on The Street. One banker said, "His money is drying up, the Wall Street Project is tanking. He is reeling."[74] Another associate said Jackson "lost his cover" with the departure of Clinton.[75] One Wall Street banker said, "Members of the New York Stock Exchange are appalled and can't understand why [Exchange Chairman] Dick Grasso is kowtowing to someone they view as anti-American."[76]

Do Jackson's negatives finally outweigh his positives?

In 1911, Booker T. Washington said, "There is [a] class of colored people who make a business of keeping the troubles, the wrongs, and the hardships of the Negro race before the public. Having learned that they are able to make a living out of their troubles, they have grown into the settled habit of advertising their wrongs—partly because they want sympathy and partly because it pays. Some of these people do not want the Negro to lose his grievances, because they do not want to lose their jobs. . . . There is a certain class of race-problem solvers who don't want the patient to get well, because as long as the disease holds out they have not only an easy means of making a living, but also an easy medium through which to make themselves prominent before the public."[77] Hmmm-mm.

Regarding racial issues, the mainstream media fails to ask proper questions because it supports "multiculturalism" or "diversity." According to William McGowan, author of *Coloring the News: How Crusading for Diversity Has Corrupted American Journalism,* "The increasing liberalism of the newsroom combined with more parochialism amplifies a disconnect from the rest of mainstream society, particularly on divisive cultural and racial issues. According to various surveys comparing opinions and attitudes of reporters and editors with those of the population at large, journalists are overwhelmingly in favor of affirmative action (81 percent, compared with 51 percent of the general public)."[78]

County Sheriff Al Cannon of Charleston, South Carolina, perhaps offers guidance. He, too, faced allegations of racism. His crime? During a heated exchange with a black legislator, the white sheriff called State Senator Robert Ford (D-Charleston), a black man, an "idiot." Cannon was publicly criticized by the Interdenominational Ministers Alliance and condemned for not apologizing.[79] Uh-oh, racism.

The local Ministers Alliance condemned Sheriff Cannon and demanded an apology, "There is no legitimate, much less important, reason for any elected official to express such vague and unrestrained remarks," said the Ministers Alliance.

But the sheriff bravely refused. He said simply, "There are black men who are idiots, and there are white men who are idiots."[80]

RACISM HERE, RACISM THERE, RACISM EVERYWHERE

Could a white reporter get away with this?

Black *Washington Post* reporter Natalie Hopkinson wrote a piece about her recent home purchase. Hopkinson and her husband bought an expensive Victorian house in Bloomingdale, a predominantly black neighborhood of Washington, D.C.

Hopkinson, who grew up in the predominately white 'burbs, explains her mission to return to the 'hood. "The fact that we had emerged victorious," wrote Ms. Hopkinson, "from a six-month battle at the height of the District real estate wars—skirmishes in which we were often the lone black faces vying for homes in historically black neighborhoods—said something else: 'We damn sure are not about to let white folks buy up all the property in D.C.' " She added, "I believe that we became part of a growing group of African Americans who are picking up where the civil rights movement left off. From our perspective, integration is overrated. It's time to reverse an earlier generation's hopeful migration into white communities and attend to some unfinished business in the 'hood."[81]

Ms. Hopkinson helpfully offers that white residents in her historically black community can play a role: "Many whites want to help out, too, and their privileged racial status can only improve the city's prospects. But this is the Chocolate City."[82]

Now, suppose a white journalist wrote, "We damn sure are not about to let black folks buy up all the property . . ."? We would, quite properly, call that white journalist a racist. What then, do we call Ms.

Hopkinson? Or is racism only a one-way road? Obviously, Ms. Hopkinson and the *Washington Post* think so.

Tiger Woods rarely discusses race and his own heritage. But the multiracial superstar expected to earn $54 million in endorsements alone in 2001. And he just signed a new deal with Disney. He receives $2–3 million just to appear at tournaments, and television viewership increases over 100 percent with a Tiger Woods in contention. The Dow averages a $45 billion gain in market value on Mondays after Tiger appears in an American tournament.[83] The word "phenomenal" doesn't begin to describe this amazing, wildly successful young man.

Yet while Tiger remains mum on racial issues, his dad, Earl, shows no such inhibition, "We live in a very racist country. The United States is one of the most racist countries in the world. It's built into the culture, the language, the movies, the books."[84] So, according to Earl Woods, the Great White Bigot still lurks, trying to keep the black man down. Apparently the Great White Bigot needs to straighten out his driver, because Tiger grows wealthier by the minute.

Los Angeles Times black columnist Sandy Banks complained about her daughter's *comfort and ease* around nonblacks. She told her daughter and her nonblack friends about the subtle racism Banks herself faces, "I uncorked a string of stories of my own: tales of party guests who lapse into Ebonics the minute I join their social circle, and hostesses who take pains to seat me next to the only other black person in the room. I imagine their gestures are well intended, meant to make me feel comfortable among folks not my own. Instead, they only let me know that I must stick out like a sore thumb. 'Now,' I told my daughter's friends, 'you see what we feel all the time.' "[85]

But Banks's daughter shocked her mother, when she said, "Not *we*, Mommy. That's how *you* feel. That's not how *I* feel. . . . I feel comfortable with my friends. I don't think people always look at me and say, 'Oh, she's black.' It's not about race all the time." Banks's rejoinder? "It disappoints me some that after all the struggles my generation waged to craft a cultural identity built on dignity and pride, our children sometimes seem determined to shuck it off and pitch it aside."[86]

So, when whites show hostility towards blacks, this is bad. When whites, however, welcome blacks with open arms, this, too, is bad. Sorry, white folks. You can't win.

BLACK LEADERS AND PATRIOTISM DON'T MIX

On September 14, 2001, Congress and the Senate passed a joint resolution authorizing the use of military force in response to the attacks of September 11. Of the 535 members of the U.S. Congress, black Representative Barbara Lee (D–California) cast the only vote against the authorization. Lee said she "agonized" over the vote, but "I felt that [someone] in this environment of grief needed to say let's show some restraint in our response. Let's not do anything that could escalate this madness out of control. . . . We need to figure out a way to stamp out international terrorism and bring these perpetrators to justice without creating more loss of life."[87]

Unfortunately, many other "black leaders" completely side with Lee. At a State of the Black World Conference in Atlanta, Mayor Bill Campbell welcomed the participants and received rousing applause for his punch line, "While the rest of the country waves the flag of Americana, we understand we are not part of that."[88]

And Reverend Al Sharpton bellowed, "We don't owe America anything; America owes us."[89] He got a standing ovation.

Jesse Jackson offered this victicrat vision, "We are in danger. The extreme right wing has seized the government. Tonight, [Attorney General John] Ashcroft and the CIA and the FBI and Homeland Security and the IRS can work together, so look out. Because without a definition of who is a terrorist, anyone can be . . . Martin Luther King could have been . . . Malcolm X, the Black Panthers. The right-wing media, the FBI, they are targeting our leadership."[90]

Author and civil rights activist Sonia Sanchez said, "You and I know we have been under assault for a long time." Referring to the terrorist attacks and the hardships New Yorkers have since experienced, she said, "White people are now enduring the black experience."[91]

NAACP Durham, North Carolina, chapter head Curtis Gatewood, four days after the terrorist attacks of September 11, issued this statement: "Black males can no longer afford to be used as sacrificial lambs at the time of war.[92]

"Those black males who make it back home alive from war are likely to come home and be discriminated against by the people whose businesses were headquartered in the World Trade Center, racially abused and profiled by an American police officer, killed in the streets in their crime-infested neighborhoods or harmed by Bush Administration policy."[93]

A right-wing Supreme Court, according to the statement, elected Bush. The statement also said the attacks were not, repeat not, an attack on freedom. This even upset NAACP President Kweisi Mfume, who issued a strong statement denouncing what Gatewood said.[94] But Gatewood remains chapter head, and his chapter members—400 to 600 strong—voted to approve his statement.[95]

At an antiwar/peace rally in Washington, D.C., Gatewood said: "But let me tell you something, patriotism is very dangerous, because sometimes I think we can fuel American patriotism with American racism because they're very closely related."[96]

The *San Francisco Chronicle,* after September 11, asked people how the tragedies changed their lives. Of the six responses printed, five talked of the ways 9–11 altered their lives. But one black man said:

"As a black man in the United States, I'm terrorized every single day. Terrorized by a criminal justice system that warehouses black men and keeps me looking over my shoulder. Terrorized by a racist corporate America that keeps my brothers and sisters from advancing beyond jobs above the level of security guard or mailroom clerk. Terrorized by legislation and court decisions aimed at keeping African Americans from ever gaining equal footing in the United States. And finally, terrorized by a president who wouldn't even consider attending a conference on racism to learn more about reconciling with the people he proposes to lead. No, September eleventh's terrorist acts have not affected my daily life."[97]

The *Los Angeles Sentinel*, a black Los Angeles weekly newspaper, publishes a weekly people's poll. They ask "people in the street" topical questions. The newspaper recently asked: "Do you think race relations are getting better or worse?" It chose six persons, publishing a photo with the response to the question underneath.

Are race relations getting better or worse?

"Worse," said Kim Benson. "Black people are prejudiced against themselves. At one time we used to support and be close as a people and a family. If we can't get along at home, how can we get along anywhere else?"[98]

"Worse," said Leslie Barnum. "People of ethnic backgrounds have not changed. The way they view other ethnic groups has been changed to disguise the way they discriminate."[99]

"Worse," said K.A.P, "because black actors are not getting the parts they should get. Black people are still on the bottom; none are on the top. We have no black leaders. The Caucasian race is pulling the strings and we have no one that can stop it."[100]

"Worse," said Gloria Robinson. "In the sixties blacks advanced. After the assassination of Martin Luther King, it seemed to change. Other ethnic groups became dominant, the focus turned towards other cultures, mainly Hispanic. Spanish-speaking people are getting jobs. I am an American! Where is my job?"[101]

"Worse," said Mark Jones. "Blacks and Mexicans are getting into disagreements every day. More and more in the streets, even more than jail."[102]

"Probably worse," said Shea Taylor, "because the state of affairs has not gotten any better. In terms of the black community, 'wait a minute!' There is no black community. Hispanics have taken over all the communities that we had. The powers that be have actually given the communities to them."[103]

JOHNNIE COCHRAN—MAN OF THE PEOPLE

In a country so allegedly racist, how has former O.J. Simpson defense attorney Johnnie Cochran managed to achieve both mainstream success as well as the affection of the black community? Wouldn't you think a racist country would turn against defense attorney Johnnie Cochran, the man who masterminded the acquittal of a black double murderer who killed two whites?

During the O.J. Simpson case, Cochran played opponent prosecutor Chris Darden the way Ali played Frazier. He suggested Darden was an Uncle Tom and a sellout. Smugly, at the end of the Simpson trial, Cochran and other black leaders put on an affair to invite Darden back into the community.[104]

Yet, "racist" America somehow managed to understand and accept that as a defense attorney Johnnie Cochran had successfully and skillfully performed his role. Where is the hatred, the anger?

Quite the contrary, *USA Today* recently ran a puff piece on Cochran, noting his membership in frequent-flier clubs, his triple-platinum cards, and his first-class travel style. Cochran, despite America's obvious racism, appears to be doing pretty well. " 'I travel so much, I can't keep track of the miles,' he says. 'I'm in all the frequent-flier clubs, and I'm extremely happy I received my American Airlines AAdvantage Million Mile Executive Platinum One World Emerald card. Now that's a lot of words, but they have lots of perks. And I'm almost at that level with United's Mileage Plus.'

"Cochran's AAdvantage status indicates at least one million miles total and one hundred thousand miles last year on American Airlines. 'The perks? They'll find me seats, even on full flights. I get upgraded, and they'll block the seat next to me, giving me more room.' "[105]

A-ah, the good life. Cochran says, "You reach a certain stage in your life, and you just have to have certain things. For me, it's thick towels. I just can't stand it otherwise. If there isn't a Ritz or Four

Seasons in town, my travel agent books the best hotel. They can be good, but sometimes you get towels so thin, you don't even want to take a shower."[106]

Tough being a black man in America.

The black community gives Cochran a pass, even as he walks on other blacks to achieve his goals. During the O.J. Simpson case, for example, Cochran put the Los Angeles Police Department (LAPD) on trial. At the time, Willie Williams, the city's first black police chief, headed the force. After Cochran's repeated allegations of racism, corruption, and sloppiness in the case, Williams ordered an internal review to examine Cochran's allegations. The findings? No corruption, no contamination, no planting, no collusion, no conspiracy. Just police work, while not letter-A-perfect, that points to Simpson's guilt. Cochran ignored the report, thus implying Williams was a boob, a stooge, or an ostrich.

In another case, the University of Southern California (USC) hired Marvin Cobb, a black man, as assistant athletic director in 1986. Do well, the school promised Cobb, and expect a promotion to associate athletic director. Enthusiastic about his job, Cobb soon found something disturbing. The black athletes graduated at a lower rate than did their white counterparts. He approached the athletic director, seeking resources for tutoring students with learning problems. "USC, like many schools," Cobb later said, "is a virtual black-athlete factory running on quarter-speed. They go out and sell these kids on the Trojan family, that a USC degree will mean the world. Yet they don't have the proper resources to make it an even chance for the kids they recruit."[107] After Cobb persisted, but got no follow-through, he was ultimately reassigned to a minor administrative position within USC's medical school.

Cobb sued for racial discrimination, accusing the school of denying his promotion because of his concern about the university's treatment of black athletes. Who defended USC and accused Cobb, a black man, of complaining about the treatment of black athletes at the university? Johnnie Cochran and his law firm. The result: A jury awarded Cobb a $2.1 million judgement, but the court ultimately reversed the award and reduced it to $1.1 million.[108]

The next black man in Cochran's crosshairs: Los Angeles police officer Tarriel Hopper.

Hopper, a former standout athlete, serves on the Los Angeles police force. Before that, he was a high school football star who went on to USC as a linebacker and safety. When he told his high school coach about his interest in law enforcement, the coach tried to talk Hopper out of it, saying Hopper was a "puppy dog" and that he didn't have enough of a mean streak for police work.[109]

Hopper insisted and persisted, and made the force. A couple years into his career, Hopper and his partner, Dave Orozco, received a call about a possible suicide jumper. "Hopper and Orozco were up on the building, edging toward a despondent forty-two-year-old Marine Corps veteran. Orozco talked while Hopper crept closer. The man let go, but Hopper and Orozco, leaning far over a railing, caught an arm and jacket, pulling the man to safety. . . . Soft-spoken and professional to a fault is the way [LAPD Captain Mike] Hillman describes Hopper."[110] Hopper and his partner were nominated for commendations.

On October 28, 2000, Hopper—now a three-year veteran—and his partner Natalie Humphreys received a call: Loud noise at a Halloween party in Benedict Canyon. A private security guard invited Hopper and his partner in and left the two of them in the kitchen while he went to get the host. Hopper decided to walk outside of the house, down a narrow pathway. He shone his flashlight on the darkened path and into a window. Through the window Hopper saw what appeared to be a large weapon aiming directly at him. He drew, and fired several shots, striking the gun-wielding partygoer. But, it turns out, the partygoer carried a replica gun. Officer Hopper shot a partygoer armed only with a rubber replica of a .357 magnum. An autopsy later found cocaine and alcohol in the partygoer's system, and the police found an Ecstasy pill in his hand.

Lieutenant Horace Frank, spokesman for the LAPD said, "Officer

Hopper's actions were based on a perceived threat to his safety."[111] An internal review board, and later the Los Angeles Police Commission, found that Hopper was justified in using deadly force, and that the shooting was "in policy." By a 3–2 vote, the commission decided that Hopper should undergo additional training to improve his tactics but determined that he should not be disciplined over the shooting.[112]

Enter Cochran. He filed a $100 million claim against the city of Los Angeles, saying that the "LAPD has never seen a shooting they didn't think they could justify."[113] As of this writing, no trial. But, if past practices hold, expect Cochran to fry this fourth-year officer.

Hopper became a cop to make things better for the inner city. "There are guys who, when you coach them, you just know they're going to be something special," said Hopper's USC defensive coach. "And then there are guys who you know aren't going to go on but are going to be a real positive example to society. And Tarriel was one of them. These are the ones who are going to work with kids and do stuff that matters in the community.[114] According to the *Los Angeles Times*, "Hopper plans to major in criminal justice and wants to be a youth counselor when he's done with football. 'Lots of kids are mixed up, they don't know what to do, they don't have solid families,' Hopper said. 'I'd like to keep them from having to deal with the law. I see kids 10 years old who are getting in trouble, it's bad news.' "[115]

So expect Cochran to put the LAPD on trial again. During the O.J. Simpson case, Cochran argued, among other things, that the police attempted to frame Simpson because he dared marry a white woman. Yet, the "Establishment" gives Cochran a pass for the same "crime." During the O.J. Simpson case, a white woman named Patty Sikora, aka Patricia Cochran, went public with their affair, a relationship that produced a son. So the police, according to Cochran, targeted Simpson despite the athlete's tremendous popularity, because of Simpson's relationship with Nicole, a white woman. Yet here's Cochran, a true "threat" to the establishment, not only enjoying a decades-long relationship with a white woman that apparently overlapped his marriages—but having a child with her, too. Where's the wrath of the establishment?

The black community's regard for Cochran remains unaffected despite allegations by his ex-wife of spousal abuse. Cochran's first wife, Barbara, wrote an autobiography, *Life After Johnnie Cochran: Why I Left the Sweetest-Talking, Most Successful Black Lawyer in L.A.* In it, she makes a serious charge. She accuses her then-husband, Johnnie Cochran, of spousal abuse, and, in fact, described how she obtained a restraining order.[116] In explaining the reason for publishing her book, Barbara Cochran says, "Over seventeen years, you do grow in courage and strength and faith. I have forgiven him for the lies and the cheating and the times he hit me. My objective now is to tell other women they don't have to take it, to get out of abusive situations and reclaim their lives."[117]

In a *Los Angeles Times* article on Cochran's life, a reporter asked Cochran about the spousal abuse. Cochran insists that he never struck his wife, and moreover, urges the reporter to contact Barbara, with confidence that Barbara will confirm Cochran's story. The reporter took Cochran up on his offer. According to the *Los Angeles Times*, this exchange followed. " 'I am very happy for Johnnie's phenomenal success,' Barbara said. That's it? I ask. She replies, 'I have nothing more to say.' I explain I am calling with the expectation she will back off, or at least soften her accusations. 'I decline comment,' she says. Are you saying Johnnie beat you? 'I will not discuss it. I never said I wanted to be interviewed.' "[118]

The *Los Angeles Times* reporter said that he went back and forth with the former Cochrans several times in the course of preparing for his article. Barbara Cochran Berry steadfastly refused to make a retraction, and Johnnie Cochran continued to deny that he had ever physically abused her.[119]

Recall the New York cops who beat and sodomized Haitian immigrant Abner Louima? Cochran entered the case on behalf of the Louima family. When *New York Post* columnist Andrea Peyser learned of his involvement, she wrote that Cochran "will say or do just about anything to win, typically at the expense of truth."[120] How dare she, huffed Cochran, who promptly filed a defamation suit against Peyser. A judge dismissed the suit.

Cochran's lucrative battle against "racist America" continues.

THE SHIFTING ZERO-TOLERANCE STANDARD

When it comes to white racism, we apply zero tolerance. Cross the line, and the victicrats will be after you in a flash. Of course, where that line is drawn has a lot to do with who's drawing it and who's stepping over it.

The NBA Denver Nuggets coach, Dan Issel, after another tough loss at the buzzer, walked off the court toward the locker room. A fan, however, taunted the white coach, calling out, "Issel sucks."

Issel angrily fired back, "Hey, go buy another beer. Go drink another beer, you f——ing Mexican piece of s——." (The fan denied being "drunk" but admitted to drinking a "few beers.")[121] Unfortunately for Issel, a tape captured the exchange, and the fit hit the shan.

The team suspended Issel for four games without pay, costing the coach approximately $112,000. He tearfully apologized to the fan, fans in general, the team, and the city of Denver[122] for what he called his "un-Christian-like conduct."[123]

The Hispanic Chamber of Commerce refused to accept his apology and threatened a boycott of the Nugget's games if the team didn't fire Issel. "He stopped and looked up and he saw that he was looking at a Mexican," said chamber member Veronica Barela, "Then he referred to him in a derogatory way. In my opinion that came from his heart."[124]

Other Hispanic leaders said the apology fell short. "This is not only the Mexican community," said Zee Ferrufino, the South American owner of a local radio station. "The community is one community: the Mexican community, the Mexican Americans, the Central Americans, the Cubans, everybody. He insulted the entire Hispanic community."[125] The Washington-based League of United Latin American Citizens called for Issel's resignation. They also demanded that his forfeited salary go to Hispanic groups in Denver, a city nearly one-third Hispanic.[126]

The Hispanic Chamber of Commerce obviously considers punishing Issel for his "racial insensitivity" more important than addressing the issue of excessive drinking within the Hispanic community. In 1998, out of the total population of whites, only 1 percent were arrested for driving under the influence (DUI). Out of the black population, 1 percent were arrested. But out of the Hispanic population, 4 percent were arrested for DUI.[127] According to Mothers Against Drunk Driving (MADD), 19 percent of Hispanic men are arrested for DUI at least once in their lifetime.[128] The fan in Issel's case may not have been "drunk" but according to a nationwide survey, 23 percent of Mexican-American men are "frequent heavy drinkers" (five or more drinks in one sitting at least once a week) compared to 15 percent of black men and 12 percent of white men.[129]

But Issel, like John Rocker, belongs to no protected class and thus receives no benefit of the doubt. Forget about Issel's twenty-five years with the team as player, coach, and in management. Never mind that he had no previous history of being accused of racism. No, he gets the John Rocker zero-tolerance-for-white-bigotry standard. "This man will have to live with this for the rest of his life," said Colorado state senator Rob Hernandez. "We should have a zero tolerance. The Hispanic community is deeply hurt."[130]

The double standards boggle the mind. Only months earlier, boxer Oscar De la Hoya, after defeating his former boxing promoter, Bob Arum in court, declared that he had beaten "one of the biggest Jews to come out of Harvard." De la Hoya, like Issel, promptly apologized. "I made certain remarks regarding Bob Arum that I sincerely regret. I did not mean to insult Bob Arum and his family or any ethnic or religious group in any way. I humbly apologize to anyone the remarks may have offended."[131] End of story.

But speaking of Bob Arum, did the promoter also engage in racial profiling? Someone told Arum about a superlightweight fighter named Dmitriy Salita, an orthodox Jew from the Ukraine. "When Arum first got a call from a friend, Rabbi Shea Harlig," according to the *Los Angeles Times*, "asking him to check out Salita, Arum rolled his eyes and acted polite. But he was thinking, orthodox Jew and bruising slugger are not descriptive terms one normally finds in the same sentence."[132] What? A Jewish promoter engaging in racial profiling, suggesting that "orthodox Jew" and "champion of the world" are mutually exclusive?

California's Hispanic Lieutenant Governor Cruz Bustamante addressed a group of black trade unionists a few months ago. Incredibly, inexplicably, Bustamante referred to blacks as "niggers"! "I was appalled he would even say it as a slip. You don't make a slip like that unless it is something you say normally," said one of the attendees of the Coalition of Black Trade Unionists' annual awards dinner.[133] Arguably, Bustamante's "slip" was worse than Issel's. At least Issel lashed out in anger, while Bustamante's racial epithet just sort of eased on out of his mouth. But Bustamante, like De la Hoya, promptly apologized. "I know it came out of my mouth, but it is not how I was taught. It is not how I teach my children."[134] All is forgiven.

DAMN THOSE CONSERVATIVES— ESPECIALLY BLACK ONES

Between Hitler, Stalin, and Ronald Reagan, many wonder why blacks place Reagan third. A black critic of Ronald Reagan once told me that he suspected that Reagan "felt uncomfortable around blacks." To which I responded, "I feel uncomfortable around you [a black victicrat] so what does that make me?"

Al Gore stoked black support in the 2000 presidential election by attending a black church and declaring, "Deep within us, we each have the capacity for good and for evil. I am taught that good overcomes evil, if we choose that outcome. I feel it coming."[135] And Al Gore's black campaign manager, Donna Brazile, referred to Republicans as "white boys," saying, "A white-boy attitude is 'I must exclude, denigrate and leave behind.' "[136] She also said, "Republicans bring out Colin Powell and J.C. Watts because they have no program, no policy. They play that game because they have no love and no joy. They'd rather take pictures with black children than feed them."[137]

For those who see the world through race-tinted glasses, attacking "Uncle Toms" provides fun and relief. *Los Angeles Times* columnist Sandy Banks once called me, in an unpublished e-mail, "a lackey for white America."

Recently, *Ebony* magazine featured the one-hundred-plus most influential black Americans. Among those most conspicuously absent was Justice Clarence Thomas. A sitting member of the Supreme Court is not one of the most influential Americans, let alone black Americans? Please.

Black conservatives scare people. After all, Al Gore received nearly 93 percent of the black vote.[138] Dependent upon the monolithic black voting block, Democrats attack black "nonliberals" not just for ideological reasons but as a matter of survival. The slightest erosion of the near-unanimous black support for the Democratic Party spells disaster. Recently, the Hawaii chapter of the American Civil Liberties Union (ACLU) rescinded a debate invitation extended to U.S. Supreme Court Justice Clarence Thomas. Several black members of the Hawaii ACLU board reportedly called Thomas an "Uncle Tom," "an anti-Christ," and "a Hitler" and likened having Thomas speak to "like having a serial murderer debate the value of life."[139]

Donald Adderton is the editor of the *Delta Democrat Times*, the first black editor of any daily newspaper in the state of Mississippi. Mississippians, in a referendum, voted on whether or not they wished to retain elements of the Confederate Flag. The voters overwhelmingly supported retaining the flag. Adderton wrote a column and in essence said that black people face more pressing concerns than the flag. He also accepted the assertion of many who claim to support the flag for reasons of history, Southern pride, and heritage rather than bigotry.

Adderton's columns angered the Mississippi black leadership. Adderton related what happened:

> Well, the so-called black leadership wanted me removed. When I joined the paper, it was owned by Freedom Communications in Southern California. Freedom is a libertarian company, so they weren't going to buy into what the black leadership were saying. But we were sold to a Mississippi company (Emmerich's Newspapers) and the so-called black leadership said, "Aha, we have an opportunity." So the black leadership mounted a campaign and they went to our new corporate owners and said "Adderton has to go because he's been disingenuous to the black community; he has unfairly attacked black elected officials."
>
> Mind you, in the midst of the Delta, there's a 65 percent black area, so you have a majority of black elected officials, and this particular editor, being a journalist, I hold people accountable. And I dared question the motives of the black elected officials in doing the people's business, which they weren't doing.
>
> Also, you had this great passion for the flag, while in Washington County where I reside, we have double-digit unemployment (10.9%). Six in ten students drop out of school. An increasing number of teenage pregnancies. And I didn't hear the so-called black leadership talking about staying in school, young ladies keeping their dress-tails down, and young black males, if you're gonna father a child, support them.
>
> Instead, it was interesting that the elected officials mounted the courthouse steps and they held a news conference here in Greenville, and they castigated me for about thirty minutes. We have an ABC affiliate and a CBS affiliate, and only one of the stations covered it, the others decided it was a personal attack and they didn't air it. But the so-called black leadership was undaunted and they demanded a meeting with the corporate owners and they met in a Baptist Church—ironic they met in a Baptist Church, which is a crucible for the civil rights movement—and said "Adderton has to go."

The white community came to my aid, and they told the ownership that
I'm doing a good job, and the people that they talked to did not speak for
the black community. Calmer heads came forward, including some moderate
and conservative voices in the community here, and I'm still writing.

But the interesting thing is that people will say, "We support the First
Amendment. We support your saying what you believe, until we disagree
with you. And then we want to shut you up."[140]

Never mind that in the year 2000, according to the 2001 Newspaper & Television Diversity Report, there were just fifteen editors
and executive editors of color for nearly 1,500 daily newspapers. Because of Adderton's ideology—a nonliberal, nonvicticrat black man—
the "black leaders" of Greenville, Mississippi, seemed determined to
reduce that number from fifteen to fourteen.

Calm down.

RESPONSIBILITY 101

A recent study by the NAACP confirms the bad news of black academic underachievement. But the report simply offers justification after
justification for the poor performance, including trotting out the tired
excuse of "cultural bias" on standardized tests. "The racial disparities
in the report," said the NAACP, "include differences in educational
resources, teacher quality, early childhood programs, class size, suspen-
sion and expulsion rates, and placement in special education and gifted
and talented courses. In higher education, the report also details racial
disparities in college preparation, retention, graduation and the availability of minority faculty."[141]

What about the simple fact that black kids fail to study as hard as
do many of their peers? Or that black households watch more television
than do their white counterparts, with black fourth-graders weighing
in at 50 percent more TV watching than their white fourth-grade
peers.[142]

While black leaders look for excuses, some parents know how the real world works. A black news weekly recently ran an article about the latest public school plan to improve education, to which one black parent objected in a letter to the editor:

I disagree with the (July 5) opinion piece, "Finally, a LAUSD Plan to Help Black Children." We (black folks) are always passing the buck and looking for someone or something to help us out of the miry clay. Black children are at the bottom of the totem pole in public schools, but we should not blame the schools for the failure of our offspring. I am a single parent with a full-time job. Nevertheless, every day for one hour, I sit with my four-year-old to do phonics, simple math, spelling, critical thinking, art, coloring, perception, and watch educational videos. On weekends, I take her to the library, or to the California Science Center where she sees chickens being hatched and the heartbeat of an elephant. I take her to parks that have ducks or other educational aspects. I read to her. I read books to her at least three times a week and I point my finger at every word that I read to her. I tell her that learning is fun—and reading and books are great. And now she enjoys creating her own stories. She is motivated and excited about learning as she explores the world around us. My child was psychologically tested one week after her fourth birthday and the results indicated that she scored between first and third grade levels in the superior range in reading, mathematics and written language skills.

It's about time we take responsibility of our own problems and stop looking for others to help us. There are times when I don't physically feel like working with my child or reading her a story, but she is MY responsibility, not the school's! If we send our children to school unprepared, the schools are not going to work with them or give them individual attention. Instead they are going to place them in special education classes and label them as "learning disabled."

I am tired of hearing that standards for black folks have to be lowered and that we need a plan to help us. We need to help ourselves! There are too many black kids who come to school with little or no interest in learning.

It is not the teachers' responsibility to motivate them. We as parents need to get off our butts, get off the Internet, get off the cell phone and take time for our children, and if we don't have the time, we need to make the time.

When my child is old enough to attend grade school, she is attending a private, predominantly white school that costs $12,000 a year. Why? I want her in a school where being black does not mean, "You need extra help." I refuse to put her in a school where she is an "exception to the rule." I want her to attend a school where she is expected to achieve. I want her to be challenged and not hindered.

—R. D. Woods[143]

R. D. Woods for president!

In the first half of the twentieth century, some black schools served as paragons of academic achievement. As early as 1899, black students at Washington's Dunbar high school often outscored white students, and many other black schools operated at similar levels of excellence.[144]

John McWhorter, a linguistics professor at the University of California–Berkeley, says that black children would benefit from learning a little more about their positive history instead of the negativity that is thrust upon them in schools and by the media. He says that "a history of horrors cannot inspire."

"Ignoring or downplaying black achievement promotes the victim attitude," says economist Walter Williams, "where people believe that in order for them to be successful somebody else must perform some benevolent act."[145]

POOR MLK III: WITH RACISM IN RETREAT, WHAT'S A BLACK LEADER TO DO?

"What's he really done in life?" A Montgomery civil rights worker posed this question about Martin Luther King III—the eldest son of legendary civil rights leader Martin Luther King Jr.[146] Pretty heavy thing, being named King III, and now he stands accused of lacking his father's vision, passion, and drive.

King III leads the Southern Christian Leadership Conference (SCLC), the legendary organization founded by his father some forty-four years ago. The board briefly suspended King for inattentiveness and for possessing an unfocused agenda that allowed the organization to "drift."

Of the forty-one-year-old bachelor's persona, the *Los Angeles Times* says, "He doesn't inspire people, his detractors say, he doesn't have his father's oratorical gifts (though few do)," and "somewhat shy, he lives with his mother in the same house where he grew up." To many SCLC members, King III lacks fire. " 'We got to get back to the streets,' said Richard Turner, a seventy-two-year-old carpenter in rural Georgia. 'Talk ain't worth a damn if you don't do something.' "[147] Poor King III.

"What's he really done in life?" Let's first place the focus on what King III has *not* done.

Unlike his brother Dexter, he was not infamously photographed shaking the hand of James Earl Ray, Martin Luther King's assassin. Incredibly, Dexter professed the King family belief in Ray's innocence. "I believe you, and my family believes you."[148] Reportedly, the entire King family believes that the authorities railroaded Ray, who confessed and pleaded guilty to the murder, but at least King III had the decency to keep a photo of himself shaking hands with his father's assassin out of the papers.

Unlike black "civil rights leader" Al Sharpton, King III never falsely accused a man of rape, with a jury later finding him liable in a defamation suit. He never referred to Jews as "diamond merchants" or "white interlopers."[149]

Unlike Nation of Islam leader Louis Farrakhan, he never called Judaism a "dirty religion" or said "[Adolph] Hitler was a very great man."[150] He never publicly ridiculed Desiree Washington, the young black woman a jury convicted Mike Tyson of raping.

Unlike the former head of the Black Congressional Caucus, Congresswoman Maxine Waters (D-California), he never justified the 1992 Los Angeles riots by calling them a "rebellion,"[151] while bellowing, "No justice, no peace,"[152] nor did he call President George Bush Sr., the forty-first president—also known as George Bush-41—a "racist" and refuse to apologize for it.[153] He never sent a letter to Fidel Castro urging him to refuse extradition of a black woman who killed a New Jersey State trooper and fled to Cuba. In her letter, Waters called this murderer a "persecuted . . . political activist" and likened her to Martin Luther King Jr.[154]

Unlike NAACP President Kweisi Mfume, King III never fathered any children out of wedlock. According to the *Almanac of American Politics*, "Mfume's original name was Frizzell Gray; he was 16 when his mother died, at which point he dropped out of school, held low-paying jobs, and fathered *five children out of wedlock*."[155] [Emphasis added.]

Unlike NAACP Chairman Julian Bond, no one ever accused Martin III of cocaine use. In 1987, Bond's wife told police that he used cocaine daily, that he consorted with a woman who had prior convictions—a felon later convicted for possession and intent to distribute—and that this woman assaulted Bond's wife. Although charges were never filed against Bond, after the allegations hit, writer-commentator Juan Williams wrote, "A number of [Bond's] friends and political allies . . . say they think Julian Bond uses cocaine. . . . He has not lived at home with his wife and family for six months. Relations with his five children are strained. He has had to give up credit cards because the bills got too big. He owes $150,000 in campaign debts. He has had a lien put on his house by the Internal Revenue Service."[156]

Unlike Rainbow PUSH leader Jesse Jackson, who hypocritically ministered to a troubled, philandering President Clinton, no one ever filed a lawsuit against King III seeking child support payments for an out-of-wedlock baby fathered by a married man. Comparing Jackson's tactics for extracting money from corporate America to the tactics of his own organization, even Al Sharpton disdainfully said, "We won't take money from companies we fight."[157]

What does the SCLC board want King to do—champion affirmative action? Affirmative action places some blacks at an artificially higher level than warranted based on grades and aptitude tests—a mismatch that produces high dropout rates.

Does the SCLC board want the son of the man who called for judgments based on "content of character" to push for reparations? Does the SCLC want King III to call on today's white nonslaveowners to pay black nonslaves money? Please.

The success of the black middle class renders a "civil rights organization" nearly obsolete. For the black "underclass"—nearly 30 percent of black Americans—"solutions" require an attack on the victicrat mentality. Eliminate the dependency-inducing welfare state; privatize Social Security; end the war on drugs; inject competition in public schools; remove the government from healthcare; reduce business taxes and regulations—but that kind of stuff gets King III called an "Uncle Tom."

"What's he really done in life?" Pity that King III's father so successfully shamed America into at last granting blacks full civil rights. Pity that King III now faces a thriving black middle class whose collective gross domestic income exceeds $500 billion,[158] enough to qualify it as one of the fifteen wealthiest countries in the world.[159]

The sixties civil rights movement demanded equal rights for all. For the most part, mission accomplished. The landscape King III faces looks entirely different. Perhaps King III rejects this victicrat mentality—the oppressed and powerless seeking aid from a benevolent Welfare State. Or, as an elderly black man said in explaining why he refused to vote for then-presidential candidate Jesse Jackson, "He's in the 'we shall overcome' business. And we done overcome."

THE DECLINE OF RACISM AND THE VICTICRATS' DILEMMA

How bad is racism in America?

A recent poll asked Americans to name their number-one hero. Americans' first choice? Jesus Christ. What about Americans' second choice? Martin Luther King. Third choice? Colin Powell. That's right. After Jesus Christ and Martin Luther King, Americans named Colin Powell as their top hero![160] Yet, Reverend Jesse Jackson calls him a "lapdog"[161] and is not met with screaming editorials or denunciations from the Congressional floor. Somewhere John Rocker says to himself, "Go figure."

In March 2001, *Forbes* magazine published their list of the one hundred most powerful celebrities. Under the definition of celebrity, they included politicians, athletes, actors, musicians, and others. The criteria to determine "most popular" included income, number of magazine cover stories, number of articles about, as well as Internet website hits. Blacks (if you include Tiger Woods) took twenty-six of the one hundred positions. While blacks are only 12 percent of the population, they occupy 26 percent of the "most powerful celebrity" positions. Kind of undermines the old "racism plays a part of everything in America" charge, doesn't it? And the number of "minorities" on the list grows even larger if you include the likes of boxer Oscar De La Hoya and singer-actress Jennifer Lopez.

A *Newsweek* cover recently featured three black CEOs of major corporations—Kenneth I. Chenault of American Express, E. Stanley O'Neal of Merrill Lynch, and Richard D. Parsons of AOL Time Warner. White CEOs preceded them, but *Newsweek* said, "To a man, all three departing executives are unanimous about one point: race wasn't a factor."[162]

Debra J. Dickerson is an author and a senior fellow at the New America Foundation. A black woman, she embodies the American success story. But life wasn't always so sweet. One of six children born to

Mississippi sharecroppers, she worked afternoons and evenings to help her family. Although an academically gifted child, she never considered going to college, expecting, as a poor black person, to work as a typist or a waitress.

But time, maturity, and exposure to a larger world lit a fire in her. She joined the Air Force, earning a B.A., an M.A., and an officer's commission. She then attended Harvard Law School (HLS). Her can-do, don't-blame-anybody attitude soon got her into trouble with other black Harvard students, however. She wrote:

Regardless of race, most of my HLS classmates came from professional, college-educated families. They'd often gone to private elementary schools, prep schools, and good colleges. One of the things my black classmates seemed to have learned along the way was what I came to think of as the Black Law Students Association mentality. When I joined the BLSA . . . I found an air of perpetual grievance and mindless opposition that often struck me as a pose. . . . You'd have thought blacks were still hanging from trees the way some of the BLSA members carried on. Worst of all, to disagree was to bring down the wrath of the BLSA in-crowd. Was I supposed to stand up to whites, but let blacks jerk me around? To be sure, most blacks sat silently at BLSA meetings; it was impossible to know what they were thinking. They weren't the problem. The BLSA politburo, the blackest of the black, were the ones who did most of the talking.[163]

Ms. Dickerson says that by the end of the first year, she rarely went to BLSA meetings, yet she still couldn't escape the black victicrat mentality. She also wrote about how blacks engage in self-segregation:

My second year a large group of our class was about to begin legal services work in a poor, minority-populated area of Boston. During sensitivity training in a large lecture hall, we were assigned to small random groups. A group of BLSA stalwarts demanded a black-only group. The temperature dropped to freezing. Needless to say, the New-Age facilitators (one black and one white) instantly caved. And, except for me and a black friend who accepted random assignments, the blacks got their segregated group. I dreaded rejoining the large group and the behind-my-back recriminations that were sure to follow.[164]

At the end of her Harvard career, Ms. Dickerson chastised her black Harvard colleagues for exaggerating racism and elevating the trivial:

After three years of watching campus turmoil breaking out along every possible political fault, I sometimes wished HLS students would face actual discrimination and oppression. Maybe then they wouldn't have felt the need to create it where it didn't exist.[165]

Amen, Ms. Dickerson. Amen.

Kids today know nothing of the blatant, overt racism suffered by blacks like my dad who grew up during the Depression in the segregated South. Through it all, my father never once complained about racism.

Yes, he told stories, like the one about the time he purchased a cab to start a jitney service. He needed to go to court to get a license, but the judge, in open court, denied the "nigger" a license. Turned out the judge owned a competing jitney service and did not want the competition.

Or the time my father walked into a clothing store, tried on a hat, and the white salesman made him purchase it, since the hat had touched my father's black skin. Like the segregated and less well-maintained public parks to which he took dates. Yet my father taught me that no matter how poor your circumstances, somebody somewhere suffers still more.

A friend recently met Bob, a successful, midthirties insurance executive. Bob never met his father. At the age of three, Bob's mother, in a fit of anger, broke Bob's arm. Social Services investigated but could find no evidence of foul play. At the age of eight, his mother, in a fit of anger, broke Bob's jaw. This time, Social Services took Bob away from her. For the next decade, Bob spent time in and out of various private boys' homes and in private foster care. He smoked, drank, and made subsistence grades. Why bother studying, he repeatedly said to himself. I'm still stuck in this home.

One day, a priest came and lectured the boys. In his speech, he said that all of us possess some talent. It was up to us, said the priest, to find and nurture that talent. After the speech, Bob came up to the priest, and told him of his life. "What talent," asked Bob, "what skill, what ability do I have?" The priest said, "Why, it is in front of you. Your gift is that you survived. Your gift is that you endured. This is what you have and this is what you must share with others."

The talk inspired Bob as never before, and he began to take school seriously, graduating with a good grade point average. He marched right into college, where he received a business degree. He then entered the insurance industry, and now, married, with two children, earns a six-figure salary.

Hard work wins. Hope, however, jump-starts the effort, which, in turn, ultimately produces the result. And hope remains a fragile thing. Environment can destroy it. So can incessant, negative babbling by today's we-shall-overcome leaders.

6.

ADVENTURES IN CONTEMPORARY RACE RELATIONS

By defining society not as an entity made up of individual people but as a
collection of cultures—such as white culture, black culture, Hispanic culture—the
Left effectively isolates us, whether we like it or not, into special-interest groups.
The culture has the identity, eclipsing the individual. We're no longer
individuals with unique minds and talents; we're defined instead by the color of
our skin, by the country in which we were born, by the religion we practice.[1]
—TAMMY BRUCE, FORMER HEAD OF THE LOS ANGELES
CHAPTER OF THE NATIONAL ORGANIZATION FOR WOMEN

Liberal activist Tom Hayden ran for mayor of Los Angeles a few years ago. Someone called my radio show and told me that at a campaign stop, Hayden said that I was "against my own people." Further, Hayden cautioned her "not to listen to Larry Elder." Hayden denied the remark, but the woman making the accusation insisted and offered to produce other witnesses.

Against my own people?

Democrats, at the presidential level, have failed to carry the "white vote" since 1964.[2] Does this make Hayden, a Democrat, against his own people?

Hayden also talks about his Irish-Catholic heritage in his book, *Irish on the Inside: In Search of the Soul of Irish America.* But starting in the sixties, the Irish became increasingly discontented with the Democratic Party's liberal social policies, and they followed the general trend of sub-urban voters to become Republican.[3] In the eighties, even the mostly working-class Irish-Catholic voters shifted their traditional allegiance from the Democrats to The Gip's Republican Party.[4] So does Hayden the Democrat go "against his own people"? Does this make Hayden an Irish Uncle Tom? Apparently, that epithet is reserved only for blacks who dare depart from the orthodoxy of their traditional leadership.

Liberal name-calling simply exposes the speaker's hypocrisy, duplicity, and double standards. White "dissenters" apparently enjoy more latitude and freedom to think as individuals than do black "dissenters." Thus, the very whites demanding civil rights for blacks actually give them less freedom of thought and self-analysis than provided fellow whites! So who's the bigot?

POST SEPTEMBER 11: BLACKS NOW SUPPORT RACIAL PROFILING

During the 2000 presidential campaign, Al Sharpton asked the Democratic candidates: "Many in our community have to live in fear of both the cops and the robbers. We are asking what concrete steps would you make if you were elected president, to deal with police brutality and racial profiling without increasing crime. How would you keep crime down, but at the same time confront the problem of police brutality and racial profiling?"[5]

Most police chiefs deny engaging in "racial profiling"—the illegal practice of stopping and questioning solely based upon race. For example, Los Angeles Police Chief Bernard Parks said, "We're not using just race. It's got to be race, plus other indicators."[6]

Then came September 11, 2001.

Nineteen "Middle Eastern–looking" men hijacked four commercial planes. Six of the nineteen apparently slipped into the United States illegally. And, of the remaining thirteen, three allowed their visas to expire and stayed. The government tells us that Middle Eastern "terrorist cells" operate in the United States and are linked to perhaps thousands of so-called "sleepers" worldwide, living assimilated lives in some fifty countries while awaiting the signal to strike.

Of the FBI's recently revealed list of the twenty-two "most-wanted terrorists," all are Middle Eastern with the exception of one born in Bloomington, Indiana, to Iraqi parents.[7] Shall the police ignore this obvious fact when on "heightened alert" for any suspicious activity?

Similarly, out of the universe of young black men comes a disproportionately large group of criminals. Blacks make up less than 13 percent of the population but account for 27 percent of all sexual-assault convictions, 38 percent of all fraud and embezzlement convictions, and 66 percent of all robberies.[8] Most Americans, post September 11, 2001, expect the police to use common sense and take into consideration someone's Middle Eastern ethnicity. But before September 11, 2001, many blacks demanded that cops ignore reality and pretend that young black men do not disproportionately commit crime.

Yet post September 11, according to a Gallup Poll, 71 percent of blacks said they favor requiring Arabs, including U.S. citizens, to undergo additional scrutiny. Asked whether they favor or oppose requiring Arabs to carry special ID's, 64 percent of blacks said yes![9] So it's OK to profile *them*.

Incredibly, Secretary of Transportation Norman Mineta favors political correctness over national security. On *60 Minutes* he talked about the pain he experienced as a World War II detainee in a relocation camp for Japanese nationals and Japanese Americans, and about heightened airport security.

MINETA: You can't say that a person, just because he is an Arab-American and a Muslim, that he should be a suspect and be considered someone who might be a terrorist.

KROFT: Are you saying at the security screening desks, that a seventy-year-old white woman from Vero Beach, Florida, would receive the same level of scrutiny as a . . . Muslim young man from New Jersey?

MINETA: Basically, I would hope so.

KROFT: We don't know much about the people that hijacked those planes on September eleventh, but we do know some-

thing. I mean, all 19 of them were young Arab or Middle
Eastern men.

MINETA: But that doesn't mean that we should be suspecting all
Arab young men.

KROFT: That's the only thing we know about these people.

MINETA: But that is not a characteristic that makes them a terrorist.

KROFT: Can you envision a set of circumstances from a security
point of view where it would make sense to use racial and ethnic profiling?

MINETA: On just that question alone, I'd say absolutely not.

KROFT: If you saw three young Arab men sitting, kneeling, pray-
ing, before they boarded a flight, getting on, talking to each
other in Arabic, getting on the plane, no reason to stop and ask
them any questions?

MINETA: No reason.[10]

Mineta's politically correct stance against racial profiling defies common sense. Perhaps Mineta should have a chat with former FAA inspector Steve Elson, who feels a *little* differently given the events of
September 11. "The Constitution doesn't say that you can't offend
anybody," says Elson, "and it doesn't say we can't discriminate against
people if they're a threat to our security. When it comes to our survival,
I really don't give a damn about Muslim sensitivities."[11]

Political correctness cost former New Jersey State Police superintendent Colonel Carl A. Williams his job. Following an accusation of
racial profiling, the colonel said, "Two weeks ago the president of the
United States went to Mexico to talk . . . about drugs. He didn't go to
Ireland. He didn't go to England. Today with this drug problem, the
drug problem is cocaine or marijuana. It is most likely a minority group
that's involved with that."[12] In an interview with Dan Rather, Williams
said, "Every law enforcement agency and every law enforcement person profiles. When you put the racial part on it, that's where it's

wrong." Rather asks him, "Were you fired for telling the truth or for being politically incorrect?" Williams replies, "I was fired, I guess, for being racially insensitive, whatever that is." Rather says, "Do you in fact think you were insensitive?" Williams says, "No, sir."[13] For that he lost his job. But Mineta's political correctness gets him the gig as secretary of transportation, where we expect his aversion to racial profiling to nevertheless protect us. Go figure.

Consider the plight of Argenbright Security, used by many airlines to provide private security. A few years ago, Argenbright fired seven Muslim women who worked at security checkpoints at Dulles Airport. They refused to remove their traditional Arab head covering, and nervous passengers were complaining. Remember, this took place shortly after the bombings of the American embassies in Africa. Four of the seven Muslim women were from Sudan, a nation on the State Department's terrorist blacklist. Another was from Afghanistan. The fired employees went to the EEOC and claimed discrimination.[14]

The EEOC forced Argenbright to rehire the women, offer a written apology, give them back pay plus $2,500 in compensation, and require their employees to undergo Muslim-sensitivity training.[15] Representative David Bonior defended the fired employees, and in a March 1999 speech on the House floor, said, "This incident raises a larger issue: that of widespread and systematic discrimination against Muslims and Arab-Americans in airports all across the country."[16]

In an ironic twist to the Argenbright story, the company now faces heat for hiring *too many* foreigners. After September 11, the Feds found that 87 percent of the checkpoint screeners at Dulles airport were not U.S. citizens. "If I were Argenbright and being investigated, I'd tell them, 'You want to sue us? Go talk to the damn EEOC. They're the ones who forced these people on us,'" says former FAA inspector Steve Elson.[17]

The frustrated FAA inspector throws his hands up. "The only standard government enforces," said Elson, "is making every minority happy and comfortable and not offending anybody."[18]

Before September 11, emotions and condescension, rather than fact, logic, and history, drove the argument against "racial profiling."

Time to revisit.

AFFIRMATIVE ACTION HURTS

The war against terrorism requires vigilance, focus, and excellence. We need the best and most capable military personnel, as well as industrial power and strength. How we succeed turns in large part on the quality of our citizens' education. But now we face another enemy—"multiculturalism." "Multiculturalism" means "inclusion" and "diversity," because, proponents tell us, "multiculturalism" is a good thing.

Multiculturalism and diversity became the basis for the University of Michigan's defense against an affirmative action lawsuit. Its president, now Columbia University's president, Lee Bollinger, maintained that diversity at the University of Michigan improved learning and made better students. According to the *Detroit Free Press*, "[Bollinger] helped establish Michigan's defense on the premise that diversity strengthens universities and benefits all students by creating an enriched learning environment."[19] Evidence? He uses a study conducted by University of Michigan psychology professor Pat Gurin,[20] concluding that, yes, Virginia, affirmative action works! Incredibly, they determined this, in part, by asking the students whether they benefited from "different" students around them.[21] Why, yes, we did, say the respondents.

Here's the problem. Prominent educational researcher Alexander Astin used the most comprehensive database available, that covers ten million students at 1,700 institutions and contains data on their "attitudes, values, behavior, learning, achievement, career development and satisfaction." The result of his exhaustive study showed that the percentage of minorities in a school has essentially no effect on learning or anything else. "With few exceptions, outcomes are generally not affected by these peer measures, and in all but one case [an esoteric detail about student perceptions of faculty] the effects are very weak and indirect."[22]

Journalist Dan Seligman studied Gurin's huge diversity-means-you-learn-better report, as well as the report's critiques and Gurin's defenses. Writing in *Forbes* magazine, Seligman summed up his findings. "What plainly emerges is that she has dodged Astin's devastating finding. Her solution, essentially, was to argue that (a) increased minority representation makes it likely that students will have more "diversity experiences"—interracial friendships, for example; (b) social science research demonstrates positive correlations between such experiences and academic learning; and (c) student self-report questionnaires substantiate the link between diversity and learning."[23]

Works out real well when you manage to find the "data" you need to back up the conclusion you want, doesn't it?

Richard Atkinson, president of the University of California (UC) system, advocates abandoning the SAT test. He favors what some call a "holistic approach." True to this vision, the UC regents recently voted to abandon their current way of admitting students. Under the current procedure, the admissions officer takes 50 percent of students solely based on grades and test scores.[24] The other half get in based on a number of subjective criteria, including extracurricular activities, a disadvantaged status, or other "obstacles" overcome by the applicant.[25]

Is the change to UC admission standards a subterfuge to ensure the admission of a certain number of blacks and Hispanics? UC president Richard Atkinson denies this, but did say, "Minority communities go off the deep end when they talk about the SAT. I think they have good reason. It's a mystery what the SAT measures and why their kids don't do as well as other kids."[26]

The UC schools adopted this scheme after voters in California passed Proposition 209, an initiative that rejected race- and gender-based preferences in college and university admissions. Uh-oh, post Proposition 209, not as many blacks and Hispanics got into the more competitive and prestigious UC schools like UCLA and Berkeley. But the overall number of minorities at the UC system remained unchanged, with lesser-qualified blacks and Hispanics attending less competitive schools,[27] where, by the way, their chances of graduating in a timely fashion actually increase.

But this displeases the toe-tag liberals who somehow believe that one must go to Yale or Cal Tech in order to lead a happy, productive life.

So now California admissions officers intend to use the subjective, "holistic" approach for *all* applicants. By law, California guarantees admission into the UC system for the top 12.5 percent of all California high school graduates.[28] So the movement toward "holism" disproportionately affects entry into the more sought-after campuses like UCLA and Berkeley.

According to the *Los Angeles Times*, "University of California regents . . . endorsed a major shift in the university's admissions policy to allow personal achievements, not just grades and test scores, to be considered for all freshman applicants. The 13–2 vote—in which the majority included one-time opponents of the plan—would allow consideration of such factors as a student's struggle against poverty or athletic or artistic ability. . . .

"Critics call the controversial proposal a backdoor method of reviving race-based preferences in admissions, which were banned by California voters in 1996, and say it could result both in litigation against the university and a lowering of academic standards. Supporters deny the charges, arguing that grades and test scores alone cannot capture all the qualities that make a good student and ultimately lead to success in college."[29]

UC Regent Sherry Lansing, also head of Paramount Pictures, exclaimed, "I have always felt that there has to be a better way [to admit students] than just looking at the numbers."[30] The holistic approach, claims the California State school superintendent, means a higher, not lower, caliber of student. Under the current policy, argues the superintendent, "We'd miss Abe Lincoln, we'll certainly bypass Oprah, and we'll miss Whoopi Goldberg and we won't bring Einstein or Edison forward. [All of them] came from dysfunctional families or had serious learning disabilities."[31]

Forget race. How about fundamental fairness?

Academics ignore another profoundly serious defect with the "holistic" approach—the students' credibility. Having worked as an executive search consultant, I personally witnessed numerous instances of résumé exaggeration. Gary Cornick, president of PeopleWise, one of the nation's largest screening firms, finds that "between 12 percent and 18 percent of the screenings his firm conducts find information that differs from a job seeker's résumé or application."[32] And Barry Nadell of InfoLink Screening Services estimates that 30 to 35 percent of the résumés he evaluates for employers contain "untruths."[33] If adults lie on résumés to get jobs or promotions, wouldn't kids lie to get into a prestigious college? Come on.

In opposing the UC regents' decision to switch to "holism," Professors Matthew Malkan and Stephen Jacobsen, former chairs of UCLA's Committee on Undergraduate Admissions, circulated a letter among the UC regents, addressing the "credibility issue." "A . . . problem that is apparent to many admissions insiders is the impossibility of verifying non-academic 'information.' We have little or no way of knowing how extensive a student's involvement has been in most of the extracurricular activities typically listed on his or her application. We cannot verify the levels of parental education which are so heavily weighted in the 'life challenges index.' We do not even know who has 'edited' the student essay! This self-reported information can already confer a substantial advantage to applicants who exaggerate and fabricate, thereby punishing honest applicants."

When you apply for a mortgage, do lenders accept your word when they ask you to name your income? Does the government accept your word about how much money you make come April 15? Yet college admissions officers blindly assume that John woke up every morning at 4:00 A.M. before cutting lawns for an hour and a half, before doing his homework by candlelight in the back of the family's 1976 Winnebago that drops him off for school five minutes before the bell rings.

The new criteria for UC admission include personal factors such as income, special talents, parents' education, overcoming personal struggles, and attending a low-performing high school.[34] What all-knowing, all-seeing, all-wise force can determine who suffered "adversity," however one defines that, versus who didn't?

Consider this. Couple A works hard, lives below their means, saves money to pay for an expensive private school for their son. The wife never made that Paris trip and the husband never took that fantasy golfing excursion in Myrtle Beach. No, they spent their money on Junior's education. Couple B, on the other hand, never worked very hard, never sacrificed, and sent their kids to a sub-mediocre public school.

But come admissions applications time, Couple B's kid gets an advantage. After all, he overcame "poverty." Never mind that the poverty resulted from his parents' irresponsibility and lack of initiative. And never mind that we now punish Couple A for their focus, and self-sacrifice and for valuing education itself.

Proponents of the "holistic system" say it offsets the advantages of wealth. First, since the wealthy did not, for the most part, steal, inherit, or marry their money, why penalize them for working harder, smarter, perhaps more creatively, and perhaps taking more risks than others? Second, does wealth automatically translate into better performance in school or on standardized tests? Explain, then, why poor Asians frequently outperform middle-class whites on standardized tests. Explain why, in the upper-class Cleveland suburb of Shaker Heights, blacks underperform on standardized tests when compared to their white colleagues.[35] After all, they live in the same neighborhood and have similar incomes.

Is it cultural bias? Nonsense. Colleges began using SATs in the '30s because, until then, admissions often turned on family connections, bloodlines, and recommendations from insiders and other influential people.[36] According to *U.S. News & World Report,* "Attacking the tests is like attacking thermometers because of cold weather. A ton of data tell us they are merely reporting the truth—that depressingly large numbers of non-Asian minority-group members arrive at college too poorly prepared to do well."[37]

The SAT—the lousy predictor of college success? Nonsense. According to Stuart Taylor, who writes on legal matters for the *New York Times,* when SATs are used as they are now, on a weighted basis with grades and other criteria, "the scores are the most reliable known predictor of academic success."[38] True, grades remain one of the best predictors of success, but given grade inflation and wildly varying teacher standards, the SAT serves as a way of comparing an A at one school with an A at another.

Why, despite no government mandate, do nearly 90 percent of all four-year colleges require SATs?[39] A three-year study by the University of Minnesota culled results from 1,700 previous studies done on the SAT from the 1940s to 1999. Their research confirmed that the SAT was a good predictor of college grades, especially in the first semester, but it was also effective at forecasting a grade point average (GPA) through the fourth year. They found the SAT was also effective— though weaker—at predicting study habits and graduation rates.[40]

Journalist Nicholas Lemann, author of *The Big Test,* an impressive new history of the SATs, states, "[The SATs] are designed to measure the developed capacity to do college work. And they do that well. One example: Far from being biased against blacks, the SAT has had a good record over two decades of predicting the actual performance of black students at selective colleges. In fact, the SAT has slightly over-predicted the success of those students, or, to put it another way, for reasons we don't understand, blacks have performed less well than their scores predicted."[41]

So why would the UC regents want to go from a system that relies on good test scores to one that gives power to admissions officers, whom we then trust to responsibly, intelligently, and fairly apply their holism? University of California at Berkeley admissions officer, Bob Laird, said, "We have no fixed weights in our scoring processes. We have no formulas. We depend upon the trained professional judgment of our readers. . . . So that an SAT I verbal score of 600 doesn't have a single meaning across our applicant pool. A score of 600 may mean one thing for a student whose first language isn't English, or whose parents didn't complete high school."[42] Some standard. Shelby Steele, research fellow at Stanford University's Hoover Institute, has a simpler answer to explain the jettisoning of test criteria. "Merit stands in the way of diversity, so they want to destroy it."[43]

Guess which group most gets screwed? Asian-Americans. This minority group represents around 40 percent of the student body at the prestigious campuses of UCLA and Cal-Berkeley.[44] If, however, admissions officers relied solely on grades and test scores, some estimate that the percentage of Asians on those two campuses could reach 55 percent![45] The de-emphasis of grades and test scores simply means fewer Asians.

Multiculturalism clearly shafted Asians at the prestigious Lowell High School in San Francisco. For years, Lowell High School required higher admission scores for certain groups. Lowell, a public magnet school with an excellent reputation, receives many more applicants per year than it has places. The prestigious Lowell High School produced an elite corps of alumni that includes ambassadors, authors, Rhodes scholars, scientists, and countless luminaries ranging from Supreme Court Justice Stephen Breyer to actress Carol Channing.[46]

School administrators, however, seeking a "diverse" campus, limit the number of Asians by requiring higher admissions standards for them. So, for years, to get into Lowell High, Chinese-Americans were required a score of 66 out of 69. For whites, Japanese-, Korean-, and Filipino-Americans the score was 59 to qualify, and blacks and Latinos needed a 56.[47]

Finally, a fed-up group of Asian parents filed suit and overturned this hideous admissions policy. But the new UC admissions policy similarly gives fiat to admissions officers, who punish academic excellence while doing nothing to improve the substandard K–12 education many receive. The new UC criteria de-emphasizes the accent on education found in many Asian households. Studies show Asian kids are less likely to take summer jobs or to work after school, feeling the time is better spent studying. Many Asian parents send their children to so-called "cram schools," after-school programs, or weekend school programs for additional education. Korean-language newspapers in Los Angeles publish the SAT test scores of students.

Nationwide, affirmative action forces a mismatching of lesser-qualified blacks and Hispanics in top-flight schools, resulting in a lower-than-average graduation rate for those students. Those admitted under "special criteria" or some other code word for lowered standards—a.k.a. affirmative action—drop out at a much higher rate than their peers.

As mentioned earlier, a study of seven Michigan colleges by the *Detroit News* reveals that "among black students who were freshmen in 1994, just 40 percent got their diplomas after six years, compared to 61 percent of white students and 74 percent of Asians. . . . The state's universities have special programs aimed at helping black students meet financial, social and academic challenges, but graduation rates for blacks haven't improved consistently over the past decade, the *News* found. . . . Universities knowingly admit students who have a high chance of failing. . . . The 10 years' worth of data analyzed by the *News* shows that the more selective a university is in choosing its students, the more likely its students are to graduate."[48]

As Thomas Sowell writes, bright black students "were perfectly qualified to be successes somewhere else" but were instead "artificially turned into failures by being admitted to high-pressure campuses, where only students with exceptional academic backgrounds can survive."[49] Sowell saw it coming as early as 1970. "I predicted back then, that when these programs failed, the conclusion would be not that they are half-baked programs, but that blacks just don't have it."[50]

How do white supporters of affirmative action justify the horrendous dropout rates? For these students, failure to complete college, according to one study, robs the black community of $5.3 billion in annual revenues.[51]

The new, liberal, condescending UC admissions policy ignores the real problem—the substandard K–12 education many students receive, especially in public, inner-city schools. Yet, many of the very same liberals willing to use "holistic" means in college admissions remain adamantly opposed to allowing parents, through vouchers, to select their children's school.

What do the UC admissions officers say to parents who bought smaller homes, didn't go on vacation, and lived below their means to ensure a better education for their children? Should they stand at the back of the bus because of the educational establishment's failure to provide a quality education for others? To those parents, the UC admissions policy says quite bluntly—"Suckers." And the possibility of getting into UCLA or Berkeley, if one is Asian, grows more difficult. Is this America or what?

Meanwhile, preferences thrust lesser-prepared, "disadvantaged" students into colleges with academic levels too challenging for success, setting the student up for failure, frustration, and anger.

Ultimately, what is better for the "disadvantaged" student—failure at a top-flight school, or success at a lower-tier school? Have the condescending affirmative action supporters get back to us on that one.

On the affirmative action issue, President George W. Bush and the Republicans appear, once again, to be heading for the hills. In Colorado, a company called Adarand Constructors applied for a U.S. Department of Transportation highway project. Although Adarand submitted the lowest bid, the department rejected it because the owner was white. Now the Supreme Court previously ruled in favor of limited, circumscribed "set-aside projects" designed to offset a previous history of discrimination. But in this case, the Department of Transportation parcels out contracts solely based on race or gender, without a finding or even an assertion that the plan tries to combat prior discrimination. A clear violation, one would think, of the color-blind premise under which George W. Bush ran. But, to the shock of many George W. supporters, the Bush Justice Department sided with the Department of Transportation![52]

Former Reagan Administration Attorney General Ed Meese wrote critically, "President Bush and Attorney General Ashcroft now have the historic opportunity to return us to the original, color-blind purposes of the Civil Rights Act and the Declaration of Independence, and to place government-sanctioned racial discrimination back where it belongs—in the course of ultimate extinction."[53]

WHITE CONDESCENSION: LOSE THE GUILT, HELP THE COUNTRY

Whites feel guilt about slavery, Jim Crow, and the racial discrimination historically faced by blacks. But this guilt frequently causes whites to expect a lower level of civility and morality from blacks. Guilty whites fear "blaming the victim."

What does white condescension mean? Consider this exchange between Tom Roeser, a spokesperson for Quaker Oats, and Bill O'Reilly. The Reverend Jesse Jackson—increasingly accused of "shaking down" corporations by exagerrating racism—criticized Quaker Oats for its lack of diversity. Quaker Oats disagreed, but later entered into a resolution of sorts with Jackson.

> O'REILLY: All right. Jesse Jackson says he has a problem with Aunt Jemima. Was that the reason for the meeting?
>
> ROESER: That's correct. Jackson's point was to extort—and I use that word advisedly—a tithe as a result of threatening a boycott of Quaker Oats. And he did it in subtle ways.
>
> O'REILLY: Walk me through it.
>
> ROESER: Well, Jackson says he wants to negotiate with us on a number of things. Certainly minority suppliers, which is a catchword for some of their friends, who want to get contracts. Certainly employment. That's okay, although there was a federal program in line for employment. Also, blacks on the board, and also foundation gifts.
>
> O'REILLY: Blacks make up about 13 percent of the American population. Did Quaker Oats have 13 percent black employment?

ROESER: It was lower.

O'REILLY: So Jackson had a point. You guys should have had
more minority workers.

ROESER: Well, he did have a point. But we were on the way toward that goal.

O'REILLY: So you took his point.

ROESER: The point is, Bill, is that we had no objection to meeting with Jackson, but we did object to what I thought was an
extortionate type of activity. I'm paraphrasing here. He says,
"We would hate to jeopardize your company. For example, if
there were a picket line thrown around the headquarters of the
company, that might hurt. We don't want to do that." It had
all the charm of a vintage Mafioso.

O'REILLY: What did you guys do?

ROESER: Well, what we did say is that we would not sign a covenant. He wanted to sign a covenant with us. We gave him some
money, but it wasn't a large amount. Some of it went to black
community organizations, some to his suppliers. We made certain concessions to him. All of them under threat.

O'REILLY: So Jackson won. He beat you.

ROESER: No, he didn't beat us, because we didn't sign the covenant. We paid him a lot of money in terms of suppliers but he
wanted us to dump the Aunt Jemima brand and we didn't.[54]

So, "Jackson has a point"? Well, what percentage of Quaker Oats's
workforce is Irish-American?

Suppose Roger Ailes, the CEO of Fox News, summoned Bill
O'Reilly to the office.

AILES: Bill, bad news. EEOC tells me that since we have you,
Sean Hannity, and others, we are overrepresented in Irish-
Americans. Somebody's gotta go, and we think it's you.

O'REILLY: What?

AILES: Seems that 10 percent of the American population is Irish-

American, but with you and the other on-air guys we have
around here, we're at 15 percent Irish-American, and down 2
percent in African-Americans.

O'REILLY: What?

AILES: After all, in your own book, you got on Quaker Oats because blacks account for 13 percent of the population, higher
than Quaker Oats's black workforce percentage. And you even
said, when Reverend Jackson criticized them, "[Jackson] had a
point."

O'REILLY: I said that?

AILES: Yes, right here, on page 78 of your book, *The No Spin
Zone.*

O'Reilly's well-meaning attitude reflects a paternalistic but condescending attitude toward blacks. "They love affirmative action," writes
Bernard Goldberg in *Bias: A CBS Insider Exposes How the Media Distort
the News,* "as long as their own kids get into Ivy League schools. They
love handing out jobs based on racial preferences, as long as they keep
theirs. It's a great deal: it's always somebody else who has to make the
sacrifice—sometimes Asian-American kids, sometimes other white students who don't get into places like Harvard and Yale and Princeton—
while the white liberal elite get to claim credit for being so decent, the
saviors of black people in America."[55]

Liberal reporters, in their own lives, use the normal formula to get
ahead—hard work. ABC's Sam Donaldson, a self-described not-so-
gifted student, talked about the military school he attended. "I learned
a couple things there," said Donaldson. "One, that it's better to be
with the winners than the losers. And second, that everybody needs to
understand something about discipline."[56] Donaldson now says his
work ethic allowed him to outperform others more intelligent and
more photogenic than he: "You have to do it the way Horatio Alger
did it. You have to work harder than the next person. You have to
take the dirty jobs. . . .You have to work on the weekends and you
have to work nights; you have to get up at two o'clock in the

morning. . . . That sounds pretty hard, pretty mean, but my observation has been that you have to give 110 percent. If you do that, you'll beat the people that are smarter than you. I've left behind a lot of people who were smarter than I am or more handsome because they weren't willing to do that."[57]

But for others, bring on the preferences!

White support of affirmative action often rests on a not-so-very-deep-down belief of black inferiority. Many supporters of affirmative action, deep down, simply find blacks incapable of competing without a change in rules and a lowering of standards. This condescension hurts both blacks and whites. President George W. Bush aptly calls this condescension "the soft bigotry of low expectations."

WHITES NEED NOT APPLY

And then there's the case of Chicago Alderman Thomas Murphy. Murphy, a white man who serves as the alderman of a predominantly black ward on Chicago's Southwest Side. Elected to represent the interests of his primarily black constituents, Murphy attempted to join the city council's black caucus.

But his three-week campaign to enter the group did not go well. Murphy met with four of the most influential members, and he later said they told him they would not support him. "The only reason I was given was that I'm not an African-American elected official," said Murphy. "I believe that the purpose of the caucus was to represent the interests of the black residents of this city. Apparently, they think otherwise." Finally, Murphy gave in and gave up his quest, saying he didn't want to inflame racial tensions.[58]

One white lady wrote to black columnist Larry Meeks about her experience when she attempted to attend a black church in her neighborhood. A lover of gospel music, she could hear the music in her home that came from the nearby church every Sunday. She said that before she even sat down, an usher rudely demanded to know what she was doing there, and told her she should go to another church—meaning a white church. She left—hurt, disappointed, and embarrassed.

Meeks responded, "Church racism is a dirty little secret that religious people try to hide and pretend does not exist. Minorities love to fault whites for their racism, but many minorities are guilty of the same behavior. Someone made the accurate observation that the most segregated time in America is Sunday mornings. . . . I would be willing to wager the pastor would appreciate your call, and he/she probably has no idea one of his members is such a racist. If the pastor does not respond positively, take the racist's advice and go where you will be accepted and loved."[59]

Let's hope the young white lady takes Meeks's advice and goes straight to the pastor.

THE COLOR OF HIS SCREENPLAY

White screenwriter Matt George, a former Navy SEAL, wrote a script called *Soul Alley*. The story revolved around the first black squadron leader in Vietnam, George's African-American godfather, Buddie Penn. George's girlfriend had a suggestion: "Why not enter the script in some movie competitions?" George agreed. Using entrance forms printed in a trade magazine, George's girlfriend happily entered the script in fifteen film competitions, including the IFP Gordon Parks screenwriting award, for "emerging African-American filmmakers."

George got a phone call. Congratulations, said the awards representative—out of all the entries, we selected yours! The organization, located on the East Coast, and George on the West Coast, spoke several times by phone to arrange his attendance at a fancy banquet in a hotel, where he expected to collect the $10,000 prize money. So George, the "emerging African-American filmmaker," flies to New York. They put him up in a nice hotel. A limo driver picks him up and takes him to the hotel. George arrived late, and hurriedly entered the banquet. But, as soon as he walked in, he felt something odd.

The notables on the panel of presenters and judges included director Spike Lee, director Bill Duke, actor-director-writer Cheryl Dunye, producer Deborah Martin Chase, writer-director Malcolm D. Lee, and actress Tonya Lee Williams. When George walked up to the organizers, their jaws dropped. George, you see, is not an "emerging African-American filmmaker," but, gasp, a white guy!

Nobody bothered to ask George his race. And in the several phone conversations, the organizers assumed George was black, and George, whose girlfriend failed to read the entrance requirements, thought his race a nonissue and therefore, never brought it up. What to do, what to do?

The committee told George they designed the award for "emerging African-American filmmakers." Spike Lee, a member of the board, even refused to shake George's hand.[60] Showing class and grace not accorded him by the organization, George decided to "stand down," agreeing that he failed to meet the entrance requirements.

"I showed up and it was a complete surprise," George told *Daily Variety*. "I was the bastard child at that banquet. We're talking about a starving Hollywood writer who has entered fifteen competitions and didn't really read the fine print. It was the most awkward situation of my life. It became so comedic that at the after-party there wasn't a human being in there that wasn't buying me a drink."[61]

Over the past several years, NAACP President Kweisi Mfume has traveled to Hollywood to whine about the alleged dearth of black writers, actors, executives, and other behind-camera personnel. But didn't George, by winning this contest for "emerging African-American filmmakers," demonstrate that one's race does not necessarily dictate one's ability to write in a poignant, sensitive way about others of a different race? Doesn't George's selection show that quality writing remains quality writing, irrespective of the sex or race of the author?

Of all the articles I've read about boxing, a piece by a woman,

Carol Joyce Oates, remains one of the most moving. And a woman, Mary Shelley, wrote the book *Frankenstein*. An American of Irish extraction, John Patrick Shanley wrote movingly about Italians in *Moonstruck* and in the *Italian American Reconciliation*. Shanley, who grew up in an Irish area in New York, said that he marveled at his Italian friends. They cared about their hair, their clothing, and their cologne, the opposite of the interests of the Irish kids in Shanley's neighborhood. Fascinated, Shanley decided to write about Italians and used his eye of "an outsider" to observe Italian-American culture in a way perhaps unique to him as a non–Italian-American.

In *Of Mice and Men*, John Steinbeck wrote powerfully and sensitively about the racism experienced by Crooks, a black stablehand.[62]

Why doesn't George's screenwriting victory demonstrate the importance of the content of the screenplay rather than the color of the writer? Isn't this, after all, Mfume's argument—that Hollywood ought not pigeonhole blacks, restricting them to writing only about things or people who "look like me"?

MUMIA ABU-JAMAL

If celebrity malpractice were a crime, Susan Sarandon, Paul Newman, Ed Asner, Whoopi Goldberg, and others might be on death row.[63] These celebrities all lent their hard-earned reputations to Mumia Abu-Jamal, the alleged "innocent" on Philadelphia's death row.

He is black, charismatic, a writer, accused of killing a symbol of the establishment—a cop—and he is undoubtedly guilty. In short he possesses all the right attributes for celebrity *cause célèbre*.

On December 9, 1981, at quarter-to-four in the morning, authorities claim Mumia Abu-Jamal shot and killed Officer Daniel Faulkner. The night in question, the police stopped Mumia Abu-Jamal's brother, William Cook. For whatever reason, Abu-Jamal, a former radio reporter now driving a cab, was in the area. He ran to his brother's aid and, according to the prosecution, shot Officer Daniel Faulkner first in the back and then in the face at point-blank range. Faulkner managed to unholster his service revolver and shot Abu-Jamal once in the chest.[64]

When authorities arrived, they found Officer Faulkner barely alive and Abu-Jamal with a bullet in his chest and his gun nearby. Several eyewitnesses implicated Abu-Jamal in the shooting.[65]

Incredibly, these celebrities, and many others, maintain not only that Abu-Jamal failed to get a fair trial but that the authorities framed a completely innocent man! Abu-Jamal now enjoys international fame. Bookstores carry his autobiography, *Live From Death Row*, now available in eight languages. Scores of colleges require the book in various courses. "Readers of the book," says Dan Flynn, executive director of Accuracy in Academia, "learn that America is 'the most violent nation on earth,' where drugs are 'carried into the U.S. by government-hired pilots to pay fledgling contra bills.' " Recently, Abu-Jamal was named an honorary citizen of Paris. The last person to receive that title was Pablo Picasso.[66]

Steve Lopez, a *Time* magazine writer, said that he, too, once believed in Abu-Jamal's innocence. Then he examined the case. "I didn't know much about the case when I moved to Philadelphia in 1985 to work for the *Inquirer*," wrote Lopez. "But I later heard it said that Abu-Jamal, a former radio reporter and Black Panther Party member, had been railroaded and that evidence pointing to another killer had been buried. Philadelphia being what it was and my politics being what they were, none of that seemed preposterous to me. But I began to educate myself, and the things Abu-Jamal supporters didn't know were shocking."[67]

Remember, Abu-Jamal allegedly rushed over to assist his brother, but the brother never testified on Abu-Jamal's behalf! In fact, in twenty years, the only statement uttered by Billy Cook came at the crime scene, when he reportedly said, "I ain't got nothing to do with this."[68] Remember, the eyewitnesses on the scene that night—except for two of them—implicated Abu-Jamal. But two of the people who witnessed the crime have steadfastly declined to say what happened. The two silent witnesses: Mumia Abu-Jamal and his brother.[69]

So the Mumia-Abu-Jamal-is-innocent crowd wants us to believe that Abu-Jamal's brother let him rot on death row for twenty years, refusing to testify on behalf of his innocent sibling!

Dan Flynn, in his exhaustively documented book *Cop Killer*, available at www.academia.org, presents the facts and dismisses all the conspiracy theories advanced by the free-Mumia bunch, which are primarily distortions piled on half-truths served up over a plate of lies.[70] Yet otherwise intelligent people gobble it up like candy, preferring to believe that Abu-Jamal is "America's Nelson Mandela," making him the poster child for a racist criminal justice system. Please.

On December 18, 2001, U.S. District Judge William Yohn reversed the sentence part of Abu-Jamal's case. Yohn upheld his first-degree murder conviction but overturned the penalty-phase verdict of the jury that sentenced Abu-Jamal to death. The judge determined that, in the penalty phase, the jury instructions seemed confusing, despite the fact that no juror has ever admitted being confused.[71] Small victory for the Abu-Jamal-is-innocent group, for the judge's ruling still means he's guilty, but now he gets a crack at having a new jury decide whether he should face the death penalty again or merely life in prison.

Shame on Susan Sarandon, Paul Newman, Whoopi Goldberg, and Ed Asner.

THE PUZZLING JEWISH
CONDESCENSION TO BLACKS

Please explain the strange Jewish outreach toward black bigots.

The Nation of Islam's Louis Farrakhan repeatedly denounces Jews. He lies about the allegedly massive Jewish involvement in slavery, wildly exaggerating the minor Jewish role in the North American slave trade. Farrakhan conveniently forgets that African and Arab slavers brought more slaves to South America and to the Middle East than any other group of slavers.

Some of Farrakhan's hits include:

- "Hitler is a very great man."—Radio broadcast, March 11, 1984.[72]

- "So, brothers and sisters, the germ of murder is already sown in the hearts of Jews in this nation and across the world, and those who sympathize with Jews, they have a heart now filled with murder for Louis Farrakhan, so some person is going to think as the scripture says, that they're doing God a favor and seek my death. Isn't that something? . . . But I wonder, are you as ready to die as you are to kill?"—Madison Square Garden, October 7, 1985.[73]

- "Narrow-minded, common Jews. . . . The Jews cannot defeat me so I will grind them and crush them into little bits."—*New York Post,* May 23, 1988.[74]

- "[Jews are] sucking the blood of the black community."—Michigan State University, February 18, 1990.[75]

- "I said that the State of Israel has not had peace and will not have peace because there can be no peace structured on injustice, lying, thievery, murder and using God's name as a shield for your dirty religion."—*Washington Times,* February 27, 1990.[76]

- "If you take the whole Jewish–Farrakhan question and put it in context, then you will see that it was not Farrakhan who started this. It was the Jews who started this. And every time Farrakhan goes some place, I'm not even speaking, Jews come out even calling for my death."—*Washington Post,* March 1, 1990.[77]

- "Until Jews apologize for their hand in that ugly slave trade; and until the Jewish rabbis and the Talmudic scholars that made up the Hamitic myth—that we were the children of Ham, doomed and cursed to be hewers of wood and drawers of water—apologize, then I have nothing to apologize for."—*Swing* magazine interview, September 24, 1996.[78]

- "They, [the Jews] are the greatest controllers of black minds, black intelligence. They write the scripts—the foolish scripts on television that our people portray. They are the movie moguls that feature us in these silly, degrading, degenerate roles. The great recording companies that portray our people in such a filthy and low-rating way, yet they would not allow such a man as Michael Jackson to say one word that they thought would besmirch their reputation, but they put us before the world as clowns and as purveyors of filth. No, I will fight that."—*Meet the Press* interview, October 18, 1998.[79]

Even with evidence of such bigotry in hand, newsman Mike Wallace sought to understand and reach out to Farrakhan. The CBS *60 Minutes* correspondent, who is Jewish, once did a documentary on the Nation of Islam called, "The Hate That Hate Produced." Why, wondered Wallace, does such a chasm exist between the black and Jewish communities? Surely, thought Wallace, if only he spoke to Farrakhan, and made Farrakhan understand the good faith of Jews, maybe blacks and Jews can come together.

So Mike Wallace arranged a dinner party for Farrakhan. Dinner? Yes, Farrahkan's "misunderstanding" of Jews so concerned Wallace that the newsman invited Seagram's CEO Edgar Bronfman, who offered his apartment for the dinner; Bronfman's wife Jan Aronson; Farrakhan's son-in-law Leonard Muhammad; Rock Newman, who was close to Muhammad; and Farrakhan and his wife, Khadijah, for dinner at Bronfman's apartment.

Bronfman told Farrakhan of his concern about Farrakhan's rhetoric, and Newman suggested that Bronfman and Farrakhan embark on a business venture, perhaps a hotel in Washington to be funded with Bronfman's help and operated by African-Americans. Said Newman, "It would be a wonderful business example to show that these two sides can work together closely and frankly in a high-profile way. It is a great embarrassment in the African-American community that we don't own a major full-service hotel."[80] Newman recalls that Farrakhan thought the hotel was a good idea, "He was interested in pursuing the spiritual, philosophical, cultural barriers that had been put up and ways to break them down."[81]

Oh-oh. But days following the dinner, Farrakhan reverted to type and publicly repeated the very anti-Semitic statements that inspired Wallace to invite him to dinner in the first place.

And then there's the Jewish Outreach's Reverend Al Sharpton, another incendiary bigot who built a career, in part, by denouncing Jews. Remember Crown Heights? In 1991, Sharpton turned the death of a black child in a traffic accident in Brooklyn, which involved a Hasidic Jew, into a racial firestorm. Sharpton led 400 protesters through the Jewish section of Crown Heights. One protester held a sign that read, "The White Man Is the Devil." There were four nights of rock and bottle throwing, and a young Talmudic scholar was surrounded by a mob shouting, "Kill the Jew" and stabbed to death.

Yet, when Sharpton announced a recent trip to the Middle East, Rabbi Shmuley Boteach helped plan his itinerary. Sharpton, according to the rabbi, promised not to meet with Yassir Arafat, yet only days later, Jewish New Yorkers opened the morning paper to see a smiling Arafat and Sharpton meeting and shaking hands in Israel. Furious, Rabbi Boteach said, "Prior to our recent trip to Israel, U.S. black leader Reverend Al Sharpton and I discussed several times that there were to be no meetings with Arab or Palestinian leaders, not because I wished to set preconditions for our travel, but because the express objective of our mission was to show solidarity with Israeli victims of terror. The idea was to provide a magnanimous gesture of friendship and solidarity with the Jewish nation that would hopefully have strong reverberations for the relationship of the Jewish and black communities back home."[82]

During the O.J. Simpson trial, defense attorney Johnnie Cochran compared the disgraced LAPD cop Mark Fuhrman to Adolf Hitler: "There was another man not too long ago in the world who had those same views, who wanted to burn people, who had racist views and ultimately had power over people in his country. People didn't care. People said he is just crazy. He is just a half-baked painter. They didn't do anything about it. This man, this scourge, became one of the worst people in the history of this world, Adolf Hitler, because people didn't care or didn't try to stop him. . . . And so Fuhrman, Fuhrman wants to take all black people now and burn them or bomb them. That is genocidal racism."[83]

An angry Fred Goldman, the father of murder victim Ron Goldman, said, "We have seen a man who perhaps is the worst kind of racist himself, someone who shoves racism in front of everything, someone who compares a person who speaks racist comments to Hitler, a person who murdered millions of people."[84]

Yet Cochran recently won the Joseph Papp Racial Harmony Award! Attorney Sanford Rubenstein, a corecipient, said of each individual, "I happen to believe you can make a difference. Each of us can make a difference."[85] Rubenstein spoke passionately about his recent trip to Israel and the effect it had on him. "I had to go to Israel because as an American Jew, I believe there should be a homeland for the Jewish people . . . particularly after the horrible experience during World War II."[86] Rubenstein shared the award with Johnnie Cochran, the man who once said, "Race plays a part of everything in America" and suggested that the "frame-up" of O.J. Simpson resulted from Simpson's interracial marriage.

And let's not forget that Jesse Jackson infamously called Jews "Hymie" and New York City "Hymie-town."[87] Jackson later apologized and, hey, no hard feelings. He probably has a few race-relation awards sitting on his mantle, too.

A recent Anti–Defamation League poll called 12 percent of Americans—an all-time low—anti-Semitic.[88] Yet, in the black community, the rate of anti-Semitism stands at nearly four times the rate for whites.[89]

September 11, 2001, also exposed "The Great Unsaid" about the relationship between blacks and Jews: many blacks dislike Jews and feel that the United States "blindly" sides with Israel. Few blacks seem to know or recall that in 1984–85 and 1991, Israel airlifted to its country some 20 thousand unwanted, famine–afflicted, black Ethiopian Jews.[90] Yet many black public figures still express "concern" over America's "lack of balance" in the Israeli–Palestinian dispute.

Recall black Congresswoman Cynthia McKinney (D–Georgia), who offered to take the $10 mil from the Saudi prince despite the prince's "our Palestinian brethren continue to be slaughtered at the hands of the Israelis" lecture.[91]

Many blacks quite simply side with the Palestinians because they consider them underdogs, victims of oppression from Israel with Western support. Al Sharpton, Johnnie Cochran, Farrakhan, Jackson, and Representative Cynthia McKinney's lack of empathy toward Jews reveals ignorance of the history of the Middle East, of why America properly and steadfastly supports Israel.

Many American blacks use Arabic-sounding or Muslim names. This appeals to them because it suggests a denunciation of Western culture. But again, look at the history of the Arab slave trade of blacks, and the fact that slavery continues in several areas of Africa and the Middle East.

I recently received the following letter:

Dear Larry:

Do you think the 9-11 attacks and the virulent expressions of anti-American feelings in the Muslim world will end or at least start the decline of African Americans romanticizing and identifying with Islam? Will people still give their kids names like Rashid, Khalid, and Abdul? Even though blacks suffered at the hands of Western Europeans throughout history, Arab Muslims have shown no particular love for them and even enslave blacks today in places like the Sudan. Since African Americans enjoy our way of life as much as anyone else and have shown the same patriotic response if not more in some cases, will they take the next step and see that Ralph and Kevin and Adam more accurately represent who they are than Rashid, Khalid, and Abdul?

—Mike

The relationship between Jews and blacks also remains one of the great paradoxes in politics. Jews, like blacks, tend to vote Democratic, irrespective of income, geography, age, or sex. Yet blacks, also steadfastly loyal to the Democratic Party, are far more anti-Semitic than other groups. Many blacks support affirmative action or preferences. Quotas hurt Jewish-Americans, who faced widespread anti-Semitism through much of this nation's history. In the late '20s and '30s, Jews faced constant discrimination when it came to finding work. Ninety-five percent of job orders were "closed" to Jews and employment agencies posted signs that said, "Jews need not apply."[92] Many colleges and universities used unofficial quotas *against* Jewish applicants. The Jewish success story in America turns not on set-asides, preferences, or special privileges. The Jewish experience in America instead stands as a shining tribute to good values, hard work, self-sufficiency, self-control, and personal responsibility, all of which enabled many Jews to achieve success despite anti-Semitism.

But the Democratic Party, and to a large extent the Republican Party, says, "Government to the rescue!" Affirmative action, set-asides, welfare—all represent the antithesis of the Jewish hard-work-wins success story. Also, as an affluent group, Jews pay disproportionately more in federal income taxes than do others. Yet they support a party that taxes, spends, and regulates. What's wrong with this picture?

Is it Israel? No, both Republican and Democratic presidents support Israel, although Presidents Clinton and Carter appeared to inject themselves personally in attempting to forge peace agreements. Is it the "right-wing Christian" flank of the Republican Party? No, more likely the reason boils down to this: Jews see Democrats as compassionate. Also, the illogical reaching out to black bigots like Farrakhan and Sharpton shows us something else—Jews like to be liked. And how can one be liked as a Republican, right?

GETTING FED UP?

Will whites drop the guilt and condescension? Maybe. A forty-year-old Long Beach, California, white man wrote:

. . . What it boils down to is, I'm tired. I'm tired of being sympathetic. I'm tired of caring about a people who don't care about themselves. I'm tired of listening to black leaders tell me how evil I am when in fact they simply prey on their own people. I am tired of throwing good money after bad providing opportunity to those that don't take advantage of the opportunity. I'm tired of the Jesse Jacksons and the Louis Farrakhans. I'm tired of the constant "digs" at me, like a [Spike Lee] production company called "40 Acres and Mule."

. . . I finally have realized that the black leaders can say whatever they want, I am not the enemy to the black people, they are. Whites are not the only race out there . . . there are Hispanics, there are Asians of all kinds, there are Indians (both native and from India), there are Persians. If the whites are such a problem for the black race, then they should deal with these other races. If the black race has problems with ALL these races, then it's clear this is not a white issue. And what does that say? What are the black leaders going to do when the white race is not the predominant race in America (which is coming soon)? Who are they going to blame then?

I'm not a racist, I'm not anti-black, I don't get up in the morning obsessed with how I can jack with some black person's life today. I have no interest in persecuting blacks, I have no interest in keeping the black man down. I'm just a guy stumbling through life trying to make the best of things, and I'm tired of being told all the problems of a whole group of people is somehow my fault.

—Brett L.

7.

MEDIA BIAS—THE DENIAL CONTINUES

*All truth passes through three stages. First, it is ridiculed. Second, it is
violently opposed. Third, it is accepted as being self-evident.*[1]
—ARTHUR SCHOPENHAUER, NINETEENTH CENTURY
PHILOSOPHER

*The problem is that Mr. [Dan] Rather and the other evening stars think that
liberal bias means just one thing: Going hard on Republicans and easy on
Democrats. But real media bias comes not so much from what party they
attack. Liberal bias is the result of how they see the world.*[2]
—BERNARD GOLDBERG, JOURNALIST

The media wield tremendous influence and power. A biased media
means information not given, a perspective not offered, resulting
in popular misunderstanding of important issues.

During the 2000 presidential election, a journalist friend called me
during the night.

"You should see the crying in the newsroom," he said, in describing
how some of his colleagues reacted to the networks' premature awarding
of the election to George W. Bush. My friend observed "objective" anchors, reporters, and editors visibly crying at the announcement of a Bush
victory. Two other friends who also work in television news offered similar observations.

A recent poll showed 74 percent of Republicans believe that the media
tilts to the left, and nearly 50 percent of Democrats agreed that "most
journalists are more liberal than they are"![3]

In *Coloring the News: How Crusading for Diversity Has Corrupted American
Journalism,* William McGowan quotes Michael Barone, a senior writer for

U.S. News & World Report: "As managers seek a more superficial racial diversity of women, blacks, Hispanics, Asians, Native-Americans, etc. . . . rather than a true variety of viewpoints, newsroom cultures move farther left every year. On any suburban street in America you will find plenty of people who vote for Republicans and Democrats and are happy to tell you why. But in most newsrooms those few who vote Republican tend to keep their mouths shut, while those who vote Democratic smugly continue to assume that every decent, thinking person does the same."[4]

Newsweek's Evan Thomas said, on September 1, 2001, on *Inside Washington*, "There is a perception, even among journalists, that the *[New York] Times* is going a little bit left, is getting more liberal, and that's disquieting." To which Jack White of *Time* magazine replied, "That's a lot of hokum, with all due respect to Evan. There is no liberal bias in the press in the whole. In fact, if there is a bias, it's on the other side. It's hard to find a person really, truly, of the liberal persuasion who are making any important decisions in any important media institutions in this country now. I've looked for them, I consider myself one, I have very few birds of a like feather around."[5]

Norman Pearlstine, editor in chief of AOL Time-Warner magazines, vehemently agrees with Mr. White. On C-SPAN's *Washington Journal*, he said, "The *New York Times* is middle of the road. There is no active, aggressive, important publication of the left in America. And so as a consequence, the *New York Times* when compared to the *Wall Street Journal's* editorial page may be considered to the left of it. But to call the *New York Times* left-wing is absurd."[6]

Apparently, Norman Pearlstine and Jack White don't do lunch with Bernard Goldberg, the self-proclaimed liberal who—for most of his life—never even considered voting for a Republican. Check out Goldberg's take on media bias, in general, and the *New York Times*, in particular, "That's one of the biggest problems in big-time journalism: its elites are hopelessly out of touch with everyday Americans. Their friends are liberals, just as they are. They share the same values. Almost all of them think the same way on the big social issues of our time: abortion, gun control, feminism, gay rights, the environment, school prayer. After a while they start to believe that all civilized people think the same way they and their friends do. That's why they don't simply disagree with conservatives. They see them as morally deficient.[7]

"The *Times* is a newspaper that has taken the liberal side of every important social issue of our time, which is fine with me. But if you see the *New York Times* editorial page as middle of the road, one thing is clear: You don't have a clue."[8]

When will the denials stop?

Goldberg, with CBS news from 1972 to 2000, recently published a book called *Bias: A CBS Insider Exposes How the Media Distort the News.* In his book, Goldberg points out the obvious—mainstream media possess a leftist bias. Among Goldberg's observations:

"It is this inability to see liberal views as liberal that is at the heart of the entire problem. This is why Phyllis Schlafly is the conservative woman who heads that conservative organization but Patricia Ireland is merely the head of NOW. No liberal labels necessary. Robert Bork is the conservative judge. Lawrence Tribe is the noted Harvard law professor. Rush Limbaugh is the conservative talk show host. Rosie O'Donnell is simply Rosie O'Donnell, no matter how many liberal opinions she shares with her audience. . . .[9]

"Conservatives must be identified because the audience needs to know these are people with axes to grind. But liberals don't need to be identified because their views on all the big social issues—from abortion and gun control to the death penalty and affirmative action—aren't liberal views at all. They're simply reasonable views, shared by all the reasonable people the media elites mingle with at all their reasonable dinner parties in Manhattan and Georgetown. . . .[10]

"The media elites can float through their personal lives and rarely run into someone with an opposing view. This is very unhealthy and sometimes downright ridiculous, as when Pauline Kael, for years the brilliant film critic at the *New Yorker,* was completely baffled about how Richard Nixon could have beaten George McGovern in 1972: 'Nobody I know voted for Nixon,' Never mind that Nixon carried forty-nine states. She wasn't kidding."[11]

Here's another example. Recently, Anthony Lewis, the respected liberal columnist for the *New York Times*, retired at the age of seventy-four. A *Times* editor asked Lewis to talk about his career.

QUESTION: What have been the large themes of your columns?

ANSWER: I've dealt with concrete things, usually quite obsessively, because particular issues seem to be dominant in my mind: Vietnam, while that was going on, South African apartheid, and then the Middle East.

QUESTION: Have you drawn any big conclusion?

ANSWER: Maybe it's a twin conclusion. One is that certainty is the enemy of decency and humanity in people who are sure they are right, like Osama bin Laden and John Ashcroft. And secondly that for this country at least, given the kind of obstreperous, populous, diverse country we are, law is the absolute essential. And when governments short-cut the law, it's extremely dangerous.[12]

Don't bother waiting for the obvious follow-up question along the lines of, "Jeez, Osama bin Laden and John Ashcroft, moral equivalents?"

MY DINNER WITH A
BIG-TIME JOURNALIST

At a charity fundraiser, I sat next to a distinguished writer for a major newspaper. I accused the media of a liberal bias, and he angrily defended his profession. "I've been in this business," he said, "for decades, and I must tell you that most reporters are professional, do a good job, and don't let their emotions get in the way."

I told him the following anecdote about Al Sharpton. *USA Today* did a *full-page* story on Al Sharpton's announced candidacy for the year 2004. In this rather flattering, upbeat article, *USA Today* tells us about

Sharpton's "growth." "But Sharpton has spent the past decade trying to polish his image. He has launched peaceful campaigns of civil disobedience and run for political office. In April, he visited Sudan to see first-hand the slave trade among the Sudanese. He was outraged at what he saw and said civil rights activists should look into this modern-day slavery. . . . Many say they believe that Sharpton has become more cautious and sophisticated."[13]

Near the end of the article, though, after forty paragraphs, comes this little nugget: "Roughly 25 percent of African Americans did not know him, compared with 44 percent of the general population. Among blacks, 37 percent rated him favorably and 29 percent rated him unfavorably, while 10 percent of the general population rated him favorably and 41 percent unfavorably."[14] What?! Fifty-four percent of blacks either don't know him or don't like him, yet *USA Today* does a full-page letter about his "growth" and, by implication, his power.

Talk about a media creation, I told my journalist friend. A puff piece about a David-Duke-in-blackface hustler like Al Sharpton, a man disliked or unknown by the majority of blacks. Who picked him?

My journalist dinner companion had no answer.

All right, then what about stories on the minimum wage, where the reporters never mention that 90 percent of economists oppose minimum-wage laws?[15] If, for example, 90 percent of cardiovascular surgeons opposed triple-bypass operations, wouldn't every self-respecting reporter certainly mention this in a story on triple bypasses? Similarly, how can someone write a story about rent control and minimum wage without noting that nearly all economists oppose these things. To this, this distinguished journalist replied, "Well, I agree, but that's just bad reporting."

I then told him about the *Los Angeles Times* story on House Majority Leader Dick Armey (R-Texas), characterizing him as a "hard-line conservative." In my first book, *The Ten Things You Can't Say in America*, I noted that, over a period of ten years, the *Los Angeles Times* used the term "hard-line conservative" 71 times. What about a hard-line liberal? Surely, such a person exists. What does one call Jane Fonda,

Ted Kennedy, Barney Frank, Maxine Waters, etc.? But, over the same period of time, how many times did the *L.A. Times* use the term "hard-line liberal"? Twice. And once in reference to Mikhail Gorbachev. I told this to my respected journalist dinner companion. To this he said, "Hmmm."

Finally, I asked my companion whether he knew *Newsweek* writer Evan Thomas. "Yes, I do," he replied, "and I respect him." "Well," I said, "Thomas publicly acknowledges a liberal bias, at least on environmental issues."

On CNN's *Reliable Sources*, Thomas said, "Certainly the press is pretty green. The press is pretty pro-environment. And I don't think there's any question that they, as a body, feel that Bush is wrong on the environment, with varying degrees of willingness to give him credit. And I'm excluding the conservative press, the *Weekly Standard* and so forth. But generally, the rank-and-file press is pretty green, and they're gonna use the Europeans to take the Bushes to task."[16]

So, after vigorously denying the liberal's leftward bias, my dinner companion grudgingly acknowledged that, "Perhaps there's something to some of the things you said." Small victories. Either that, or he just wanted to end the conversation, so he could enjoy his dessert.

THE BIG DENIAL

Despite the denials, little by little, the cover gets peeled back. Author William McGowan, a past reporter for *Newsweek* and the BBC, quotes Arthur Sulzberger Jr., the publisher of the *New York Times*, as noting, "We can no longer offer our readers a predominantly white, straight male version of events and say that we, as journalists, are doing our job."[17] "Straight male version"? So newspapers push for "diversity." This way, "minority perspectives" receive attention. But does this affect the quality, fairness, and even-handedness of the reporting?

Many newspapers write uncritical stories about affirmative action, because of the ideological biases of the writers. Like stories on minimum wage, stories of affirmative action seldom include critical analyses of the very premise of race-based preferences. That is, diversity inherently "works." Does it? In *The Shape of the River: Long-Term Consequences of Considering Race in College and University Admissions*, Derek Bok of Harvard and William Bowen of Princeton argue that affirmative action students graduating from elite schools perform well upon graduation, thus confirming affirmative action's inherent value. But do they?

In *Coloring the News*, McGowan says, "The average black student at the elite schools that Bok and Bowen studied graduated with a GPA in the bottom quarter of his class, and the black dropout rate was triple that of whites in the same places. This seemed to suggest that black students admitted under racial preference programs were in fact at a disadvantage at these elite schools. Blacks also did far less well on bar exams; over the last twenty years, between 57 and 70 percent of the blacks who took the New York and California bar exams each year failed, as compared with 18 to 27 percent of whites, a disparity that seems to cast doubt on Bok and Bowen's assertion that though given a break on law school admissions, they performed just as well in their careers afterward."[18]

For purposes of balance, why not include stuff like this in articles on affirmative action?

Double standards abound. Remember the Supreme Court case, *Bakke v. Regents of the University of California*? UC Davis medical school denied admission to Allan Bakke, a white man, in favor of a less-qualified black man, Patrick Chavis. In defending affirmative action, Senator Ted Kennedy,[19] Tom Hayden, and black activist Constance Rice praised Dr. Patrick Chavis. Affirmative action works! After all, Chavis operated a clinic in the inner city and provided services that are anathema to any self-respecting white, Westside-living, Lexus-driving doctor. The *New York Times* magazine, in June 1995, ran a glowing 9,000-word puff piece on Chavis. The writer admiringly portrayed him as a physician who ministers to neglected black communities. The *Time* mag piece managed a brief mention of Dr. Bakke, saying "he does not appear to have set the world on fire as a doctor."[20]

But, oh-oh, Dr. Chavis lost his license to practice medicine after a number of lawsuits that alleged medical malpractice.[21] How many articles did the *New York Times* write when Chavis lost his license? An online search found exactly zero.

"Coverage of black political figures," says McGowan, "also tends to wink at the politics of excommunication practiced by black intellectuals and political activists on those who dare to dissent from liberal racial orthodoxy. The rhetorical abuse heaped on those who do speak out is often ugly, and would certainly be deemed impermissible if it came from whites. Yet political reporters and commentators often either ignore it or echo it, with black journalists functioning as hit men against those painted as 'traitors to the race.' "[22]

The media gave Jackson a pass on the "nonstory" of his hiring Representative Mel Reynolds. In 1995, Reynolds was convicted of charges of sexual misconduct with a sixteen-year-old campaign worker, for which he served 2½ years in prison. Reynolds was also convicted in 1997 on federal campaign fraud charges.[23] Only months after the end of the January 2001 commutation of his prison sentence by former President Clinton, Reverend Jesse Jackson hired Reynolds to work in Chicago's Rainbow/PUSH coalition, where he consults on prison reform.[24]

How many papers carried the story? A handful.

The evidence of media bias is so strong that at least some journalists find it difficult to deny. In the *Chicago Tribune,* writer John Kass belatedly and bluntly admitted the media's liberal white, guilt-ridden bias. After Jesse Jackson's brief fall from grace following allegations of an extramarital affair, Kass admitted his colleagues had long treated Jackson with kid gloves, and he attempted to explain why the intense media scrutiny of Jesse Jackson, his finances, and his modus operandi were long overdue:

For years, Jackson has been treated kindly. Here's my explanation.

In the media, we're white people, mostly, and mostly suburban born, mostly Democrats, terrified of being called racists, even if the charge comes from a hustler. Black reporters don't want to become targets, either.

So news organizations skip timidly around Jackson's finances, though we've known his race baiting has carried a price tag.

Perhaps it's because we in the media, particularly TV news, have also used him for decades, installing Jackson as chief black translator of the black American experience.

Through this condescending bargain, this queasy media pact laced with white liberal guilt and white liberal racism, the crafty Jackson has prospered.

His profile increased, while other black voices, those with legitimate yet differing views, were diminished.

We didn't want true diversity. We wanted it easy. We used him. And he used us.

Jackson understood this brazen contract.

. . . When the Karin Stanford story broke, Jackson said he would take a hiatus from public appearances, perhaps for months. He came back just three days later.

That's because in that short time, other black leaders were demanding to be heard. So he came back, and fast.

Jackson's finances, his deals, it's all a worthy story. Even more important is the urgency of other black voices, pushing for recognition, finally, in the aftermath of his disgrace.

But those of us who write this Jackson story shouldn't forget that there's another part too.

It's about us.[25]

Kass nailed it. The mostly white, overwhelmingly liberal media bears a large responsibility for the iconization of Jesse Jackson, a hands-off status that left him virtually shielded from deeper scrutiny. That kind of status is injurious to the corporations he hounded, and ultimately to us all.

The leftward bias of the mainstream media on issues of race, minimum wage, the glass ceiling, the alleged gap between the rich and the poor, racism, bilingual education, the continued monopoly of public education, Medicare, Medicaid, campaign finance reform, taxes, and spending misinforms the public.

This media mind-set of don't-hit-me-with-facts-that-challenge-my-worldview explains the amazing ignorance on matters of fertility. A recent *60 Minutes* piece found that most *women* were shocked when they found out how difficult it is to conceive while in their forties. But fertility specialists have known for years that the odds of a forty-year-old woman conceiving naturally is less than 10 percent. In a piece published the same week, *Time* magazine said, "Last fall [2001] the . . . [American Infertility Association] conducted a fertility-awareness survey on the women's website iVillage.com. Out of the 12,524 respondents, only one answered all fifteen questions correctly. Asked when fertility begins to decline, only 13 percent got it right (age 27); 39 percent thought it began to drop at forty. Asked how long couples should try to conceive on their own before seeking help, fully 42 percent answered thirty months. That is a dangerous combination: a couple that imagines fertility is no problem until age 40 and tries to get pregnant for thirty months before seeing a doctor is facing very long odds of ever becoming parents."[26]

The media routinely ignores counterviews from economists, scholars, and nonliberal members of academia. This shutout of alternative voices, says McGowan, helped spark the rise of talk radio. "While it may not always have its facts nailed down," says McGowan, "this populist, largely conservative medium does get out the news that mainstream journalists have long ignored or suppressed."[27]

Bernard Goldberg's *Bias* did to the media what *The Valachi Papers* did to the Mafia. The book quotes CBS News president Andrew Hayward: "Look, Bernie, of course there's a liberal bias in the news. All the networks tilt left."[28] Oh-oh.

Maybe, just maybe, they're finally starting to get it.

In 2002, MSNBC hired conservative Alan Keyes to host his own show. Earlier, Fox News hired Greta Van Susteren away from CNN. In general, no big deal, but Erik Sorenson, MSNBC's president and general manager, sniffed, "We did not know Fox was going to program one of the leading Clinton supporters [Greta Van Susteren]."[29] A network chief dissing another network's selection by calling her "one of the leading Clinton supporters"? Well, well.

And here's a saving grace. At least Geraldo Rivera admits media bias. Consider this exchange between the *Today Show*'s Matt Lauer and talk show host-correspondent-reporter Rivera:

> LAUER: As a journalist, now a member of NBC News, why should I expect that Geraldo Rivera is going to be objective when covering a story about O. J. Simpson or Ken Starr in the future?
>
> RIVERA: I think objectivity is a fantasy. I don't believe reporters are objective. Everyone comes to a story with their own bundle of personal experiences.
>
> LAUER: But most keep it secret or keep it private.
>
> RIVERA: But they secretly influence the take on the story or the angle, even if only subconsciously. What I do is lay out, 'Here I am.' I am—my heart is right here on my arm. Read it. The question to ask is whether I misrepresent anything? Am I factually correct? Is my program balanced and fair?[30]

Still, the leftist, mainstream media remain alive and well. The American public must learn to spot the subtle and not-so-subtle signs of bias. That way one can watch and read news the appropriate way—defensively.

GOOD MORON, AMERICA

Lack of balance means people remain uninformed.

On the *Today* show, for example, NBC News correspondent Keith

Miller reported from Paris, "Break out the band, bring on the drinks. The French are calling it a miracle. A government-mandated thirty-five-hour work week is changing the French way of life. Two years ago, in an effort to create more jobs, the government imposed a shorter work week on large companies, forcing them to hire more workers. . . . Sixty percent of those on the job say their lives have improved. These American women, all working in France, have time for lunch and a life."[31]

At the end of Miller's piece, Katie Couric—who, remember, just signed a $60 mil contract—gushed, "So great that young mother being able to come home at three every day and spend that time with her child. Isn't that nice? The French, they've got it right, don't they?"[32] Yeah, but does it really work out that smoothly? Cut hours, hire more workers—and everybody's happy.

Never mind that in an article on part-time workers, the *Wall Street Journal* argues the opposite case. "Even as some economists declare the recession over," writes the *Journal*, "one little-followed development in labor suggests that the downturn could be lengthier than the rosier projections indicate. Many employers, uncertain about how long this recession might last and wary of losing valued workers altogether, are reducing the workweek rather than the work force. The trend may soften the short-term effects of the recession and leave employers in better shape when it ends. But for many workers shifted from full-time work to part-time, the belt-tightening that results could help delay the recovery."[33] So, according to Couric, the French have it right, but according to the *Journal*, this kind of thing postpones an economic recovery. Agree or disagree, but Couric's remark shows that this "objective journalist" takes a side. That's the point.

CBS newsman Dan Rather attended a Texas fundraiser, cohosted by his daughter, a possible Democratic Party candidate for mayor of Austin. Like Al Gore's famous amnesia after visiting a Buddhist temple, Rather claims ignorance about the true nature of the meeting, "I didn't ask the question, and I should have," says Rather. "I take full responsibility for it. I'm responsible and I'm accountable."[34]

Rather's excuse? Said Rather, rather lamely, "When I got there, I was very aware that it was a fundraising event. I'm not going to say I had no idea what was going on. . . . If someone wants to fault me for that, I wouldn't blame them."[35] Fine. How much can one fairly make out of this?

But what did Rather do during Congressman Gary Condit's media frenzy over Chandra Levy, the missing intern? For eleven weeks, Rather incredibly failed to air a single story about the missing intern until the story had completely unfolded.[36] Even the *Times of London* weighed in on Rather's lack of coverage: "[Rather] has done his best to ignore the story. For eleven weeks he held the high moral ground, saying that unless the congressman was charged, no crime had been committed, and that one girl's disappearance in a country of 280 million people was not, on its own, a valid news story."[37]

Eleven weeks. Refusing to mention a story about a congressman whom the police had interviewed several times during that eleven weeks, even though other media were reporting that investigators considered charging the congressman with obstruction of justice and suborning perjury?! Rather remained silent. Restraint is one thing. Concealing a newsworthy story from the masses puts this on a whole different level. Media bias?

When he finally broke his silence, Rather explained to radio host Don Imus why he finally caved in and aired a report on the story: "What happened was they [CBS management] got the willies, they got the Buckwheats. Their knees wobbled and we gave it up."[38]

Yes, he said "the Buckwheats." *Investor's Business Daily* said, "Had such a reference—Buckwheat was the timid black child in the 'Our Gang' films—tumbled from Rush Limbaugh's mouth, the elite media might have taken notice."[39]

And how, when Congressman Gary Condit got into trouble over the missing intern, Chandra Levy, did he suddenly become "conservative"? The *Washington Times* calls him a "conservative."[40] The *Times of London* referred to him as a "right-winger."[41] The *Washington Post* called him a "Blue Dog Democrat."[42]

According to the *National Journal,* this "conservative" opposed school vouchers, the North American Free Trade Agreement (NAFTA), and the privatization of Social Security. Condit supported banning Mexican-registered cars unless they met California's clean air standards. He pushed for tougher air standards in the San Francisco Bay Area. And while he was one of thirty-one House Democrats to vote for the Clinton impeachment *inquiry,* he later voted against impeachment. In 1999, Democratic House Minority Leader Dick Gephardt invited Condit to serve on the party's leadership council—the "centrist" Democratic organization once led by Bill Clinton.[43] In fact, the liberal Americans for Democratic Action gives Condit a lifetime 52 percent rating, while he receives a lower 48 percent score from the American Conservative Union.[44] *That's* a "right-wing" Democrat?

What's more, the mostly liberal mainstream media seem reluctant to remind us that Condit even *is* Democrat. The Media Research Center (MRC) analyzed ABC, NBC, and CBS morning and evening news programs from May 14 through July 11. Of the 179 stories mentioning Gary Condit, only fourteen identified him as a Democrat. The MRC reported that, "Normally, a 'Republican' or 'Democrat' label is presented nearly every time a member of Congress is cited, as in 'Rep. Gary Condit (D-California).' But since May, the three broadcast networks have practically erased the 'D' from Condit's political identity, detaching the scandal-plagued politician from the rest of his party." And of the fourteen times that Condit actually was identified as a Democrat, nearly half were preceded with "conservative" or "right-wing" adjectives.[45]

ABC's *Good Morning America* (*GMA*), according to the MRC, rather belatedly mentioned Condit's party. After airing 26 stories on the Levy case, *GMA* first hinted that Condit was a Democrat when, on June 25, analyst George Stephanopoulos said, "A political maverick who rides a Harley, Condit founded the Blue Dog coalition of conservative Democrats."[46]

The Media Research Center pointed out, "Six additional stories conveyed Condit's affiliation without using a straightforward label. On the July 8 *CBS Evening News*, for example, Sandra Hughes didn't quite say that Condit was a Democrat but remarked that 'the Republican Party also sees weakness and may focus on gaining his congressional seat.' But even adding those six stories to those that plainly labeled Condit leaves 159 network stories, or 89 percent of the total coverage, which offered viewers no clue he was a Democrat. . . . Before he became controversial, Condit's party label was normally presented on those few occasions he appeared on a network news program. But now that the Levy case has made him a household name, you have to listen for a long time to hear a network reporter acknowledge Gary Condit's membership in the Democratic Party."[47]

Here's Bill Maher chatting about Condit on *Larry King Live*:

> BILL MAHER: OK. Talking about the fact that Gary Condit was one of those guys who called for Clinton to resign, right? He's one of those religious types.
>
> LARRY KING: Very conservative.
>
> MAHER: Very conservative.[48]

And Maher also managed to blame former independent counsel Ken Starr for Condit's troubles:

> MAHER: I do think, if it turns out that this beautiful young girl is gone, I think—and he is responsible in some way—you have to look to Ken Starr for a little bit of guilt.
>
> KING: Why?
>
> MAHER: Because, you know, Ken Starr made it so that you—in the old days, you had an affair with somebody, and you know, OK, you had an affair. The press didn't report it. They didn't make a political case of it. Now it's almost like you have to get rid of them. That is really what——
>
> KING: Ken Starr put that on them.
>
> MAHER: Yes, I think that's what Gary Condit . . . was going through his mind, is you know, I can't get caught with some-

one. If she's coming to me and saying she's pregnant or she's
going to the press——

KING: You're going to figure out a way to blame Ken Starr for
something, aren't you, Maher?

MAHER: I'm telling you, it's like that's a whole new wrinkle in
it.[49]

On July 9, George Stephanopoulos predicted on *Good Morning
America*: "I don't think the rest of the Democratic Party is going to get
tarred by Gary Condit."[50] No kidding. The more trouble Democrat
Gary Condit gets in, the more out-of-touch, conservative, and
"Republican-like" his voting record becomes. Odd.

THE CLINTON NO-FLY ZONE

After September 11, former President Bill Clinton gave a speech at
Georgetown University before approximately one thousand students.
Both the *Washington Times* and CNN wrote articles about the speech,
and both articles contained verbatim quotes from Clinton's speech.

CNN's Brad Wright covered the speech in his article entitled,
"Clinton Sees Struggle for 'Soul' of Twenty-first Century." Wright's
article on CNN's website ran the following quotations from the speech:

*There is a war raging within Islam about what they should think about the
United States in particular and the West in general. And we've now reached
a point with all these people lying dead and with all these terrorists, with the
anthrax and everything, where people need to actually say what it is that
they believe. What do you believe is right and wrong?*

*. . . We need to do a better job of getting the facts out. Most Muslims
in the Middle East, I guarantee you, don't know [that] the last time we
used our military power was to protect poor Muslims in Bosnia and Kosovo. . . .*

In the complex combustible mixture of a lot of these countries, a lot of the governments allow people to go into the mosques and demonize us, and demonize the West and demonize Christianity and demonize Jews, because as long as they do that, they think they're shifting the heat of popular distress off of the governments.[51]

Washington Times writer Joseph Curl also covered the speech. His article, entitled, "Clinton Calls Terror a U.S. Debt to Past," suggested that Bill Clinton practically blamed America for September 11, 2001. According to Curl, "Bill Clinton . . . said . . . that terror has existed in America for hundreds of years and the nation is 'paying a price today' for its past of slavery and for 'looking the other way when a significant number of native Americans were dispossessed and killed.' "[52]

The two reporters seemed to almost hear two entirely different speeches!

Curl's article also included this quotation from the speech: "It's no accident that most of these terrorists come from non-democratic countries. If you live in a country where you're never required to take responsibility for yourself, where you never even have to ask whether there's something you should be doing to solve your own problems, then people are kept in kind of a permanent state of collective immaturity and it becomes quite easy for them to believe that someone else's success is the cause of their distress."[53] Wow. Out of the mouth of Bill Clinton.

Let's put aside, for a moment, the Clintonesque gall. Imagine Bill Clinton lecturing someone on assuming personal responsibility. This, from a man who once rhetorically asked what to do about our budget surplus, and said, "We could give it all back to you and hope you spend it right."[54] In short, Clinton finds taxpayers too "collectively immature" to spend their own money.

How's this for media bias: Let's compare what the Big Three anchors had to say about our current and our previous presidents' first day in office. Background: as one of President Bill Clinton's first initiatives, he reversed some antiabortion policies of Presidents Reagan and Bush-41. During his first day in office, President George W. Bush reversed a proabortion policy of Bill Clinton's.

Clinton's First Day in Office
January 22, 1993

Peter Jennings, ABC News:
"President Clinton keeps his word on abortion rights. President Clinton kept a promise today on the twentieth anniversary of the Supreme Court decision legalizing abortion. Mr. Clinton signed presidential memoranda rolling back many of the restrictions imposed by his predecessors."[55]

Tom Brokaw, NBC News:
"Today, President Clinton kept a campaign promise and it came on the twentieth anniversary of *Roe vs. Wade* legalizing abortion."[57]

Bush's First Day in Office
January 22, 2001

Peter Jennings, ABC News:
"One of the president's first actions was designed to appeal to anti-abortion conservatives. The president signed an order reinstating a Reagan-era policy that prohibited federal funding of family planning groups that provided abortion counseling services overseas."[56]

Tom Brokaw, NBC News:
"We'll begin with the new president's very active day, which started on a controversial note."[58]

Dan Rather, CBS News:
"On the anniversary of *Roe vs. Wade*, President Clinton fulfills a promise, supporting abortion rights. It was twenty years ago today, the United States Supreme Court handed down its landmark abortion rights ruling, and the controversy hasn't stopped since. Today, with the stroke of a pen, President Clinton delivered on his campaign promise to cancel several antiabortion regulations of the Reagan–Bush years."[59]

Dan Rather, CBS News:
"This was President Bush's first day at the office and he did something to quickly please the right flank in his party: He reinstituted an anti-abortion policy that had been in place during his father's term and the Reagan presidency but was lifted during the Clinton years."[60]

Any questions?

So President Bill Clinton "keeps his word," "kept a campaign promise," "fulfills a promise." And despite the controversial nature of abortion, none of the anchors called Clinton's move "controversial," as if, of course, any fair-minded, responsible person would have done the same thing.

But in Bush's case, the anchors' tones appear almost prosecutorial. Bush didn't "keep a campaign promise." No, Bush acted "to appeal to antiabortion conservatives," "to quickly please the right flank in his party," and he "started on a controversial note."

The not-so-subtle theme: Clinton practices good government by honoring his promises. Bush, in contrast, caters to, and becomes the errand boy for, the "right flank" in his party, as if the party's non-right flank feels a whole lot different about abortion.

Much of the media also gave Hillary Rodham Clinton another pass. Shortly after September 11, Mrs. Clinton appeared on NBC's *Dateline*. Where, Senator Clinton, was daughter Chelsea on that fateful day? Here's what Senator Clinton told Jane Pauley:

SENATOR CLINTON: She'd gone on what she thought would be
   a great jog. She was going down to the Battery Park, she was
   going to go around the towers. She went to get a cup of coffee and—that's when the plane hit.

PAULEY: She was close enough to hear the rumble.

CLINTON: She did hear it. She did.

PAULEY: And to see the smoke . . .

CLINTON: That's right.

PAULEY: . . . in person, not on television.

CLINTON: No . . . [61]

But Chelsea Clinton wrote a first-person article about that fateful morning for the December 2001 issue of *Talk* magazine. Where did *Chelsea* say she was on September 11? "On the morning it happened I was at my friend Nicole Davison's apartment, near Union Square in Manhattan. . . . That morning we had gotten up and grabbed coffee, and then she took the subway to work while I bought a paper and headed back to her apartment. I had just walked in when she called from work. A plane had just crashed into the World Trade Center, she said. I should stay put and she'd call me back when she knew more. I turned on the television and watched as the second plane hit."[62]

Just a bit of a discrepancy.

A major news item, right? After all, Internet publisher Matt Drudge noted the conflicting accounts in his November 9 *Drudge Report*.

And, yes, the next day, the *Washington Times* and *New York Post* ran the story, both quoting Mr. Drudge. The *Times* said, "There are thousands of stories about the September 11 terrorist attacks that chronicle the human condition from every angle. But for now, public attention has focused on just two, and they do not jibe. Sen. Hillary Rodham Clinton and her daughter, Chelsea, have opposing accounts about that day."[63] The *Post* put it more bluntly. "Hillary and Chelsea Clinton should have gotten their stories straight. It turns out there are glaring discrepancies in their accounts of what Chelsea was doing on the morning of September 11."[64] But, by November 14, an on-line search of 550 U.S. newspapers turned up no other papers bothering to mention this, uh, discrepancy.

HELEN THOMAS'S GRANDMOTHER CLAUSE

Watch any White House press conference and UPI's Helen Thomas generally asks the first question. But there's one slight problem. Though Thomas spent nearly fifty years as a UPI correspondent, she no longer works for the wire service. And even though she's earned the respect of colleagues as well as presidents with her dogged questions, she now works for the *Houston Chronicle* as a *columnist*. This makes her an opinion giver, not a news gatherer and reporter.

She not only no longer serves as a reporter, but her columns and statements expose her as a President Clinton-loving, welfare-state-supporting leftist. On October 9, 2001, before the Greater Washington Society of Association Executives, Helen Thomas introduced former President Bill Clinton at a gathering of worshipful supporters. Shedding any doubt of where her politics lie, Thomas gushed, "He [has] . . . brought unprecedented prosperity to our nation, and because of that, President [Bush] can use the surplus Mr. Clinton left behind to pay for many of the nation's needs in this time of crisis. . . . He is the man from Hope, and that is what he has given us, hope." And to tie it up in a nice big bow, Thomas ended the coronation with, "We miss him."[65]

Former President Clinton then joked, "When I was told Helen Thomas was going to introduce me, I said, 'God, I hope she doesn't get to ask a question.' I thought her questions to me were term-limited. You know, when Helen left the UPI, some reporters wrote that she had given up her front row seat at the White House Press Conferences, but it turned out not to be so. In a town where power is supposed to be vested in the office and not the individual, she is the exception to the rule—the only person powerful enough to quit her job and still keep her seat, and I am profoundly honored to be with her tonight. America is a better place today because of the fifty-plus years she has given to the noble work of journalism."[66]

So Thomas credits Clinton with the economic boom of the nineties, completely neglecting the role played by Republicans. Remember Clinton's $31 billion stimulus package, touted as necessary for an economic recovery? Congress defeated it, yet the economy boomed. Remember Hillary's attempt to grab one-seventh of the nation's economy via Hillary-care, a horrendous intrusion of government into the healthcare system that threatened economic disaster? Congress stopped it. Clinton signed the immensely successful Welfare Reform Act of 1996 with more Republican support than Democratic, with party members calling it immoral and predicting starvation and death for the nation's poor. And, yes, Clinton signed NAFTA and the General Agreement on Tariffs and Trade (GATT), but again these received more Republican support than Democratic.

Thomas ignores this, crediting Clinton with the economy as a rooster credits himself with the sunrise. Fair enough, lots of people feel this way—that's what makes them Democrats. But this places Thomas firmly on the idea-giving side of the aisle, not on the news or reporting side.

In a recent column, Thomas defended "Taliban John" Walker as a simple, misguided youth deserving of a break. Thomas urged President George W. Bush to show leniency toward Walker, snidely reminding the president that he positioned himself as a "compassionate conservative."[67] Again, the column reveals her as an advocate for leniency for Walker, a position not shared by most Americans, but more importantly inconsistent with the press corps' job—that of serving as objective questioners of matters of the national interest. Sorry, despite Thomas's entertaining and feisty questions, she no longer qualifies to continue sitting there! And she isn't even subtle. "I used to write about things as they were and as I saw them," says Thomas. "Now I write about things as I want them to be."[68]

Why does she retain her position as a member of the White House correspondents' corps, retaining the privilege to ask the president a question? Could a male reporter retire, show up to work the following Monday, while retaining the same perks, powers, and privileges?

Arguably, Thomas gets kid gloves because of her advanced age. Yet aging Senators Strom Thurmond and Jesse Helms consistently serve as fodder for late-night comedians' "growing old" jokes, while Helen Thomas gets a no-fly zone.

Why not grant Clinton aide-turned-critic columnist/Fox TV analyst Dick Morris a ringside seat near the presidential podium? Why not, during the Clinton years, assign a front-row seat to columnist George F. Will, who once suggested Clinton was a rapist and said that Clinton "surely . . . is the worst person to be president?"[69]

In dismissing the charge of a leftist media bias, Elaine Povich, former Capitol Hill reporter for the *Chicago Tribune*, said, "One of the things about being a professional is that you attempt to leave your personal feelings aside as you do your work." Only the naïve consider reporters soulless automatons who always successfully set aside biases. Worse, in Thomas's case, we know her "personal feelings."[70] Now that we know, she loses credibility in performing the most important function of a free press—to serve as our watchdog over government.

Sorry, Helen.

MAINSTREAM MEDIA'S UNQUESTIONED SUPPORT FOR THE WELFARE STATE

The late Beatle George Harrison sounded positively Libertarian with his antitax song *Taxman*:

Don't ask me what I want it for . . .
And you're working for no one, but me.[71]

But unlike Harrison, many in the mainstream media seem to believe money falls from the sky. The *Los Angeles Times*, for example, recently ran an article about House approval of a bailout bill for the insurance companies. Its title, "House Votes to Aid Insurers if Terrorists Attack U.S. Again," tells it all.[72] "House Votes to Aid Insurers . . ."? No, the House agreed to spend some of your and my money.

The article says, "But industry officials say they cannot continue to insure against the incalculable liability from a future attack without government assistance." Without "government assistance"? *No*, without spending *your* and *my* money. Later, the article discusses "government assistance" and a "federal safety net," "federal assistance," "assistance," "the government," "protection."[73] But not one word about the taxpayer. Nothing about the individual on whose back the insurance companies receive the "assistance."

Peter Jennings, in an interview with Larry King, offered this reassuring assessment of the media's neutrality. "I think there is a mainstream media," said Jennings. "CNN is mainstream media, and . . . ABC, CBS, NBC are mainstream media. And I think it's just essentially to make the point that we are largely in the center without particular axes to grind, without ideologies which are represented in our daily coverage, at least certainly not on purpose."[74]

Nonpartisan? Mr. Jennings, after airing a story on childhood aggression in daycare centers, said, "The U.S. is actually the least generous of the industrialized nations. In Sweden, a new mother gets eighteen months of maternity and parental leave, and she gets 80 percent of her salary for the first year. Mother or father can take the parental leave any time until a child is eight. England gives eighteen weeks maternity leave. For the first six weeks, a mother gets 90 percent of her salary from the government and $86 a week thereafter. German women get two months of fully paid leave after giving birth. The government and the company kick in, and either parent has the option of three full years in parental leave with some of their salary paid and their jobs protected."[75] Journalism, or editorializing?

Bernard Goldberg writes of reporters' general ignorance of Economics 101. "Part of the problem is that most reporters and editors— television and print—are total dunces when it comes to the economy.

Most don't know a capital gain from a mutual fund. This, as much as bias, in some cases leads to the kind of reporting we see on the flat tax and a lot of other economic issues."[76]

Los Angeles Times business writer Warren Vieth called "deficit spending, a potent recession cure."[77] Deficit spending, "a potent recession cure"? Sure, lots of economists believe that, as did John Maynard Keynes, who advocated deficit spending. But many economists disagree, and urge spending cuts and low taxation.

"The Keynesian reflex has been around since the 1930s," editorialized *Investor's Business Daily*. "It's based on stimulating the demand side of economy with increased government spending or short-term tax cuts. Trouble is, there is no link between increased government spending and economic recovery . . . The failure of Keynesian economics is not unique to the U.S. Japan has been practicing Keynes's theories since 1990 and still can't rally its stagnant economy. Over that time, the country has passed ten stimulus packages, totaling more than $1 trillion. All that spending has produced nothing but staggering debt that's 120 percent of its stagnant economy, more than twice the debt of the U.S. . . . Far from government manipulation of the economy, supply-side policies give workers incentives to be more productive. Instead of shifting cash about, supply-side solutions boost growth. Cuts to taxes on capital gains, corporations, and individuals provide those very incentives."[78]

In his book *Basic Economics*, Thomas Sowell said, "John Maynard Keynes argued that government spending could put more money back into circulation and restore the economy to full employment faster than by waiting for prices to fall into balance with the reduced amount of money in circulation."[79] Sowell noted that both Herbert Hoover and Franklin Delano Roosevelt attempted this. "Scary as it may seem, neither president understood this much basic economics. Moreover, it did not just seem scary, it *was* scary, because the livelihoods of millions of Americans were at risk and many suffered disastrously. Although some have tried to depict FDR as the man who got us out of the Great Depression, all previous depressions had ended much sooner, without any major government intervention. This was in fact the first depression in which the federal government intervened so much, first under Hoover and then even more so under Roosevelt."[80] Indeed, ill-advised government intervention and policies transformed a severe economic slowdown into the "Great" Depression.

But not according to the *Los Angeles Times* business writer who offers theories as facts and editorials masquerading as journalism. In another article on the economy, Vieth tells us how the federal surplus, however temporary, came into being: "That [surplus] window was opened as a result of a series of politically painful budget reforms; tax increases and spending restraints approved during the administrations of Ronald Reagan, the elder George Bush, and Bill Clinton."[81] Penalty flag. Note the bias: the writer argues that the nineties surplus came about, in part, because of tax increases. Why, then, does Ronald Reagan describe his tax increases as the biggest mistake of his administration, even bigger than Iran–Contra? If tax increases keyed the surplus, why does George Bush-41 regret ever having broken his "no new taxes" pledge?

But the spend-to-get-us-out-of-trouble mantra lives on. About "Keynesians" economist Paul Craig Roberts sniffs, "As the adage goes, it is hard to teach old dogs new tricks, and Keynesians, who have spent four decades thinking in terms of spending and demand, find it hard to understand arguments about incentive and supply."[82]

Well, if the economists don't get it, what hope for Joe and Joan Sixpack, especially with newspaper articles like this—"deficit spending, a potent recession cure when administered properly."[83]

The writer doesn't even say, "Many economists argue . . . ," or "Some say. . . ." No, the writer states "deficit spending, a potent recession cure . . ." as if it were a certainty, a fact, not debatable in economic circles.

Again, the problem lies not with Mr. Vieth's Keynesian philosophy. Vieth's article implies that economists universally approve of deficit spending, ignoring the body of research and the large number of economists who disagree.

MEDIA BIAS AND LABELS

Toe-tag liberals simply assume darkness in the hearts of "conservatives." Take a look at Microsoft Word 98. Look up the word "liberal" in Word's thesaurus. Now look up conservative. Notice anything? Under liberal we see "reform, progressive, tolerant, generous." Now check out conservative: "inflexible, right-wing, unprogressive, obstinate, champion of the status quo."

Following the September 11 tragedy, the *New York Times* ran wonderful profiles of those who died in the World Trade Center attacks. About Edward C. Murphy, the newspaper wrote, "Defying Easy Categorization: Edward C. Murphy's life brimmed with contrasts and deep loyalties. He was a staunch Republican who invested in real estate and racehorses. *But* [emphasis added] he also helped nonprofit groups raise money for food and clothing for poor children in his native Clifton, N.J."[84] On the one hand, he voted like a "me first" Republican, but shockingly developed the giving dimension of his character such that he helped nonprofits raise money for food and clothing? Stop the presses! Conservative, bad. Progressive, good.

The use of ideological labels in describing think tanks and experts also reveals bias. Most newspapers, for example, properly call the Heritage Foundation, a Washington, D.C., think tank, "conservative." And most call the Cato Institute a "libertarian" think tank. And most call the Brookings Institution, another Washington, D.C., think tank, "liberal."

A *Los Angeles Times* article on November 10, 1999, for example, referred to the "conservative Heritage Foundation."[85] In the *New York Times*, the paper referred to the Brookings Institution as a "liberal-leaning research group."[86] And in a *Washington Post* article on "privatizing" Social Security, the paper called it the "liberal Brookings Institute."[87] And in a *Los Angeles Times* article by Robert Jackson, it referred to the "liberal Brookings Institute."[88] But not always.

In an August 30, 2001, *Los Angeles Times* article on the status of

George W. Bush's presidency, eight months or so into his term, co-author Hook used an anti-Bush talking head: "Thomas Mann, a scholar of the American presidency at the non-partisan Brookings Institution in Washington said . . ."[89]

"Nonpartisan"? In his book *Bias*, Bernard Goldberg chastised CBS for failing to point out "Brookings's decidedly liberal orientation."[90]

A recent "nonpartisan" Brookings Institution study, for example, found that blacks suffer from something they call a "segregation tax." What is a "segregation tax"? Well, according to the Brookings Institution, blacks live in "segregated" neighborhoods, avoided by many home buyers, which diminishes the competition for homes in these black neighborhoods, thus lowering the price. Never mind that predominantly black areas like Baldwin Park or Ladera Heights in Los Angeles have beautiful, appreciating housing stock. No, according to the "non-partisan" Brookings Institution, the great majority of white homeowners don't buy homes in black neighborhoods. "If there is less competition for a home that comes on the market," said a consultant on urban and suburban policy, "that is likely to keep the price down."[91]

Does it ever occur to the Brookings Institution that the diminished competition for homes in certain area stems from crime, poor schools, or a lack of labor opportunities? No. According to the "non-partisan" Brookings Institution, blame racism.

Nonpartisan? On November 10, 1999, the *Los Angeles Times* called the Brookings Institute "liberal," but by August 30, 2001, it suddenly became "non-partisan." Not bad, from liberal to objective and non-partisan in less than two years.

Read defensively. Sometimes things slip by in quite subtle ways. For example, the *Los Angeles Times* wrote about the replacement of the chairman of the Federal Energy Regulatory Commission. The newspaper described former Chairman Curtis L. Hebert Jr. as a "free-market apostle." Apostle? Get it? A blind believer in free markets. Never mind that in 4,000 years of recorded human history, price controls show abject failure. Never mind the collapse of the Soviet Union, founded on the premise that capitalism does not work.

The same article, however, described Hebert's replacement as a "pragmatist" who believes that "government should intervene if dysfunctional markets do not produce benefits for consumers."[92] So an all-knowing, benevolent body of bureaucrats who know precisely when to intervene in order to rescue "dysfunctional markets"—this constitutes pragmatism. No, it constitutes idealism, a quaint, romantic notion that suggests bureaucrats possess superior wisdom and judgement than individuals making their own decisions as they see fit. Pragmatism, indeed.

Fight media bias—read defensively.

8.

GUN CONTROL—WE TRIED
IT ROSIE'S WAY

*Between April and November 2001, the number of murders in the Metropolitan
Police area [of London] committed with a firearm soared by almost 90 percent
over the same period a year earlier. . . . Although all privately-owned handguns
in Britain are now officially illegal, the tightened rules seem to have had little
impact in the criminal underworld. No one knows how many illegal firearms there
are in Britain, although estimates range from between 200,000 to several million.
Whatever the true figure, it is said to be growing daily.*[1]

—BBC NEWS, *A COUNTRY IN THE CROSSHAIRS*

G un control" proponents shift the balance of power from the good
guys to the bad guys. Suppose the government did not mandate
waiting periods, or licensing, or registration, or safety locks, or trigger
locks, or one-per-month purchase limits. What then? The Wild West?
Road-rage shootouts on thoroughfares in our cities? Shootouts between
pistol-packing spectators at the Oakland Raiders football game? These
scary scenarios are absurd. In fact, according to the National Center for
Policy Analysis, "Licensees were 5.7 times less likely to be arrested for
violent offenses than the rest of the general public."[2]

We need to trust the law-abiding citizens. In reality, crime falls when
the bad guys don't know who's packing.

Recently, a Canadian wrote to the late Ann Landers bemoaning America's "love affair" with guns:

Dear Ann Landers:

*I am a Canadian who cannot understand why you Americans are so naïve
regarding your safety and the safety of your children. I know the Second*

Amendment states, *"The right of the people to keep and bear arms shall not be infringed,"* but I cannot believe your Founding Fathers would still feel this way if they knew innocent children were being slaughtered daily in one of the most advanced countries in the world.

A couple years ago, the Toronto Star *printed some very disturbing facts regarding guns in America. An article by Kathleen Kenna stated:*

Fifteen American children die from gunshot wounds every day.

In 1996, 9,390 Americans were murdered by gunfire. Compare that to 106 in Canada, thirty in Britain, fifteen in Japan and two in New Zealand.

The United States leads the world in using guns to kill its children. In 1997, of all the firearm deaths of kids under the age of fifteen in twenty-six industrialized nations, 86 percent of the victims were in the United States.

Gun-related murder is the leading cause of death among African-Americans age 15–24.

Guns are the second most frequent cause of death overall for Americans age 15–24, and they are the top killer of youth in California.

More kids are killed every year by guns in Washington state (population 5.5 million) than in Canada and Great Britain combined (total population 90 million).

Guns are the second leading cause of traumatic death related to a consumer product. (Automobiles are first.)

Wake up neighbors! Your children are being killed—thanks to the National Rifle Association and its lobbyists.
—Happy to Be Safe Living in Canada

Dear Safe in Canada:
Thanks for a sane and sensible letter. A while back, the National Rifle Association was touting its defense: "Guns Don't Kill People. People Kill People." How ridiculous can you get? Yes, people kill each other, but it is a lot easier if you have a gun.

Thanks for those statistics. I hope they open the eyes of your neighbors to the south. I have long believed that Canadians are a lot more civilized in this area than Americans.[3]

Landers's response speaks volumes about the emotionally driven, fact-free way gun-control supporters make their case. Nothing about the number of lives *saved* by people brandishing a gun to break off an attack. Japan's per capita suicide rate exceeds ours even with the island nation's stringent gun-control laws. Seventeen out of 100,000 people commit suicide in Japan compared to the U.S. rate of 11.1 per 100,000.[4]

The *Journal of the American Medical Association* (*JAMA*) examined the effects of the Brady Bill on the remaining thirty-two states that in 1994 the federal law required to adopt the Brady provisions. The JAMA study compared the homicide and suicide rates of the thirty-two "treatment" states to the eighteen "control" states that already had Brady-type gun restrictions prior to 1994. If the Brady Bill was being effective, shouldn't the "treatment" states show a post-1994 comparative decline in homicide and suicide rates? But the study found no statistical difference in homicides, and only one statistically significant change for suicide. While the *gun* suicide rate for persons fifty-five-and-over did decline by 6 percent, their *overall* suicide rate remained unchanged. Clearly these people simply chose another means to accomplish their objective.[5]

Ann Landers omits any mention, of course, of the Second Amendment, the Constitutional right to keep and bear arms. The term "right" means just that—not a shifting privilege subject to a cost/benefit analysis. She fails to mention the decreasing crime in the thirty-three states that allow citizens to carry concealed weapons.

We think of other countries as civilized, crime-free havens. But examine recent crime rates in Japan. According to the International Crime Survey, Japanese crime rates seem low compared to ours. But murder, rape, and arson in Japan increased 95 percent in the last decade, and the rates continue to climb.[6] Guns are outlawed in Japan, so the weapon of choice is often a knife. Japan is culturally and historically different from the United States, so comparisons are difficult. But the murder rate in Japan—a nation with outlawed guns—is about one per 100,000. In the United States, there are about 3.2 murders per 100,000 people each year by *weapons other than firearms*. In other words, even *without* guns in the United States, we would still have about three times the murder rate of the Japanese.[7]

What about Great Britain? That country suffers one of the highest contact crime (assault, robbery, sexual attack) rates in the world, with 3.6 percent, in a recent year, victimized by crime.[8] While the UK enjoys a lower murder rate, many other categories of crime exceed ours. According to the Department of Justice, British crooks rob, assault, and steal cars at twice the rates found in the United States.[9] While robberies rose 81 percent in England and Wales in the last several years, they fell 28 percent in the United States.[10] Similarly, assaults increased 53 percent in England and Wales, but declined 27 percent in the United States.[11] Burglaries doubled in England, but fell by half in the United States. Authorities call half of all burglaries in Britain "hot"—meaning a resident is at home when the criminal strikes. The U.S. "hot" burglary rate is 13 percent.[12]

All states should allow qualified citizens to apply for a permit to carry concealed weapons. But are guns too dangerous?

Widely publicized shootings frighten people into supporting further gun restrictions. For example, a jury convicted Nathaniel Brazill, a fourteen-year-old accused of murdering his middle-school teacher by pointing a gun at the teacher's face and pulling the trigger. The gun went off "accidentally," claimed the teenager from the stand. The gun went off accidentally? Therein lies a problem. Only someone unfamiliar with guns would buy the argument that "it accidentally went off." Ignorance and unfamiliarity with guns drives the debate. Women buy into gun-control arguments because many lack an understanding of guns. And since guns "go off by themselves," many women quite naturally fear them. But it's the fear—not the facts—that drive the debate. Follow the facts. They show that gun restriction helps the bad guys while hurting the rest of us.

Even though America remains "awash" with guns, police shootings continue to drop. When states allow citizens to apply for permits to carry concealed weapons, the violent crime rate drops.

MORE GUNS, FEWER TERRORISTS

Now pilots get it. On the morning of September 11, four planes took off while governed by FAA rules. FAA policy assumed those who hijacked planes did so with a political objective and a desire to land the plane safely, which would then be followed by negotiations. But the World Trade Center, the Pentagon, and western Pennsylvania changed all that.

Hijackers boarded with box cutters, permissible under FAA rules, and the hijackers commandeered planes, easily breaking through the flimsy, FAA-approved cockpit doors.

The government grounded planes for several days after September 11, and for several days after resuming flights, airlines proceeded without specific FAA guidance. But without guidance, airlines made commonsense decisions. On one of the first post–September 11 flights, a United Airlines plane flew out of Denver. The plane's pilot, noting the lack of FAA direction, gave the following announcement to the passengers over the intercom:

> I want to thank you brave folks for coming out today. We don't have any new instructions from the federal government, so from now on we're on our own. . . . Sometimes a potential hijacker will announce that he has a bomb. There are no bombs on this aircraft and if someone were to get up and make that claim, don't believe him.
>
> If someone were to stand up, brandish something such as a plastic knife and say 'This is a hijacking' or words to that effect, here is what you should

do: Every one of you should stand up and immediately throw things at that person—pillows, books, magazines, eyeglasses, shoes—anything that will throw him off balance and distract his attention. If he has a confederate or two, do the same with them. Most important: Get a blanket over him, then wrestle him to the floor and keep him there. We'll land the plane at the nearest airport and the authorities will take it from there.

Remember, there will be one of him and maybe a few confederates, but there are 200 of you. You can overwhelm them. "[13]

Not bad, given the lack of guidance by the Feds.

According to *Washington Times* columnist Peter Hannaford, who wrote about this incredible pilot announcement, it took no federal law for a United Airlines captain to instruct his passengers on a September 15, 2001, flight. Hannaford said, "The end of this remarkable speech brought sustained clapping from the passengers. He had put the matter in perspective. If only the passengers on those ill-fated flights [on September 11] had been given the same talk, I thought, they might be alive today."[14]

The Air Line Pilots Association, with a membership some 67,000 strong, has long opposed arming pilots.[15] They assumed, as many antigun folks do, that guns offer more risks than benefits. Then they got religion.

El Al, the Israeli airline, understands terrorism. Double-steel cockpit doors seal off the pilot and copilot, and they do not come out until and unless the plane lands safely. The pilots also carry firearms, as do several plainclothes sky marshals on each plane. The flight attendants also undergo hours of training in martial arts and self-defense.

After September 11, the Air Line Pilots Association pulled a 180 and now strongly supports allowing any pilot who wishes to carry a firearm to do so.[16] "It is probably safe to say that the entire aviation industry . . . enjoyed a false sense of security before September 11," union president Captain Duane Woerth told the House Transportation Aviation Subcommittee. "We must replace that false sense of security with a genuine sense of security." His union's revised post–September

11 guidelines state, "The pilot must be prepared to kill a cockpit intruder."[17]

"Those men and women operate $100 million pieces of equipment," says aviation consultant Michael Boyd. "They can sure learn to operate a .38 snub-nose if they want to. I'd rather have the gun in the hand of the pilot than the gun in the hand of some guy . . . who wants to kill people."[18]

Congress, however, balks at allowing pilots to carry firearms. House Majority Leader Dick Armey, skeptical about the proposal, said he would "have more of an affinity for" arming pilots with stun guns.[19] Dick Gephardt said, "I don't think we need pilots to be trying to be security officers and pilots."[20] Even President George W. Bush, whom opponents once derided as a Texas cowboy, failed to back the pilots' request.[21]

But in a letter to the Federal Aviation Administration, Boeing 737 Captain W. J. "Skip" Hapeman said, "It seems quite incredible to me that I am entrusted daily with a $40 million aircraft and the lives of many hundreds of passengers, but the FAA, in their questionable wisdom, does not trust me with a firearm."[22]

The airline pilots refuse to take this lying down. The union passed a resolution demanding the right to carry firearms and insisting that, if refused, the planes will stay parked.

The LAPD Protective League sided with the airline pilots and suggested that airlines allow flying off-duty police officers to carry their weapons. League President Mitzi Grasso sent a letter to Attorney General John Ashcroft demanding the right for off-duty law enforcement personnel to carry their weapons while traveling.[23] After all, over 600,000 people serve in law enforcement in America,[24] many of whom fly at any given time. The current rules, however, forbid off-duty law enforcement personnel from carrying a firearm without a special purpose and without written permission. So, with off-duty personnel allowed to carry firearms, the bad guys cannot identify the one or two plainclothes sky marshals, assault them first, and assume no further professional resistance. Not if among the two hundred or so passengers lurked two or three undercover, off-duty cops trained to act.

In their letter, the LAPD union chief said, "If the public knows that additional protection is available to them through trained and credentialed officers, they will feel much safer traveling via airplane. . . . We request that the federal government expand this permission to all off-duty state and federal peace officers. . . . If this program can be launched in California through an existing course . . . we believe it can easily be implemented in other states. However, should you feel that taking this program nationally is not a viable option, then we suggest that you consider allowing officers to be armed on flights within their own state or between states that approve of their training."[25]

The one-size-fits-all government solution remains predictable—the feds should take a *greater* role in airport security. But how often does the FAA issue a ruling only to have the ruling ignored or enforced so infrequently that the rule ceases to exist?

On the television show *Crossfire*, former Secretary of Transportation Rodney Slater confronted Michael Boyd, aviation analyst and cofounder of the Boyd Group. Boyd called the FAA's oversight "pat," and launched into a diatribe concerning all the different things the FAA has promulgated and never done:

> [*The Secretary of Transportation*] *stood behind President Bush when he signed the bill, and then a week later, he said, "Oh, George, we can't do this." The point of the matter is, let's be honest with the American public. There is no hard way and no totally effective way of checking all the checked luggage for explosives. There are things we could do . . . that Europe does. For example, they X-ray all checked luggage, and we should do that. They also then, with exceptions, put them through these computer tomography machines—that's a tongue twister—and they check those on a random basis. What Congress has mandated to do—I think Congress thought all we need to do is bless something and say, "We legislate it," it'll take place. It can't. Secretary of Transportation came out last week and said . . . "Dogs? They*

can only sniff for thirty minutes. No one told us that." Now that's outra-
geous. We knew this was an unattainable thing. And secondly, the machinery
they're picking to do it doesn't work very well. We have ample evidence of
that. The problem is we need to deter this, not play hide and seek. But don't
lie to the American public by saying, "We can check every bag with any
kind of certainty." The equipment doesn't exist.[26]

Or—here's a thought—how about letting pilots carry guns? One expert told me that there are one hundred ways to bring down a plane, and 100 percent safety is unrealistic. Well, do you refuse to lock your front door because a burglar can enter the window?

REVISITING THE ARGUMENT
FOR "GUN CONTROL"

The same arguments for allowing off-duty police officers to carry guns apply to civilians in the streets. The bad guys don't know who's packing. The thirty-three states which allow a citizen to carry concealed weapons also rely on this notion of "randomness."

After September 11, even gun-control-supporting liberals now revisit their positions. Antigun correspondent Geraldo Rivera dispatched himself to Afghanistan for a close-up look at the war. On *The O'Reilly Factor*, Bill O'Reilly asked Rivera whether Rivera traveled with a gun. After all, on CNBC Rivera once reacted to a video excerpt of NRA president Charlton Heston, "That smell of bulls——t. . . . How much longer are we gonna be wrapping in the flag of patriotism to justify 250 million guns out there?"[27]

On April 27, 2001, on *Rivera Live*, he said, "It was an off-the-cuff, I think politically brilliant speech today as President Clinton evoked his own Arkansas childhood and its gun culture then challenged all of us, all his fellow citizens to change their long-held ways of thinking. Guns are incredibly easy to buy in this country. I've mentioned it and I think it is the most bitter irony of all that in Colorado you can get a gun at eighteen and you can't buy a drink until you are twenty-one. I mean what the hell is that about? What? What genius thought up that scheme? I mean it makes me sick to my stomach. . . .

"Conservative commentators have been so willing and so able to point the finger of responsibility for the Littleton massacre at violent movies or video games. I think it is criminally irresponsible not to talk about the need for gun control. So God bless the president and the first lady. I'm telling you, though, if the popularity of these gun shows are any indication, it is easier said than done to get this thing changed."[28]

At the time of the antigun Million Mom March, Rivera said, "I hate the things [guns]."[29]

And now? Afghanistan Rivera told O'Reilly, "I think that if you're traveling, if you're a journalist traveling outside the central city or . . . the capital city without an armed escort, you're a fool. The old days when a journalist could hold up a press card and say, I'm a neutral, I'm not taking sides, I'm here to report honestly, fair and balanced, what's going on, those days are gone."[30]

The same day, on another program, Rivera also said, "My brother, Craig, and I—I said this yesterday. We refuse to be crime victims. We're not the victim types. If they're going to get us, it's going to be in a gun fight. It's not going to be a murder. It's not going to be a crime. It's going to be a gun fight."[31]

Note that Rivera and his brother refused to be "crime victims." Rivera did not say, "We refuse to be killed in a war zone, or as a war correspondent in a treacherous and dangerous area." No, he declared himself not a "victim type."

According to Jared Taylor in *Paved With Good Intentions*, "In Harlem, there are so many killings that a black man living there is less likely to reach age sixty-five than is a man living in Bangladesh."[32] What about people in the inner city who refuse to be "victim types"? What about them?

Pre September 11, *Time* magazine featured a story on the rise of gang violence in Los Angeles. *Time* says, "From 1996 to 1999, gang murders in the city increased 143 percent [in 2000]."[33] Call them domestic terrorists, for they often prey on the innocent, intimidating neighbors, and terrifying witnesses who testify.

The Los Angeles Police Department, currently rocked by the biggest scandal in its history, faces mounting criticism over alleged excessively aggressive tactics. In Los Angeles' so-called Rampart Scandal, Rafael Perez, from the special antigang unit—CRASH (Community Resources Against Street Hoodlums)—admitted fabricating evidence and falsely testifying against gang members suspected of serious crimes.[34] While the scandal involves less than a fraction of 1 percent of all police officers, it gave the "hate-the-cops" crowd all the ammo they needed. "O.J. Simpson was right," many cried. "The cops do plant evidence."

Predictably, the cops pulled back. No longer "proactive," the cops fear negative community reaction if they aggressively police, and they fear being called "racist," prompting an official investigation that many cops deem unfairly tilted in favor of the criminal.

Gang members grow brazen in the face of police passivity. For example, *Time* magazine says, "On a Saturday night in the Playboys' neighborhood, three young gang members are hanging out—Rowdy, Spotter and Mad Dog. Spotter has taken a sniper's position with a rifle on top of a building overlooking Pico. Rowdy is down at the corner with a Beretta handgun in a pocket of his baggy pants, and Mad Dog is standing in the street, flashing gang signs at passing cars and looking to draw fire from any rival gangster who might be passing.[35]

" 'That is what you call bait,' says Spotter with a laugh, looking down the sights of the rifle. He whistles a warning to his homeboys on the street. A black-and-white comes into view, doing a slow lap around four or five blocks, up Pico, across Mariposa, down and back around. Then it leaves. The Playboys laugh at the departing cops. Two years ago, CRASH teams were all over them, jumping out of their patrol cars to search them for weapons and drugs, getting them to pull up their shirts to show their tattoos, pumping them for information about shootings. These days the cops barely engage."[36]

Yet LAPD Chief Bernard Parks refuses to grant permits to carry concealed weapons, no matter how crime-ridden the neighborhood, no matter whether your job requires you to catch a bus at 2 A.M. headed for downtown. Too bad.

To whom do poor inner-city residents turn? Certainly not their lawmakers. Most lawmakers who represent inner-city residents also fear an "out-of-control" armed public. Can inner-city residents, like Congress, pass a resolution refusing to leave their homes and go to work unless granted the right to carry concealed weapons? Can inner-city residents grind air traffic to a virtual halt if they don't get their way, as the Air Line Pilots Association now threatens?

Three weeks after the terrorist attacks, a man armed with a box cutter boarded a Greyhound bus in Louisville, Kentucky. As the bus traveled along the highway near Manchester, Tennessee, in the Nashville area, the passenger jumped up and slit the bus driver's throat with the box cutter. The bus lurched off the road, and six people died, including the assailant. The driver survived.[37] Federal laws prevent even those with permits to carry concealed weapons while traveling interstate unless traveling from a state where one may lawfully possess a firearm to another state where one may lawfully possess a firearm. But even here, federal law imposes strict conditions.[38] Even though Kentucky, like Tennessee, allows citizens to arm themselves, federal rules control interstate traveling, and those rules offered a guarantee to the assailant that no one would resist with a gun. In Tennessee, more than 86,000[39] residents out of over five million[40] possess permits to carry concealed weapons. In concealed-carry states, only about 2 percent of the population ever apply for a concealed weapon permit,[41] but the bad guys don't know which 2 percent. That's the whole point. Odds suggest, on that Tennessee bus, there might have been one civilian with a gun—but federal law would have required him to turn in the unloaded gun to the driver. Who knows, maybe one armed civilian, and we have a different result.

Even the police brass seem on board with the idea of responsible citizens carrying concealed weapons. According to a survey by the National Association of Chiefs of Police, over 60 percent of police chiefs and sheriffs wish to allow law-abiding citizens to carry concealed weapons. For the first time in the survey's fourteen-year history, the survey asked the following question: "Do you agree that a national concealed handgun permit would reduce rates of violent crime as recent studies in some states already reflected?" Sixty-two percent of respondents said "yes."[42]

GUN CONTROL PROPONENTS— LYING TO PERSUADE

Some of the antigun crowd simply lie to make their case. Emory University historian Michael Bellesiles wrote a widely reviewed book, *Arming America: The Origins of the National Gun Culture*. Bellesiles argued that, contrary to popular belief, few early Americans and settlers possessed guns! Guns were costly, unreliable, with parts hard to find.[43] When Bellesiles published his book in September, 2000, anti-gunners cried, "Hallelujah," as if they had uncovered the antigun "Rosetta stone" that dismantles the arguments of the "gun lobby."

Reviewers embraced the book. *Los Angeles Times* reviewer Fred Anderson said, "The availability of guns, together with the conviction that they could be used to serve political or social ends (the preservation of the union, the expansion of freedom, the perpetuation of white supremacy, the protection of the family and so on) created America's modern gun culture in the 1860s and 1870s. The mystique of an armed citizenry and myths of minutemen, frontiersmen and gunslingers sustain it to this day, despite mounting social costs. With thorough scholarship, lucid writing and impassioned argument, Bellesiles offers a brief against the myths that align freedom with the gun."[44]

New York Times reviewer Gary Wills gushed, "Bellesiles deflates the myth of the self-reliant and self-armed virtuous yeoman of the Revolutionary militias."[45]

At *The Chronicle of Higher Education*, one could hear the high-fives as the publication practically performed the scholarly equivalent of "the

Wave." It featured the book on its front page, with the headline, "Exploding the Myth of an Armed America."[46]

And *The American Prospect* wrote, "The image of . . . the American founders believing in an individual's right to keep and bear arms . . . turns out to be a myth."[47]

The *Atlantic Monthly* referred to the notion of guns as instruments of liberty and equality as "self-evidently crazy."[48]

The antigun crowd embraced Bellesiles's book because he provided ammo against a "pro-gun argument"—namely, that America was founded upon a "gun culture," with guns as American as Mom and apple pie. Not so, says Bellesiles.

But, iceberg ahead. Northwestern University law professor James Lingren said, "In virtually every part of the book examined in detail, there are problems."[49] In an article called "Gun Control Book Based on Faulty Data," University of Tennessee law professor Glenn Harlan Reynolds reveals that Bellesiles, in making his argument that few early Americans owned guns, relied on probate records. Presumably, since people list their possessions in their wills, Bellesiles felt he could determine gun ownership percentage. But, says Professor Reynolds, "The data sets Bellesiles drew from the probate records he claims to have examined are unavailable; Bellesiles says they were destroyed in a flood. Even more damning, one set of records that Bellesiles says he relied on were destroyed in the 1906 San Francisco earthquake and have been unavailable to anyone since then *without access to a time machine*."[50] [Emphasis added.]

Still more trouble for Bellesiles. His school, Emory University, has questioned whether the data provided "prima facie evidence of scholarly misconduct" and ordered a probe.[51] And the National Endowment for the Humanities (NEH), apparently seeking to distance themselves from the controversy, withdrew its name from a fellowship for Bellesiles, saying, "The name of the National Endowment for the Humanities represents a standard that Professor Bellesiles's application . . . did not meet."[52]

But while reviewers failed to question Bellesiles's data, lay readers did not. Nonprofessional reviewers, notes Professor Reynolds, wrote and posted skeptical reviews on Amazon.com. Reynolds said, "Amazon reader Sondra Wilkins did something that [*New York Times* reviewer] Garry Wills did not: She checked some of Bellesiles's sources and reported: 'In checking his sources, often the ones he lists, even the particular pages that he lists, contain evidence that contradicts his claims. He quotes parts of sentences from those sources and ignores the contradictory information on that same page.' "[53]

According to Reynolds, "Another reader, David Ihnat, said he couldn't believe Bellesiles's claim that it took three minutes to load and fire a muzzle-loading rifle. His report: 'Never having fired a flintlock before, I tried to load and fire ten times in succession, and was able to average fifty seconds per load.' His conclusion: 'Bellesiles has an axe to grind, and worked it throughout this book.' "[54]

How do they get away with it? They know that the antigun sentiments of most reporters ensure little scrutiny. Professor Reynolds said, "But for our purposes, it doesn't matter whether Bellesiles is a fraud. . . . Because there's another failure here. . . . The people who should have examined his evidence rushed to embrace it, because *it told them what they wanted to hear.*"[55] [Emphasis added.]

A red-faced *New York Times*, upon learning about the apparent faulty data, said, "Over the past year a number of scholars who have examined his sources say he has seriously misused historical records and possibly fabricated them."[56] But even here, the *New York Times* gave Bellesiles some love. "Without doubt," said the *New York Times,* "Mr. Bellesiles's research would not have received such careful scrutiny if he had not stepped into the politically and ideologically charged struggle over guns." Still, Bellesiles's research forced the *Times* to say, "Yet the scholars who have documented serious errors in Mr. Bellesiles's book— many of them gun-control advocates—do not appear to have any sort of political agenda."[57] They don't *appear* to have any sort of political agenda—or at least, the writer couldn't find one before his deadline. But hey, let's keep that door open, just in case we find out one of them has a cousin in the NRA!

And what does Mr. Bellesiles have to say? Not much. "Mr. Bellesiles has refused all media comment for months," says the *Washington Times*. "He has responded to the charges only in an article in the *William and Mary Quarterly* in which he impugned the motives of the book's critics."[58]

Post September 11, gun stores report record sales. This alarmed people like Sarah Brady, head of the organization formerly known as the National Council to Control Handguns. Now called Handgun Control, Inc., they recently posted data designed to discourage people from using guns for self-defense. After all, goes their thinking, guns kill, and their absence must mean fewer deaths, suicides, and accidents. The Brady Center to Prevent Handgun Violence recently posted an article called, "In the Wake of Terrorist Attacks, Sarah Brady Warns About Risks of Guns in the Home." The article contains these frightening "statistics."

1. A gun kept in the home is twenty-two times more likely to be used in an unintentional shooting, a criminal assault or homicide, or an attempted or completed suicide, than to be used to injure or kill in self-defense.
2. When someone is home, a gun is used for protection in fewer than 2 percent of home invasion crimes.
3. The risk of homicide in the home is three times greater in households with guns.
4. The risk of suicide is five times greater in households with guns.[59]

I asked John Lott, author of the book *More Guns, Less Crime*, to comment on these statistics. He says that if a gun is physically present in the house when a crime occurs, for the purposes of these stats, they assume that the good guys own the gun, even if the bad guy brought the gun inside the house. So even if the good-guy victim owns no gun—he goes into the gun-in-the-home column.

These sharply skewed stats also don't inform the reader that in a self-defense case, 98 percent of the time simply brandishing a gun is sufficient to stop the crime. According to John Lott, research at Florida State University and at the University of Chicago indicates that only one out of 1,000 defensive gun uses results in the attacker's death.[60]

Surely, one would think, reporters grew skeptical about Brady's claim? Wrong. Antigun stories confirm the gut instincts of reporters, many of whom simply dislike the Second Amendment.

Can we expect a diminished bias against guns from the media? Not any time soon, but a sliver of hope appears from time to time. For example, the *Los Angeles Times* issued a challenge to Professor John Lott: Take a week and find citizens who use guns for defensive purposes.

Now, understand the difficulty of this assignment. Citizens who use guns for defensive purposes seldom call the police, let alone reporters— thus the ignorance of how frequently Americans use guns for defensive purposes. Professor Lott, however, accepted the challenge. He produced twenty examples in that week alone.[61]

To their credit, the *Los Angeles Times* published his findings. In one case, in Salt Lake City, "Two robbers began firing their guns as soon as they entered a pawn shop. The owner and his son returned fire. One of the robbers was shot in the arm; both later were arrested. The shop owner's statement said it all: 'If we did not have our guns, we would have had several people dead here.' " Another example was in Baton Rouge, "A crack addict kicked in the back door of a house and went in. The attacker was fatally shot as he charged toward the homeowner."[62]

A copy of *The American Rifleman* put out by the National Rifle Association would have saved the *L.A. Times* a great deal of time. Every month they run a column called *The Armed Citizen*, giving real-world stories of defensive uses of guns. A recent issue contained the following:

Bobby Wolfe was locking the front door of his Moon Lake, Miss., store one night when a man came around the icebox near the door, pointed a gun and demanded money. "He had a gun in his hand, and the other hand was over his face," Wolfe recalled. The storekeeper dropped and pulled a .38-cal. revolver from his pocket. "We think the robber shot first and Mr. Wolfe returned fire," stated Cuohoma County Sheriff Andrew Thompson of the exchange that followed. When Wolfe took off running for his nearby home, he encountered a second gunman who began firing at him. "He shot two or three times, and I shot one more time," said Wolfe. Within five minutes of the robbery, one gunman was dead, Wolfe was wounded, and police picked up three suspects—one of whom was mortally wounded—making a getaway. Wolfe later said of the men, whom he recognized, "I'm sure they intended to kill me because they knew I'd recognize them." (The Clarksdale Press Register, Clarksdale, Miss., 10/29/01)

A 32-year-old man was shot and killed in North Hollywood when he slashed through a door screen with a knife and threatened to kill everyone inside. The man, identified as Tony Saucedo, allegedly had assaulted his ex-girlfriend in her home. She then ran to a neighbor's home. A witness said Saucedo, knife in hand, began searching for her. He approached the wrong house and was shot once in the chest as he cut through the screen and attempted to force his way inside. (The Los Angeles Times, Los Angeles, Calif., 10/16/01)

A 78-year-old Franklin, Ind., woman was rudely awakened at 1 o'clock one morning by a loud banging sound at the back of her house. When she discovered a man kicking in the wall next to her back door, she picked up her .25-cal. handgun and dialed 9-1-1. While she was on the phone with police, the would-be intruder kicked a large hole in her wall and tried to push his way into the house. The resident ordered him to stop and, when he did not cooperate, she fired a shot at him. The man backed out of the hole and was met by police, reported Officer John Moore. (Indianapolis Star, Indianapolis, Ind., 10/24/01)

When a Leesville, Ohio, store owner discovered an unwelcome after-hours visitor in his bait and tackle shop, he pulled out a .22-cal. revolver and held the burglary suspect for police. Lieutenant Shane Steele of the Carroll County Sheriff Dept. said there were no struggles or injuries involved *in the capture. The owner "detained the suspect until we got down there," said Steele. (*The Times-Reporter, *New Philadelphia, Ohio, 10/24/01)*

*The manager of a Citgo gas station/mini-mart shot and killed a robbery suspect when the man appeared to be reaching for his gun. The manager had observed a female clerk being robbed at gunpoint on the store's video monitor. When the manager confronted the suspect at the front of the store, he said the robber appeared to be reaching into his waistband, so the manager shot him. According to Angelique Cook-Hayes, a police spokeswoman, the would-be robber was carrying a BB gun that resembled a semi-automatic handgun. (*The Baltimore Sun, *Baltimore, Md., 10/28/01)*

*An elderly man shot an intruder after the man forced his way into a house and assaulted the homeowner and his wife. The couple had heard noises from the back of their house, then they saw a stranger walking from the back yard to the front yard. When they went to their front door to see what was going on, the stranger forced his way into the home and a brief struggle ensued, with the intruder pushing and grabbing at the homeowners. When the interloper then bolted toward the back of the house, the homeowner grabbed his gun from a bedroom and shot his attacker when he again tried to assault him. (*The Post and Courier, *Charleston, S.C., 10/7/01)*

*A seventy-seven-year-old woman shot one of two men as they tried to break into her home early one morning. The woman told deputies she had been awakened about 1:30 in the morning when she heard someone banging loudly on her back door. The homeowner, who lives alone, grabbed her .38-cal. handgun and fired four shots, striking one intruder as he attempted to climb through a bedroom window. The suspects fled in a car and then crashed into a guardrail on a nearby highway. (*Lexington Herald-Leader, *Lexington, Ky., 10/30/01)*[63]

Now let's apply this to September 11, 2001. What if airline personnel carried weapons? Al Marchand, one of the stewards on United Airlines Flight 175, the second plane that crashed into the World Trade Center tower, spent 21 years as a highly decorated police officer. An ex-military man, Marchand frequently traveled for pleasure. "Why couldn't we trust someone like Marchand with a gun?" asks Professor

Lott. "The terrorists knew the planes were gun-free zones and they didn't have to worry about someone on the plane being armed. Possibly police or military personnel might need to take a short course before qualifying. There are about 600,000 active state and local law enforcement officers in the U.S. today, and many travel on vacation. Discount fares could be given to those who fly with their guns."[64]

Following September 11, an off-duty cop told me that he called to participate in the federal sky marshal program. Sorry, they told him. He was ineligible for the program. Why? The program refuses anyone over thirty-seven years of age! Thus, we kick to the curb all these over thirty-seven, retired, often-distinguished law enforcement personnel. This is simply beyond dumb.

Before September 11—just like the arguments against racial profiling—emotions, rather than fact, logic and history drove the argument against guns.

Let's revisit.

9.

REPUBLICANS VERSUS DEMOCRATS

Talking the Talk, but Not Walking the Walk

*Your representative owes you, not his industry only, but his judgment; and he
betrays instead of serves you if he sacrifices it to your opinion.*[1]
—EDMUND BURKE, SPEECH TO THE ELECTORS OF BRISTOL,
NOVEMBER 3, 1774

No man's life, liberty or property is safe while the legislature is in session.[2]
—JUDGE GIDEON J. TUCKER

*Politics is the art of looking for trouble, finding it, misdiagnosing it
and then misapplying the wrong remedies.*[3]
—GROUCHO MARX

Irrelevant differences and overwhelming similarities define our two major political parties. The Republican Party professes to support limited government, while expanding it. At least the Democratic Party makes no pretense of adhering to the Founding Fathers' vision of a limited government that trusts its people.

The Founding Fathers envisioned an America with Americans providing for their own retirement, education, and health care. They saw a country of free people, making their own personal and financial decisions, spending their money as they see fit, and assuming responsibility—for ill or for good—of their own decisions.

Indeed, recall that George W. Bush's Treasury Secretary Paul O'Neill said, "Able-bodied adults should save enough on a regular basis so that they can provide for their own retirement and, for that matter, health and medical needs."[4]

Too bad this does not appear to be the *administration's* policy.

Shortly after the 2000 presidential election, I interviewed Vice President Dick Cheney. Name the department, agency, bureau, program, or cabinet position scheduled for closure, I asked. The answer: none.

The Republicans and Democrats claim to trust the American people. But do they?

In 2000, we elected George W. Bush, a "compassionate conservative." George W. Bush's first budget *increased* government beyond inflation. He expanded the federal government's role in education and sought to expand Medicare even further by providing prescription benefits for seniors. He wished to increase government's role in charity by providing federal funds for so-called "faith-based initiatives."

President George W. Bush replaced Curtis Hebert, the former head of the Federal Energy Regulatory Commission. Hebert, a staunch free-market advocate, opposed price controls in any form. Suddenly, he "resigned." Bush replaced him with Pat Wood, considered more "practical" in his approach.

Sure, former Republican Senator James Jeffords of Vermont switched to independent status, citing the vast ideological differences between the parties. "Looking ahead," said Jeffords, "I can see more and more instances where I'll disagree with the president on very fundamental issues: the issues of choice, the direction of the judiciary, tax and spending decisions, missile defense, energy and the environment, and a host of other issues, large and small."[5]

Vast ideological differences? Just look at the actions of both parties.

People intuitively think Democrats issue more regulations than Republicans. But George Mason University economist Jay Cochran examined new regulations issued under both Democrats and Republicans. In looking at the *Federal Register,* the roster of regulations issued by government, Cochran found little difference between Republicans and Democrats. "There's a perception in D.C. that Democrats are regulators and

Republicans are deregulators," said Cochran, "but the data just don't support that conclusion. The partisan effect is zero."[6] Bill Clinton broke Jimmy Carter's regulation record, but regulation expanded at about the same pace under Nixon, Ford, Reagan, and Bush.

Both parties participated in the creation, expansion, and defense of the welfare state. Both parties supported and expanded Medicare, perhaps the largest intrusion into private industry in the history of America. Both parties supported and expanded the federal government's role in education and watched as urban schools continued to underperform.

Yes, the Jeffords defection panicked the Republicans, who put on a full-court press to keep him in the fold. Question: If, as Jeffords claims, the differences between the parties are so stark, why would Republicans want to keep someone so allegedly out-of-step with the party's ideology? Power over principle.

Remember Secretary O'Neill's position, requiring able-bodied adults to fend for themselves? Liberals pounced on the statement. Calling O'Neill's statement a "gaffe," *Los Angeles Times* columnist Robert B. Reich said, "Secretary Paul O'Neill . . . offer[s] a glimpse into the real philosophy of the Bush corporation that now runs the United States."[7]

If O'Neill's position truly reflected the Republican Party—not just in word but in deed—this chapter need not be written. Unfortunately, few Republicans seem to believe in O'Neill's philosophy of limited government and self-reliance. Words are one thing, deeds another. Republicans constantly show a willingness to maintain and increase the scope, size, and intrusiveness of government.

The government's so-called "social safety net" assaults the Constitution's vision of a limited government, as well as the principle of self-sufficiency and personal responsibility. People fear freedom, because with freedom comes responsibility. Fragile rests a country's foundation when its government shields people from the responsibility for and the consequences of their own actions.

LIBERTARIANS—A *REAL* DIFFERENCE

Former Representative Bob Dornan (R–California) accused the Libertarian Party of causing the Republicans to lose seven House seats in the 1996 election. "Seven good Republicans . . . lost their seats because a Libertarian was in the race," said Dornan, who identified himself as one of the seven. "Libertarians knocked off seven fiscal conservatives and replaced every one of them with a flaming liberal Democrat."[8] Damn those Libertarians!

Why abandon the Republican Party to vote Libertarian? Why do some sane, rational people vote Libertarian? Many, quite understandably, see the Republicans as Democrat-lites. They see Republicans passing regulatory measures, raising taxes, and either opposing or not encouraging competition in public education.

Many are Riordan Republicans. In California, Richard Riordan served two terms as mayor of Los Angeles. A decent, likeable man, Riordan, a multimillionaire businessman, termed out as a mayor and ran for governor. He markets himself as a "moderate" Republican, but look at his record.

The *California Political Review*'s George Neumayr, in an article called "Republican Self-Mutilation," asks a simple question. Why is this man a Republican? Many of Riordan's views sound like a playbook from the Democratic platform.

In a letter sent to the *California Political Review* in 1991, Richard Riordan criticized Democratic California Senator Dianne Feinstein and Republican former Governor Pete Wilson for lacking the political courage to *increase* taxes. "I would like to say that Californians have been consuming far more than they have been producing the last 15 to 20 years. This 'undertaxing' is reflected in the state's deteriorating infrastructure—particularly in education. The Proposition 13 Syndrome [the 1978 measure overwhelmingly passed to halt drastic rises in property tax] continued into the 1990 election. Neither Feinstein nor Wilson would dare come out for new taxes, especially not for a reversal of

Proposition 13. The 'pull up the ladder' (I've got mine) attitude was particularly evident in the propositions dealing with expenditures and new taxes (even on alcohol)."[9]

On gun control, Riordan made statements reminiscent of Rosie O'Donnell. He said he "favored removing guns even if it necessitated a citywide police sweep. . . . [A police sweep] gets very complicated but if that's the only answer we could come up with, yes, I would be in favor of much stronger control of gun dealers even to the point of shutting them down."[10] He brags about California's longer-than-the-Brady-Bill waiting period, saying that the Brady bill "didn't go far enough," and says that, "We should try to as much as we can keep handguns in the hands of police." Even Clinton began taking notes from Riordan on how the government could license gun owners like they do motorists.[11]

Riordan not only supported extremely liberal Democratic candidates but did so against Republican opponents! Riordan gave $500,000 to former Democratic Los Angeles Mayor Tom Bradley's various campaigns, including Bradley's gubernatorial race against Republican candidate and eventual winner George Deukmejian. In the recent mayoral contest between Democratic liberal James Hahn and Democratic hyperliberal Antonio Villaraigosa, Riordan supported Villaraigosa.[12]

He also gave money to Congresswoman Maxine Waters (D-California). Waters personifies the toe-tag liberal: pro gun control, pro high taxes, pro high regulation, pro Johnnie-Cochran-doctrine ("Race plays a part of everything in America"), and on and on. About Waters, *The Almanac of American Politics* says, "Waters comes from a background of poverty and believes with fervor in federal aid for the poor and for racial preferences to help blacks overcome years of slavery, segregation and discrimination; she favors drastic reductions in defense spending and was one of six members [of the House] who voted against supporting the Gulf war once it started, asking how urban gang members could be expected to stop fighting when America's own leaders were waging battles. She brings to her work a fury that is almost palpable, and an insistence that she will assert herself regardless of protocol, publicity and results. 'I don't have time to be polite,' she says."[13]

Guess who contributed to Maxine Waters's campaign? You got it, Richard Riordan.[14] For his part, Riordan apologizes for supporting Maxine Waters, noting that she later called him a "plantation owner."[15] But why did it take that for the former mayor to come to his senses?

Riordan also gave money to current California Governor Gray Davis (Democrat), his would-be opponent! According to the Cato Institute, the libertarian think tank, "[Davis's] first budget, prepared under the specter of a $2 billion deficit, included spending increases of the magnitude common during [Pete] Wilson's administration. When the revenue estimates were updated and the state government found itself swimming in excess revenue to the tune of $4.3 billion, Davis's big-spending instincts kicked into high gear. He increased his spending proposals massively and requested growth in the state budget twice as great as was needed to keep up with population growth and inflation. . . . With the likelihood of large surpluses on the horizon in this high-tax state, Davis's spendaholic appetite will be well fed, and the prospects for substantially lower taxes will likely take a back seat to towering growth spurts in the budget."[16]

On the issue of taxes and "social justice," he sounds almost Ted Kennedy-esque. "As the gap between the haves (the vast majority of the voters) and the have-nots continues to grow," said Riordan, "we can expect the number of homeless, welfare recipients, drug addicts, and criminals to increase rapidly."[17] And, in a recent debate, Riordan stated that everyone, including those who enter the country illegally, "has a God-given right to have a quality education and quality health care."[18]

Congressman David Dreier (R-California), who calls himself a conservative-libertarian Republican, serves as Riordan's cochair for governor. How does he explain the support of a pro–gun–control, non–limited-government person like Riordan? Dreier says that he wants to win. What about principles? What about values? Why not explain the principles of limited government and personal responsibility and assume a populace smart enough and intelligent enough to get it?

CAN "LOSERTARIANS" WIN?

How to explain the timidity of so-called conservative-Republican-limited-government pundits in challenging the welfare state? After all, not up for reelection, with no party to answer to, they could swing for the fences. Why their timidity in challenging the welfare state? Why not inform people about the moral, philosophical, economic, and constitutional basis for the vision of limited government?

Losertarians.

A pundit thus described those who vote Libertarian. Libertarians, some claim, cost the Republicans control of the Senate.

In Colorado, Republican Governor Bill Owens ran against Democrat Gail Schoettler, winning by just 7,928 votes. The Libertarian candidate, Sandra Johnson, received 22,159 votes—three times the victory margin.[19] And conventional wisdom suggests that a vote for a Libertarian means one less vote for a Republican, thus increasing the chances of a Democratic victory. Therefore, if just a few more Republicans had been lured to the Libertarian candidate, there would have been a Democrat in Colorado's state capitol.

Ralph Nader "cost" the Democrats the state of Florida. Almost 100,000 people voted for Nader in that state, likely siphoning off Democratic voters. Yet Nader remains a hero to many in the Democratic Party because he ran on principles and values, however wrong-headed.

Believers in freedom and limited government see a Republican Party that often abandons its principles and unnecessarily compromises its values. But when conscientious Republicans vote their principles, this invites the wrath of other Republicans and their "Just win, baby" philosophy.

Americans respond to plain, simple, commonsense talk. In the 1992 presidential race, billionaire Ross Perot made appearances on *Larry King Live*. A plainspoken, tough-talking Texan, he seemed a fresh antidote to the phoniness and "gridlock" of politics. King suggested Perot run for president, and Perot decided to jump in. Soon polls gave Perot almost a third of the presidential vote, placing him on even footing with the Republican and Democratic candidates.

Few had heard of Ross Perot until his appearances on Larry King. A multibillionaire, Perot spent his own money on his campaign. He took to the airwaves and spoke plainly about the need to control the nation's debt and annual deficit. He literally jump-started a national debate over fiscal policy. The day after his modern-day fireside chat, replete with charts and graphs, I called on a client at a large downtown office building. As I waited in the lobby for my elevator, I overheard two janitors discussing the Perot appearance the night before, saying that the nation needed to get its hands around the problem of debt and deficit. Pretty impressive. Two janitors, who most likely never thought until the night before about deficit spending, engaging in this kind of conversation. Ross Perot's candidacy ultimately spun out of control, and the more people learned, the less impressive Perot seemed. Still, his meteoric rise to national prominence suggests that the formula for success is: man (or woman) plus message plus money.

In the 2000 elections, the Libertarian Party ran more than 1,430 candidates, more than twice as many as all other third parties combined. It was the first time in eighty years that any third party contested a majority of the seats in Congress. Currently, over 300 Libertarians hold elective office, more than twice as many as all other third parties combined.[20] It can be done.

When Libertarian Party National Director Perry Willis heard Bob Dornan blasting his party for costing a seven-seat Republican loss in the House, he was pleased. "We know we have a significant impact on congressional elections," said Willis, "but we're delighted that a leading Republican thinks we cost them so many seats. Republicans apparently believe we've become very influential."[21]

In Minnesota, Jesse "The Body" Ventura became governor, besting his better-established and better-funded Republican and Democratic opponents. Here's how. During a debate, reporters asked the candidates about their plans for the state's budget surplus. The Republican emphasized less government and tax cuts. The Democrat talked about the importance of public education and a "balanced approach" to deal with the surplus. But Ventura suggested that a state surplus results from over-taxation. He would, as governor, return the money to the taxpayers.[22] What?! And, later, when an art student asked Ventura what he intended to do to help art students like her, Ventura suggested that she produce some art, and sell it. What?!

At another debate, the Minnesota gubernatorial candidates were asked to outline their agenda to fight crime. Minnesota writer Bill Holm reported, "[The Democrat] just blathered, and [the Republican] said he was going to increase spending on prisons, throw away the keys, and reintroduce the death penalty. And here's Ventura, who's twice the size of these guys. 'What would you do, Mr. Ventura?' 'Nothing,' he replies. 'That's not the governor's job. Crime is for city and county officials.' And it's absolutely true. He's the one guy who read the job description."[23]

Critics laughed at Ventura and wrote him off as having no chance. One opponent called him "Typhoon Jesse," and the other dismissed him as irrelevant. Hillary Rodham Clinton called him a "traveling road show." On election night, CBS News anchor Dan Rather said "there is a better chance of seeing Cuba's Fidel Castro riding a hippopotamus down the street than Jesse Ventura being elected governor."[24]

Ventura won. Much of his support came from first-time voters, many of whom felt unmotivated by the other mainstream establishment candidates. "At our party caucus in June," says Ventura, "we had four-teen people. Six of them were eighteen years old. I can't get my teen-age son to clean his room, but I got six 18-year-olds to the caucus. That's when I first knew I could win."[25]

A man, a message, and some money.

Perot and Ventura attempted to explain, to teach, and to enlighten. They assumed a certain amount of intelligence from the American people and found them capable of understanding when given the facts in a plain and honest way. But, all too often, Republicans don't even try, assuming people too incapable of accepting freedom and respon-sibility. Thomas Jefferson once said, "I know no safe depository of the ultimate powers of the society but the people themselves; and if we think them not enlightened enough to exercise their control with a wholesome discretion, the remedy is not to take it from them, but to inform their discretion by education. This is the true corrective of abuses of constitutional power."[26]

Educate the people. Inform them. It works.

WHY NOT A LIBERTARIAN?

At Robert Kennedy's funeral, Ted Kennedy quoted his slain elder brother Bobby, "Some men see things as they are and say why. I dream things that never were and say why not."[27]

In college, I took a class from a Nigerian professor. We discussed South Africa and another apartheid country, then known as Rhodesia. The professor soberly predicted apartheid's unfortunate enduring success, sadly predicting that he would not see apartheid's demise in his lifetime. Well, in March of 1992, apartheid fell, and within two years, the people elected former imprisoned dissident Nelson Mandela!

Several years ago critics doubted whether we could reform welfare. For the first time in over a generation, Congress passed measures placing time restraints and so-called "family caps." Over the screams of many Democrats, Clinton held his nose and signed the bill. Welfare rolls plummeted nearly 50 percent,[28] substantially more than predicted by economists.

Well, why not a Libertarian? Can we reverse course toward a small, limited, and humane government?

Take your voting-Libertarian-wastes-my-vote argument to Leadville, Colorado, City Councilman Joe Swyers. The Leadville City Council enjoys a unique reputation as the only city council dominated by Libertarians. Of the seven city council seats, Libertarians hold four.[29] Why Leadville? And can others duplicate Leadville's success? How did Swyers accomplish this? On my radio program I asked Mr. Swyers whether others could duplicate his success:

"One of the ways to deal with that," said Swyers, "is smaller juris-dictions—smaller cities, smaller counties. In the L.A. area, you've got three portions of L.A. that are trying to do that. And it will be less expensive, for instance, in the San Pedro area for a Libertarian to get on council there, if they were their own city. Right now, for a Lib-ertarian to try to get into the L.A. city council, or the county govern-ment, good luck. . . .

"Well, we hope to lead by example here, and show that it is possible to other small towns. We talked earlier, Larry, about the bigger races, the bigger cities, where people can make a change in their neighbor-hoods, their wards, small towns and small counties. They can do it if they get together."[30]

Size matters. The population of Leadville stands at 3,000. Getting the word out in a hamlet like this costs a lot less than, say, a guber-natorial race in California. And therein lies the rub. Money helps to win elections. And television and radio ad time costs plenty.

To win, change campaign finance laws.

In New York City, Michael Bloomberg was elected mayor in No-vember, 2001. The multimillionaire overcame a forty-point deficit in the polls to defeat frontrunner Mark Green for mayor of New York.[31] How did he do it? Money. Lots of it. Five months before he became mayor of New York, how many New Yorkers could spot Michael Bloomberg out of the lineup? Bloomberg, a lifelong Democrat, switched parties so that he could run. He spent nearly $70 million of his own money on his campaign[32] and eked out a victory.

Of Bloomberg's candidacy, the *New York Times* said, "Michael R. Bloomberg spent at least $50 million [later found to be almost $70 million] of his own fortune running to become the mayor of New York, setting a record that raises new questions about how well the city's nationally recognized campaign finance law can limit the influ-ence of money in politics when one candidate chooses to ignore it."[33]

Unfortunately, campaign finance laws only allow unlimited spend-ing on one's own candidacy! (Even that has limits for the candidate to be eligible to receive federal funds.) Campaign finance laws place caps on people who wish to donate money to others. Thus, multimillion-aires like Bloomberg enjoy an advantage that nonmultimillionaires don't. So, if, for example, Bill Gates or Warren Buffett wishes to support a candidate, the various campaign laws limit the size of their check—usually to between $500 to $2,000, depending on the type of race. This presumably limits the pernicious influence of money on politics.

This campaign finance law certainly prevents someone from writing a big check to a candidate, but does it also prevent bad government? The answer, according to the Cato Institute, is, "No." A politician votes the way he or she votes for three reasons: party interest, constituent desire, and personal ideology. If only a matter of money, a smart lobbyist would simply give his political opposition money in order to buy their votes or silence.

Why shouldn't an Internet gazillionaire be able to whip out a checkbook for his favorite limited-government, low-regulation, free-enterprise type of candidate? To spark a large-scale Leadville, we need to repeal laws stopping wealthy individuals from giving what they want to give and to whom.

So, to the honest, sincere, limited-government Republicans out there, here's a challenge. Repeal the campaign finance laws that prevent an individual from giving as much as he or she wishes to a candidate. Believers in freedom and limited government could then donate as much as they want to candidates who share their vision of a small, humane, and moral government that trusts the judgment of its people.

LIBERTARIAN FOREIGN POLICY

Conservative Republicans, especially post September 11, criticize Libertarians for promoting "open borders."

Regarding "open borders," the official Libertarian Party platform says: "The Libertarian Party has long recognized the importance of allowing free and open immigration, understanding that this leads to a growing and more prosperous America. . . . At the same time, we recognize that the right to enter the United States does not include the right to economic entitlements such as welfare. The freedom to immigrate is a freedom of opportunity, not a guarantee of a handout."[34]

"Open borders" does not mean no-questions-asked entrance into the country. Nor does it mean we allow students to overstay their visas with no follow-up means to determine their location and activities. Numbers matter. Given our welfare state, and the magnet it presents for those in the third world, "open borders" remains an ideal for a world where people live in political and economic freedom. But coming to America is a privilege, not a right. And any country's number-one responsibility remains protecting its citizens from foreign and domestic enemies. Government could and should ensure that people entering the country do so for peaceful purposes and do not overstay their visas and melt into the population with no follow-up.

Libertarians make Republicans uncomfortable because they must deal with the gap between rhetoric and action. Several pundits, for example, viciously attacked former Libertarian presidential candidate Harry Browne when he suggested that America's foreign policy provoked the attacks of September 11.

A conservative Republican pundit said, "This sort of idiocy would be altogether unworthy of attention were it not for the sad fact that many thoughtful, patriotic people voted for Browne in his presidential campaigns. . . . The next time someone tells you he's backing a Libertarian candidate as a means of 'voting his conscience,' please recall the party's unconscionable incoherence at a moment of national crisis. From now on, the leaders of this oddball political operation deserve the designation 'Losertarians.' "[35]

Never mind that the Libertarian Party platform position strongly disagrees with Browne. A look at the Libertarian Party platform shows no blanket prohibition against foreign intervention, let alone suggests blaming America for something like September 11. On foreign policy, the Libertarian Party says, "There is no excuse for such savage acts. No legitimate political or religious ideology can justify the murder of thousands of innocent people. . . . The Libertarian Party hopes these attacks will elicit a thoughtful national discussion about how we can prevent similar tragedies in the future."[36]

A member of the Executive Committee of the Libertarian Party of California wrote to me: "Please note that Harry Browne's position regarding the Afghan War and whether the U.S. deserved to be attacked on September 11 are [sic] NOT shared by Libertarians. . . . He [Browne] morally blames the U.S. for a foreign policy of opposing foreign dictatorships like Iraq and Libya, and for aid to Israel. Whereas, the view of the vast majority of Libertarians is that U.S. foreign policy is, at worst, stupid, not evil, as Harry Browne implies. . . . He implies that the U.S. morally deserved to be attacked because we 'bullied' dictatorships. . . . Browne has been very slimy and disingenuous about this, trying to smuggle in a message that the U.S. bears guilt. . . . Most Libertarians do not believe the U.S. has sinned against foreign dictatorships, as Harry Browne does, rather against its own people by subjecting them to risk of terrorist attack and loss of civil liberties, and by coercing taxpayers into supporting an interventionist misguided foreign policy. Harry Browne has earned the resentment of many libertarians."

Libertarian Party National Director Steve Dasbach said:

Declaring that all suicidal killers are irrational is, well, irrational. Japanese kamikaze pilots were suicidal killers. But they clearly weren't irrational. Otherwise they might have randomly chosen their targets, hitting a wayward tugboat here, taking out a fishing boat there.

Likewise, the Palestinian suicide bombers who terrorize Israel are not irrational. When they strap on explosives and charge into an ice cream shop or discotheque, they know exactly what they're doing and to whom they're doing it: Jews. . . .

Like it or not, bloodthirsty terrorists—like most criminals—do act rationally. And politically. In the case of September 11, their motives aren't a mystery: They wanted to punish the U.S. for aiding Israel and for a perceived foreign policy bias against Arab nations; and for a host of other foreign policy sins, real or imagined. . . .

To acknowledge a connection between military interventionism and terrorism isn't to condone terrorism, any more than acknowledging a connection between walking through Central Park at midnight and getting mugged is to condone violent crime. Recognizing that link is the first step toward avoiding more terrorism.[37]

Cautioning against unnecessary foreign involvement and blaming America are two different things. Indeed, George Washington, in his farewell address, similarly warned against foreign misadventure. Washington said, "Against the insidious wiles of foreign influence (I conjure you to believe me, fellow citizens) the jealousy of a free people ought to be constantly awake, since history and experience prove that foreign influence is one of the most baneful foes of republican government, but that jealousy, to be useful, must be impartial, else it becomes the instrument of the very influence to be avoided, instead of a defense against it. Excessive partiality for one foreign nation and excessive dislike of another cause those whom they actuate to see danger only on one side, and serve to veil and even second the arts of influence on the other. . . . The great rule of conduct for us in regard to foreign nations is in extending our commercial relations to have with them as little political connection as possible. So far as we have already formed engagements let them be fulfilled with perfect good faith."[38]

Winston Churchill acknowledged that the harsh conditions of the World War I Treaty of Versailles angered Germany, adding to conditions conducive to the rise of a demagogue like Adolph Hitler. "The triumphant Allies continued to assert that they would squeeze Germany till the pips squeaked.' All this had a potent bearing on the prosperity of the world and the mood of the German race."[39]

As we fight the war against terrorism and maintain our support of the State of Israel, we must avoid foreign involvements where we lack vital national security interests. Post September 11, we cannot afford to ignore the lessons of history or the words of our first president. On foreign policy, the Libertarian Party platform urges return to the non-interventionist foreign policy of Thomas Jefferson, who articulated a foreign policy consisting of, "Peace, commerce, and honest friendship with all nations, entangling alliances with none." The latest foreign policy press release from the Libertarian Party says, "As our nation embarks on this new war, the words of Thomas Jefferson echo down the centuries, and point in the direction of an America that can be at peace with the world—and have less to fear from foreign enemies."[40]

WHAT DO REPUBLICANS STAND FOR?

Republican critics of Libertarians invite a counter question. What do Republicans stand for?

Richard Nixon created the first federal affirmative action program with goals and timetables. Does the Republican Party stand for wage freezes and price controls? After all, even before Nixon signed into order the Office of Minority Business Enterprise (OMBE), which expanded federal procurement from firms owned by minorities,[41] he imposed wage and price freezes under the Economic Stabilization Act of 1970.[42]

Does the Republican Party stand for socialized medicine? After all, President Nixon signed the Women's, Infants and Child Act, once again extending health care at taxpayers' expense. Does the Republican Party stand for protectionism? The Feds passed a ten-year $170 billion farm bill, providing corporate welfare to mostly well-to-do farmers.[43] Does the Republican Party support the continued government near-monopoly on education? Sure. About the Title I program, Secretary of Education Rod Paige said, "After spending $125 billion of Title I money over the last 25 years, 'for the disadvantaged,' we have virtually nothing to show for it."[44] But what did Republican President George W. Bush do? He signed legislation that extended the life of and provided more funds for the Title I program.

Of Bush's leftward tilt on education, columnist Bob Novak quoted an unnamed "loyal Republican congressman" as saying, "We always knew that . . . [Bush] would go left on education, but that is a small price to pay for a president who is pro-life and pro-defense."[45]

Does the Republican Party oppose the principle of states' rights? After all, Oregonian voters twice approved a bill allowing doctor-assisted suicide.[46] With several restrictions and conditions, doctors may prescribe a lethal drug. A troubled Republican Attorney General John Ashcroft said if any doctor prescribes lethal drugs under this law, he would revoke their privileges to dispense drugs. This, for all practical purposes, shuts down a doctor's ability to practice.[47] Where is the outcry from principled Republicans, believers in the Ninth and Tenth Amendments?

Does the Republican Party stand for regulation? Didn't President George Bush-41 sign the Americans With Disabilities Act, one of the most monstrous pieces of legislation ever conceived, with tentacles that reach into virtually every American business? And didn't he raise taxes while reregulating cable?[48]

For one brief moment, in 2001, Republicans controlled the House, the Senate, and the presidency. As a result, Americans did get a tax cut—$300 per eligible wage earner, or less than $1 a day. Our "rebate" reminds me of a story a waitress once told me. After receiving a $1 tip for a $25 bill, my waitress friend politely returned the money to the customer: "If this is all you can spare, you probably need it more than I do."

Many Republicans and Democrats seem disinclined to battle the newfound love for Big Government. Using September 11 as a justification for an expansion of government, New York Senator Charles "the-era-of-Big-Government-is-back" Schumer (Democrat) wrote:

The recent disputes in Congress over airline security and stimulating the economy, like so many other arguments in Washington, revolve around a fundamental question: How big should the federal government be? Since the election of Ronald Reagan in 1980, those who believe the federal government should shrink have had the upper hand. September 11 changed all that. For the foreseeable future, the federal government will have to grow. The next few years will more closely resemble the mid-1930s, when federal power dramatically increased; but this new deal will involve an overarching federal effort to bring physical, not economic, security to our people.

. . . The era of a shrinking federal government has come to a close. From 1912 to 1980, the federal government grew with little interruption. The modern conservative movement, beginning with Barry Goldwater in 1964 and attaining power with Ronald Reagan's victory in 1980, argued that Washington had grown too large, too inefficient and too out of touch. Even liberals had to admit there was some truth to this argument. For the next two decades, the federal government stopped growing, and by some measures even shrank, with Bill Clinton doing more of the shrinking than any other president. But our new situation has dramatically reversed that trend. Within a few years, those like Dick Armey and Tom DeLay, who believe that any time the federal government moves, its fingers should be chopped off, will be fighting an increasingly desperate rear guard action.[49]

Tax, spend, and regulate simply makes Americans work longer and harder and pay more for the things we buy. Eliminate the IRS, remove the federal government from education, privatize Social Security, support medical savings accounts for emergency medical needs, and dramatically slim down the government. Americans stand ready to hear the message of limited government and personal responsibility which the Founding Fathers created in that extraordinary document called the Constitution. The Constitution limited government and denied the federal authority the power to interfere with our lives. Americans now work until July to pay all their taxes.

We need to spend billions of dollars in the coming years to fight this war on terrorism. Americans can no longer afford to shoulder this welfare state behemoth, with its tax grab at a post–World War II high. Every dollar spent on non-federally-mandated functions like education and health care becomes one less dollar spent on our military or domestic self-defense. Americans across the country ask, "How can we help in the war against terrorism?" "By assuming responsibility," the president should answer, "for that which you can and should do for yourselves."

Let's stop the madness. Vote your principles.

10.

NO MORE WELFARE
STATE. NOW WHAT?

*A wise and frugal government, which shall restrain men from injuring one
another, which shall leave them otherwise free to regulate their own pursuits of
industry and improvement, and shall not take from the mouth of labor
the bread it has earned. This is the sum of good government.*[1]

—THOMAS JEFFERSON

*Any type of welfare state is unjust to the productive individuals who are forced
to finance it. Perhaps equally bad, however, is the horrible harm it perpetrates
on the poor. Poverty is not like an incurable disease. It is a problem that is
resolved by full-time employment. But the poor individual must be willing to
examine and change the destructive values that underlie and give rise to his
poverty. In some terms, if only implicitly, he must grasp both the nature of
selfishness and the role of the mind, if he is to achieve prosperity and happiness.
The welfare state militates against such understanding and supports his most
irrational premises. This is one of the most important reasons
why it must be eliminated.*[2]

—ANDREW BERNARD, PHILOSOPHY PROFESSOR

No federal income taxes, mandates, or regulations. What? No federal health-care social safety net? What if my grandfather gets sick? What if my grandmother needs to go into a nursing home? Unfortunately, Americans are actually *worse off* now that the federal government has entered the complicated fields of medicine, health, and nursing care. If government would butt out, the private sector would provide drugs, health care, and long-term care less expensively, more accessibly, and of higher quality.

Even those who rail against the welfare state accept its existence as a given. Bill O'Reilly, for example, in his book *The No Spin Zone,* properly attacks what he calls a "tax culture" by pointing to out-of-control government spending. "Government waste is staggering. Incompetence, apathy, and fraud permeate D.C. like humidity in summer. Your hard-earned money is being thrown into the incinerator and nobody in power seems to care. . . . According to the Tax Foundation, the average American working person works three hours out of eight *each day* in order to pay his or her federal taxes. Bottom line for the typical American worker: Forty percent of your pay is being torn out of your wallet by various forms of government. Forty percent! Talk about an outrage."[3]

Fine, but O'Reilly accepts the welfare state as a given, apparently content to accept the extortion so long as the feds spend the money properly. "Let's be clear: If our tax dollars were being used effectively to solve social problems, to alleviate suffering and provide protection for American families, I'd shut up. If we all share in strengthening the nation by contributing monies that are honestly and fairly used, then we all benefit."[4] So O'Reilly, like so many others, accepts the existence and persistence of the welfare state, seemingly content only to trim a bit around the edges.

Republicans also accept the welfare state as a given. Incredibly, the Senate recently voted to increase federal spending on education. And remember the failed Title I program? Well, Congress passed a bill that expanded it. The *Los Angeles Times* happily noted the bipartisan convergence of Republicans and Democrats: "Passage of the legislation marked a high point for cross-party cooperation in what has been a year of on-again, off-again bipartisanship. Republicans and Democrats lined up to praise the legislation."[5] Education Secretary Rod Paige looked forward to an expanded federal role in education. "We're going to have a hands-on approach and a partnership approach with the states in implementing the law."[6]

Americans get the government they vote for. But don't politicians nevertheless owe voters their judgment? For example, both Republicans and Democrats tentatively agreed, post September 11, to expand unemployment compensation and health benefits. Good idea?

For fifteen years, I ran a firm that specialized in placing experienced attorneys. One day a few years ago I ducked out of work to hit some tennis balls at a local public park. I began hitting with a young man in his midtwenties. As we sat and toweled down, he asked what I did for a living, and I told him that I worked in the employment field. "Great," he said, "I'm looking for a job. May I leave you a résumé?" "If you're looking for a job," I said, "why are you out here hitting tennis balls?" He responded, "Oh, I don't intend to get serious until my unemployment compensation runs out."

Larry Katz, the chief economist at the Labor Department during the Clinton Administration, demonstrated that extending unemployment benefits decreases one's incentive to get out and look for a job. He found workers are almost three times more successful in finding jobs when benefits are just about to run out.[7] So powerful evidence exists showing that extending unemployment benefits simply steals initiative from those otherwise motivated to get out and find a job. Still, they vote to spend more of our money.

THE BEHAVIOR OF RISK

Helmet and bicycle laws demonstrate the folly of nanny legislation designed to protect us. Most states require motorcycle drivers to wear helmets. But do they save lives? Not according to the Motorcycle Industry Council Statistical Annuals. They show that in 1989, the first full year that the mandatory helmet law was in force in Oregon, the ratio of fatalities to accidents actually increased 50 percent.[8] But what about helmets for bicycle riders? Surely those work? Again the data paint a cloudy picture. Recall that according to the Consumer Product Safety Commission, even though fewer people are riding and more are wearing helmets, the data suggest the rate of head injuries among cyclists has actually increased 51 percent in the past ten years.[9]

The law rests on the following arrogant premise. Government cares more about your children than you do. What's more, lawmakers ignore what insurance companies call "risk homeostasis." How does risk homeostasis apply to the welfare state?

In "Risk Homeostasis and the Futility of Protecting People from Themselves," author Dwight Filley says, "The theory of risk homeostasis predicts that people become accustomed to some acceptable level of risk, and that when they are required to reduce a risk they are exposed to, they will increase other risks until they have re-established the level of risk they have become accustomed to. If they are required to wear seat belts, the evidence suggests they drive faster, pass other cars more dangerously, put on make-up, and so on, so as to maintain the level of risk they are comfortable with. In effect, they 'consume' the additional safety they are required to have by changing their driving behavior so as to attain other desirable ends."[10]

If, for example, the government mandates the wearing of motorcycle helmets, expect head injuries to increase, not decrease. Why? The more the risk-taker assumes an aura of protection—in this case provided by the helmet—*the more he or she engages in even more risky behavior.*

"There is a growing body of evidence," says Filley, "that points to the surprising conclusion that most coercive measures intended to increase safety either have no effect or an opposite effect. Thus for example, when the government mandates the use of automobile seat belts, fatality rates do not decrease as expected. . . . When subjects who normally did not wear seat belts were asked to do so, they were observed to drive faster, [they] followed more closely, and [they] braked later. Statistics from the United States indicate that as more and more states required seat belt use, the percentage of drivers and passengers killed in their seat belts increased. The cliché that seat belts save lives is true in the lab and on paper, and it's true if driver behavior does not change. *But behavior does change.*"[11] [Emphasis added.]

In biology, homeostasis means the human body adapts. We maintain a body temperature of 98.6 despite numerous variations in both internal and external factors. People adjust.

Filley concludes that, "This counter-intuitive result is consistent across a broad range of governmental attempts to protect people from themselves. Such lack of progress suggests that government regulators may be wasting their time and ours, that they are wasting tax money, and that other approaches are needed."[12]

Someone recently wrote to me:

> *Most of your ideas are good. However, the Libertarian concepts cannot work. You make the assumption that everyone will do the right/best things. It will not and doesn't happen. I own a mid-size real estate company. The realtors are self-employed. Some of them make really good money. I have had many financial people come in to my meetings to try to help them set up retirement accounts. Guess how many have set up an account? None. My realtors are typical of the American public. . . . Only one out of the bunch could make it without the current laws.*
>
> —*Steve R.*

What a charming analysis of human nature. Undoubtedly, the planners of Social Security never considered risk homeostasis, but the very existence of Social Security induces some to do nothing more to provide for retirement. And polls overwhelmingly show that young people simply do not believe that Social Security will even exist when they retire, let alone provide enough income to pay for a comfortable living. Accordingly, many young people already take steps to ensure their futures. Never forget the Elvis Factor. I once read that 10 percent of the American people think Elvis is still alive, and 8 percent believe that if you send him a letter, he will receive it.

But what about the slow, the stupid, the irresponsible, the lazy— the Elvis Factor folks? Should the minority of the irresponsible curtail the rights and freedoms of the responsible majority? A perfect world is not an option. Never was. But for power-grabbers, the inability of some to act responsibly serves as a justification for denying freedom for the responsible. If my neighbor cannot responsibly plan for his retirement, should I, too, be prevented from investing my money in stocks and bonds, thus creating an inheritance for my loved ones?

Nanny-staters oppose the privatization of Social Security. After all, what if you know nothing about the stock market? What if you're completely ignorant about bonds, debentures, options, puts, and margin calls? What if you're gullible and easily fall prey to schemes and scams? What if someone is simply dumb, doesn't know a stock from a sock, an equity from an eyelash, and a bond from a bodega? Not to worry— an idiot could outperform the meager "returns" from our current federal Social Security system.

According to the book *Millionaire*,[13] one need only follow several easy steps:

- Save.
- Start now.
- Be patient.
- Take risk.
- Put the odds in your favor.
- Invest.
- Diversify.
- Keep your money working.
- Avoid costs . . . at all costs.
- Avoid taxes.
- Never sell.
- Don't talk to anyone about your investing—and never listen to braggarts.

Thomas Jefferson said the solution for irresponsibility lies not in removing choices from the irresponsible. Rather, the solution is to inform, educate, and allow people to suffer the consequences of their own actions. Like laws, irresponsible behavior creates a deterrent effect for others unwilling to end up in the same plight.

With Social Security and Medicare, people engage in a kind of risk homeostasis. When one assumes a certain amount of Social Security retirement income, do we not save less, plan less, and learn less about investments and managing our own finances? In the case of Medicare, does its availability cause some to avoid healthful eating and beneficial activity? After all, professionals tell us that the most successful health-care measure remains prudence—don't smoke, avoid excessive drinking, eat nutritious foods, don't overeat, get plenty of sleep, exercise, and drink plenty of water. If people paid directly for their health-care costs and saw their own premiums go up, you could confidently expect more Americans to engage in these simple, healthful habits.

ZERO-TOLERANCE ACCOUNTABILITY

Hold the Red Cross accountable!

The headlines seemed unmerciful. Red Cross CEO Bernadine Healy, on the job only two years, suddenly announced her retirement. According to the *Los Angeles Times*, "Healy resigned . . . saying she had been forced out by her board over policy disputes."[14]

A *USA Today* editorial urged Americans to hold the Red Cross's feet to the fire. The organization had raised over $500 million since the tragedy of September 11, 2001. People gave, said *USA Today*, expecting the victims to receive all of the monies, "Now the Red Cross appears intent on diverting a significant share to other purposes. That isn't illegal, and the other causes may be worthy, but the switch appears a mismatch with donors' intent. . . . The Red Cross and all non-profits need to make certain that donors' wishes are followed and that money flows quickly and efficiently to those who deserve it."[15]

Let's string the CEO up. Trial to follow!

The Red Cross, according to its web page, had given out $153,800,000 of the over $320 million donated specifically for its September 11 disaster relief fund less than two months after the attack.[16] Healy's resignation concerns policy disputes rather than, say, missing money.

Let's apply this Red Cross zero-tolerance standard elsewhere. Remember the high-profile lawsuits against tobacco companies? In selling its citizens on these lawsuits, state attorneys general said they filed suit to collect monies for antismoking programs. But what happened? When the states agreed to a settlement of $246 billion, some spent much of the money on non-tobacco-related programs. Rhode Island, having repealed its state auto tax, used the money to replace the "shortfall." In Alabama, legislators debated a proposal to spend some of its $3.2 billion for programs designed to fight gangs and satanic worship. In Montana, legislators wanted to spend some on a boot camp for juvenile offenders.[17]

And remember the sales pitch for state-run lotteries? Why, after all, the lottery monies will go to education. But, for the most part, the states' lotteries failed to expand the total educational budget. Instead, legislators anticipated a certain dollar amount from lotteries and simply subtracted an equal amount from what they otherwise expected to spend on schools.

And what about the accountability of the federal government? Senator Fred Thompson (R-Tennessee), ranking minority member on the Senate Governmental Affairs Committee, issued a two-volume report, *Government on the Brink*, addressing waste, fraud, and abuse within the federal government. According to the Thompson report, "Because of its size and scope, and the terrible way it is managed, the federal government wastes billions and billions of your tax dollars every year. The waste, fraud, and abuse reported to the Governmental Affairs Committee each year is staggering. Of course, no one knows exactly how much fraud, waste, and mismanagement cost the taxpayers because the federal government makes no effort to keep track of it."[18]

Insight on the News magazine analyzed Thompson's report:

Department of Defense: Despite the massive audit effort, the Department of Defense could not overcome the fundamental inadequacy of its financial-reporting systems and produce reliable data. The department continues to confront pervasive and complex financial-management problems that can seriously diminish the efficiency of the military services' support operation. There is no major component of the Defense Department that can balance its books.

Department of Agriculture: Because its financial management is so defi-

cient, the department can't ensure that its financial statements are reliable and presented in accordance with generally accepted accounting principles. For fiscal 2000—the seventh straight year—the Agriculture Department failed its annual financial audit.

Department of Education: With the exception of fiscal year 1997, the Department of Education has not received an unqualified or "clean" opinion on its financial statements since its first agency-wide audit. That means it can't even balance its books once a year. Needless to say, it can't manage its money on a day-to-day basis.

Department of Health and Human Services: The Department got an unqualified or "clean" opinion on its financial statements for fiscal year 2000. However, it still can't use its financial systems for day-to-day management. The department's clean opinion came only after billions of dollars of discrepancies were figured out many months after the end of the fiscal year.

Department of the Treasury: GAO [the General Accounting Office] has reported that the federal government is not able to properly and consistently compile financial statements, identify and eliminate intragovernmental transactions or reconcile the results of operations in the financial statements with the budget results.[19]

"These summaries" says *Insight,* "are just a sample of nearly a dozen departments plagued with financial problems. Eleven of the twenty-four major federal agencies and departments have financial-management problems, and of those eleven none received a grade higher than D-plus from Representative Steve Horn (R–California), chairman of the House Government Reform subcommittee on Government Efficiency, Financial Management and Intergovernmental Relations. For years he has reported on the state of federal management in an annual report card.

"Despite the inability of the federal bureaucrats properly to account for their funds, their budgets remain the same or have been increased. For fiscal 2002 the president requested increases for both the DOD [Department of Defense] and the Department of Education. The total amount requested for the eleven departments and agencies unable to properly account for their money comes to nearly $1.4 trillion—some 86 percent of the total fiscal 2002 budget request of $1.9 trillion."[20]

In fact, following a Department of Defense audit of their fiscal year 2000 financial statement, *Insight* said, "At the end of the last full year on Bill Clinton's watch, more than $1 trillion was simply gone and no one can be sure of when, where or to whom the money went."[21]

How about a little zero tolerance for *that* kind of mismanagement?

In *Feeling Your Pain: The Explosion and Abuse of Government Power in the Clinton–Gore Years,* James Bovard wrote, "The vast majority of government agencies can neither be reinvented nor reformed. If Americans want good government, hundreds of failed government programs must be abolished and legions of laws that turn government into a public nuisance must be repealed. All other 'reforms' will merely prolong the abuse of the American people."[22]

Yet Representative Dick Gephardt (D-Illinois) wants to use federal workers for airport security. "If . . . [federalization of workers] is good enough for . . . [Congress], it's good enough for the American people."[23] Let's hope not. Americans deserve more. How about the Red Cross zero-tolerance standard?

AMERICA, THE GENEROUS—THE STRENGTH OF PRIVATE CHARITY

Overthrowing the stranglehold of the victicrats calls for the elimination of the Internal Revenue Service, Medicaid, Medicare, as well as the numerous federal "poverty programs." President Jimmy Carter once called America, "the stingiest nation on earth." This suggests a country too stingy to care about the poor, the sick, the mentally handicapped, except for a kind of forced compassion exacted through taxation and the redistribution of money to "the needy."

Carter's wrong. Americans care about other Americans. September 11 demonstrated that.

Ask Pastor Denny Bellesi about the allegedly cold, uncaring American spirit.

The pastor of the Coast Hills Community Church in Aliso Viejo, California, asked for a few volunteers. Similar to the parable of the talents, where a master entrusts three servants to invest a few coins, the pastor gave $100 bills to one hundred members of his church, urging them to give the money to the needy. "I dumped a huge responsibility on them," said Bellesi, "But it turned out to impact more people than any of us thought possible."[24]

The conditions? "I told them it had to be invested outside the church," Bellesi said. "It had to be glorifying to God and it had to be benefiting to others."[25] Some bought hamburgers for the hungry, provided blankets for those in the cold, aided shelters, helped destitute families, and performed other good deeds.

Bellesi started out with $10,000. And he simply said find people who need the money and give it to them. Word spread of Pastor Bellesi's plan, and so many donated to Bellesi's "fund" that the original $10,000 multiplied fifteenfold![26]

People magazine said, "Bellesi and his wife, who helps run the church's youth programs, first thought of reenacting the parable of the talents (Matthew 25:14–30) fifteen years ago. But even they have been surprised by the resourcefulness of parishioners like homemaker Terry Zwick, forty-five, who told friends at a party about the pastor's challenge and left with $1,700."[27]

Bellesi said, "I could never have imagined all this. When the truth of something is applied in a way people can see, it is transforming."[28]

President George Bush, the forty-first president, urged community involvement, referring to activists and organizations for the needy as "a thousand points of light." No, President Bush. Not a thousand. Many, many, many more than that.

Alexis de Tocqueville, in *Memoir on Pauperism,* lays out the case against guaranteed pubic welfare. "I have said," wrote Tocqueville, "the inevitable result of public charity was to perpetuate idleness among the majority of the poor and to provide for their leisure at the expense of those who work."[29]

Tocqueville felt reliance on public charity bred irresponsibility, illegitimacy, and a sense of entitlement on the part of the recipient: "But I am deeply convinced that any permanent, regular administrative system whose aim will be to provide for the needs of the poor will breed more miseries than it can cure, will deprave the population that it wants to help and comfort, will in time reduce the rich to being no more than the tenant-farmers of the poor, will dry up the sources of savings, will stop the accumulation of capital, will retard the development of trade, will benumb human industry and activity, and will culminate by bringing about a violent revolution in the State, when the number of those who receive alms will have become as large as those who give it, and the indigent, no longer being able to take from the impoverished rich the means of providing for his needs, will find it easier to plunder them of all their property at one stroke than to ask for their help."[30]

In railing against the George W. Bush budget, Senate Majority Leader Tom Daschle (D-South Dakota) played the class envy card. Standing with Democratic House Minority Leader Richard Gephardt (Missouri), Daschle said, "This is a Lexus. It is a fully loaded, every-luxury-option-available Lexus, a 2000 Lexus GS-300, just like the Bush tax cut—fully loaded. If you're a millionaire, under the Bush tax cut, you get a $46,000 tax cut, more than enough to pay for this Lexus. But if you're a typical working person, you get $227, and that's enough to buy this muffler."[31]

How can America urge the rest of the world to embrace free enterprise when our very own politicians seem confused by the concept? Bob got his at the expense of Ed's. Moreover, Senator Daschle believes that Bob deserves the high-rate taxing of his money and that Ed deserves receiving his money out of Bob's taxes.

Bob may indeed feel pity for Ed and wish to help him out. But not by pointed bayonet, not by government dictates and mandates issued on high by some all-knowing party. Does government possess the wisdom and judgment to sort out the deserving from the undeserving? All without inducing financial and spiritual dependency?

WHEN GOVERNMENT CHOOSES THE DESERVING

After September 11, Americans opened their hearts and wallets to the survivors of the terrorist attacks. And in addition to Red Cross donations and contributions from many other charities, Congress passed a new federal program to provide compensation for the families of those killed. The Victim's Compensation Act enables surviving families to receive an average award of $1.65 million.[32]

But what of those whose loved ones died on April 19, 1995, when Timothy McVeigh bombed the Oklahoma City Federal office building? Yes, the government paid death or disability benefits, but Congress never passed a law to directly compensate those families, thus making an apparent distinction between homegrown terrorism and that of a foreign variety.

Marsha Kight, who lost a daughter on April 19, 1995, said, "I don't want to do a hierarchy on terrorism here, but that's kind of minimizing what happened to the people of Oklahoma City. The individual loss was just as great for us."[33] How do you explain this?

In *Memoir on Pauperism,* Tocqueville talked about the inability of government to sort out worthy victims from those less worthy. "Nothing is as difficult to distinguish as the nuances that separate unmerited misfortune from an adversity produced by vice. How many miseries are simultaneously the result of both these causes! What profound knowledge must be presumed about the character of each man and of the circumstances in which he has lived, what knowledge, what sharp discernment, what cold and inexorable reason! Where will you find the magistrate who will have the conscience, the time, the talent, the means of devoting himself to such an examination? . . . Who, being judge of the joy or suffering, life or death, of a large segment of his fellow men, of its most dissolute, its most turbulent, its crudest segment, who would not shrink before the exercise of such terrible power?"[34] In other words, do we want government to distinguish between the deservedly and undeservedly needy?

Who stands a better position?

Enter nonprofits, churches, civic activists, and other charitable institutions. The concept of neighborhood includes mosques, churches, synagogues, and other places of caring. And who may better determine who deserves assistance—a local philanthropic worker or some bureaucrat on the Potomac?

And since neighbors no longer look to Washington for money or assistance, they turn inward and must, through necessity, become more cooperative. This creates greater localized interdependence and increases community civility. People look to friends, family, and others, rather than government, for help when in need. Local charities' representatives frequently know the needy, how they got into trouble, and what steps to take to improve behavior. The faceless bureaucrat in Washington lacks the information about you and your personal circumstances that a neighbor or member of the community has. A neighbor or minister can talk specifically about your behavior and what you can do to change. Neighbor Bob shows up at Ed's door with a check in hand, and says, "Ed, we're covering this month's food and rent. And I'll help you find a job. But here's what *you* have to do in return . . ." If Ed has no government welfare options, you better believe that Ed will listen.

Each year, the *Los Angeles Times* features stories on needy families, complete with phone numbers so that people may donate funds. The uncritical, nonjudgmental profiles almost never even suggest a "plight" caused by irresponsibility. Take the article about a family of seven sleeping in a garage.

The story begins this way. "Paolo Chaparro, her husband and five children live in a twenty-by-twenty-foot room in a partitioned garage in Santa Ana, a place without plumbing.

"The seven family members squeeze into 400 square feet, sleeping in bunk beds and surviving on potatoes, ramen noodles and food handouts. They seldom use the kitchen and bathroom of the adjoining house, doing so mostly when the residents are not home.

"It's the best they can do in Orange County's tight housing market, where median monthly rents have climbed to more than $1,000. . . . Chaparro rents the garage for $480 a month from a relative."[35]

How much money does the head of the household make? Three hundred dollars a week, stocking shelves in an auto parts store. His wife suffers from a blood ailment, a condition that prevents her from working regularly, although she does work some weekends at a hotel. Their five children range in age from three to fifteen. Question: When did Mrs. Chaparro contract her blood ailment, and did they continue having children after her condition became evident?

The article does not mention the family's legal status, although it says that Chaparro is "a native of Toluca, Mexico." If the family arrived here illegally, presumably to seek a better life than in Mexico, wouldn't they suffer more back home in Mexico? And, of course, what of the Chaparros's responsibility for subjecting their children to these conditions? Miriam Gonzales, a health worker at Maternal Outreach Management Systems, says, "The housing is affecting the children. They are embarrassed. They don't want their classmates to find out where they live. The family is really trying, but things keep happening to them. They are in a real bad spot, worse than anyone could imagine."[36]

The children feel embarrassed. The *Times* uncritically assumes that the Chaparros have no responsibility for their own plight. But how about those parents who violate the most basic of rules—not to have children without the ability to feed, clothe, house, discipline, and educate?

A story like the Chaparros's points out the superiority of private charity over government. Private charity can attach strings—maybe, where appropriate, a lecture about having more children until such time as you can care for ones already in the world. Religious instruction may follow, something the government constitutionally cannot provide.

PUBLIC EDUCATION, THE WELFARE STATE, AND THE LACK OF PERSONAL RESPONSIBILITY

In addition to the media and Hollywood, supporters of limited government also face academia. The government monopoly on public education ensures a leftward indoctrination of many of our children.

A letter I recently received read in part, "You see, I'm a teacher for the Los Angeles Unified School District. If I'm not mistaken, the Libertarians (and you) would like public schools to be privatized. I don't know if that's a good thing or not. Public education is a cornerstone of our democracy."

Public education, a cornerstone of our democracy? But America enjoyed high levels of literacy before government began to monopolize education.

In his book *Market Education*, Andrew J. Coulson calls the public-education-good-for-democracy argument flat-out wrong:

> *Perhaps the most revealing aspect of nineteenth-century American education is the impact of public versus private schools on religious and ethnic relations. One of the central beliefs of modern educators is that public schooling has a unifying effect on American society, and that without it, the various racial, religious, and political groups that comprise that society would become polarized and antagonistic to one another. They would, in modern political jargon, be balkanized. Based on the experiences of the 1800s, this belief is not only wrong, it is exactly backward.*
>
> *Prior to the government's involvement in education, there were nondenominational schools, Quaker schools and Lutheran schools, fundamentalist schools and more liberal Protestant schools, classical schools and technical schools, in accordance with the preferences of local communities. Some had*

homogeneous enrollments, others drew students from across ethnic and religious lines. In areas where schools of different sects coexisted, they and their patrons seldom came into conflict, since they did not try to foist their views on one another. They lived and let live in what were comparatively stable, though increasingly diverse, communities. It was only after the state began creating uniform institutions for all children that these families were thrown into conflict. Within public schools, many parents were faced with an unpleasant choice: accept that objectionable ideas would be forced on their children, or force their own ideas on everyone else's children by taking control of the system.[37]

Many schools celebrate "diversity" and "multiculturalism" but support a one-size-fits-all public education system.

A "cornerstone of democracy"? It practically takes an act of Congress to get a bad teacher fired. Glenn Sacks, who taught high school, both in public and private schools, and who was named to *Who's Who Among America's Teachers,* talked about the public schools' "code of silence" regarding inferior, dumbed-down education provided the children, and detailed the way the system protects bad teachers, many of whom end up at the worst schools where parents are less likely to complain. Sacks writes:

Sometimes, a failing teacher's classroom is a daily battleground. In other cases, failing teachers and their students reach an unspoken agreement—the teacher pretends to teach and the students pretend to learn. The students are given a light amount of busy work and the students use the extra time to do work for their other classes, pass notes, or chat in low voices. Everybody is happy— the class is relatively quiet (often an administrator's judge of a teacher's competence goes no deeper than the question— "Is it quiet in there?"), the failing teacher survives, and the students have less work to do. When it is necessary, the students will put on a show in front of any bothersome visitors.

Failing teachers often compound their problems by refusing to refer out disruptive students. Failing teachers know that most administrators know little about what is really happening in the classroom and that, as long as they do not bring attention to themselves, the teacher will be presumed to be "doing fine." Referrals serve to draw unwanted attention from administrators.

One of the reasons that administrators often would rather not know about failing teachers is that it is frequently difficult to find suitable replacements. This is particularly true of teachers who work in crime-ridden areas where few teachers want to go, or who teach one of the many subjects where there is a shortage of qualified teachers. According to former U.S. Secretary of Education Richard W. Riley, 28 percent of high school math teachers and 55 percent of physics teachers have neither majors nor minors in their subjects. Over a third of all teachers in grades seven through twelve are teaching a subject that they have not studied.

More importantly, because of the union and tenure protections teachers enjoy, it is costly and time-consuming to terminate a teacher, particularly once their probationary period is over. Nationally, it takes between two and three years and costs roughly $60,000 to fire a teacher.[38]

A recent Dartmouth Medical School study found that, contrary to the stereotype of the rebellious teenager, parental attitude remains the most influential factor in determining whether a teenager starts smoking cigarettes. Dr. James Sargent, associate professor of pediatrics at Dartmouth Medical School, said, "We overrate the rebelliousness of teenagers."[39] Researchers found when kids came from homes where parents disapproved of smoking, even if the parents themselves smoked, the children were far less likely to pick up the habit than if the parents were lenient about smoking. Well, if the parents play this strong a role in whether their kids smoke, what role do parents play in their children's attitudes toward education?

Another public school education warrior wrote me the following letter:

This is my third year in public education, and I am not certain that I want to stay. For a "back-to-basics" philosophy teacher like me, the system is a maddening mental sickroom of administrators willing to try the latest gizmo to plug the burgeoning dike of failing schools and students. The system seems so overloaded with ineffective bureaucratic paperwork requirements that one cannot just teach for the worrying of what an administrator may require next. Far too many of the students are ill-behaved, rude, foul-mouthed, and greatly feel entitled to grades that are beyond what they deserve. Effective classroom management only earns a female teacher the rank of "Bitch." I have desperately tried to work through some basic skills that my students clearly lack only to be labeled boring and met with hostile stares. This is the land of education where tenured teachers can have no classroom management and allow their problem students to roam the halls or library unmonitored. This is the land of education where to try to instill some basic skills, like vocabulary building, is met with such resistance, it is like meeting a bulldozer head-on. I have to call students' parents when they are failing, and they fail due to flat-out laziness, not lack of ability. I know this because I have had to oversimplify my curriculum. I teach English to seniors in the Inland Valley, but as I say, this is probably my last year. With my skills and dedication, it will be simple to find a job. I show up and work.

—Anonymous

Unfortunately, many parents don't care. They send their children to school undisciplined, and sometimes even hostile. This kid then sits next to one who does care, whose parents did emphasize education. What about that child?

True, parents of private school students expect their kids to receive a superior education. But most private school parents cite security and civility as their top concerns. Learning suffers amidst disorder and disruptions. In the private sector, authorities do not tolerate acting out. Parents spent good money and signed a contract forcing them to live up to their end of the bargain. Parents must provide a reasonably well-behaved child who has done his or her homework. If not, that child suffers and gets kicked out because if the teachers or administration refuse to do anything about it, the other cash-paying parents will.

Brazenly, politicians admit their reluctance to "subject" their own children to a public education. In Los Angeles, mayoral candidate Antonio Villaraigosa, a champion of public schools, provides his children a parochial school education. When asked why, incredibly, Villaraigosa said, "I'm doing like every parent does. I'm going to put my kids in the best school I can. My kids were in a neighborhood public school until just this year [2001]. We've decided to put them in a Catholic school. We've done that because we want our kids to have the best education they can. If I can get that education in a public school, I'll do it, but I won't sacrifice my children any more than I could ask you to do the same."[40]

Sacrifice, indeed.

END THE WAR ON DRUGS

Abraham Lincoln said, "Prohibition will work great injury to the cause of temperance. It is a species of intemperance within itself, for it goes beyond the bounds of reason in that it attempts to control a man's appetite by legislation and makes a crime out of things that are not crimes. A prohibition law strikes a blow at the very principles upon which our government was founded."[41]

As to fighting a "War on Drugs," Republicans and Democrats march in virtual lockstep. Just as Bill Clinton got "tough on drugs," new Attorney General John Ashcroft pronounced "reinvigorating" the war on drugs to be one of his top three agenda items. We face high crime, in part, because of the war on drugs. Many instances of motorists being stopped by the police—who later face allegations of racial profiling—result from the police crackdown on the drug trade.

Recently England announced a policy of decriminalization for possession of small amounts of marijuana. A number of U.S. state legislatures now consider laws to provide for the medical use of marijuana, and some now even consider decriminalizing small amounts of certain drugs. A step in the right direction, but not enough.

The war against drugs increases street crime. It increases our prison population, filling jail cells with people who never committed violent offenses. It corrupts our criminal justice system because drug busts rely on notoriously unreliable and self-dealing informants to rat out those involved. It increases the use of wiretaps and asset forfeitures. And a large number of drug offenders now seek work with "ex-con" stamped on their résumés.

How about saving lives and increasing prosperity?

According to a newsletter from the Advocates for Self-Government:

Approximately 7,000 people die each year from drug overdose, compared to 100,000–200,000 annual deaths from alcohol and 320,000–390,000 from tobacco. However, 80 percent of drug deaths (5,600) are due to impurities and other factors that would not be present in legal preparations. Because needle sales are banned, shared needles have become the primary mode of AIDS transmission in the U.S. (approximately 3,500 new cases/year). The turf wars over drug territory result in gang shootings in which innocents (1,600 annually) are killed. Because drug prohibition makes the price of drugs almost 100 times higher than they otherwise would be, addicts rob to support their habit, killing many of their victims in the process (about 750 each year).

Thus, the death toll caused by the War on Drugs (5,600 + 3,500 + 1,600 + 750 = 11,450) is about 8 times higher than it would be if drugs were legal (20% of 7,000 = 1,400/year). Since almost one out of eight people in the U.S. use [sic] illegal drugs regularly, the whole population would have to use them in a legal setting for the death toll to be as high as it is under drug prohibition.[42]

Economist Thomas DiLorenzo tells of the emergency room carnage spawned by the War on Drugs. "A former MBA student of mine," said DiLorenzo, "was the director of emergency medicine at a large hospital in the city of Baltimore. He once told me that he and his colleagues spent about 90 percent of their time treating the knife and gunshot wounds of drug gang members. Drug war-related injuries are bound to dominate the emergency room services of virtually all inner-city hospitals. The incredible violence in America's inner cities that most Americans have become numbed to is almost exclusively the result of the war on drugs."[43]

Disputes between suppliers, or between supplier and customer, in a legal market resolve themselves without violence. But since a disappointed drug customer cannot file a lawsuit or call a cop, street violence remains the only means of enforcement. "The workload of hospital emergency rooms in America's cities," said DiLorenzo, "could probably be cut at least in half by ending the failed war on drugs. That would make room for more genuine emergencies and reduce the financial burden on taxpayers as well, since the big majority of hospitals are either government-run or government-subsidized nonprofit hospitals. The cycle of violence in America's cities would be reversed, property values there would soar, and the lives of literally thousands of Americans would be saved."[44]

If these reasons do not persuade, here's another: The War on Drugs provides badly needed money for terrorists. John Thompson of the Mackenzie Institute, a Canadian think tank, says, "As the Soviet Union weakened in the 1980s, more and more insurgent groups, terrorist groups, started to resort to organized criminal activities to pay their bills."[45] The big money-earner for most of them seems to be narcotics, and, as early as 1994, Interpol's chief drug officer, Iqbal Hussain Rizvi, said, "Drugs have taken over as the chief means of financing terrorism."[46]

Yoseff Bodansky, director of the congressional Task Force on Terrorism and Unconventional Warfare, and who also wrote a biography of Osama bin Laden, says, "The Afghans are selling $7 to $8 billion of drugs in the West a year. Bin Laden oversees the export of drugs from Afghanistan. His people are involved in growing the crops, processing and shipping. When Americans buy drugs, they fund the jihad (holy war)."[47]

Indeed, laughably, the United States gave the Taliban $43 million to "fight" its drug war.[48] Never mind that, according to the *Washington Post*, the Taliban's very existence depends on the good graces of Osama bin Laden, who gave the regime $100 million in the last five years.[49] Does anyone really believe the U.S.'s $43 million actually went to fighting the drug war?

End the war against drugs to help fight terrorism? Author and journalist Alan Bock says:

> Drugs are as profitable as they are almost entirely because of prohibition. If we're serious about reducing terrorism, or at least reducing the resources terrorists have available for their dastardly activities, we need to think about de-profitizing the drug trade by ending drug prohibition, or at least substantially altering the way the government approaches the many aspects of drug use.
>
> It isn't just the money that drives terrorists and drug traffickers into one another's arms. Terrorists and drug traffickers have similar needs—untraceable cash, weapons, safe hiding places, secure infiltration routes, ruthless associates who have little incentive to help authorities—and thus have been and are natural allies.
>
> If terrorism is to be the main focus of the Bush administration's attention for the next few years, it is reasonable to argue that resources devoted to the drug war should be reoriented toward the main goal, as Steve Trinward has argued in a recent issue of Sierra Times. And the national debate on drug decriminalization, which would carry myriad benefits in the realms of restoration of freedom, reduction of corruption, sensible priorities in law enforcement and reduction of violent crime, should be intensified.
>
> Decriminalize drugs to fight terrorism? It might be the single most effective step that could be taken.[50]

After September 11, House Speaker Dennis Hastert (R–Illinois), said, "The illegal drug trade is the financial engine that fuels many terrorist organizations around the world, including Osama bin Laden." But Hastert doesn't get it. "By going after the illegal drug trade, we reduce the ability of these terrorists to launch attacks against the United States."[51] Right problem, wrong solution.

According to *Reason* magazine, "Actually, 'going after the illegal drug trade' is what allows terrorists to fund their operations with profits inflated by prohibition. In that sense, the $40 billion or so the U.S. spends on drug law enforcement each year represents a subsidy for murderers. . . . Stronger enforcement, Hastert's favored solution, would tend to increase the risks of drug trafficking, eliminate competitors, and raise profits. So it hardly makes sense to fight terrorism by cracking down on drugs."[52]

To save lives, save hard-working Americans' money and fight terrorism, end the war on drugs. Now.

HATRED AND CLASS ENVY AGAINST THE WEST: WHAT ABOUT HATRED AND CLASS ENVY WITHIN THE WEST?

In one of his first speaking appearances after September 11, former President Jimmy Carter said the chasm between rich and poor countries was "by far the most important single problem in the world."[53]

Incredible.

What fuels radical Islam's hatred toward the West? An angry, ill-informed, misguided, devoid-of-perspective worldview based on a victicrat mentality. Statements like the former president's merely give aid and comfort to this worldview.

The Arab world feels exploited, misused by a mean-spirited, war-mongering, imperialistic West. But in the court of historical equity, the Arab world does not enter with clean hands, either.

At a post–September 11 forum at Princeton, actor Danny Glover practically indicted America for worldwide anti-Americanism and the American sentiment, saying that, "One of the main purveyors of violence in this world has been this country, whether it's been Nicaragua, Vietnam or wherever."[54] Actually, Glover's own extremely violent movies *Lethal Weapon 3* and *Lethal Weapon 4* purveyed over $150 million each in foreign film receipts.[55]

America as the main purveyor of violence? Unfortunately, the published reports don't show how, if at all, Mr. Glover amplified his remarks. If Mr. Glover's "wherever" means Hiroshima and Nagasaki, many historians believe that the dropping of those bombs saved over a million lives on both sides. Presumably, this club of "main purveyors of violence" includes, say, Stalin at seven to ten million victims during his man-made Ukrainian famine,[56] Hitler at almost twelve million victims,[57] Pol Pot of Cambodia at about one million,[58] and the Rwanda civil war at half-a-million.[59]

As for our involvement in Vietnam, we can debate our commitment, focus, and lack of exit strategy, but America did not enter for purposes of imperialism. Former President Bill Clinton suggested that Americans should feel shame about our prosperity and success. After declaring that America is "paying a price today" for its history of slavery and treatment of Native Americans, Clinton said, "We have to be smart enough to get rid of our arrogant self-righteousness so that we don't claim for ourselves things we deny for others."[60]

President Clinton offers the traditional welfare-state vision of the world: Give the Afghans things—money, "humanitarian aid," loans, grants, etc. What about the importance of economic freedom, allowing citizens to utilize their time and money in a way they think most meaningful and productive? What about lecturing on the brilliance of a bold yet wonderful principle—that of the nonestablishment of a state religion?

In a 1962 speech to Congress, Senator Robert Byrd (D–West Virginia) noted that of the fifty-five delegates to the Constitutional Convention, over half were Anglicans, nearly one-third were Calvinists, and among the rest were two Methodists, two Lutherans, two Roman Catholics, and one lapsed Quaker/sometimes Anglican. There was only one open Deist—Benjamin Franklin—and he attended all Christian worships and called for public prayer.[61]

The Founding Fathers, in their personal, spiritual lives, believed in God and spoke often of their faith and of its importance in civic life:

From the day of the Declaration . . . they [the American people] were bound by the laws of God, which they all, and by the laws of The Gospel, which they nearly all, acknowledge as the rules of their conduct.

—John Quincy Adams, sixth U.S. president[62]

Providence has given to our people the choice of their ruler, and it is the duty, as well as the privilege and interest of our Christian nation to select and prefer Christians for their rulers.

—John Jay, first chief justice of the Supreme Court[63]

It cannot be emphasized too strongly or too often that this great nation was founded, not by religionists, but by Christians; not on religions, but on the gospel of Jesus Christ. For this very reason peoples of other faiths have been afforded asylum, prosperity, and freedom of worship.

—Patrick Henry, revolutionary leader[64]

But the God-fearing Founding Fathers saw the danger in fusing politics with religion, and the arrogance and intransigence of a faith-based religious legislative process, and of a legislative body committed to the Bible rather than the Constitution. "In a free government," James Madison declared, "the security for civil rights must be the same as that for religious rights. In one case, it consists of a multiplicity of interests and, in the other, a multiplicity of sects. This is presumed to depend on the extent of the country and number of people comprehended under the same government."[65]

For the most part, the Arab world lacks religious freedom. And envy over American success blinds many to the unparalleled generosity of the American spirit.

Over two decades ago, Gordon Sinclair, a Canadian radio commentator, said:

This Canadian thinks it is time to speak up for the Americans as the most generous and possibly the least appreciated people on all the earth.

Germany, Japan and, to a lesser extent, Britain and Italy were lifted out of the debris of war by the Americans who poured in billions of dollars and forgave other billions in debts. None of these countries is today paying even the interest on its remaining debts to the United States.

When France was in danger of collapsing in 1956, it was the Americans who propped it up, and their reward was to be insulted and swindled on the streets of Paris. I was there. I saw it.

When earthquakes hit distant cities, it is the United States that hurries in to help. This spring, fifty-nine American communities were flattened by tornadoes.

Nobody helped.

The Marshall Plan and the Truman Policy pumped billions of dollars into discouraged countries. Now newspapers in those countries are writing about the decadent, warmongering Americans. I'd like to see just one of those countries that is gloating over the erosion of the United States dollar build its own airplane. Does any other country in the world have a plane to equal the Boeing Jumbo Jet, the Lockheed Tri-Star, or the Douglas DC10? If so, why don't they fly them? Why do all the international lines except Russia fly American planes?

Why does no other land on earth even consider putting a man or woman on the moon? You talk about Japanese technocracy, and you get radios. You talk about German technocracy, and you get automobiles. You talk about American technocracy, and you find men on the moon—not once, but several times—and safely home again.

You talk about scandals, and the Americans put theirs right in the store window for everybody to look at. Even their draft-dodgers are not pursued and hounded. They are here on our streets, and most of them, unless they are breaking Canadian laws, are getting American dollars from ma and pa at home to spend here.

When the railways of France, Germany and India were breaking down through age, it was the Americans who rebuilt them. When the Pennsylvania Railroad and the New York Central went broke, nobody loaned them an old caboose. Both are still broke.

I can name you 5,000 times when the Americans raced to the help of other people in trouble. Can you name me even one time when someone else

raced to the Americans in trouble? I don't think there was outside help even
during the San Francisco earthquake.

Our neighbors have faced it alone, and I'm one Canadian who is damned
tired of hearing them get kicked around. They will come out of this thing
with their flag high. And when they do, they are entitled to thumb their
nose at the lands that are gloating over their present troubles. . . .

Stand proud, America![66]

Yes, post September 11, many of our allies did stand with us, but Europeans criticize America for its support of Israel. In the last couple of years, Israel experienced over one hundred so-called suicide-bombing attacks. In response, Israel's Prime Minister Sharon ordered the military into the West Bank in an effort to root out terrorists. Europe's response? Because of their large Arab population, trade with the Arab nations, and need for oil, European leaders— with the exception of Britain's Tony Blair—place the Israelis and the Palestinians on the same moral plane.

THE TIME IS NOW

Republicans often condescendingly refer to plans for "outreach" to black Americans. "Outreach"? How about just plain, simple, under-standable English? No, Ronald Reagan was not the devil incarnate. In fact, under Ronald Reagan, black adult unemployment and black teen unemployment fell faster than did white teen unemployment. And, no, the Republican Party is not the Klan in suit and ties. As a percentage of the party, more Republicans voted for the passage of the Civil Rights Act of 1964 than did Democrats. And the old Southern red-necks who defied integration—Orville Faubus of Arkansas, Lester Maddox of Georgia, George Wallace of Alabama—Democrats all.

The president faces a historic opportunity. Bush could launch an-other war, a war against the welfare state.

After September 11, Americans gave him a 90 percent approval rating on his performance, the highest rating for any president in modern history.[67] Although he received only 8 percent of the black vote, Bush now enjoys the support of three out of four black Americans![68] Now is the time to deliver simple, plainspoken lectures to the American people on the perils of ever-growing government. He should inform the American people that the federal government's involvement in education produced worse results, not better. He should make the case for extracting the federal government from the business of education, leaving it to the states or to local communities and the private sector.

A war against the welfare state compliments our war against terrorism. Every dollar spent on a pork-barrel project, on expanding failed programs like Title I, on a social program for the able-bodied and able-minded is one less dollar spent on domestic self-defense, and to combat this international war against terrorism.

The president possesses the tools. His plainspoken style in his first post–September 11 speech endeared him to millions of Americans. Polls now show Americans embracing the Republican approach to the economy more so than the Democratic tax, spend, and regulate approach.

The president also possesses two underutilized secret weapons—Secretary of Treasury Paul O'Neill and Office of Management and Budget head Mitch Daniels.

O'Neill was the one who dared to tell us a simple truth—that able-bodied adults should save enough so that they can provide for their own retirement.[69] And Mitch Daniels literally threw up his hands at the post–September 11 cries of poor mouth by private industry. Daniels described Congress's willingness to lay down and pony-up to the special interests this way: "Congress may not believe it, but it takes a long time to spend $40 billion. . . .Their motto is, 'Don't just stand there, spend something.' This is the only way they feel relevant."[70]

Daniels also said, "It is our lot in life to disappoint people on a daily basis,"[71] in reference to his job as budget chief. And, lambasting the post–September 11 spending pressures, he said, "It might be autumn everywhere else, but in Washington it is springtime for spenders."[72]

But O'Neill never repeated his blunt prescription—self-reliance—to attack the welfare state. Similarly, Mitch Daniels pulled back from his anti-big-government statements, noting, "To be effective for the president, I need to be able to work with [Congress]."[73]

The president took time and patience to educate Americans on the politics, religious history, geography, and strategic importance of the war against terrorism. The president urged us to examine the religion of Islam, and we reexamined our commitment to Israel in the Israeli–Palestinian dispute. Americans happily embarked on this learning curve because the president stamped it important, and we listened. And now the president enjoys a historic opportunity to reshape the debate on the welfare state.

The president should inform the American people that, no, Lyndon Johnson's War on Poverty did not reduce poverty. Indeed, the "war" created dependency, with a significant percentage of those on welfare facing a life of indefinite government dependence.

The president should remind voters about President John Kennedy's justification for reduced taxes, "It is a paradoxical truth that tax rates are too high today and tax revenues are too low—and the soundest way to raise revenues in the long run is to cut rates now.

"The experience of a number of European countries has borne this out. This country's own experience with tax reductions in 1954 has borne this out, and the reason is that only full employment can balance the budget—and tax reduction can pave the way to full employment. The purpose of cutting taxes now is not to incur a budgetary deficit, but to achieve the more prosperous expanding economy which will bring a budgetary surplus."[74]

The president should discuss the Ponzi-scheme qualities of Social Security. In 1940, a few years after Congress passed Social Security, forty-one workers supported every retiree. Soon, less than three workers will support each retiree.[75] The system, quite simply, can no longer operate.

Medicare, too, faces the same demographic pressures. As the large class of baby boomers become eligible for benefits, the system can enlist only an ever-smaller number of young workers to pay for it. This, too, cannot continue.

The president should remind Americans that for over a century, this country somehow managed to survive without government regulatory oversight. It wasn't until 1887 that the first independent regulatory commission—the Interstate Commerce Commission—was established.

In 1822, Congress authorized monies to extend the Cumberland Road, a roadway that ran from Cumberland, Maryland, to Wheeling, West Virginia. James Monroe, our nation's fifth president, used the only veto of his presidency to defeat the congressional bill, arguing that the road's extension should not be done by the federal government but by the states it passed through—present-day Pennsylvania, Virginia, Ohio, Indiana, and Illinois.

According to Monroe's biography on www.americanpresident.org, "Although Monroe personally supported the idea of internal improvements, he balked at the federal government's role in the American System being proposed by Congressmen Henry Clay and John C. Calhoun. They wanted a series of federally financed projects designed to improve and update the nation's roads, bridges, and canals. Monroe worried, however, that federal payments for such internal improvements would expand even further the power of the federal government at the sake of state power. Where would the limits be drawn?"[76]

The massive welfare state, the president should tell Americans, tears away at the fabric of society. When families rely on government to provide health care, retirement benefits, and medical care, why rely on family, friends, and community?

The often-misunderstood general welfare clause simply outlines specific responsibilities and powers of the federal government, leaving all others to the states and to the people. James Madison, the father of the Constitution, warned against using the document to dispense money, no matter how well-intended or deserved: "With respect to the words general welfare, I have always regarded them as qualified by the detail of powers (enumerated in the Constitution) connected with them. To take them in a literal and unlimited sense would be a metamorphosis of the Constitution into a character which there is a host of proofs was not contemplated by its creators."[77]

Franklin Pierce, our fourteenth president, in 1854 vetoed a bill to help the mentally ill saying, "I cannot find any authority in the Constitution for public charity," adding that to approve such spending, "would be contrary to the letter and the spirit of the Constitution and subversive to the whole theory upon which the Union of these States is founded."[78]

President Grover Cleveland, our twenty-second and twenty-fourth president, in 1887, said when vetoing an appropriation to help drought-stricken counties in Texas, "I feel obliged to withhold my approval of the plan to indulge in benevolent and charitable sentiment through the appropriate of public funds. . . . I find no warrant for such an appropriation in the Constitution."[79]

Americans want to know what they can do to help fight the War on Terrorism. During World War II, people willingly and patriotically assumed hardships, accepted shortages. and adjusted their lives for a higher cause. So, too, do contemporary Americans wish to shoulder their responsibility and help win this war. They can by understanding that a growing welfare state weakens the nation, strengthens their enemies, and hinders our ability to prosecute and win this War on Terrorism.

Lead, Mr. President. This historic opportunity exists now. Seize it. Americans will follow.

ENDNOTES

1. LIBERAL FASCISM

1. Pearcy, Thomas, and Mary Dickson, "The Basic Philosophy of Fascism," [On-line] Available http://www.wwnorton.com/college/history/ralph/workbook/ralprs.35.htm.

2. Carson, Clarence B., "C.S. Lewis on Compelling People to Do Good," [On-line] Available: http://www.libertyhaven.com/noneoftheabove/religionand christians/lewiscompel/html.

3. Dailey, Keli, "Putting Out the Welcome Mat," *Westside Weekly,* [On-line] Available: http://www.latimes.com/tcn/westside/front/20010701/tws0002138.html.

4. Pool, Bob, "Los Angeles Santa Monica Divided Over Rehiring Labor Law," *Los Angeles Times,* November 30, 2001, p. B-4.

5. Wartzman, Rick, "Falling Behind: As Officials Lost Faith in the Minimum Wage, Pat Williams Lived It," *Wall Street Journal,* July 19, 2001, p. A1.

6. Friedel, Frank, *Franklin D. Roosevelt: A Rendezvous With Destiny* (Hyde Park, New York: Back Bay Books), 1990.

7. Ibid, p. 162.

8. Ibid, p. 163.

9. Ibid, p. 226.

10. Ibid, p. 231.

11. Ibid, p. 239.

12. Williams, Walter, "Could They Be Elected Today," *Creators Syndicate,* August 17, 2000.

13. Anderson, Edgar B., "The 'Progressive' Plan To Save Our Lives." [On-line] Available http://www.frontpagemag.com/guestcolumnists/anderson06-29-01.html, June 29, 2001.

14. Ibid.

15. Ibid.

16. Ibid.

17. Ibid.

18. Ibid.

19. Ibid.

20. Ibid.

21. Ibid.

22. Ibid.

23. Deutsch, Linda, "Allred Wins Cash, Apology From Schmitz Over 'Butch' Comment," Associated Press, August 21, 1986.

24. Ibid.

25. *Allred & Taylor,* KABC Talkradio, January 3, 2001.

26. Welch, William M., "Stark Calls Sullivan a 'Disgrace to His Race,' " Associated Press, August 2, 1990.

27. Hume, Brit, *This Week With David Brinkley,* ABC, August 5, 1990.

28. Boliek, Brooks, "Bill Offers Place for Gripes About Portrayals in Media," *Yahoo News,* August 6, 2001.

29. Jipping, Thomas L., "ABA Is (Surprise!) Solidly Partisan," *Long Beach Press-Telegram,* August 17, 2001, p. A15.

30. Ibid.

31. Goldberg, Bernard, *Bias* (Washington, DC: Regnery Publishing, 2002), p. 57.

32. Goldliner, Dave, "TV Prez Brands 'W' a 'Moron' and 'Scary,' " *New York Daily News,* February 14, 2001, p. 23.

33. *The Guardian,* "Acting Up: Friends and Enemies in Tinseltown," July 10, 2001.

34. Wilker, Deborah, "Cher to Voters: 'Has Everyone Lost Their Minds?' " [On-line] Available: http://daily.news.yahoo.com/htx/ws/2 . . . cher_to_voters_has_everyone_lost_their_minds__1.htm, October 31, 2000.

35. "Film Figures Vow to Leave U.S. If Bush Wins," *National Post,* September 19, 2000, p. A14.

36. Malvern, Jack, "We're Off, But Not Yet," *Times of London,* January 24, 2001, p. 1DD.

37. "Actress' Play on Words Falls Two Ways," *USA Today,* September 22, 2000, p. 16A.

38. "Roberts Endorses Bush Girl Boozing," *Daily News,* June 25, 2001, p. 2.

39. Fink, Mitchell, and Lauren Rubin, " 'Apes' Actor Held Their Fire When Heston Made His Cameo," *New York Daily News,* June 6, 2001, p. 19.

40. Ibid.

41. "Making His Mark," *People,* August 6, 2001, p. 74.

42. Codrea, David, "Planet of the Ape," *Keep and Bear Arms,* August 10, 2001, [On-line] Available: http://www.KeepAndBearArms.com/information/XcIBViewItem.asp?id=2360.

43. Ibid.

44. Ibid.

45. Dutka, Elain, "Arts and Entertainment Report," *Los Angeles Times*, December 6, 2001, p. F-54.

46. Doran, D'Arcy, "Hollywood Cell-ebrities," *Toronto Star*, August 12, 1999, p. 1.

47. Gladwell, Malcolm, "Rapper Tupac Shakur Robbed, Shot in N.Y.," *Washington Post*, December 1, 1994, p. A1.

48. Fink, Mitchell, "Penn Drips Some Venom on Talkmeisters O'Reilly, Stern," *New York Daily News*, January 2, 2002.

49. Smith, Liz, *New York Post*, February 15, 2001.

50. Smith, Liz, *Star-Ledger*, October 6, 2001.

51. "Jeers 2001," *TV Guide*, January 5, 2002, p. 18.

52. Dalton, Stephen, "It's No Walk in the Park," *Times of London*, January 21, 2002, pp. 2–16.

53. Condor, Bob, "America's Obesity Crisis Grows Again," *Chicago Tribune*, November 18, 2001, p. 3.

54. Mokdad, Ali H., Barbara Bowman, Earl S. Ford, Frank Vinicor, James S. Marks, and Jeffrey Koplan, "The Continuing Epidemics of Obesity and Diabetes in the United States," *JAMA*, September 12, 2001, vol. 286, no. 10.

55. Vanzi, Max, "Lawmaker Targets On-Screen Smoking Health," *Los Angeles Times*, October 26, 1997, p. A-3.

56. Sullum, Jacob, "Lighten Up, America!" *Reason On-line*, December 25, 2001 [On-line] Available: http://reason.com/sullum/122501.shtml.

57. Mann, Judy, "A Whiff of Absurdity Wafts From Montgomery," *Washington Post*, November 30, 2001, p. C08.

58. *The Larry Elder Show*, KABC Talkradio, November 21, 2001.

59. "Bush Praises Americans With Disabilities Act in Radio Address," Associated Press, July 28, 2001.

60. "Bush Lauds Success of Americans With Disabilities Act," Dow Jones International News, July 28, 2001.

61. Bolt, Bill, "Commentary: The Disabled Are Bound by Chain of Unemployment Laws," *Los Angeles Times*, June 28, 1999.

62. Butler, Kevin, "How Successful Is Disabilities Act? Unintended Results Are Showing Up," *Investor's Business Daily*, August 22, 2000.

63. Ibid.

64. Margasak, Larry, "High Court Says Golfer Casey Martin Has Right to Use Cart," Associated Press, May 29, 2001.

65. Ibid.

66. Ibid.

67. Mehren, Elizabeth, "Governor's Pregnant State Is the Big News," *Los Angeles Times*, May 10, 2001, p. A-28.

68. Marantz, Steve, "AFL-CIO Pushes Plan for Parent Leave," *Boston Herald,* July 17, 2001.

69. Islas, Jason, "Controversial Speaker Sparks Political Debate," *The Samohi,* December 20, 2001, vol. XCII, no. 6, p. 1.

70. Johnson, Peter, "Couric Gets $60M Payday to Keep Her at NBC," *USA Today,* Decmber 20, 2001, p. 1.

71. Ibid.

72. Anderson, Nick, "Pelosi Makes History as New Minority Whip," *Los Angeles Times,* October 11, 2001, p. A-31.

73. "NOW's New Leader Vows Political Fight," *USA Today,* July 2, 2001, p. 3A.

74. Shaikin, Bill, "Their Playing Field Is the Executive Suite," *Los Angeles Times,* July 16, 2001, p. D-7.

75. "Free Choice Will Create Gender-Based Science Careers," *Daily University Science News,* November 26, 2001 [On-line] Available: http://unisci.com /stories/20014/1126014.htm.

76. Ibid.

77. Hopkins, Jim, "A Woman's Work is Rarely Funded," *USA Today,* August 15, 2001, p. 1B.

78. Ibid.

79. Ibid.

80. Ibid.

81. Barnes, Julian E., "Helmet Use Up; So Are Injuries," *Orange Country Register,* July 29, 2001.

82. Ibid.

83. Ibid.

84. Ibid.

85. "Acting Up Friends and Enemies in Tinseltown," *The Guardian,* July 10, 2001.

86. Maher, Bill, interview with Larry King, *Larry King Live,* CNN, July 27, 2001.

87. "Nancy Pelosi's Moment." *San Francisco Chronicle,* August 26, 2001, p. C6.

88. Knudson, Tom, "Fat of the Land," *Sacramento Bee,* April 22, 2001.

89. "Martin Sheen Honored by Sierra Club," Associated Press, April 18, 2001.

90. Jackson, David, "Democrats Cooking Up a Comeback," *Dallas Morning News,* May 7, 2001, p. 1A.

91. Charen, Mona, "Dangers in Life," *Orange County Register,* April 2, 2001.

92. Easterbrook, Gregg, "W. The Environmentalist Health Nut," *The New Republic,* April 30, 2001.

93. Ibid.

94. Browne, Harry, "The Top 10 Misconceptions About Government," *WorldNetDaily,* June 26, 2001, [On-line] Available: http://wnd.com/news/article.asp?ARTICLE_ID=23379.

95. Babbitt, Bruce, "Bush Isn't All Wrong About the Endangered Species Act," *New York Times,* April 15, 2001, p. 11.

96. "Progressive Environmentalism: Principles for Regulatory Reform," *National Center for Policy Analysis,* July 6, 1995, p. 28.

97. "An Environmental Report Card on the 104th Congress," *National Center for Policy Analysis,* January 14, 1997, p. 13.

98. Cheney, Dick, Interview with Larry Elder, *The Larry Elder Show,* KABC, April 25, 2001.

99. Lindzen, Richard, "The Press Gets It Wrong," *Wall Street Journal,* June 11, 2001.

100. Ibid.

101. "Networks Exclude Critics of 'Global Warming,' " [On-line] Available: http://www.newsmax.com/archives/articles/2001/5/9/174405.html.

102. Holtz, Robert Lee, "Melting Releases Riddles on Global Warming," *Los Angeles Times,* April 1, 2001, p. A-1.
Report, ABC, June 29, 2001.

103. Stossel, John, "Tampering With Nature," *Special Report, ABC,* June 29, 2001.

104. Ibid.

105. Singer, Dr. S. Fred, Interview, *The New American,* January 31, 2000,p. 21.

106. Stossel, John, "Tampering With Nature," *Special Report,* ABC, June 29, 2001.

107. Ibid.

108. Knudson, Tom, "Fat of the Land," *Sacramento Bee,* April 22, 2001.

109. Ibid.

110. Stossel, John, "Tampering With Nature," *Special Report,* ABC, June 29, 2001.

111. Knudson, Tom, "Fat of the Land," *Sacramento Bee,* April 22, 2001.

112. Heinlein, Peter, "Danish Scientist Claims Kyoto Treaty Useless," Voice of America, www.voanews.com, October 1, 2001.

113. Wavell, Stuart, "Wonderful World," *London Sunday Times,* July 15, 2001, p. 6.

114. Ibid.

115. Heinlein, Peter, "Danish Scientist Claims Kyoto Treaty Useless," Voice of America, www.voanews.com, October 1, 2001.

116. "Scientific American Beats Up *The Skeptical Environmentalist,*" Center for the Defense of Free Enterprise, [On-line] Available: http://www.cdfe.org/scientific.htm.

117. Ibid.

118. Ibid.

119. Ibid.

120. Kaku, Michio, *Hyperspace* (New York: Anchor Books, Doubleday, 1994), p. 320.

121. Reisman, George, *Capitalism* (Chicago: LPC Group, 1998), p. 87.

122. Willman, David, "Drug Tied to Deaths Is Pulled," *Los Angeles Times,* August 9, 2001.

123. "Audacious First Aid," *Los Angeles Times,* September 5, 2001.

124. "Britain to Pay for Treatment Abroad," *New York Times,* August 26, 2001.

125. Houston, Kerri, "Beware Free Care," *Investor's Business Daily,* June 20, 2001.

126. Charen, Mona, "The Economics of Health-Care Reform," *Orange County Register,* June 23, 1999.

127. Ibid.

128. Morris, Charles R., "Health-Care Economy Is Nothing to Fear," *Atlantic Monthly,* December 1999, p. 92.

129. Thompson, Greg, "Red All Over," *Physical Therapy Products,* September 2000, p. 8.

130. Ibid.

2. SELF-DEFENSE IS JOB NUMBER ONE

1. Moore, Stephen, "Sept. 11's Lesson: By 'Doing It All,' Government Fails to Do Anything," *Investor's Business Daily,* October 25, 2001.

2. "Byrd to the Barricades," *Wall Street Journal,* Review & Outlook (Editorial), November 9, 2001, p. A14.

3. Winston, Judith A., "Helping Poor Children Learn," *Washington Post,* April 26, 2001, p. A-26.

4. Coile, Zachary, "Accord on Major Education Reform Bill: Annual Testing of All Students," *San Francisco Chronicle,* December 12, 2001, p. A-1.

5. Norton, Rob, "Rough Around the Edges: Why Does Paul O'Neill Make People So Hot Under the Collar?" *Washington Post,* August 19, 2001, p. B-01.

6. Moore, Stephen, "Tax Cut and Spend," *National Review,* October 1, 2001, pp. 30–31.

7. Ibid.

8. Ibid.

9. O'Donnell, Jayne, "Frequent Fliers Airlines Really Must Please: Congress," *USA Today,* July 31, 2001, p. B16.

10. Ibid.

11. Editorial, *Wall Street Journal,* October 25, 2001.

12. Associated Press, "Drug Maker Lowers Price of Cipro," *New York Times,* October 24, 2001.

13. Ibid.

14. Ibid.

15. "The Cipro Circus," Editorial, *Wall Street Journal,* October 25, 2001.

16. O'Donnell, Jayne and Laurence McQuillan, "Airlines seek $24B in Government Aid," *USA Today,* September 19, 2001, p. 1A.

17. Koenig, David, "American Airlines Prepares for Cuts," Associated Press, September 18, 2001.

18. McCartney, Scott, Susan Carey, and Greg Hitt, "Mayday Call: U.S. Airlines Industry Faces Cash Crunch, Pleads for a Bailout," *Wall Street Journal,* September 17, 2001, p. A1.

19. McKenna, Barrie, "Canada Follows N.Z.'s Flight Path," *Globe and Mail,* March 13, 1995, p. B1.

20. Ibid.

21. Poole, Robert W. Jr. "Let's Privitize Air Traffic Control," *USA Today,* February 5, 2001, p. A8.

22. Dolan, Thomas G., "Evil From Above, or Incompetence From Within," *Security Technology & Design,* October, 2001.

23. Firestone, David, "Rules Will Allow Airport Screeners to Remain in Jobs," *New York Times,* December 30, 2001.

24. Ibid.

25. Utt, Ronald, "Taking Advantage of Tragedy," The Heritage Foundation, October 3, 2001.

26. Williams, Walter, "Tests of Loyalty?" *Orange County Register,* December 12, 2001, p. 9.

27. Shogren, Elizabeth, "House Defies White House by Passing Farm Bill," *Los Angeles Times,* October 6, 2001, p. A-26.

28. Williams, Walter, "Tests of Loyalty?" *Orange County Register,* December 12, 2001, p. 9.

29. Pear, Robert, "Lobby Groups Find Congress in Giving Mood," *New York Times,* December 18, 2001.

30. Shogren, Elizabeth, "House Defies White House by Passing Farm Bill," *Los Angeles Times,* October 6, 2001.

31. Lynch, Michael W., "Money for Nothing," *Reason,* November 2001, p. 25.

32. Ibid.

33. Broder, John M., and Dwight Morris, "Urban 'Farmers' Reap Rich Harvest of Crop Subsidies Agriculture," *Los Angeles Times,* March 16, 1995, p. 1.

34. Shogren, Elizabeth, "House Defies White House by Passing Farm Bill," *Los Angeles Times,* October 6, 2001, p. A-26.

35. Williams, Walter, "Tests of Loyalty?" *Orange County Register,* December 12, 2001, p. 9.

36. Lynch, Michael W., "Money for Nothing," *Reason,* November 2001, p. 25.

37. Pear, Robert, "Lobby Groups Find Congress in Giving Mood," *New York Times,* December 18, 2001.

38. Ibid.

39. Utt, Ronald, "Taking Advantage of Tragedy," The Heritage Foundation, October 3, 2001.

40. Ibid.

41. Williams, Walter, "Legal Looting," *Orange County Register,* October 17, 2001, p. 9.

42. Marriott, J.W., Interview with Cokie Roberts, *This Week With Sam Donaldson & Cokie Roberts,* ABC, December 23, 2001.

43. Utt, Ronald, "Taking Advantage of Tragedy," The Heritage Foundation, October 3, 2001.

44. "Post Office Asks Congress For Financial Help After Attacks," *Dow Jones International News,* November 8, 2001.

45. Ibid.

46. Von Mises, Ludwig, *Human Action* (San Francisco: Fox & Wilkes, 1996).

47. Hook, Janet, "Response to Terror: Capitol Hill OMB Chief's Blunt Talk Could Point to Trouble," *Los Angeles Times,* November 26, 2001, p. A-1.

48. Ibid.

49. Friedman, Milton, "No More Economic Stimulus Needed," *Wall Street Journal,* October 10, 2001.

50. Gosselin, Peter G., "White House Seeks to Curb Tax Cuts, Spending," *Los Angeles Times,* October 17, 2001, p. C-1.

51. Boxer, Barbara, Interview with Larry Elder, *The Larry Elder Show,* KABC Talkradio, September 14, 2001.

52. Williams, Walter, "Legal Looting," *Orange County Register,* October 17, 2001, p. 9.

53. "Terror-Relief Donations Exceed $840 Million," *Los Angeles Times,* October 9, 2001.

54. Kiely, Kathy, "Importance of Foreign Aid Is Hitting Home," *USA Today,* December 4, 2001, p. A11.

55. Curl, Joseph, "Clinton Calls Terror a U.S. Debt to the Past," *Washington Times,* November 8, 2001.

56. Ibid.

57. Solzhenitsyn, Aleksandr, *A Warning to the West* [On-line] Available: http://www.alor.org/WordsofWarning.htm#1a.

58. Roll, Richard, and John Talbott, "Why Many Developing Countries Just Aren't," November 20, 2001, p. 19.

59. Ibid.

60. Ibid., p. 17.

61. "Stimulus Politics," *Investor's Business Daily,* November 29, 2001.

62. Roll, Richard, and John Talbott, "Why Many Developing Countries Just Aren't," November 20, 2001, p. 15.

63. Ibid., p. 16.

64. Ibid., p. 16.

65. Ibid., p. 26.

66. "Leader Says Islam Is Inferior to West," *Chicago Tribune,* September 28, 2001, p. 9.

67. Ibid.

68. Boudreaux, Richard, "Clerics Say Religion No Basis for Terror," *Los Angeles Times,* October 6, 2001.

69. Miller, Christain, "Bin Laden's Voice Out of Nowhere," *Los Angeles Times,* October 16, 2001.

70. Kavanaugh, John F., "The Logic of Terror," *America,* February 28, 1998, p. 23.

71. Emerson, Steve, *American Jihad: The Terrorists Living Among Us* (New York: The Free Press, 2002) p. 127.

72. Ibid, p. 130.

73. Ibid, p. 132.

74. "The UK's Bin Laden Dossier in Full," *BBC News,* October 4, 2001. [On-line] Available: http://news.bbc.co.uk/hi/english/uk_politics/newsid_1579000/1579043.stm.

75. "Osama bin Laden Lashes Out Against the West," *Time* magazine, January 11, 1999.

76. Ibid.

77. bin Laden, Osama, "Talking With Terror's Banker," Interview with John Miller, *ABC News,* June 9, 1998, [On-line] Available: http://abcnews.go.com/sections/world/dailynews/terror_980609.html.

78. Sowell, Thomas, *Conquests and Cultures* (New York: Basic Books, 1998) p. 9.

79. Ibid, p. 111.

80. Ibid, p. 112.

81. Murphy, Dennis, "A Case of Modern-Day Slavery," *Dateline,* NBC, December 28, 2001.

82. Blair, David, "Bin Laden Buys Child Slaves for His Drug Farms in Africa," *Sunday Telegraph,* March 28, 1999, p. 36.

83. Ibid, pp. 32–3.

84. Collins, Larry, and Dominique Lapierre, *O Jerusalem* (New York: Simon & Schuster Inc., 1988) p. 26.

85. Peters, Joan, *From Time Immemorial: The Origins of the Arab–Jewish Conflict Over Palestine* (Chicago: JKAP Publications, 2000), p. 3.

86. Ibid, p. 12.

87. Ibid, p. 13.

88. Ibid, p. 14.

89. Ibid, p. 16.

90. Ibid, p. 11.

91. Ibid, p. 25.

92. Ibid, p. 411.

93. Keinon, Herb, "Peres to Complain to UN About Anti-Semitic Skit on Abu Dhabi TV," *Jerusalem Post,* November 19, 2001.

94. Winton, Richard, "Hate Crimes Soar Following Attacks," *Los Angeles Times,* December 21, 2001, p. B-1.

95. Khan, Muqtedar, "An Open Letter to U.S. Muslims," *Orlando Sentinel,* November 18, 2001, p. G1.

96. Special Dispatch 288, *The Middle East Media Research Institute,* [On-line] Available: http://www.memri.org/sd/SP28801.html, October 17, 2001.

97. Special Dispatch 270, *The Middle East Media Research Institute,* [On-line] Available: http://www.memri.org/sd/SP27001.html September 20, 2001.

98. Dobbs, Michael, "Myths Over Attacks on U.S. Swirl Through Islamic World," *Washington Post,* October 13, 2001, p. A22.

99. "Bin Laden's Warning: Full Text," *BBC News,* October 7, 2001 [On-line] Available: http://news.bbc.co.uk/hi/english/world/south_asia/newsid_1585000/1585636.stm.

100. Watanabe, Teresa, "Extremists Put Own Twist on Faith," *Los Angeles Times,* September 24, 2001, p. A-13.

101. "Prominent Muslim Cleric Denounces Bin Laden," *UPI,* October 17, 2001.

102. "Saudi Describes Arab Perspectives of War on Terrorism," *Dow Jones International News,* September 20, 2001.

103. Dhondy, Farrukh, "The Danger Within," *Australian Financial Review,* December 14, 2001, p. 1.

104. Rushdie, Salman, "Yes, This Is About Islam," *New York Times,* November 2, 2001, p. 25.

105. Maas, Peter, "Emroz Khan Is Having a Bad Day," *New York Times Magazine,* October 21, 2001, pp. 48–51.

106. Ibid.

107. Khan, Muqtedar, "An Open Letter to U.S. Muslims," *Orlando Sentinel*, November 18, 2001, p. G1.

108. Robin, Joshua and Bobby Cuza, "Rudy Rejects Prince's $10M," *Newsday*, October 12, 2001, p. A10.

109. Goldman, John J., and Marisa Schultz, "Giuliani Refuses Saudi's Check Donations," *Los Angeles Times*, October 12, 2001, p. A-3.

110. "Text of McKinney Letter," *Atlanta Journal-Constitution*, October 12, 2001.

111. Ibid.

112. Zakaria, Fareed, "Why Do They Hate Us?" *Newsweek*, October 15, 2001, pp. 22–40.

113. Willman, David, and Greg Miller, "Saudi Aid to War on Terror is Criticized," *Los Angeles Times*, October 13, 2001, p. A-1.

114. "The Buying Power of Black America—2000," *Target Market News*, [On-line] Available: http://targetmarketnews.com/numbes/index.htm, November 2001.

115. *The World Almanac 2002*, Ed. William A. McGeveran Jr. (New York: World Almanac Education Group, 2002), p. 106.

116. Talal, Prince Walid bin, Interview with Larry King, *Larry King Live*, CNN, October 12, 2001.

117. Schumer, Charles E., "Big Government Looks Better Now," *Washington Post*, December 11, 2001, p. A33.

118. Reynolds, Maura, "Response to Terror Change," *Los Angeles Times*, December 9, 2001, p. A-5.

119. Ibid.

120. Ibid.

3. EDUCATION BIAS: NO WONDER JOHNNY CAN'T READ

1. "Fist Control," *Keep and Bear Arms*, January 23, 2002, [On-line] Available: http://www.keepandbeararms.com/information/XclBPrintltem.asp?ID=137.

2. Nichols, Hans S., "College Grads Hear Mostly From the Left," *Insight*, July 2–9, 2001, p. 16.

3. Bockhorn, Lee, "The Ivy League Left," *Weekly Standard*, January 17, 2002.

4. York, Byron, "Ganging Up on the Tax Cut," *National Review*, April 2, 2001, pp. 20–22.

5. Ibid.

6. "Private Schools More Integrated Than Public," *School Reform News*, November, 1998.

7. Ibid.

8. "How Members of Congress Practice School Choice," *The Heritage Foundation Backgrounder,* June 14, 2000 [On-line] Available: http:www.heritage.org/library/backgrounder/bg1377.html.

9. Henry, Tamara, "NAACP Issues a Call to End Inequality in USA's Schools," *USA Today,* November 16, 2001, p. A.04.

10. Clowes, George A., "Should Classes be Smaller . . . or Simply More Orderly?", *School Reform News,* September 2001.

11. Farahmandpur, Ramin, and Peter McLaren, "Critical Literacy for Global Citizenship," *Center X Forum*—UCLA Graduate School of Education & Information Studies, Spring/Summer 2001, vol. 1, no. 2, p. 1.

12. Ibid.

13. Ibid.

14. Ibid.

15. Ibid.

16. Davis, James E., and Phyllis Maxey Fernlund, *Civics: Participating in Government* (Upper Saddle River, New Jersey: Prentice Hall, 2001), p. 346.

17. Ibid.

18. Ibid, p. 347.

19. Chaney, Helen, "Feds Didn't Learn From AT&T Case," *Orange County Register,* June 8, 2000, p. 9.

20. Ros, Juan C., "Who's the Monopoly?" *Daily News,* May 12, 2000.

21. Locke, Edwin A., "Microsoft Harmful?" *Orange County Register,* November 10, 1999, p. 11.

22. Davis, James E., and Phyllis Maxey Fernlund, *Civics: Participating in Government* (Upper Saddle River, New Jersey: Prentice Hall, 2001), p. 347.

23. Sinclair, Upton, *The Jungle* (Doubleday, 1906).

24. Davis, James E., and Phyllis Maxey Fernlund, *Civics: Participating in Government* (Upper Saddle River, New Jersey: Prentice Hall, 2001), p. 347.

25. Brasher, Phillip, "Government Wants to Drop Pizza Rules," *Long Beach Press Telegram,* November 8, 2001, p. A7.

26. Kemp, Jack, "Clinton Mischief Risks Economy," *Seattle Post-Intelligencer,* November 22, 2000, p. A15.

27. Davis, James E., and Phyllis Maxey Fernlund, *Civics: Participating in Government* (Upper Saddle River, New Jersey: Prentice Hall, 2001), p. 347.

28. Romney, Lee, and Karen Robinson-Jacobs, "Jobless Blacks Face Steepest Challenge," *Los Angeles Times,* November 26, 2001, p. A-13.

29. Ibid.

30. Ibid.

31. Harris, Bonnie, "In Fast Food, Some See Fast Track, "*Los Angeles Times,* March 12, 2001.

32. Ibid.

33. Ibid.

34. Ibid.

35. Davis, James E., and Phyllis Maxey Fernlund, *Civics: Participating in Government* (Upper Saddle River, New Jersey: Prentice Hall, 2001), p. 347.

36. Reisman, George. *Capitalism* (Ottawa, Illinois: Jameson Books, 1998), p. 514.

37. Ibid. p. 920.

38. Davis, James E., and Phyllis Maxey Fernlund. *Civics: Participating in Government* (Upper Saddle River, New Jersey: Prentice Hall, 2001), p. 347.

39. Rockwell, Llewellyn, "The Education Tax Racket." [On-line] Available: http://www.wnd.com/news/printer-friendly.asp? ARTICLE ID=24167, August 23, 2001.

40. Warder, Michael, "Check Out Urban Private Schools," *Los Angeles Times,* August 25, 2001, p. B21.

41. Hayes, Elizabeth, "A School System That Works," *Los Angeles Business Journal,* February 28, 2000.

42. Cloud, John, and Jodie Morese, "Home Sweet School," *Time* magazine, August 23, 2001.

43. Ibid.

44. "Traits of Home Schooled Are Similar," *Washington Times,* August 4, 2001.

45. Ibid.

46. Shapiro, Ben, "Effects of Campus Liberalism Far-Reaching," *Daily Bruin On-line,* November 20, 2001.

47. Hentoff, Nat, "1st Amendment Trampled on College Campuses," *E&P,* July 2, 2001.

48. Bockhorn, Lee, "The Ivy League Left," *Weekly Standard,* January 17, 2002.

49. Leo, John, "The No-Speech Culture," *U.S. News & World Report,* March 19, 2001, p. 16.

50. Hentoff, Nat, "1st Amendment Trampled on College Campuses," *E&P,* July 2, 2001.

51. LaGanga, Maria L., "College Paper Apologizes for Anti-Reparations Ad," *Los Angeles Times,* March 2, 2001.

52. "To Our Readers," *Daily Californian,* March 1, 2001.

53. Daily Cal Staff, "Daily Cal Issues Apology Over Controversial Ad," *Daily Californian,* March 2, 2001.

54. The California Aggie On-line—Campus Section 3.2.2001.

55. Daily Cal Staff, "Daily Cal Issues Apology Over Controversial Ad," *Daily Californian,* March 2, 2001.

56. Horowitz, David, [On-line] Available: http://www.frontpagemag.com /notepad/default.htm, March 2, 2001.

57. Daily Cal Staff, "Daily Cal Issues Apology Over Controversial Ad," *Daily Californian,* March 2, 2001.

58. Agopian, Eleeza V., Interview with Larry Elder, *Larry Elder Show,* KABC Talkradio, March 8, 2001.

59. Burress, Charles, "UC Newspaper Apologizes for Insensitive Ad," *San Francisco Chronicle,* March 2, 2001. p. A21.

4. More Dads, Less Crime

1. Stetson, Brad, "The Hollow Eyes of Fatherlessness," *Orange County Register,* August 27, 2000.

2. Anderson, Eloise, "Father's Day Or Fatherless Day?" *Investor's Business Daily,* June 19, 2000.

3. Glascock, Ned, "Out of Wedlock Births on Rise," *Raleigh News & Observer,* October 14, 2001.

4. Ibid.

5. Ibid.

6. Ibid.

7. Ibid.

8. Bernstein, Andrew, "The Welfare State Versus Values and the Mind," *Intellectual Activist,* October 2001, p. 15.

9. Ibid, p. 14.

10. *Larry Elder Show,* KABC Talkradio, April 16, 2001.

11. Sports Desk, Photo: Quotebook, *Los Angeles Times,* November 25, 2001, p. D-2.

12. Teaford, Elliot, "Gentry Rips His Players' Work Ethic," *Los Angeles Times,* November 27, 2001, p. D-6.

13. Ibid.

14. Plaschke, Bill, "Tough Love," *Los Angeles Times,* June 9, 2000, p. D-1.

15. Ibid.

16. Ibid.

17. Orlov, Rick, "Suspect Charged: Parks Grateful," *Los Angeles Daily News,* June 9, 2000, p. N1.

18. Stetson, Brad, "The Hollow Eyes of Fatherlessness," *Orange County Register,* August 27, 2000.

19. Anderson, Eloise, "Father's Day Or Fatherless Day?" *Investor's Business Daily,* June 19, 2000.

20. Parker, Kathleen, "The Sorry Legacy of a Lonely Father's Day," *USA Today,* June 17, 1998.

21. Anderson, Eloise, "Father's Day Or Fatherless Day?" *Investor's Business Daily,* June 19, 2000.

22. McCarthy, Terry, "L.A. Gangs Are Back," *Time* magazine, September 3, 2001, p. 48.

23. Ibid., p. 46.

24. Ibid.

25. Ibid.

26. Ibid., p. 48.

5. BLACK VICTICRATS

1. Dionne, E.J., "Struggling to Find a Way to Teach Values," *Washington Post,* July 9, 1990, p. A-5.

2. Holmberg, Mark, "Is One Pitcher Really Worth All These Words?" *Richmond Times-Dispatch,* June 11, 2000, p. B-1.

3. Lioi, Rachel Hoskins, "Blacks Say Racism Is Ongoing Problem," *Washington Times,* July 11, 2001.

4. "The Dog Days of July: White House Bites Back at NAACP's Attack," *Washington Post,* July 10, 2001, p. A7.

5. Jacoby, Jeff, "Liberals Love Their Hate Talk," *Orange County Register,* January 2, 2002, p. 9.

6. Murphy, Kim, "Group Boycotts Starbucks Over Police Shooting," *Los Angeles Times,* June 20, 2001, p. A-8.

7. Simon, Stephanie, "From Cincinnati's Mayhem Come Signs of a Better Day," *Los Angeles Times,* April 14, 2001.

8. Ted Koppel, *Nightline,* ABC, April 12, 2001.

9. Osborne, Kevin, and Kimball Perry, "Mfume Wants Federal Probe of City Police," *Cincinnati Post,* April 13, 2001, p. 7A.

10. Hortsman, Barry M., "15 Black Men Killed Since 1995," *Cincinnati Post,* April 10, 2001.

11. Edwards, Jennifer, "City Records 100th Shooting," *Cincinnati Post,* August 17, 2001, p. 1A.

12. Miller, Steve, "Cincinnati in Grip of Crime Wave Months After Riots," *Washington Times,* July 18, 2001, p. A6.

13. MacDonald, Heather, "Why Cincinnati's Crime Rate is Exploding," *Knight-Ridder Tribune Business News,* July 26, 2001.

14. Miller, Steve, "Cincinnati in Grip of Crime Wave Months After Riots," *Washington Times,* July 18, 2001, p. A6.

15. Leo, John, "Cincinnati Cops Out," *U.S. News & World Report,* July 30, 2001, p. 10.

16. Hasson, Judi, "Mayor D.C.: Crime Rate's Low," *USA Today,* March 24, 1989, p. 2A.

17. Frank, Robert and Eleena de Lisser, "Research in Affirmative Action Finds Modest Gains for Blacks Over 30 Years," *Wall Street Journal,* February 21, 1995, p. A2.

18. Eastland, Terry, *Ending Affirmative Action* (New York: Basic Books, 1996), p. 43.

19. Vandenabeele, Janet and Jodi Upton, "Colleges' Retention of Blacks Dismal," [On-line] Available: http://www.detnews.com/2001/schools/0107/15/a01-247739.htm, July 15, 2001.

20. Ibid.

21. Washington, Booker T., *Up From Slavery* (New York: Doubleday, Page and Company, 1901), p. 49.

22. O'Neill, June, "Welfare Reform Worked," *Wall Street Journal,* August 1, 2001.

23. Thernstrom, Stephen and Abigail, *America in Black and White* (New York: Simon & Schuster, 1997), p. 240.

24. Peterson, Karen S., "Health & Behavior," *USA Today,* June 17, 1999, p. 10D.

25. Zinsmeister, Karl, "Illegitimacy in Black and White," *Wall Street Journal,* November 16, 1987.

26. Waters, Maxine, *Larry Elder Show,* KABC Talkradio, June 8, 2000.

27. Seper, Jerry, "Agents Cite 'Political Interference': DEA Ends Probe After Profiling Claim," *Washington Times,* December 7, 2000, p. A4.

28. Editorial, "Cuba No Enemy to U.S. Fugitives," *Palm Beach Post,* February 7, 1999, p. 1E.

29. "New Jersey Top Cop Rips Lawmaker on Chesimard," *Star-Ledger,* January 14, 1999, p. 004.

30. Editorial, "Cuba No Enemy to U.S. Fugitives," *Palm Beach Post,* February 7, 1999, p. 1E.

31. Friedman, Milton, "There's No Justice in the War on Drugs," *New York Times,* January 11, 1995.

32. Schlesinger, Arthur, Jr., "A New Era Begins—But History Remains," *Wall Street Journal,* December 11, 1991, p. A16.

33. Glazer, Nathan, "The Shape of the River: A Case for Racial Preferences," *Public Interest,* April 1, 1999, pp. 45–63.

34. *SAG Newsletter,* April, 2000, p. 13.

35. Angeli, David H., "A 'Second Look' at Crack Cocaine Sentencing Policies," *American Criminal Law Review,* March 22, 1997.

36. Price, David Andrew, "A Good Man Is Hard to Find," *Wall Street Journal,* February 21, 1995.

37. Colvin, Richard Lee, "Education Bill Getting Closer to Completion," *Los Angeles Times,* September 19, 2001, p. A30.

38. Lawrence, Curtis, "Jackson Faults U.S. on Talks: Says Ducking Issues at Racism Conference Smacks of Isolation," *Chicago Sun-Times,* September 9, 2001, p. 28.

39. "U.S. Media Considers Blacks as Sub-Human," *Business Day (Johannesburg),* September 6, 2001, [On-line] Available: http://allafrica.com/stories/printable/200109060456.html.

40. Miller, Steve, "Jackson to Make Reparations a Priority," *Washington Times,* September 7, 2001, p. A1.

41. Ibid.

42. Lawrence, Curtis, "Jackson Faults U.S. on Talks: Says Ducking Issues at Racism Conference Smacks of Isolation," *Chicago Sun-Times,* September 9, 2001, p. 28.

43. Knickmeyer, Ellen, "African Leaders: 'Forget Reparations,' and 'Remember Slavery's Wrongs'," *Los Angeles Sentinel,* September 6, 2001.

44. Ibid.

45. Pittman, Todd, "Liberia Struggles With Its Own Past of Slavery," *Washington Times,* September 20, 2001.

46. Bandow, Doug, "A Look Behind the Marshall Plan Mythology," *Investor's Business Daily,* June 3, 1997.

47. "Mary Francis Berry's 'Propaganda Mill,' " *Washington Times* (Editorial), July 1, 2001.

48. Price, Joyce Howard, "Berry Evokes Passions," *Washington Times,* December 9, 2001.

49. Miller, Steve, "NAACP Address Called Excessive," *Washington Times,* July 10, 2001.

50. Price, Joyce Howard, "Berry Evokes Passions," *Washington Times,* December 9, 2001.

51. "Mary Francis Berry's 'Propaganda Mill,' " *Washington Times* (Editorial), July 1, 2001.

52. Ibid.

53. Price, Joyce Howard, "Berry Evokes Passions," *Washington Times,* December 9, 2001.

54. Sammon, Bill, and Steve Miller, "Bush's Pick Has Job, No Seat," *Washington Times,* December 7, 2001.

55. Ibid.

56. Ibid.

57. Abel, David, "Harvard 'Dream Team' Roiled," *Boston Globe,* December 22, 2001, p. A1.

58. Ibid.

59. Keller, Julia, "Poisoned Ivy," *Chicago Tribune,* January 11, 2002, p. 1.

60. Hunt, Albert R., "The Phony Protest . . . and Leaders," *Wall Street Journal,* January 10, 2002, p. A13.

61. Miller, Steve, "Toyota Faces Jackson's Deadline," *Washington Times,* July 31, 2001, p. A1.

62. Babwin, Don, "Toyota Aims to Hire More Minorities," Associated Press, August 9, 2001.

63. Miller, Steve, "Toyota Faces Jackson's Deadline," *Washington Times,* July 31, 2001, p. A1.

64. Noel, Peter, "Is Jesse for Sale?", *Village Voice,* January 2, 2000.

65. Ibid.

66. "Chavis Ousted by NAACP Board," *Chicago Tribune,* August 21, 1994, p. 1.

67. Morano, Marc, "Jesse Jackson Accused of 'Racketeering' by Top Black Businessman," Cybercast News Services, October 22, 2001, [On-line] Available: http://www.cnsnews.com/ViewPrint.asp?Page=\Culture\archive\200110\CUL 20011022a.html.

68. Ibid.

69. Ibid.

70. Morano, Marc, "Jesse Jackson's Empire Crumbling, Associates Say," Cybercast News Services, January 11, 2002, [On-line] Available: http:www.cnsnews. com/ViewPrint.asp?=\Politics\archive\.

71. Ibid.

72. Ibid.

73. Morano, Marc, "Jesse Jackson's Empire Crumbling, Associates Say," Cybercast News Services, January 11, 2002, [On-line] Available: http://www. cnsnews.com/ViewPrint.asp?=\Politics\archive\.

74. Ibid.

75. Ibid.

76. Ibid.

77. "A Curriculum of Indoctrination," *Issues and Views,* Fall, 1992.

78. McGowan, William, *Coloring the News: How Crusading for Diversity Has Corrupted American Journalism* (San Francisco: Encounter Books, 2001), p. 228.

79. "Unrepentant Sheriff Condemned; Black Ministers Say Senator Deserves Apology After Being Called Idiot," *Charlotte Observer,* November 30, 2001, p. 2Y.

80. Ibid.

81. Hopkinson, Natalie, "I Won't Let D.C. Lose Its Flavor," *Washington Post,* June 17, 2001, p. B1.

82. Ibid.

83. Tannenbaum, Rob, "Eyes on the Tiger," *TV Guide,* June 9, 2001, pp. 17–20.

84. Ibid., p. 43.

85. Banks, Sandy, "Mocha Girls and a Changing World View," *Los Angeles Times,* August 12, 2001.

86. Ibid.

87. Cooper, Marc, "Rowing Against the Tide," *Los Angeles Times,* September 23, 2001, p. M-4.

88. Miller, Steve, "Black Leaders Rally on Racial Rhetoric at Conference," *Washington Times,* November 30, 2001.

89. Ibid.

90. Ibid.

91. Ibid.

92. "NAACP Branch President to Speak Against War," *St. Petersburg Times,* November 28, 2001, p. 14.

93. Bickley, Rah, "Durham NAACP Supports Its Leader," *News & Observer,* September 25, 2001, p. B1.

94. "Nation At a Glance Column," *St. Louis Post-Dispatch,* September 20, 2001, p. A8.

95. Bickley, Rah, "Durham NAACP Supports Its Leader," *News & Observer,* September 25, 2001, p. B1.

96. *Larry Elder Show,* KABC Talkradio, October 2, 2001.

97. "Is Fear of Terrorism Affecting Your Way of Life?" *San Francisco Chronicle,* October 21, 2001.

98. Goodloe, Valerie, "The People's Pulse: Do You Think Race Relations Are Getting Better or Worse?" *Los Angeles Sentinel,* August 16, 2001, p. A-6.

99. Ibid.

100. Ibid.

101. Ibid.

102. Ibid.

103. Ibid.

104. Holden, Benjamin, "Trying Times," *Wall Street Journal,* February 5, 1996, p. A1.

105. Merin, Jennifer, "Hitting the Road Again: Celebrity Status Keeps Cochran Surrounded," *USA Today,* April 11, 2000, p. 01E.

106. Ibid.

107. Brubaker, Bill, "Ex-USC Official: Study of Athletes, Academics Halted," *Washington Post,* October 1, 1991, p. C01.

108. White, Matt, "Cobb's Award Reduced $1 Million in Ruling by Superior Court Judge," *Los Angeles Times,* July 16, 1994, p. 8.

109. Meyer, Josh, Carla Hall, and Kurt Streeter, "Two Lives Shattered in a Moment at the Castle Shooting," *Los Angeles Times,* November 5, 2000, p. 1-A.

110. Ibid.

111. Streeter, Kurt, "$100 Million Sought in Shooting of Actor Violence," *Los Angeles Times,* December 12, 2000, p. B-1.

112. Lait, Matt, and Scott Glover, "Los Angeles 2nd Panel Says Police Slaying Was Justified Probe," *Los Angeles Times,* October 24, 2001, p. B-3.

113. Streeter, Kurt, "$100 Million Sought in Shooting of Actor Violence," *Los Angeles Times,* December 12, 2000, p. B-1.

114. Meyer, Josh, Carla Hall, and Kurt Streeter, "Two Lives Shattered in á Moment at the Castle Shooting," *Los Angeles Times,* November 5, 2000, p. 1-A.

115. Gonzales, Greg, "Hopper Takes His Football Career One Step at a Time," *Los Angeles Times,* July 25, 1991, p. 10.

116. Hadnot, Ira J., "Cochran's Ex-Wife Makes Her Defense," *Dallas Morning News,* September 27, 1995, p. 1C.

117. Ibid.

118. Goodman, Michael J., "For the Defense: Johnnie Cochran's Whole Career Has Been a Prelude to What Is Happening in Courtroom 103," *Los Angeles Times,* January 29, 1995, p. 11.

119. Ibid.

120. "News Corp's N.Y. Post Moves To Dismiss Cochran Libel Suit," *Dow Jones News Service,* May 11, 1998.

121. Kreck, Carol, "Issel Suspended Over Insult," *Denver Post,* December 13, 2001, p. A01.

122. "Denver's Issel Apologizes for Remark," *Washington Post,* December 16, 2001, p. DO9.

123. Kreck, Carol, "Issel Suspended Over Insult," *Denver Post,* December 13, 2001, p. A01.

124. "Hispanic Groups Boycotting Nuggets," *New York Times,* December 14, 2001, p. 6.

125. Kreck, Carol, "Issel Suspended Over Insult," *Denver Post,* December 13, 2001, p. A01.

126. Crosson, Judith, "Denver Team to Meet With Hispanic Leaders Over Insult," *Reuters English News Service,* December 13, 2001.

127. Nazario, Sonia, "Sobering Facts: Heavy Drinking by Some Mexican-American Men Is Taking a Severe Toll on Families. Cultural Sensitivity Has Held Back Discussion in the Community," *Los Angeles Times,* March 21, 1999.

128. Caetano, Paul, and Catherine Clark, "1995 National Alcohol Survey," Mothers Against Drunk Driving (MADD), [On-line] Available: http://www.madd.org/madd/stats/printable/0,1068,1690,00.html.

129. Nazario, Sonia, "Sobering Facts; Heavy Drinking by Some Mexican-American Men Is Taking a Severe Toll on Families. Cultural Sensitivity Has Held Back Discussion in the Community," *Los Angeles Times,* March 21, 1999.

130. "Denver Nuggets Coach Suspended for Racial Slur," *Reuters English News Service,* December 12, 2001.

131. Springer, Steve, "De La Hoya Issues Apology for His Remark About Arum," *Los Angeles Times,* March 31, 2001, p. D-7.

132. Springer, Steve, "Arum Finds a New Talent," *Los Angeles Times,* October 13, 2001, p. D-7.

133. "Calif. Lt. Gov. Uses Racial Slur During Black History Speech," *Dow Jones International News,* February 13, 2001.

134. Ibid.

135. Kass, John, "Good Vs. Evil?" *Chicago Tribune,* November 6, 2000, p. 3.

136. Lambro, Donald, "GOP Leaders Condemn Gore Aide's Remarks," *Washington Times,* January 7, 2000, p. A4.

137. Ibid.

138. Sack, Kevin, "Blacks Who Voted Against Bush Offer Support to Him in Wartime," *New York Times,* December 25, 2001.

139. Vincent, Norah, "Baiting 'the Beast,' " *Village Voice,* July 24, 2001.

140. *Larry Elder Show,* KABC Talkradio, December 7, 2001.

141. "NAACP Calls For Local School Systems, Colleges and Universities to End Racial Disparities," *NAACP News,* November 13, 2001.

142. Jeter, Jon, "Glued to Their TV Sets," *Washington Post National Weekly Edition,* July 1–7, 1996.

143. "Don't Give Me or My Child Crutches!" *Los Angeles Sentinel,* July 19, 2001.

144. Williams, Walter, "Blacks: Look Ahead, Not Backward," *Orange County Register,* August 23, 2001, p. 9.

145. Ibid.

146. Gettleman, Jeffrey, "M.L. King III: Father's Path Hard to Follow," *Los Angeles Times,* August 4, 2001, p. A-1.

147. Ibid.

148. Willing, Richard, "King's Son Says He Believes Ray is Innocent," *USA Today,* March 28, 1997, p. A01.

149. Peyser, Andrea, "True or Not, Sickening Story Is All Too Easy to Believe," *New York Post,* July 18, 2000, p. 5.

150. "Min. Farrakhan and the Jews," [On-line] Available: http://blacksandjews.com/Farr_&_Jws.html#anchor359844.

151. Ford, Andrea, and Michael K. Frisby, "Maximum Effect," *Emerge,* April 1997, p. 46.

152. Newman, Marie, "The Angry Insider U.S. Rep. Maxine Waters is a Combative But Effective Voice of the Disenfranchised," *Kansas City Star,* May 30, 1992.

153. Murphy, Dean E., "Waters: No Apologies for Her Calling the President a Racist," *Los Angeles Times,* August 9, 1992, p. A-14.

154. Mulshine, Paul, "California Congresswoman Comes to Cop-Killer's Defense," *Star-Ledger,* December 27, 1998, p. 3.

155. *Almanac of American Politics 1992,* Ed. Michael Barone, Grant Ujifusa, (Washington, D.C.: National Journal, 1991), p. 559.

156. Williams, Juan, "What Next?" *Washington Post,* June 21, 1987, p. W18.

157. Hosenball, Mark, and Evan Thoms with Vern E. Smith, "Jesse and Al's Food Fight," *Newsweek,* April 9, 2001, p. 41.

158. "The Buying Power of Black America—2000," *Target Market News,* [On-line] Available: http://targetmarketnews.com/numbers/index.htm, November 2001.

159. *The World Almanac 2002,* Ed. William McGeveran Jr. (New York: World Almanac Education Group 2002), p. 106.

160. "Harris's Interactive Annual Report on America's Heroes," *PR Newswire,* August 15, 2001.

161. Jackson, Jesse, "From General to Lapdog," *Tribune Media Services,* August 6. 2001

162. Roberts, Johnnie L., "The Race to the Top," *Newsweek,* January 28, 2002, p. 44.

163. Dickerson, Debra J., "Pride and Prejudice," *California Lawyer,* January 2001, p. 96.

164. Ibid.

165. Ibid.

6. ADVENTURES IN CONTEMPORARY RACE RELATIONS

1. Bruce, Tammy, *The New Thought Police: Inside the Left's Assault on Free Speech and Free Minds* (Roseville: Prima Publishing, 2001), p. 166.

2. Barabak, Mark Z., "Campaign 2000: For Many Blacks, Election Isn't on Radar," *Los Angeles Times,* October 17, 2000, p. A-1.

3. Helmick, Kristiana, "Support O' the Irish Dear to Clinton," *Christian Science Monitor,* October 18, 1995, p. 4.

4. "If You're Irish, You're a Target," *Irish Voice,* August 20, 1996, p. 6.

5. "Democratic Presidential Candidates Participate in Debate, Apollo Theatre, New York," *Political Transcripts by Federal Document Clearing House,*" February 21, 2000.

6. Roane, Kit R., "A Risky Trip Through 'White Man's Pass' In New Jersey, a Losing War on Racial Profiling," *U.S. New & World Report,* April 16, 2001, p. 24.

7. Brune, Tom, "America Strikes Back," *Newsday,* October 11, 2001, p. A05.

8. Cloud, John, "What's Race Got to Do With It?" *Time* Magazine, July 30, 2001, p. 42.

9. Worrill, Conrad W., "The Fallout of the Attack on the United States and African People," *Los Angeles Sentinel,* October 25, 2001, p. A-6.

10. Mineta, Norman, "That Dirty Little Word 'Profiling,' " *60 Minutes,* Interview with Steve Kroft, CBS, December 2, 2001.

11. Sperry, Paul, "Airport-Security Firm at Mercy of Muslims," *WorldNetDaily,* [On-line] Available: http://www.worldnetdaily.com/news/article.asp? ARTICLE ID=25259, November 16, 2001.

12. Kalita, S. Mitra, "N.J. State Police Leader Fired for Racist Remarks," *Portland Oregonian,* March 1, 1999, p. A05.

13. Williams, Colonel Carl, "New Jersey Police Superintendent Connection Between Race and Crime," Dan Rather, *CBS News: 60 Minutes II,* October 19, 1999.

14. Sperry, Paul, "Airport-Security Firm at Mercy of Muslims," *WorldNetDaily,* [On-line] Available: http://www.worldnetdaily.com/news/article.asp? ARTICLE ID=25259, November 16, 2001.

15. Ibid.

16. Ibid.

17. Ibid.

18. Ibid.

19. Lords, Erik, "University of Michigan Says Its Cause Stronger Than Ever: Devotion to Affirmative Action to Uphold Bollinger's Vision," *Detroit Free Press,* October 22, 2001, p. 1B.

20. Winkler, Jaimie, "U. Michigan: Expert Witnesses in U. Michigan Lawsuit Discuss Diversity," *U-Wire,* March 18, 1999.

21. Seligman, Dan, "Mr. Diversity," *Forbes,* November 26, 2001, p. 81.

22. Ibid.

23. Ibid.

24. Locke, Michelle, "UC Moves Closer to Admissions Overhaul," *Los Angeles Times,* November 14, 2001.

25. Ibid.

26. Weiss, Kenneth, "UC Chief Seeks to Drop SAT as a Requirement," *Los Angeles Times,* February 17, 2001.

27. Weinkopf, Chris, "Racial Preferences No Longer Important," *Los Angeles Daily News,* April 12, 2000, p. N15.

28. Weiss, Kenneth R., "Education: The 4% Solution," *Los Angeles Times,* March 31, 1999, p. B-2.

29. Trounson, Rebecca, "UC Admissions Plan Would De-Emphasize Grades, Tests," *Los Angeles Times,* November 15, 2001.

30. Ibid.

31. Ibid.

32. Higuera, Jonathan J., "Several Factors Drive More Firms to Do Background Checks on Job Applicants," *Arizona Daily Star,* November 27, 2001.

33. Useem, Jerry, "The Art of Lying," *Time,* December 20, 1999.

34. Ibid.

35. Ohlemacher, Stephen, "Test Scores Reveal Width of Racial Gap," *Cleveland Plain Dealer,* November 4, 2001, p. A1.

36. Weiss, Kenneth, "UC Chief Seeks to Drop SAT as a Requirement," *Los Angeles Times,* February 17, 2001.

37. Leo, John, "Let's Attack Merit," *U.S. News & World Report,* November 24, 1997, p. 22.

38. Ibid.

39. Schemo, Diana Jean, "Head of U. of California Seeks to End SAT Use in Admissions," *New York Times,* February 17, 2001.

40. "Study: SAT Good Predictor of Grades, Graduation Rate," *Fox News,* April 28, 2001, [On-line] Available: http://www.foxnews.com/study/0,2933, 18138,00.html.

41. Leo, John, "Flogging the SATs," *U.S. News & World Report,* October 25, 1999, p. 16.

42. Laird, Bob, "Secrets of the SAT," *Frontline,* PBS, [On-line] Available: http:// www.pbs.org/wgbh/pages/frontline/shows/sats/interviews/laird.html, January 11, 2002.

43. Ibid.

44. Hong, Peter Y., "The Changing Face of Higher Education Trends," *Los Angeles Times,* July 14, 1998, p. A-1.

45. Lubman, Sarah, "Campuses Mull Admissions Without Affirmative Action," *Wall Street Journal,* May 16, 1995.

46. Asimov, Nanette, "A Hard Lesson in Diversity: Chinese Americans Fight Lowell's Admissions Policy," *San Francisco Chronicle,* June 19, 1995, p. A1.

47. Billingsley, K. L., "Quota Foes Attack Judge's Decision on Racial Admissions," *Washington Times,* May 15, 1997, p. A10.

48. Vandenabeele, Janet, and Jodi Upton, "Colleges Retention of Blacks Dismal," *Detroit News,* July 15, 2001.

49. Krauthammer, Charles, "Lies, Damn Lies and Racial Statistics," *Time,* April 20, 1998, p. 32.

50. Greenberg, Paul, "A Trio of Sensible Thinkers on the Subject of Affirmative Action," *Chicago Tribune,* September 7, 1990, p. 21.

51. Ibid.

52. Biskupic, Joan, "Bush to Defend Affirmative Action Policy Support of Race Conscious Program Surprises Many," *USA Today,* August 3, 2001, p. A1.

53. Meese, Edwin, and John C. Eastman, "The Death Throes of Preference," *Washington Times,* August 10, 2001, p. A21.

54. O'Reilly, Bill, *The No Spin Zone* (New York: Broadway Books, 2001), pp. 78–79.

55. Goldberg, Bernard, *Bias* (Washington, D.C.: Regnery Publishing, 2002), p. 108.

56. Schleier, Curt, "Newscaster Sam Donaldson: Dedication Keeps Him at the Top," *Investor's Business Daily,* May 1, 2001, p. A3.

57. Ibid.

58. Richards, Sarah, E., "Murphy Drops His Caucus Bid," *Chicago Tribune,* July 17, 2001.

59. Meeks, Larry, "Segregated Sundays a Sad Secret," *The Sun,* May 29, 2001.

60. Garchik, Leah, "The In Crowd: And the Winner Is . . ." *San Francisco Chronicle,* October 25, 2001, p. B-10.

61. Graser, Marc, "Parks Winner Red-Faced," *Daily Variety,* October 23, 2001, p. 1.

62. Steinbeck, John, *Of Mice and Men* (New York City: Penguin Books, 1993).

63. Lopez, Steve, "Wrong Guy, Good Cause," *Time,* July 31, 2000, p. 25.

64. Flynn, Dan, *Cop Killer* (Washington, D.C.: Accuracy in Academia, 1999).

65. Ibid.

66. "Convicted Murderer Abu-Jamal Named Honorary Citizen of Paris," *Fox News,* December 6, 2001.

67. Lopez, Steve, "Wrong Guy, Good Cause," *Time,* July 31, 2000, p. 24.

68. Ibid., p. 25.

69. Flynn, Dan, *Cop Killer* (Washington, D.C.: Accuracy in Academia, 1999) p. 13.

70. Flynn, Dan, *Cop Killer* (Washington, D.C.: Accuracy in Academia, 1999).

71. Flynn, Dan, "Mumia Is Still Guilty," *American Enterprise,* December 20, 2001.

72. "Min. Farrakhan and the Jews," [On-line] Available: http://blacksand jews.com/Farr_&_Jws.html#anchor359844.

73. "Louis Farrakhan, Madison Square Garden, October 7, 1985," Simon Wiesenthal Center Research Department.

74. *Daily Variety,* February 24, 1994.

75. Ibid.

76. Ibid.

77. Simon Wiesenthal Center Research Department.

78. "Minister Louis Farrakhan: In His Own Words," [On-line] Available: http://www.adl.org/special_reports/farrakhan_own_words/on_slave_trade.html.

79. "Minister Louis Farrakhan: In His Own Words," [On-line] Available: http://www.adl.org/special_reports/farrakhan_own_words/on_jews.html.

80. Gaiter, Dorothy J., "'Quiet Diplomacy': How Mike Wallace Set Up a Meal to Mend Black-Jewish Relations," *Wall Street Journal,* February 25, 1997, p. A-1.

81. Ibid.

82. Boteach, Shmuley, "Sharpton's Missed Opportunity," *Jerusalem Post,* November 9, 2001, p. B-8.

83. Rutten, Tim, and Andrea Ford, "Families Anger Erupts Outside the Courtroom," *Los Angeles Times,* September 29, 1995.

84. "'Do the Right Thing,' Defense Tells Simpson Jury," *Seattle Post-Intelligencer,* September 29, 1995, p. A-1

85. Boyd, Herd, "Johnnie Cochran Receives Racial Harmony Award," *The Black World Today,* [On-line] Available: http://www.tbwt.com/views/specialrpt/specialrpt_0012.asp.

86. Ibid.

87. Faw, Bob, and Nancy Skelton, "The 'Hymie' Incident," *Los Angeles Times,* October 19, 1986, p. 20.

88. "Anti-Semitism and Prejudice in America. How Prevalent Is Anti-Semitism in America?" [On-line] Available http://www.adl.org/antisemitism_survey/survey_i.html.

89. "Anti-Semitism and Prejudice in America. Which Americans Are Most Likely to Hold Anti-Semitic Views," [On-line] Available: http://www.adl.org/antisemitism_survey/survey_iii.html.

90. Parmelee, Jennifer, "Israel Evaluates Ethiopian Jews," *Washington Post,* May 25, 1991, p. A-1.

91. Goldman, John J., and Marisa Schultz, "Giuliani Refuses Saudi's Check Donations," *Los Angeles Times,* October 12, 2001, p. A-3.

92. Weiss, Albert, *Patterns of Discrimination Against Jews* (New York: Friendly House Publishing, 1958) p. 46.

7. MEDIA BIAS—THE DENIAL CONTINUES

1. Shermer, Michael, "How to Be a Skeptic," *Natural History,* April 1, 1997, p. 8.

2. Goldberg, Bernard, "On Media Bias, Network Stars Are Rather Clueless," *Wall Street Journal,* May 24, 2001, p. A 22.

3. Ibid.

4. McGowan, William, *Coloring the News: How Crusading for Diversity Has Corrupted American Journalism* (San Francisco: Encounter Books, 2001), p. 226.

5. Media Research Center, *The Best Notable Quotables of 2001,* December 24, 2001, vol. Fourteen, no. 26, p. 6.

6. Ibid., p. 7.

7. Goldberg, Bernard, *Bias* (Washington, D.C.: Regnery Publishing, 2002.), p. 24.

8. Ibid., pp. 221–222.

9. Ibid.

10. Ibid.

11. Ibid.

12. "Fifty Years of Covering War, Looking for Peace and Honoring Law," *New York Times,* December 16, 2001, p. 9.

13. Jones, Charisse, "A Once-shunned Sharpton on a Comeback," *USA Today,* August 15, 2001, p. A.04.

14. Ibid.

15. Glassman, James K., "Don't Raise the Minimum Wage," *Washington Post,* February 24, 1998, p. A21.

16. Thomas, Evan, interview with Howard Kurtz, *Reliable Sources,* CNN, June 16, 2001.

17. McGowan, William, *Coloring the News* (San Francisco: Encounter Books, 2001), p. 19.

18. Ibid., p. 169.

19. Sowell, Thomas, "Consequences of Affirmative Action," *Las Vegas Journal-Review,* September 14, 2001, p. 2d.

20. Lasswell, Mark, *Wall Street Journal,* "The Fall of an Affirmative Action Hero," August 27, 1997.

21. Ibid.

22. McGowan, William, *Coloring the News* (San Francisco: Encounter Books, 2001), p. 57.

23. Ciokajlo, Mickey, "Reynolds Set to Return to Work in Community," *Chicago Tribune,* January 29, 2001, p. 1.

24. Warren, Ellen and Terry Armour, "Jackson CNN Show May Not Go on Now That Pay Is Public," *Chicago Tribune,* March 7, 2001, p. 2.

25. Kass, John, "Even National Media's Love for Jackson Lost," *Chicago Tribune,* March 28, 2001.

26. Gibbs, Nancy, "Making Time For a Baby," *Time,* April 15, 2002, p. 51.

27. McGowan, William, *Coloring the News* (San Francisco: Encounter Books, 2001), p. 246.

28. Drudge, Matt, *Drudge Report,* November 30, 2001.

29. Jensen, Elizabeth, "MSNBC Schedules Alan Keyes Talk Show," *Los Angeles Times,* January 8, 2002.

30. *Notable Quotables,* vol. 11 no. 12, Media Research Center, June 1, 1998.

31. *The Best Notable Quotables of 2001,* vol. 14 no. 26, Media Research Center, December 14, 2001, p. 6.

32. Ibid.

33. Eig, Jonathan, "Do Part-Time Workers Hold the Key to When the Recession Breaks?", *Wall Street Journal,* January 3, 2002.

34. Kurtz, Howard, "Rather Spoke at Democratic Fundraiser," *Washington Post,* April 4, 2001, p. A01.

35. Ibid.

36. Editorial, "Rather Restrained," *Christian Science Moniter,* July 26, 2001, p. 10.

37. Coles, Joanna, "Unlike Clinton, Gary Condit Is Facing a Media Onslaught Completely Unarmed," *Times of London: News International,* July 30, 2001, p. 27.

38. Limbacher, Carl Jr., "Civil Rights Leader Dan Rather Slurred Blacks with Chandra Comments," *NewsMax,* July 23, 2001, [On-line] Available: http://www.newsmax.com/archives/articles/2001/7/22/190650.shtml.

39. "The Gall of This Gatekeeper," *Investor's Business Daily,* July 27, 2001.

40. "Condit's Redrawn District is Tougher," *Washington Times,* September 15, 2001.

41. Whitworth, Damien, "What About The Girl, Gary?" *The Times of London: News International,* July 6, 2001.

42. McGrory, Mary, "Intern Saga's Sorry Sequel," *Washington Post,* July 12, 2001, p. 03.

43. "Rep. Gary Condit (D-CA)," *National Journal,* July 9, 1999, [On-line] Available: http://www.nationaljournal.com.

44. "Avoiding Gary Condit's Democratic ID," vol 5, no. 22, Media Research Center, July 12, 2001.

45. Ibid.

46. Ibid.

47. Ibid.

48. Maher, Bill, Interview with Larry King, *Larry King Live,* CNN, July 27, 2001.

49. Ibid.

50. "Avoiding Gary Condit's Democratic ID," vol. 5, no. 22, Media Research Center, July 12, 2001.

51. Wright, Brad, "Clinton Sees Struggle For 'Soul' of 21st Century," *CNN.com,* [On-line] Available: http://www.cnn.com, November 7, 2001.

52. Curl, Joseph, "Clinton Calls Terror a U.S. Debt to Past," *Washington Times,* November 8, 2001, p. A1.

53. Ibid.

54. Shogren, Elizabeth, "Clinton Gives New Plans, Job Ratings a Public Trial," *Los Angeles Times,* January 21, 1999, p. A-15.

55. " 'Controversial" Abortion Order;' " January 23, 2001, [On-line] Available: http://www.mediaresearch.org/news/cyberalert/2001/cyb20010123.asp#1.

56. Ibid.

57. Ibid.

58. Ibid.

59. Ibid.

60. Ibid.

61. Clinton, Hillary Rodham, "New York Senator Hillary Rodham Clinton Discusses Attack on the World Trade Center with Jane Pauley," *Dateline NBC,* NBC, September 17, 2001.

62. Clinton Chelsea, "Before & After," *Talk,* December 2001/January 2002, p. 100.

63. Harper, Jennifer, "Details of 'Terror Day Tale,' Pit Hillary vs. Chelsea," *Washington Times,* November 10, 2001, p. A1.

64. "Chelsea Rebuts Mom's Story," *New York Post,* November 10, 2001, p. 10.

65. Rosen, Mike, "2001 Doozies From the Media," *Rocky Mountain News,* December 28, 2001, p. 49A.

66. Clinton, President Bill, "Remarks of President William Jefferson Clinton to the Greater Washington Society of Association Executives in Washington, D.C., on October 9, 2001," [On-line] Available: http.//www.gwsae.org/SpeakersSeries/Clintontranscript. html.

67. Thomas, Helen, "John Walker Needs Bush's Compassion," *Houston Chronicle,* December 28, 2001.

68. Scott, Walter, "Personality Parade," *Parade,* April 14, 2002, p. 2.

69. Will, George F., "She, Even More Than He, Personifies Clintonism," *Orlando Sentinel,* March 30, 2000, p. A15.

70. Greenberg, Paul, "Is the Press Biased? Are Bluebirds Blue?" *Houston Chronicle,* August 22, 1996, p. 32.

71. Harrison, George, Composer: 1966. Recorded April 21–22 and May 16, 1966; Released UK, August 5, 1966 (LP: *Revolver*); Released U.S.: August 8, 1966 (LP: *Revolver*).

72. Simon, Richard, "House Votes to Aid Insurers if Terrorists Attack U.S. Again," *Los Angeles Times*, November 30, 2001, p. A-16.

73. Ibid.

74. Media Research Center, *The Best Notable Quotables of 2001*, December 24, 2001, vol. 14, no. 26, p. 7.

75. Ibid, p. 6.

76. Goldberg, Bernard, "Networks Need a Reality Check," *Wall Street Journal*, February 13, 1996, p. A14.

77. Vieth, Warren, "States Revenues Now Sagging Under Weight of Recession," *Los Angeles Times*, December 25, 2001, p. A–1.

78. "The Pump-Priming Fallacy," *Investor's Business Daily*, Editorials, October 3, 2001.

79. Sowell, Thomas, "Basic Economics: A Citizen's Guide to the Economy" (New York: Basic Books, December 26, 2000), p. 327.

80. Ibid., p. 328.

81. Vieth, Warren, "New Deficits Force Boost of Debt Ceiling," *Los Angeles Times*, January 3, 2002.

82. Vedder, Richard E., and Lowell E. Gallaway, *Out of Work: Unemployment and Government in Twentieth Century America* (New York: New York University Press, 1993, 1997), p. 230.

83. Vieth, Warren, "States' Revenues Now Sagging Under the Weight of Recession," *Los Angeles Times*, December 25, 2001, p. A-1.

84. Barstow, David, Robert Hanley, Jan Hoffman, Kirk Johnson, Sarah Kershaw, N.R. Kleinfield, John Leland, and Terry Pristin, "A Nation Challenged: The Victims," *New York Times*, October 19, 2001, p. 11.

85. Brownstein, Ronald, and Janet Hook, "A Bruised Clinton Prepares to Grab Legislative Victory Policy," *Los Angeles Times*, October 14, 1998, p. A-1.

86. Stevenson, Richard W., "A Finale in Three-Part Harmony," *New York Times*, December 12, 2001, p. 27.

87. Chandler, Clay, "Hill Weighs Stock for Social Security," *Washington Post*, April 27, 1998, p. A01.

88. Jackson, Robert, "Darkest Days of Nixon Years," *Los Angeles Times*, November 10, 1999, p. A-5.

89. Gerstenzang, James, and Janet Hook, "Rejuvenated Bush Prods Congress on Education, Defense," *Los Angeles Times*, August 30, 2001.

90. Goldberg, Bernard, *Bias: A CBS Insider Exposes How the Media Distort the News* (Washington, D.C.: Regnery Publishing, 2002), p. 218.

91. Clairmont, Julie, " 'Segregation Tax' Paid," [On-line] Available: http://www.inman.com, December 26, 2001.

92. Alonso-Zaldivar, Ricardo, "Federal Energy Panel Chair Herbert Steps Down," *Los Angeles Times,* August 7, 2001.

8. GUN CONTROL—WE TRIED IT ROSIE'S WAY

1. *A Country in the Crosshairs,* BBC News, January 4, 2002.

2. Chapman, Steve, "Guns in Michigan," *Orange County Register,* June 9, 2001, p. 9.

3. Landers, Ann, "Neighbor Up North Gives Us a Shot of Our Own Medicine," *Chicago Tribune*, July 24, 2001.

4. "In Japan and England, The Murder Rate Is a Fraction of What It Is Here," [On-line] Available: http://www.guntruths.com/Myths/Japan_England.htm, June 8, 2001.

5. Ludwig, Jens, and Philip J. Cook, "Homicide and Suicide Rates Associated With Implementation of the Brady Handgun Violence Prevention Act," *JAMA,* August 2, 2000, vol 284, no. 5, p. 585

6. Reitman, Valerie, "School Slayings Horrify Japan," *Los Angeles Times,* June 9, 2001.

7. "In Japan and England, The Murder Rate Is a Fraction of What It Is Here," [On-line] Available: http://www.guntruths.com/Myths/Japan_England.htm, June 8, 2001.

8. Dougherty, Jon, "Britain, Australia Top U.S. in Violent Crime," *WorldNetDaily*, February 2001.

9. Faria Jr., Miguel A., "Great Britain and Gun Control: With Neither Liberty Nor Safety," *NewsMax.com*, July 11, 2000.

10. Ibid.

11. Ibid.

12. Lott Jr., John R., "Unraveling Some Brady Law Falsehoods," *Los Angeles Times*, July 2, 1997.

13. Hannaford, Peter, "Aboard Flight 564," *Washington Times,* September 19, 2001.

14. Ibid.

15. Associated Press, "Pilots Union Urges Congress To Let Pilots Carry Weapons," *Dow Jones International News,* September 25, 2001.

16. Ibid.

17. Ibid.

18. Ibid.

19. "America on the Brink," *Detroit Free Press,* September 26, 2001, p. 1A.

20. Ibid.

21. "Pilots Won't Be Armed," *National Post,* September 28, 2001, p. A05.

22. Jones, Del, "Pilots Ready to Fight to Defend Friendly Skies," *USA Today,* September 25, 2001, p. 1B.

23. Glover, Scott, and Matt Lait, "Response to Terror," *Los Angeles Times,* September 28, 2001.

24. Dorning, Mike, "Decreasing Rate of Gun Triggers Debate," *Chicago Tribune,* June 4, 2000, p. 1.

25. Glover, Scott, and Matt Lait, "Response to Terror," *Los Angeles Times,* September 28, 2001.

26. Slater, Rodney, and Michael Boyd, "Interview with Mike Farrell; Interview with Rick Sanford," Bill Press and Larry Elder, *Crossfire,* CNN, December 19, 2001.

27. *Notable Quotables,* vol. 12 no. 10, Media Research Center, [On-line] Available: http://www.mediaresearch.org/news/nq/1999/nq/19990517.html, May 17, 1999.

28. *Notable Quotables,* vol. 12 no. 9, Media Research Center, May 3, 1999.

29. Winegar, Garvey, "Give Million Mom March a Second Look," *Richmond Times-Dispatch*, May 12, 2000, p. D-4.

30. Rivera, Geraldo, Interview with Bill O'Reilly, *The O'Reilly Factor*, Fox News, November 29, 2001.

31. Rivera, Geraldo, Interview with Laurie Dhue, *Fox News*, November 29, 2001.

32. Taylor, Jared, *Paved With Good Intentions: The Failure of Race Relations in Contemporary America* (New York: Carroll & Graf Publishers, 1992), p. 10.

33. McCarthy, Terry, "With Police in Retreat and Gangsters Winning Parole, Mayhem Returns to the Streets," *Time,* September 3, 2001, p. 46.

34. Glover, Scott, and Matt Lait, "Police in Secret Group Broke Law Routinely," *Los Angeles Times,* February 10, 2000, p. A-1.

35. McCarthy, Terry, "With Police in Retreat and Gangsters Winning Parole, Mayhem Returns to the Streets," *Time,* September 3, 2001, p. 49.

36. Ibid.

37. "Wrap: Greyhound Bus Crashes As Driver Attacked; 6 Killed," *Dow Jones International News,* October 03, 2001.

38. "A Citizen's Guide to Federal Firearms Laws," NRA Institute For Legislative Action, [On-line] Available: http://www.nraila.org, January 16, 2002.

39. "Handgun Carry Permits," Tennessee Department of Safety, [On-line] Available: http://www.state.tn.us/safety/handguns.html, January 17, 2002.

40. *The World Almanac and Book of Facts 2002* (New York: World Almanac Education Group, 2002), p. 377.

41. Ratnesar, Romesh, "Should You Carry a Gun?" *Time*, July 6, 1998, p. 48.

42. Burns, Jim, "Survey: Top Cops Favor Concealed Carry Laws," CNSNews.com, November 30, 2001.

43. Anderson, Fred, "Guns, Rights and People Arming America, The Origins of a National Gun Culture," *Los Angeles Times,* September 17, 2000, p. 1.

44. Ibid.

45. Reynolds, Glen Harlan, "Gun Control Book Based on Faulty Data, [On-line] Available: http://www.foxnews.com/story, October 10, 2001.

46. Ibid.

47. Ibid.

48. Ibid.

49. Ibid.

50. Ibid.

51. Ibid.

52. McCain, Robert Stacy, "NEH Halts Backing for Gun Historian's Grant," *Washington Times*, May 22, 2002.

53. Reynolds, Glen Harlan, "Gun Control Book Based on Faulty Data," [On-line] Available: http://www.foxnews.com/story, October 10, 2001.

54. Ibid.

55. Ibid.

56. Worth, Robert F., "Historian's Prizewinning Book on Guns Is Embroiled in a Scandal," *New York Times,* December 8, 2001, p. 13.

57. Ibid.

58. McCain, Robert Stacy, "NEH Halts Backing for Gun Historian's Grant," *Washington Times*, May 22, 2002.

59. "In the Wake of Terrorist Attacks, Sarah Brady Warns About Risks of Guns in the Home," Brady Center to Prevent Gun Violence, [On-line] Available: http://www.bradycampaign.org, September 18, 2001.

60. Lott, John R. Jr., "Others Fear Being Placed at the Mercy of Criminals," *Los Angeles Times,* March 30, 2001, p. 9.

61. Ibid.

62. Ibid.

63. *Armed Citizen,* NRA Publications, [On-line] Available: www.nrahq.org, January 2002.

64. Lott, John, unpublished work, October 9, 2001.

9. REPUBLICANS VERSUS DEMOCRATS

1. Bartlett, John, *Familiar Quotations* (Boston: Little, Brown and Company, 1980), p. 372.

2. "Quotes: Liberty/Politics," [On-line] Available: http://www.duke.edu/~gnsmith/quotes/quotes03.htm.

3. "Humorous Quotes Attributed to Groucho Marx,"[On-line] Available: http://www.workinghumor.com/quotes/groucho_marx.html.

4. Reich, Robert B., "Commentary: Back of the Hand to the Safety Net," *Los Angeles Times,* June 21, 2001.

5. Mehren, Elizabeth and Greg Miller, "A Shift in Power," *Los Angeles Times,* May 25, 2001, p. A-19.

6. Lynch, Michael W., "Midnight Scramblers," *Reason,* April 2000, p. 15.

7. Ibid.

8. "High Profile Republican Says LP Cost GOP Seven U.S. House Seats in 1996," *LP News,* July 1997, [On-line] Available: http://www.lp.org/lpn/9707-GOP.html.

9. Neumayr, George, "Republican Self-Mutilation," *California Political Review,* November/December 2001, p. 20.

10. Clifford, Frank, "Candidates for Mayor Receive Radio Grilling Politics," *Los Angeles Times,* January 7, 1993, p. 1.

11. Neumayr, George, "Republican Self-Mutilation," *California Political Review,* November/December 2001, p. 20.

12. Ibid.

13. "Thirty-Fifth District," *The Almanac of American Politics,* (Washington: National Journal Group, 2001), pp. 250–251.

14. Neumayr, George, "Republican Self-Mutilation," *California Political Review,* November/December 2001, p. 20.

15. Marinucci, Carla, "GOP Maverick to Make Run for Governor," *San Francisco Chronicle,* November 6, 2001, p. A15.

16. Moore, Stephen, and Stephen Slivinski, "Fiscal Policy Report Card on America's Governors: 2000," *Cato Institute Policy Analysis, No. 391,* February 12, 2001, pp. 3, 26

17. Neumayr, George, "Republican Self-Mutilation," *California Political Review,* November/December 2001, p. 20.

18. Barabak, Mark Z., and Michael Finnegan, "GOP Rivals for Governor Debate Their Differences," *Los Angeles Times,* January 23, 2002, p. A-1.

19. Ewegen, Bob, "Will Libertarians Bolt the Stupid Party?" *Denver Post,* November 24, 2001.

20. "Libertarian Campaigns," Libertarian Party, January 19, 2002, [On-line] Available: http://www.lp.org/campaigns/.

21. "High Profile Republican Says LP Cost GOP Seven U.S. House Seats in 1996," *LP News,* July 1997, [On-line] Available: http://www.lp.org/lpn/9707-GOP.html.

22. "Governor Report," *The Hotline,* October 10, 1998.

23. Redekop, Bill, "In Search of Jesse Ventura," *Winnipeg Free Press,* April 11, 1999, p. B1.

24. O'Keefe, Kevin, "Body Politic Jesse Ventura Grasps Voters' Discontent in Minnesota," *San Antonio Express-News,* November 15, 1998, p. G1.

25. Ibid.

26. Jefferson, Thomas, "We Owe Him Our Thanks," *Investor's Business Daily,* November 25, 1998, p. A20.

27. Kennedy, Senator Edward M., "Tribute to Senator Robert F. Kennedy," [On-line] Available: http://www.cs.umb.edu/jfklibrary, June 8, 1968.

28. O'Neill, June, "Welfare Reform Worked," *Wall Street Journal,* August 1, 2001.

29. "Leadville Libertarians Sworn into Office," [On-line] Available: http://www.lpcolorado.org/cl/2002/01leadville.html, January 18, 2002.

30. Swyers, Joe, Interview with Joe Swyers, *Larry Elder Show,* KABC Talk-radio, November 29, 2001.

31. Saltonstall, Dave, "Bloomberg in Need of Poll Vault," *New York Daily News,* May 2, 2001, p. 3.

32. Kowal, Jessica, "Bloomberg's Record Spending a Key to Campaign," *Newsday,* December 4, 2001, p. A7.

33. Cooper, Michael, "The 2001 Elections: Campaign Finance—Record Spending by Bloomberg Raises Questions About City's Acclaimed Law." *New York Times,* November 8, 2001, p. 4.

34. Tanner, Michael, "The Benefits of Open Immigration," [On-line] Available: http://www.lp.org/issues/platform, January 18, 2002.

35. Medved, Michael, "Blaming America: Libertarians See U.S. at Fault for September 11 Terrorism," *Investor's Business Daily,* November 5, 2001.

36. "Response From the Libertarian Party to the Terrorist Attacks of September 11," Libertarian Party, [On-line] Available: http://www.lp.org/lpnews/results.php, September 12, 2001.

37. Dasbach, Steve, "An Obvious Link: U.S. Adventurism Laid Groundwork for Sept. 11 Attack," *Investor's Business Daily,* November 27, 2001, p. A17.

38. "George Washington, Farewell Address, Philadelphia, PA," [On-line] Available: http://odur.let.rug.nl/~usa/usa.htm, September 17, 1796.

39. Churchill, Winston, *Memoirs of the Second World War* (Mariner Books, September 1962), p. 6.

40. "Libertarian Party Press Releases," Libertarian Party, October 15, 2001, [On-line] Available: http://www.lp.org/press/archive.php?function=view& record=540.

41. Kotloeski, Dean, "Black Power—Nixon Style: the Nixon Administration and Minority Business Enterprise," *Business History Review* (Harvard College), September 22, 1998.

42. *New York Times Abstracts,* September 18, 1971, p. 1.

43. Gordon, Greg, "House Starts Debate on $170 Billion Farm Aid Bill," *Star-Tribune,* p. 3A.

44. Kondracke, Morton M., "If Fourth-Graders Can't Read, Congress Is Failing to Lead," *Roll Call,* April 23, 2001.

45. Novak, Robert, "Bush Gives in on Education," *Chicago Sun-Times,* May 14, 2001, p. 29.

46. Ritter, John, "Ashcroft's Crackdown Outrages Many in Oregon," *USA Today,* November 12, 2001, p. 4A.

47. Verhovek, Sam Howe, "Federal Judge Stops Effort to Overturn Suicide Law," *New York Times,* November 9, 2001, p. 16.

48. Pine, Art, "'92 National Elections," *Los Angeles Times,* November 5, 1992, p. 5.

49. Schumer, Charles E., "Big Government Looks Better Now," *Washington Post,* December 11, 2001, p. A33.

10. No More Welfare State. Now What?

1. "We Owe Him Our Thanks," *Investor's Business Daily,* November 25, 1998, p. A20.

2. Bernstein, Andrew, "The Welfare State Versus Values and the Mind," *The Intellectual Activist,* October 2001, p. 22.

3. O'Reilly, Bill, *The No Spin Zone* (New York: Broadway Books, 2001), pp. 111–112.

4. Ibid.

5. Anderson, Nick, "Congress OKs Overhaul of Public Schools," *Los Angeles Times,* December 19, 2001.

6. Ibid.

7. Lott, John, "Stimulus Bull: Congress May Simply Deepen the Recession," *Investor's Business Daily,"* December 20, 2001, p. A16.

8. Saxton, Frank Wycoff, "Motorcycle Helmet Laws Don't Save Lives," *Portland Oregonian,* May 2, 1997, p. D13.

9. Van Allen, Jackie, "Exercise Judgement, Not Just Numbers," *Spokane Review,* July 31, 2001, p. B6.

10. Filley, Dwight, "Risk Homeostasis and the Futility of Protecting People From Themselves," Independence Institute, January 20, 1999.

11. Ibid.

12. Ibid.

13. Wagner, Wayne and Al Winnekoff, *Millionaire* (Los Angeles: Renaissance Books, 2000).

14. Huffstutter, P.J., and Scott Gold, "Red Cross Chief Quits Amid Policy Disputes," *Los Angeles Times*, October 27, 2001.

15. "Red Cross Diverts Money Raised for Sept. 11 Victims," *USA Today*, October 30, 2001, p. 14A.

16. "Your Donations at Work," [On-line] Available: http://www.redcross.org/news/ds/0109wtc/donationwork/index.html, November 5, 2001.

17. Swanson, Stevenson, "States Poised to Inhale Tobacco's Windfall: $246 Billion Settlement Lights Up Lawmakers' Dreams," *Chicago Tribune*, April 2, 2000, p. 4.

18. O'Meara, Kelly Patricia, "Wasted Riches," *Insight on the News,* October 22, 2001, pp. 10–12.

19. Ibid.

20. Ibid.

21. O'Meara, Kelly Patricia, "Investigative Report: Rumsfeld Inherits Financial Mess," *Insight*, September 3, 2001.

22. Bovard, James, *Feeling Your Pain: The Explosion and Abuse of Government Power in the Clinton–Gore Years* (New York: St. Martin's Press, 2000), p. 349.

23. "Text of House Democratic Leader Dick Gephardt Floor Statement on Airline Security Bill," [On-line] Available: http://www.usnewswire.com.

24. Plummer, William, and Jill Movshin Singer, "Angels Seed Money: Pastor Denny Bellesi Planted a Notion of Charity in His California Congregation . . .," *People*, May 21, 2001, p. 139.

25. Carter, Chelsea J., "Pastor's Lesson Inspired Good Deeds," Associated Press, January 1, 2001.

26. Plummer, William, and Jill Movshin Singer, "Angels Seed Money: Pastor Denny Bellesi Planted a Notion of Charity in His California Congregation . . .," *People*, May 21, 2001, p. 139.

27. Ibid.

28. Ibid.

29. Tocqueville, Alexis de, *Memoir on Pauperism* (New York: Harper & Row, 1968), p. 61.

30. Ibid, p. 70.

31. Zuckman, Jill, "Daschle Takes Hits Before He Takes Reins GOP Scoffs at His Vow to Compromise," *Chicago Tribune,* June 3, 2001.

32. Associated Press, "Oklahoma City Victems Feel Slighted Over Aid to WTC Families," *Dow Jones International News*, December 22, 2001.

33. Ibid.

34. Tocqueville, Alexis de, *Memoir on Pauperism* (New York: Harper & Row, 1968), p. 56.

35. Mena, Jennifer, "Los Angeles Steep Rents and Health Problems Squeeze Family of 7 Living in Garage," *Los Angeles Times*, November 30, 2001, p. B-4.

36. Ibid.

37. Coulson, Andrew J., *Market Education: The Unknown History* (New Brunswick [USA] and London [UK]: Transaction Publishers, 1999), p. 85.

38. Sacks, Glenn, "The Failing Teacher and the Teachers' Code of Silence," *Los Angeles Daily News*, December 2, 2001.

39. Tanner, Lindsey, "Parental Disapproval Cuts Chances Kids Will Smoke," *Chicago Tribune,* December 3, 2001, p. 5.

40. "Campaign 2001: Excerpts From the Debate Between Mayoral Hopefuls," *Los Angeles Times*, p. B-9.

41. "Letters to the Editor: End the Prohibition on Drugs," *Pittsburgh Post-Gazette,* November 25, 1997, p. A-18.

42. "The Liberator On-line," Vol. 7, No. 1, Advocates for Self-Government, January 8, 2002.

43. DiLorenzo, Thomas J., "The Other War," www.mises.org, November 19, 2001.

44. Ibid.

45. Bock, Alan, "Eye on the Empire: Anti-Terrorism for the Long Haul," [On-line] Available: http://www.Antiwar.com, October 3, 2001.

46. Ibid.

47. Rosen, James, "After the Attack: Drug Trade Filled Coffers of Taliban, Bin Laden Group," *Star-Tribune*, Minneapolis-St. Paul, September 30, 2001, p. 21A.

48. Scheer, Robert, "Bush's Faustian Deal With the Taliban, *Los Angeles Times*, May 22, 2001.

49. Woodward, Bob, "Bin Laden Said to 'Own' the Taliban: Bush Is Told He Gave Regime $100 Million," *Washington Post*, October 11, 2001.

50. Bock, Alan, "Eye on the Empire: Anti-Terrorism for the Long Haul," [On-line] Available: http://www.Antiwar.com, October 3, 2001.

51. Sullum, Jacob, "Drugs and Thugs," *Reason*, December, 2001, p. 29.

52. Ibid.

53. Hansen, Jane O., "Gap Between Rich, Poor Nations a Growing Risk, Carter Says," *Atlanta Journal-Constitution,* November 15, 2001, p. A19.

54. Sommers, Dave, Staff Writer, "Lethal Lesson," *Trentonian*, November 16, 2001

55. Welkos, Robert W., "A Few New Tricks to the Hollywood Trade," *Los Angeles Times,* August 8, 1999.

56. "The Artifical Famine/Genocide in Ukraine 1932–1933," [On-line] Available: http://www.infoukes.com/history/famine, January 21, 2002.

57. McFee, Gordon, "Are the Jews Central to the Holocaust?" [On-line] Available: http:www.holocaust-history.org/jews-central, January 21, 2002.

58. Crossette, Barbara, "The World: Before Rwanda, Before Bosnia; Waiting for Justice in Cambodia," *New York Times,* February 25, 1996.

59. Simons, Marlise, "An Awful Task: Assessing Four Roles in Death of Thousands," *New York Times,* April 30, 2001.

60. Curl, Joseph, "Clinton Calls Terror a U.S. Debt to Past," *Washington Times*, November 8, 2001.

61. Pearlston, Carl, "America, a Christian Nation?" *California Political Review,* March–April 2001.

62. Ibid.

63. Ibid.

64. Ibid.

65. *The Federalist Papers: In Modern Language Indexed for Today's Political Issues* (Washington: Merril Press, 1999), p. 213.

66. "A Timeless Message About the United States," *Contra Costa Times*, September 14, 2001, p. A-10.

67. Hutcheson, Ron, "Bush's Approval Rating Tops Father's," *Milwaukee Journal Sentinel,* September 25, 2001, p. A1.

68. Sack, Kevin, "Blacks Who Voted Against Bush Offer Support to Him in Wartime," *New York Times,* December 25, 2001.

69. Norton, Rob, "Rough Around the Edges; Why Does Paul O'Neill Make People So Hot Under the Collar?" *Washington Post,* August 19, 2001, p. B01.

70. "Byrd to the Barricades," *Wall Street Journal,* Review & Outlook (Editorial), November 9, 2001, p. A14.

71. Hook, Janet, "OMB Chief's Blunt Talk Could Point to Trouble," *Los Angeles Times*, November 26, 2001.

72. Ibid.

73. Ibid.

74. "Kennedy's Latest Word on Tax Cuts, Plans for Business," *U.S. News & World Report*, December 24, 1962.

75. "The Ghost of Social Security," *Wall Street Journal,* July 12, 2000.

76. "The 'Era of Good Feelings' President. The Monroe Presidency: Domestic Affairs." [On-line] Available: http://www.americanpresident.org/KoTrain/Courses/JMO/JMO_Domestic_Affairs.htm, August 12, 2001.

77. Williams, Walter, "Could They Be Elected Today?" Creators Syndicate, Inc., August 17, 2000.

78. Ibid.

79. Ibid.

INDEX